ANTI-ROCK

ANTI-ROCK
The Opposition to Rock 'n' Roll

Linda Martin and Kerry Segrave

DA CAPO PRESS • NEW YORK

Library of Congress Cataloging in Publication Data

Martin, Linda, 1950–
    Anti-rock: the opposition to rock'n'roll / Linda Martin and Kerry
Segrave.
        p.   cm.
    Originally published: Hamden, Conn.: Archon Books, 1988.
    Includes bibliographical references and index.
    ISBN 0-306-80502-2
    1. Rock music—History and criticism. I. Segrave, Kerry, 1944–   . II. Title.
ML3534.M414   1993   92-44438
781.66′09—dc20   CIP

First Da Capo Press edition 1993

This Da Capo Press paperback edition of *Anti-Rock* is an unabridged republication
of the edition published in Hamden, Connecticut in 1988.
It is reprinted by arrangement with Archon Books.

Published by Da Capo Press, Inc.
A Subsidiary of Plenum Publishing Corporation
233 Spring Street, New York, N.Y. 10013

Contents

Part III 1974–1986

Preface

Rock and roll fans, if even a portion of what the critics have said was true, by now would be stone deaf, with their minds burnt out by drugs, and their bodies wasted by excessive fornication. That none of this is true has never bothered rock opponents nor caused them to pause in their attacks. Rock-bashing has remained constant since the mid-1950s both in content and style. This book is about the history of opposition to rock and roll from its beginnings up to the mid-80s, written from a pro-rock point of view. We have not attempted to define the term in any rigid way, preferring to consider it "music of the young," for rock-bashing ultimately represents an age-old problem: the generation gap.

PART I
1953-1962

1

Rock 'n' Roll Rises
and the Opposition Forms

With its black roots, its earthy, sexual or rebellious lyrics, and its exuberant acceptance by youth, rock and roll has long been under attack by the establishment world of adults. No other form of culture, and its artists, has met with such extensive hostility. The music has been damned as a corrupter of morals, and as an instigator of juvenile delinquency and violence. Denounced as a communist plot, perceived as a symbol of Western decadence, it has been fulminated against by the left, the right, the center, the establishment, rock musicians themselves, doctors, clergy, journalists, politicians, and "good" musicians.

Rock has been blasted for promoting drugs and sex; for destroying hearing; and, by insidiously adding backward messages to records, pimping for Satan. And that's just a beginning. Rock and roll singers have been subjected to as much abuse as the music itself. No one ever received such a torrent of bile delivered over so short a period of time as did Elvis Presley. And then there's Mick Jagger of the Rolling Stones—Lucifer himself, in many eyes.

While rock and roll became a national phenomenon beginning in 1955, the first rock record dates prior to that and there were many contenders for the crown. Some name the 1954 hit by the Chords, "Sh-Boom," as the first. Others prefer "Gee" by the Crows, released the same year. Still another goes back to 1951, "Rocket 88" by Ike Turner, sung by Jackie Brenston. Bill Haley has a number of releases to be considered, including "Rock the Joint" (1952) and "Crazy, Man, Crazy" (1953). The crown should go perhaps to the latter song as it was the first rock and roll record to sell over a million copies. It is not coincidental that the first

3

million-seller was recorded by a white male. With the limited airplay they were allowed, black records had no chance of selling a million copies.

Until the early 1950s black music was segregated almost totally from the white world. Black records were played only on black stations and the records were available only in black record stores, located in the black sections of cities. Jukeboxes were similarly segregated, with boxes in white areas containing only material by white artists. The number of black singers who "crossed over" and were popular with whites during the 1940s and early 1950s were few and far between. Nat "King" Cole and Billy Eckstine were among the exceptions and they performed the innocuous white pop that was nonthreatening, and so popular with the white audiences.

The term for this black music in the early 1950s was "rhythm and blues." It was a phrase dreamed up and applied by Jerry Wexler and others who worked at *Billboard* magazine in the late 1940s. It was meant to replace "race" music, the derogatory term then applied to popular black music. This new designation caught on, although Wexler claimed the music was not true blues nor was it "particularly rhythmic." He admitted that "rhythm and blues" was also a euphemism which "meant the music of black people."[1]

R&B was largely urban black music, a linear descendent of the blues since it maintained the tradition of sensual lyrics. It differed in that it added a dancing rhythm, the big beat, and mixed lead vocals and background vocal harmony groups. These three points gave the music a strong appeal to white youths searching for music alternatives to the white pop of the day which featured banal lyrics, nondanceable melodies, and solo singers.

Before R&B could turn into rock and roll it was necessary for the music to be heard by whites; this came about through radio, which responded to a number of pressures of the 1940s and early 1950s. During the labor shortage of World War II many blacks moved to northern and western cities to work in relatively high-paying defense jobs. During that decade over three times as many (1,260,000) blacks left the South as in the 1930s.[2] This comparatively full employment and affluence was met by an increased number of radio stations that programmed for a black audience.

Television radically altered the course of radio further in the late 1940s and early 1950s when the networks switched all of their comedy, drama, and variety programs over to the new medium. This left a large vacuum for the radio stations, particularly the network ones, to fill. They began to

4

program more for specialty markets — country music, black music, and so on. One obvious specialty market then forming, in terms of increasing numbers and economic clout, was the teen market.

The significant increase in radio stations that programmed black music — many of which were located in large cities — exposed the music to any white listener bored enough with white pop to flip the radio dial. And the whites did listen. Not only that, they started going to black record stores to buy the records. In May 1952 the Dolphin record store in Los Angeles claimed that forty percent of its business was done with whites, whereas a few months earlier white business had been negligible.[3] Jukeboxes were also affected as requests for R&B disks mounted.

A growing number of white disk jockeys who were programming R&B material spread the music to their listeners. The most notable of these was Alan Freed, then working in Cleveland, Ohio. Like Wexler before him, Freed, in 1952, used a new term, "rock and roll," to get around the racial stigma attached to "rhythm and blues," inventing a name easier for whites to swallow. It would be a few more years before the white world would fully "discover" rock and roll but the process was well under way. For blacks it was nothing new, it was just the same old music with yet another name.

In marked contrast to white pop material some R&B tunes dealt openly with sex, a topic the white music industry pretended didn't exist. Struggling to survive in a hostile, racist society, blacks didn't have time for the subtleties of behavior and morality that marked white society. Their music was less inhibited, less bound by convention, and more celebratory of whatever they had that was enjoyable.

Popular R&B songs of the early 1950s included "Sixty Minute Man," about delayed ejaculations, and "Work with Me Annie," which implored, "Annie, please don't cheat. Give me all my meat." Not all the R&B disks were about sex. The difference was that whites never sang openly about sex. This crucial feature of R&B was one of the reasons white youth embraced the music wholeheartedly. It was also one of the factors which horrified white adults and caused them to attack the music vociferously.

Earthy lyrics could be found in black music going back for decades and apparently no one had minded. Of course, that material was directed solely at the black market; the lyrics only became a problem when they filtered through to the white market. It was almost a call to arms for whites. Consider the racist and conservative society that America was in 1954. Consider a group of middle-aged and middle-class whites watching five black men in outlandish purple and yellow costumes, jiving around, and belting out "Work with Me Annie." What you had was a white nightmare containing all the demons of a white hell.

For teens and young adults this expressive and sexual music was a welcome beacon in the repressed white world—a welcome relief from the asexual, antiseptic pop of such white stars of the day as Patti Page, Eddie Fisher, and Rosemary Clooney. It was a white society so uptight that it objected to the use of the words "virgin" and "seduction" in *The Moon is Blue*, a 1953 film by Otto Preminger. The music was sensual, a celebration of sex, but white puritans perceived it as a threat to what they considered "respectable" behavior.

While R&B was seeping into the white world and undergoing a name change, American teenagers were also undergoing changes which would lead them to a happy union with R&B. The atmosphere of the early 1950s was a conservative and oppressive one. Eisenhower was president and Senator Joseph McCarthy was not vanquished in his witch-hunting until 1954. That same year the U. S. Supreme Court struck down racial segregation in the public schools as unconstitutional. This put an end, in law if not in fact, to the racist "separate but equal" notion. Hanging over everything was the cold war and the threat of nuclear destruction.

Teenagers tended to stay in school longer, remaining financially dependent upon their parents even though they were mature in other ways. These young people did have money to spend, due to a trickling down effect from the affluent society. This allowance belonged to the youth who would spend it as they determined, not necessarily as their parents directed or wished. And the money would be spent on teen products, a market opened up specifically for this age group. The postwar baby boom ensured that this market would grow proportionately faster than that of any other age group.

In this atmosphere youth began to seek out values and a culture of their own as they rejected that of their parents. Music was not the only area where this happened: they also turned to car customizing. A whole industry sprang up to cater to teens who wanted to make their cars faster and noisier than those of their parents—to make them distinctive. Different clothes, hairstyles, and cosmetics were adopted and teenagers modeled themselves after their film heroes, Marlon Brando in *The Wild One* (1953) and James Dean in *Rebel without a Cause* (1954). In one memorable exchange from the Brando film a character asked, "What are you rebelling against?" Brando replied, "What've you got?" It struck a note with many teens. A sense of alienation from adult norms and frustration with adult authority was brewing.

Urban gangs and juvenile delinquency became a particular fixation in the 1950s. Teen fashions such as leather jackets, synonymous with delinquency and gangs, came under attack. Adults had tied juvenile delinquency to a number of such instigating factors as movies, comic books, TV and radio crime shows, and drive-in restaurants. Rock and roll became the instigator of choice, the scapegoat, because it was the most deviant of all. Rock was something virtually all teens loved and virtually all adults hated. It was also the one possible cultural form over which teens had the greatest control. Television produced programs for young people but they were designed by adults. Some of the rock music was written, played, and performed exclusively by the youths themselves. Clearly then, rock and roll was the prime cause of delinquency, at least in the collective adult mind. No matter that juvenile delinquency had arisen after World War II and long before rock emerged.

When Bill Haley's "Rock around the Clock" appeared on the soundtrack of the 1955 film *Blackboard Jungle* it marked the beginning of rock and roll's full breakthrough as a popular music form among the young. It also laid the groundwork for a firm association of rock and roll and juvenile delinquency. The cowriter of "Rock around the Clock," Jim Myers, was intent on promoting the song. With single-minded determination he sent two hundred copies of the tune to Hollywood producers. His persistence paid off when it was selected as the opening song for *Blackboard Jungle*. The first shot in the film showed kids in a schoolyard, with a high, chain link fence in the foreground — a symbolic jail — while "Rock around the Clock" blared away in the background.

The movie dealt with the problems faced by a young teacher (Glenn Ford) in dealing with his tough teenage students/delinquents. In one scene Ford tries to "communicate" with the kids and give them an appreciation of "good" music by bringing his prized collection of jazz records to the classroom. The kids show their appreciation by smashing the records to pieces.

The meaning and importance of this imagery was not lost on anybody. For teens the song represented a call to break out of their "jail" and to celebrate. It was a stand against parents and teachers. "Rock around the Clock" became a youth anthem, the "Marseillaise" of rock and roll, and moved to the top of the charts. Adults arrayed in almost unanimous opposition. They believed *Blackboard Jungle* advocated violence and disrespect, and they could point to its theme song to confirm their own beliefs. This film had a great impact on the public since it represented a cross section of underprivileged teens at a city high school, a more representative population than that in *The Wild One*, which portrayed a limited section of lawless youths, the bikers. In *Blackboard Jungle*, the students made defiance and insolence the norm, committed acts of vandalism, and assaulted their teachers. In fact, the film simply reflected what was already a national problem.

Much was made of the so-called riots which accompanied many of the live rock concerts and dances in the mid-1950s; they cemented the link between rock and delinquency. Most of these incidents just involved kids dancing in the aisles at theaters; jiving in their seats; and stomping, clapping, and yelling a lot—having a good time, in short. The authorities thought an audience should sit quietly and sedately, perhaps clapping a little at the end of the performance. When they tried to enforce this kind of behavior, the kids reacted.

Many of the "riots" were also a reaction to heavyhanded police tactics. Imagine a professional football game where the police roam the aisles, ordering people to sit down and shut up every time they jump or holler at an exciting moment. Imagine these same police immediately breaking up any group which lingered after the game outside the stadium, on their own. This was precisely what police did during rock and roll shows. Is it any wonder that "riots" broke out?

Police provocation worked out well for the establishment and anti-rock forces since they could then point to the riots, blame the music, and attack it more vigorously. One of the few pieces of research on the subject of violence and rock during this time indicated that the music "had a tendency to absorb violence, and to redirect violent energies into making music or into partisan but essentially nonviolent support for particular groups and singers."[4]

While all of this was going on, the white music industry was responding in its own fashion. From the 1920s to the early 1950s the industry aimed its products at a family audience. Music reached the listener by radio and by the phonograph. The average home had one of each. As one observer noted, "to be popular a record had to transcend the differences between listeners; it had to appeal to all ages and classes and races and regions, to both sexes, to all moods and cultures and values."[5]

This observation was not quite accurate. White pop music didn't make any attempt to appeal to blacks, or to young people, for example. The music strove for a broad, mass appeal only among white adult society. It was WASP culture the music spoke to, and it did so in the most benign way. It sang of no taboos, nor did it question any values. White popular music was one hundred percent white bread, unenriched. In

8

1954, the established stars from this field included: Patti Page, Tony Bennett, Doris Day, Rosemary Clooney, Frank Sinatra, Perry Como, Jo Stafford, and Eddie Fisher. Chart hits during the period from 1949 to 1954 included: "Goodnight Irene" by Gordon Jenkins, "Doggie in the Window" by Patti Page, and Eddie Fisher with "Oh, My Papa."

The white pop market was dominated by five record companies: RCA, Mercury, Columbia, Capitol, and Decca — the majors. The R&B market had been shared by the majors and the smaller independent companies in the 1920s but most of the independents got wiped out in the depression of the 1930s. The majors set up subsidiary labels, for example, a "Sepia" series for its "race" artists.

Due to wartime shortages in the early 1940s, the majors had trouble obtaining all of the shellac they needed, then an essential ingredient in record production. As a result they dropped most of their sidelines, such as black material, to concentrate solely on popular songs. This left a vacuum into which many independents, mostly black-owned, stepped to service the R&B field. Estimates are that as many as four hundred such companies were formed in the 1940s while only one hundred were surviving in 1952. A few of the more important independents were Atlantic (New York), Chess (Chicago), and Specialty (Los Angeles).

By the early 1950s the R&B market was large and growing, and the majors made an attempt to reenter it. A couple of the majors set up subsidiary labels again but they quickly failed, probably because they tried to impose white standards and values on music which tended to ignore such standards. The tactic most often used by the majors was that of covering a black record. When a record was released and a second company produced a copy with one of its own singers doing the same song, it was termed a "cover." Whites who covered black material for the majors included: the Crew-Cuts covering "Earth Angel" by the Penguins and "Sh-Boom" by the Chords; Perry Como and Tony Bennett covering "Kokomo" by Gene and Eunice; and the McGuire Sisters covering "Sincerely" by the Moonglows. Pat Boone gained most of his early fame as a rock star by covering songs sung originally by Fats Domino and Little Richard.

The practice of covering records, of exploiting blacks, and even the consolidation of the music industry into a small number of companies were all aided greatly by the Copyright Act of 1909, still in effect in the 1950s. Under the act, once a songwriter allowed his song to be recorded then anybody else was permitted to record it as well. The composer was entitled to his royalty of two cents a record but he had absolutely no say over who recorded his songs, or under what circumstances.

In addition, under a system known as compulsory licensing, the performance of a song couldn't be copyrighted, only the underlying sheet music. This meant that record companies never had to compete for a song, only for the performance of a song. The system worked like this: a record company could pass over a good song thinking it wouldn't be a hit. The song is then produced by another company, becoming a hit. The first company could then release a version with one of their top singers, who was under exclusive contract, and reap the benefits of a hit song. What became important for the record industry was in signing up top draw singers for long-term contracts; the hunt for music was secondary.

Compulsory licensing explained why there might be half a dozen or more versions of the same song circulating at the same time. This system worked against the small independent company who might make a big investment in producing a record destined to go on to be a hit. If that happened a major could come along and rush out a version by a "name" like Sinatra for example, and take all the sales away from the independent and its unknown singer.

It was not surprising that a handful of companies came to dominate the market. John Schulman, counsel for the Songwriters' Protective Association, whose members were responsible for most of the pop songs produced by the majors, commented in the mid-1950s on the effect of this system. "The very existence of the compulsory license therefore has a tendency to smother competition for new and fresh musical material. . . . The competition for the new and fresh material is stifled [and the compulsory licensing explains] the monotony, repetition and impersonal music offered to the American public."[6]

For black companies the process was made more difficult by compulsory licensing. When white stations refused to play a black song and demanded a white cover, another company was legally free to produce one. This siphoned off potential sales from the black version, although the songwriter got the same money. However, as often as not, the black songwriter was exploited by the independent label and gave the company the copyright for a small lump sum, or even less. "Composer rights were bought for a few dollars or even signed away for the 'privilege' of recording. . . . The majors had been no more principled when they controlled black music. Even the best musicians were only paid $5 for performing on one side of a record, $10 to the leader."[7]

The singer was the loser during a period of heavy cover activity since he got royalties only on the sales of his record. For the black independent record company the compulsory licensing system encouraged them to obtain the copyright to a song from the composer, for that way they would get a share of the money if a major did a cover, a share denied them in the white market. It even made sense for these companies to encourage a white cover. The woman who wrote "Hound Dog," Big Mama Thornton, received, according to her, one check for $500 and no more. An early Presley tune, "That's All Right," was written by Arthur "Big Boy" Crudup, who received nothing at all.[8]

At first the majors did well with cover versions, often racking up big sales and outselling the original, even though the cover was weak by comparison. Many stations simply wouldn't play the black material. Due to jockeys like Alan Freed, who refused to play the cover and insisted on using the original, and a growing sophistication on the part of the audience, and perhaps a lessening of racist attitudes, the practice of covering failed to give the majors a sufficiently dominant share of the emerging rock and roll market. Pat Boone's copies of "Tutti-Frutti" and "Long Tall Sally" are inane compared to Little Richard's originals.

An indication of the changing market division can be seen for the period 1946 to 1957. From 1946 to 1952, 162 million-selling records were produced but only five were produced by independent companies; all the others came from the majors. For the R&B field, of the top thirty records for 1954, the independents produced twenty-two. In 1956, when rock and roll had come to dominate the white charts, the independents produced ten of the top nineteen tunes, and this exaggerated the importance of the majors since their share came mostly from two performers: Bill Haley (Decca) and Elvis Presley (RCA). By the end of 1957 the independents had twenty-nine of the top forty-three songs and were beginning to dominate the entire pop market.[9]

The rock market was growing rapidly, but the majors did not enter the market directly. While they did have a few rockers, besides Presley and Haley—there was Gene Vincent at Capitol and Buddy Holly with Decca—generally, the majors joined in with everybody else and condemned rock and roll. They left the field mainly to the independents. There were a number of reasons why the majors didn't turn to rock. One objection was on "aesthetic" grounds. Executives at the majors considered rock a "rather shoddy" music and they thought the singers were poorly educated and were uneasy in dealing with them. Executives felt that Cole Porter or Gershwin or classical music was "better." According to Ahmet Ertegun of Atlantic Records, these executives "thought rock 'n' roll was for morons."[10] In addition, all the majors had producers and talent departments which had been providing traditional popular music for decades and rock music went against all of those values. Trained in middle-of-the-road music, they were incapable of distinguishing one act from another, and were unable to predict which groups teens would like and which they wouldn't. Moreover, the majors had many of the big name pop stars under long-term contracts for large salaries, and they didn't want to see these investments crumble away.

Compulsory licensing made signing a big star more important than getting song material. Crooners like Fisher and Sinatra were not going to sell rock. Therefore, the rise of rock would mean a corresponding drop in the market value of the crooners. The majors fervently hoped rock and roll was only a passing fad and were reluctant to re-tool, as it were, for a new product. Another reason to avoid rock and roll was the sexual content of some of the songs; the objections raised around the country to "leerics" made the executives wary, as did the annoying fact that so many black people sang them. The majors were more comfortable with sterile, white material.

Added to this was the ASCAP factor. The American Society of Composers, Authors and Publishers was an organization which registered and licensed music, but only mainstream pop material. It ignored country and black material. A similar and rival organization, Broadcast Music Incorporated (BMI), had been set up in 1940 to break the ASCAP monopoly. BMI licensed the vast bulk of rock tunes, as it still does, and had most of their material produced through independent record companies. ASCAP had the bulk of its material produced through the majors. While some "crossover" took place, it was minor. ASCAP had only a thousand or so members and as a percentage of the American population they were miniscule. But they wielded enormous power, out of all proportion to their numbers. They attacked both rock and roll and BMI vigorously in the press, Congress, and the courts. While they failed to defeat BMI in most ways, they were effective in generating a good deal of negative publicity against rock. This, too, tended to keep the majors out of the rock and roll market.

ASCAP also had strong ties with Hollywood and Broadway and given their relationship with the majors it was not surprising that the majors resisted rock, and joined in blasting it. Mitch Miller, A&R director at Columbia Records through the early 1960s, was one rock opponent. A&R is an abbreviation of artist and repertoire, a term used for a person who signed up talent and songs for his label, and then matched them up. It was an industry term for a producer. ASCAP was particularly effective because Miller "maintained close relations with Broadway producers and despised rock 'n' roll."[11]

The majors' share of the market continued to decline, being halved between 1955 and 1958. A comparison between 1939 and 1959 shows how much rock music had opened up a virtually closed industry and gave opportunities to a variety of different people and companies who otherwise might never have had the chance. For the first nine months of each year the number of hits — 72 (1939), 70 (1959) — and songwriters — 118 (1939), 104 (1959) — were similar. In 1939 the publishers were all based in New York, in 1959 they were spread over eight states. Songwriters came from eighteen states instead of just three. In 1939 the top sellers were made by only three companies (all in New York), while in 1959 the songs were produced by thirty-nine companies located in ten different states.[12]

The fact that the majors ignored rock and roll for so long, leaving the independents to dominate until the mid-1960s, was undoubtedly healthy for rock and roll and allowed it to keep its vigor and energy. All the companies involved in rock, majors and independents, kept a wary eye on lyrics and practiced some degree of self-censorship. But it is hard to imagine that the majors wouldn't have put a tighter rein on both the song content and style of such artists as Little Richard or Jerry Lee Lewis.

So who hated rock and roll? In the beginning it seemed almost every adult did, and that's not much of an exaggeration. At the industry level, it was ASCAP that commanded a good deal of media attention and exerted a great deal of influence. They presented their negative views in a number of forums and were a factor in keeping the major recording companies largely out of the field. They harassed rock and roll, and its main licensing agency, BMI, involving the government and eventually bringing about the payola hearing which altered the face of rock music.

Another major objection to rock was based on racist grounds, sometimes unspoken and sometimes blatant as in the southern United States. Many whites resisted the music because of its black beginnings and the large number of black performers. Combined with sexual lyrics the music became a double threat and therefore had to be resisted twice as hard.

The major reason for attacking rock and roll was that it was the music of the young. It symbolized the generation gap. Rock expressed the kind of freedom that was unavailable to a responsible adult. By presenting an alternative to established norms, the music threatened those standards. Parents were accustomed to influencing their children's values, but America's youth had different ideas. They had more economic power than in the past. They experienced more protracted periods of living at home which left them older, maturer, and more desirous of directing their own lives. They identified partially with black music because blacks were outcasts from the white world. Teens considered themselves outcasts from the adult world. By adopting rock they could listen to music that talked about things they cared about — sexuality, school, or hot rod cars. Youth used rock as a way of setting their own standards and disseminating them through peer interaction.

Adults resisted teen culture in order to regain their authority over the young. The battle took place in many areas, but nowhere was the conflict more intense than in music. Rock was particularly threatening because young people often wrote, played, and performed it themselves. A teenage boy could alter a car to suit himself, but first he had to buy a standard off the assembly line, one produced by the adult world. A teenage girl might dress differently than her mother, but they would buy from the same manufacturer. With rock and roll it was possible for the young to produce the finished product themselves. From the beginning rock and roll was viewed by the adult world as the clarion call to teenagers to rise up and defy their elders, to flaunt their morality, to mock their ideals, to break away from adult control, to reject the adult world. The adult world was determined to undermine rock and roll. They would fight it tooth and nail, every step of the way.

2

Leerics

The opening shots in the battle against rock began to be fired about 1954, before the term "rock and roll" became part of the national vocabulary, and before rock had produced what would be its first super hit. At that time the music business was divided along color lines. Whites had their pop artists such as Perry Como, all their music was produced under ASCAP, and it was pressed on the half dozen or so major record labels such as Columbia and Capitol. Black artists produced rhythm and blues under BMI and the music was pressed on small, independent labels such as Chess of Chicago. Radio stations programmed themselves for either a white or a black audience. An R&B fan in New York City had to journey to Harlem record stores to buy an R&B disk because the downtown outlets stocked only the white material. Likewise, the Harlem stores stocked only the black artists.

This division began to erode during the early years of the 1950s, an erosion which would eventually produce rock and roll. It was a trend the white music establishment was not happy to see. The major labels, the Tin Pan Alley songwriters of ASCAP, major radio stations, and trade publications such as *Variety* and *Billboard* all made their money from white music. They feared that the growth of R&B would be at their expense. They had a vested interest in keeping R&B down. America of the mid-1950s was also a very racist society and another objection to the music was simply that it was black.

In 1954 a hue and cry began to be raised around the United States against R&B music, due to its supposed poor quality and obscene content. Peter Potter, a disk jockey in Los Angeles and host of the CBS television show "Juke Box Jury" (which rated new tunes), condemned record companies

15

for inculcating poor taste in teenagers. He considered it impossible that companies would be issuing songs such as "Sh-Boom" twenty years hence. "Sh-Boom," recorded in 1954 by the Chords, and covered by the white Crew-Cuts, is considered by some as the first rock and roll song. It has become a classic and was indeed still available twenty years later. Potter noted the popularity of R&B among teenagers in his area, including whites, and termed much of it "obscene and of lewd intonation, and certainly not fit for radio broadcast."[1] A little later he commented that "all rhythm and blues records are dirty and as bad for kids as dope."[2]

In its September 25, 1954 issue the trade magazine *Billboard* editorialized, under the headline "Control the Dim-Wits," that a number of R&B record companies had produced a rash of double entendre disks that stepped out side the bounds of propriety and flew in the face of good taste. In response, the sheriff's office in Long Beach, California banned one such record from local jukeboxes and police in Memphis, Tennessee confiscated jukeboxes and fined the operators. West coast radio stations had banned one such record and area newspapers were said to be complaining to all and sundry about obscene R&B records. *Billboard* urged the industry to control itself lest someone else do it.

The very next week, *Billboard* urged radio stations to exercise their obligation to the public and carefully examine a record before spinning it on the air: "distasteful disks must be weeded out." Ironically, *Billboard* advised stations not to accept its own top ten charts as a recommendation to play the songs. *Billboard* felt that the charts reflected sales and "cannot be tampered with" but that they still might contain unacceptable material and radio stations should eliminate from their playlists any of these songs that the station felt didn't "qualify as home entertainment."

The Music Publishers' Protective Association (MPPA), which represented most of the pop publishing companies, joined the bandwagon and passed a resolution condeming "dirty" songs. They regarded such tunes "as showing bad taste and a disregard for recognized moral standards and conventions."[3] They claimed to have been urged on by a number of civic groups who wished to stop juvenile delinquency. This stance by the MPPA was to be expected as none of their virtually all-white material was under attack. Another organization, the Songwriters' Protective Association, passed a similar resolution.

The record industry in general was said to be in agreement that there was a problem with double entendre R&B records getting a big airplay. This agreement didn't extend to the R&B companies themselves. At the end of September such labels as Apollo, Savoy, and Atlantic all denied that R&B was guilty. They felt that the proportion of off-color tunes in R&B was no higher than in country or pop and that R&B was being singled out unfairly.[4]

Others fell into line more quickly. In New York the president of Music Operators of New York, an association with ten thousand jukeboxes in that city, announced his group would no longer allow off-color songs in their jukes. The president, Albert Denver, announced he would stick to any list of objectionable records that *Billboard* would care to provide. Record distributors in various places such as Texas and Tennessee also stated they wouldn't handle anything suggestive and had started a thorough screening of records. It shouldn't be surprising that they reviewed mainly R&B material. In New York City an ad hoc group of disk jockeys had formed and agreed not to play off-color R&B material; they lobbied to get other jockeys to join them in the clean-up drive.

Perhaps the most perceptive comment came from an R&B industry source in Chicago who refused to be identified. With regard to off-color songs he said, "The R&B field has been doing this sort of thing all along. It only came into prominence when the pop kids [white] started buying R&B disks and playing them at home. . . . The pop kids are buying the R&B records because of the beat rather than the lyrics. After all, some of the old-time pop disks had entendres too."[5] When *Billboard* had editorialized about "Control the Dim-Wits" they noted that it was regrettable that the law had to step in just as R&B was enjoying greater acceptance, not only among blacks "but also in the pop market." *Billboard* did not see, or wish to see, the causal connection the way the source in Chicago did.

At the beginning of October 1954, Memphis radio station WDIA, which programmed for the black market, announced it would no longer play any record it considered off-color. Concerned about what they considered to be the increased trend toward suggestiveness and double meaning in R&B songs, WDIA established a policy whereby they critically listened to records and removed those that violated their idea of good morals, The station then informed the record company, the distributor, and other radio stations as well. By the end of October the station had axed twenty-five records as being unfit, including "Honey Love" on Atlantic, "Forget It" on Apollo, and the "Annie" series on King. The latter was done by Hank Ballard and the Midnighters and involved a series of songs about a mythical character named Annie and featured titles such as "Work With Me Annie" and "Annie Had a Baby." Ballard went on to later fame with "Finger Poppin' Time" and "The Twist," although Chubby Checker's cover of "The Twist," written by Ballard, achieved the greatest popularity.

WDIA claimed they weren't bluenoses but urged other stations to join their campaign. They claimed to have received congratulatory letters from the R&B companies on their stance, including ones whose songs were banned. According to WDIA, the R&B companies were "all for it." When the station received a request to play a song from the banned list the following announcement was made on the air, "WDIA, your good-will station, in the interest of good citizenship, for the protection of morals and our American way of life does not consider this record, [name of song], fit for broadcast on WDIA. We are sure all you listeners will agree with us."[6]

This stance was greeted ecstatically by the editors of *Billboard* who offered hearty congratulations and a bravo to WDIA for its "courageous program of self-regulation, conceived by a thoughtful station management [which] highlights its respect for—and devotion to—the rhythm and blues field."[7]

The other major trade publication, *Variety*, took a similar position to *Billboard*. The former felt music had an "alchemist effect" on kids and there was thus "the obligation to feed them the right type of lyrics." The fast buck that the smutty R&B people were reaping was coming at the expense of juvenile morals and should be decried. *Variety* editors clearly favored the good old days when the white establishment writers of pop held unchallenged ascendancy—a time when "Tin Pan Alley's obligation to its public has been almost idealistically manifest over the years. The treasury of American pop songs that inspire the sentimental, nostalgic and rhythmic moods is a tribute to the ingenuity and productivity of the American music business."[8]

Other groups outside of the music business joined in the fray. The Boston Catholic Youth Organization (CYO) began to police record hops in their area, demanding that disk jockeys eliminate the sexual songs from their programming. The Boston CYO was upset because some of the hops had turned into orgies and the group was convinced it was those obscene R&B tunes which were the trigger. The CYO was also lobbying the jockeys to keep them from playing these records on their radio programs.

Black organizations also joined the campaign to eliminate their own music. In Chicago a weekly black paper, *The Courier*, fought to clean up the smutty disks by printing stories on irresponsible jockeys. *The Courier* organized a write-in campaign and encouraged letters from parents and ministers. The paper also advised its readers to write letters condemning the smutty R&B tunes to other area newspapers.

By 1955 rock and roll had become firmly established in the national psyche. Its popularity grew exponentially. While 1954 had seen a surge of complaints against the off-color music, 1955 produced a tidal wave of opposition, led by the trade papers, but then quickly picked up by various segments of the general population. For the trades it was a continuation of the attempts by the white, pop music ASCAP to remove its growing competitor, the black, rock and roll BMI.

Variety ran a three-part series in February and March on what they called "leer-ics," their term for alleged obscene lyrics. For the editor, Abel Green, songs had touched new lows, were generated by people interested only in a fast buck, and were breaking down all reticence toward the subject of sex. R&B was a raw musical idiom which stank up the environment; it was dirty postcards translated into songs. Variety acknowledged that leerics had existed for years but that, until recently, they had been hidden away in some sort of musical underworld and were available only to a few people, not the bulk of the general population. The paper had no use for songwriters who justified "their leer-ic garbage by declaring that's what the kids want."[9] Even at that early date, payola was described as one of the roots of the evils of the current music business. The paper urged the industry to clean up and police itself lest outside influences do it for them.

This Variety editorial was widely picked up by the wire services and many newspapers, including the New York World-Telegram & Sun, who gave it front page treatment. All of this indicated how much animosity existed toward this new musical format. Parts two and three of the Variety series on leer-ics ran in the next two issues. It is likely that their writing was an afterthought, due in part to the intense reception and publicity generated by part one. When the initial article ran, no mention was made that it was to be a series, nor was it labeled as part one. In that first article, the paper had tried to present a semblance of impartiality by claiming the major record companies were as guilty as the small independent ones. In part two their true bias showed through when the editor stated that there were "any number of independent diskery labels which neither know nor care about ethics and concern about potential juvenile delinquency."

Part three consisted mostly of the paper congratulating itself on taking the bull by the horns in addressing this thorny issue. Variety claimed to have received a flood of letters putting public opinion clearly behind the trade paper's position. Newspapers that had picked up the editorial were said to have received large volumes of mail commending them for printing the editorial. Major labels like Decca and RCA also endorsed the paper's position. Herman Finkelstein, the general counsel for ASCAP, promised his group's complete cooperation and claimed that the members of ASCAP, pop writers and publishers, condemned the "smutty and suggestive lyrics as much as Variety did.

The pressure was so great that some of the independent R&B labels felt the need to publicly confess their sins and promise to offend no more. *Variety's* March 16, 1955 issue featured a letter from King Records of Cincinnati in which John S. Kelley, Jr., the vice-president, admitted his company was "not without guilt in having in the past allowed some double-entendre tunes to reach the public." Kelley promised to reject any songs in the future that his company considered unsuitable for teens. A letter had gone out to the three labels within the company warning them that if material from part of a recording session had to be thrown out due to improper lyrics, the company employee responsible for the session would personally have to pay for that part of the session that was rejected. In Kelley's words, the company would "never relent again and allow off-color lyrics."

A couple of weeks later *Variety* was still patting itself on the back for the "almost embarrassingly" wide pick-up of its leer-ics editorial. Feeling at least a twinge of guilt, the paper tried to address the charge that pop songs had also included questionable lyrics. Although agreeing that the charge was warranted, the paper argued that this was not an appropriate defense of this type of lyrics for rock and roll to offer to the public. For the pot to call the kettle black was to offer no constructive thought. For the editor, rock would first have to cleanse itself before it could point the finger at smut in other music areas.

Billboard took a much more ambivalent, but perceptive, stance. They decried the blue material and got some satisfaction from the anti-rock activites taking place around the country. But they were also worried that so much of the opposition came from outside the industry. *Billboard* wanted the industry to clean itself up without attracting outside regulation. The editor also commented that, "Most disgraceful is the fact that much of the hue and cry was fostered and abetted by elements within the industry who acted in order to guard their own selfish interests."[10] This clearly was a veiled reference to ASCAP's war against BMI, fought under the guise of clean songs versus filthy degeneracy. *Billboard* was on ASCAP's side but wanted ASCAP to castrate and strangle BMI, and rock, quietly, without outside interference. *Billboard* worried that outside intervention might shackle all of pop music in some way, without eradicating BMI and rock.

The carry-over of hostility to rock and roll music to society in general had nothing to do with the ASCAP and BMI battles. Some of the hostility was racial and some of it came from those who were uptight about anything remotely sexual. Most of it had to do with the opposing values between youth and adult, between children and parents, as teenagers developed their own set of values and morality.

Radio station WDIA in Memphis had a banned list of about forty songs, all from BMI, in early 1955. In Mobile, Alabama, WABB aired an editorial before each major program titled, "About the Music You Won't Hear on WABB." They also ran the editorial as an ad in the local paper, the *Mobile Press Register*. Directed especially to teachers, clergy, parents, and teenagers, the station announced it was banning all records it considered off-color and all records containing double entendres. They resolved to play only new songs which met the standards established by "perennial favorites." Anything offensive would be discarded. At another Mobile station, WKRG, it was estimated that forty to fifty percent of all submitted records went into the garbage. In Shenandoah, Iowa, station KMA launched a "Crusade for Better Disks." They set up their own screening board and barred records they deemed too blue. Included in the first banned list were "Dim, Dim the Lights" and "Rock and Roll, Baby."

Other disk jockeys took the initiative and spoke out on their own. A group of four jockeys at New York's black-oriented WLIB sent a joint warning letter to record companies urging them to cut out the blue material. They knocked the industry for not cracking down on the independent labels that were selling "filth passing under the guise of pop lyrics." The jockeys felt that R&B had broken out of the black market only because some independent labels had hooked listeners with "strange singing groups," and that once the money started to roll in, they quickly reverted to blue material. These blacks also laid the blame for the R&B problems to a time when "they bypassed all the Negro disk jockeys to put a non-Negro on a fifty-thousand watt outlet and this stuff got the biggest push ever."[11] This was a shot at disk jockey Alan Freed, then at New York's WINS.

Longtime New York jockey Martin Block, then with the ABC network, considered the majority of current songs to be "abysmal" and stated he "cringed" before each hour that he was scheduled to play new records. Block felt that teenagers were the prime cause of the failing of the music scene because it was extremely difficult to get them to accept a "good" song. They only wanted something with a beat.

Other radio stations joined in the assault, with a little assist from outside pressure groups. In the Windy City the Chicago Inter-Student Catholic Actionists, comprised of teenage students, demanded an industry-wide board of review that would listen to all songs and screen out objectionable ones. This coalition of Catholic groups bombarded radio outlets with an estimated fifteen thousand letters in one week as part of their "Crusade for Decent Disks." Their goal was the eventual establishment of some sort of national board which would bestow a seal of approval on acceptable records; media outlets would be allowed to play only those tunes carrying the seal.

As a result of this pressure two stations, WGN and WGN-TV, established a special review panel comprised of jockeys and station executives to review records after, and in addition to, the station's normal screening process. The panel promised to "reinforce traditionally strict music clearance policy." While WGN did ban a couple of songs, they did not ban some songs from the top of the charts. The students were unhappy and claimed that a whitewash had taken place. WGN replied that those songs had been played for two months without protest. This particular student protest was somewhat blunted since many of their letters of complaint were sent to stations and jockeys who never played rock, and since the letters largely named no specific songs.

Public censure and press attacks were severe enough in Boston that representatives of six city radio stations met with local journalists and religious leaders and formed their own board to review and censor records. The Boston jockeys acknowledged the need to keep their record programming "clean" and promised to keep offensive lyrics off the air. The action was prompted by local newspapers, an area Catholic publication, *The Pilot*, and a visit by songwriter Jimmy McHugh who called current lyrics "very disgusting" and urged parents, the clergy, and teens to write in an all-out effort to eliminate the blue material. "Wake Up Little Susie" by the Everly Brothers did manage to get itself banned in Boston when several stations deemed it "too suggestive." "Susie" got the same reaction that much of the heavy metal material would get in the future. It was the same adults who enjoyed Cole Porter's double entendres who found it so damnable when their kids heard the relatively mild lyrics of the Everly Brothers.

In San Antonio, Texas, the San Antonio Commission, with members from the local police and judiciary, had drawn up a list of objectionable records and it was reported that virtually all city radio outlets would honor the list and not play the cited tunes. Station KITE had begun plugging itself as the "clean music" station.

Bob Haymes, a jockey at New York City's WCBS and ASCAP songwriter of a Julius LaRosa ballad, publicly condemned rock and roll. This prompted Freed's WINS, a rock outlet, to place an unofficial ban on

Haymes's songs. Haymes called rock and roll "poor music, badly record-ed, with lyrics that are at best in poor taste . . . and at worse obscene . . . this trend in music (and I apologize for calling it 'music') is affecting the ideas and the lives of our children." He then defended himself by claiming he didn't single out rock over any other kind of "bad music."[12]

At that time ASCAP limited itself to registering and licensing music while BMI, in addition to these functions, was engaged in inspection of music, perhaps as a result of all the pressure. The BMI music editor screened incoming material before it passed to a further screening committee. A blackball at that stage sent it to yet another committee of higher executives for a final say.

On the West Coast the National Audience Board (NAB), a group that strove for better television broadcasting, was active through its auxiliary, the Junior NAB. This group had gotten peititions asking for better lyrics and circulated them among Los Angeles disk jockeys. A total of twenty-five leading jockeys at nine different radio stations had agreed to cooperate in eliminating blue material from the air.

In Houston, Texas the Juvenile Delinquency and Crime Commission prepared a list of objectionable records it wanted banned from the air. The subgroup of the commission which undertook this task was called the "Wash-Out-The-Air" Committee. The group claimed that radio represen-tatives had asked them to produce the list and that they had support from ASCAP executives in New York. The group was looking for records that were "suggestive, obscene, and characterized by lewd intonations." In ad-dition, city record stores and jukebox operators were asked to cooperate and not handle any of the objectionable disks.

The list contained twenty-six records, all on independent labels, all BMI, and almost all by blacks. The list included: "I Got A Woman" by Ray Charles, "Watcha Gonna Do Now" by Clyde McPhatter, "Annie Had A Baby" by Hank Ballard and the Midnighters, "Sixty Minute Man" by the Dominoes, "Honey Love" by the Drifters, "Work With Me Annie" by the Midnighters, and "Good Rockin' Tonight" by Roy Brown. One of the few white artists on the list was Elvis Presley singing "Good Rockin' Tonight."

The commission made it clear to the stations in Houston that if they played any of the songs on the list the group would complain to the Federal Communications Commission (FCC), which granted and renewed radio licenses. All nine of Houston's radio outlets were monitored by as many as eleven committee members. According to the group's head, Dr. H. A. Bullock, a black professor of sociology at Texas Southern University, all nine stations cooperated "sooner or later." The effect was to erase most "suggestive or obscene race music" from Houston's air. Bowing further to this group's pressure tactics, some of the radio stations used committee suggestions as a guide to record selection and some set up their own screening panels.

A columnist for the jazz magazine *Down Beat*, Leonard Feather, took the view that the lyric question was really unimportant. It masked the real issue which was the appalling musical level of rock and roll itself. The artists were provided with only two types of material: love songs that could have been penned by any "reasonably bright third grader in grammar school" and novelty songs written by the younger brothers of the aforesaid. For Feather, "music as a creative art, and the average R&B performance, by today's standards, are about as close together as Eisenhower and Bulganin."[13]

The situation was carried to its illogical extreme by veteran songwriter Jimmy Kennedy (ASCAP) who agreed fully that R&B lyrics were obscene and who thought that such material should not have been allowed on the air. He put much of the blame on writers he termed "new boys," not-yet songwriters who thought smut was smart, who lacked taste, judgment, literacy, and most of all, talent. The idea that teens might want the material being produced cut no ice with Kennedy since he felt that the tail should not be allowed to wag the dog. He also condemned record companies for letting the industry "be fouled by marketing filth." His biggest worry was that such material was being distributed worldwide and was creating a negative global impression of the United States. He wrote, "what is bad for the youth of America is also bad for the youth of England and other countries."[14]

Censorship and condemnation of rock lyrics for sexual and other reasons would continue over the years but the first fever pitch attacks on rock leerics peaked in 1955, the year that rock swept the land. Whites continued to cover black tunes but artists like Chuck Berry and Little Richard cracked the color lines as superstars among both white and black fans. Rock also produced its own white stars doing original hits. While R&B had its share of tunes dealing with sex, the majority of them dealt with other topics. As rock came to dominate the music scene, it would have been futile for forces opposing rock to continue to attack only leerics. Even if successful in eliminating such tunes, the majority of rock tunes would be unaffected.

After 1955 the anti-rock advocates moved into broader attacks on the music. Attacking with just a sexual brush could only "tar" a few songs. By moving into wider areas of attack the opposition hoped to "tar" the full spectrum of rock and roll. Henceforth attacks would center more on the poor and abysmal quality of rock music, its supposed effect in creating juvenile delinquency, and the lewdness of performers themselves. For example, artists such as Presley would be condemned for the way they performed a song, regardless of its lyrics. However, the furor over leerics certainly had its effect on rock music. Many artists such as Bill Haley and Little Richard "cleaned up" songs before they cut and released them. The artists and their management people imposed censorship on themselves, before the fact, anticipating a possible storm over their material.

The actions of the Mutual Broadcasting System provided an example of the broader type of attack. In 1958 the twenty-one hours a week of record programming service they provided to affiliates was changed from "Top 50" to "Pop 50" and some rock and roll was banned. The company eliminated rock and roll songs which contained "distorted, monotonous, noisy music and/or suggestive or borderline salacious lyrics."[15] Some examples of banned rock were "Splish Splash" by Bobby Darin, "Yakety Yak" by the Coasters, and "Hard Headed Woman" by Elvis Presley.

NBC was also hostile to rock and sent a special LP to advertising agencies knocking rock and roll. Called "Music To Buy Time By" the album featured excerpts from rock and roll songs, with derogatory comments added. "Peggy Sue" by Buddy Holly was described as "mood music for stealing hub caps." The Coasters, who performed "Yakety Yak," were called "four fugitives from the hog-caller seminar." When this tune was excerpted the commentator said, "let's see what other garb-uh-rock and roll music we have."[16] Only ABC, with Dick Clark's "American Bandstand," was receptive to rock. Mutual's music director, Phil Lampkin, went so far as to claim that the major record companies only released rock records "under duress."

The Catholic Youth Center (CYC), high school students in Minneapolis, and jockeys around the country launched an anti-rock campaign in 1958 to combat records which lowered teenagers' moral standards. "Secretly" and "Wear My Ring Around Your Neck" were on their blacklist because they both advocated going steady. This group sponsored a contest for high school students to write "fresh and decent" song lyrics and submit them to local radio stations. They sent promotional material to jockeys across the country, addressed to "the most disk-criminating diskjockey at your station."[17] The CYC issued a newsletter to teens in Minneapolis and urged them to buy only the "wholesome" records that were listed weekly in the *Catholic Bulletin*. The group also advised its readers to "Smash the records you possess which present a pagan culture and a pagan concept of life. . . . Phone or write a disk jockey who is pushing a lousy record. Switch your radio dial when you hear a suggestive song. . . . Some songwriters need a good swift kick. So do some singers. So do some jockeys."[18]

Even ABC was far from wholeheartedly behind rock and roll. The network's music supervisor, Harold Parkyn, opined that censors were becoming more lenient at the end of the 1950s, and while he said rock and roll was popular enough to deserve radio and TV time and that Dick Clark's "Bandstand" gave little trouble, he was still wary of Presley. "Elvis has been a naughty boy on some disks, so we listen to his new ones carefully."[19] "Bandstand" was not without its own problems. Link Wray had an instrumental hit called "Rumble," a slang word for a teenage gang fight. Some New York stations wouldn't play the song because Manhattan was in the midst of a teenage crime wave and some critics tied the record to the problem. When Wray was booked to do "Bandstand," the network at first refused to allow him on the air. His song, with no words whatsoever, was banned. After much discussion a compromise was reached. Wray could appear but the song title couldn't. Clark simply said, "now here's Link Wray" and Wray did "Rumble" although the word was not mentioned. This song was judged as acceptable by the previously mentioned Catholic Youth Center in Minneapolis.

The odd diehard still clung to the leerics issue. Columnist Don Morrison of the *Minneapolis Star* saw in rock and roll music in 1962 a moral menace worse than Henry Miller's novels, then under the gun for pornography. Morrison made it clear he wasn't upset by the music quality, "unspeakable" as he found it, but he was offended by the lyrics. He felt they were worse than Miller's work because even an illiterate could come under rock's influence while literacy, an attribute of few rock fans, was required to read Miller. Morrison even coined a new term: if Miller's works were pornographic, then rock was pornophonic, or even stereopornophonic, which was twice as bad. *Variety* reprinted the column, perhaps hoping to create another stir as they had in 1955, but it didn't have much of an impact.[20] Morrison was seven years out of date, or perhaps twenty years too early.

3

"Riots in the Streets"

Live rock and roll shows came under the gun from authorities almost immediately. In March of 1955 the first bans on such affairs were announced as both Bridgeport and New Haven in Connecticut put the clamps on. This happened when a rock and roll teenage dance in New Haven resulted in a brawl after which several youths were arrested. Police in those cities barred such events and said they would issue no more permits for them. Bridgeport police superintendent John A. Lyddy felt the situation was getting out of hand. While Lyddy had received no specific requests from community or church groups to block rock and roll shows, he did claim to have received complaints from parents and added, "Teenagers virtually work themselves into a frenzy to the beat of fast swing music."[1]

For the most part though, 1955 saw attacks on rock directed mainly at the so-called obscene lyrics, or leerics, as they were often termed. It was in 1956 that live rock shows and dances came under the heaviest fire as these events increased in number and appeal. Illustrating the change in emphasis was a *New York Times* review of a live rock and roll stage show at New York City's State Theater early in 1956. The reviewer felt compelled to first define this still very new music form before going on to decry it as "commercialized wailing," "crude and noisy," and far removed "from the kind of popular song that can delight the heart." The reviewer hoped rock was just a craze that would pass, and the sooner the better. Two girls got up to dance in the aisle but were soon seated again by a policeman. The writer also pointed out that words of rock were "aptly described" as leerics, although the reviewer grudgingly had to admit that none of the words at this show were suggestive.[2]

March of 1956 saw a "teen riot" at the Massachusetts Institute of Technology (MIT) in Cambridge, Massachusetts. The event was a live rock concert emceed by local disk jockey Bill Marlowe of station WCOP, a youth favorite. A crowd of three thousand paid ninety-nine cents apiece to come to what many thought was going to be a dance. However, the event was exclusively a concert with no room for dancing. After two acts had performed, the audience crowded closer and closer to the stage. The seven police who had been in attendance all evening, fearing problems, ordered Marlowe to bring the concert to a halt. The crowd then commenced to smash tables and generally trash the place. Twenty additional police were called in to quell the disturbance which lasted for about ninety minutes.

A number of factors were likely involved in triggering the incident: overcrowding, poor stage arrangement, a large number of the audience thinking it was a dance, and the police shutting it down before anything had actually happened. Marlowe said that while he had advertised the show all week on his radio program, he never said it was a dance. Whatever the cause, the blame fell squarely on the music and on the disk jockey. After the incident, "a wave of criticism against rock and roll music for teenagers and the custom of following one's favorite disk jockey around from one record hop to another" broke out.[3]

It was then ominously noted that at recent record hops at nearby Somerville some youths had been seen consuming a mixture of Coca Cola and benzedrine pills. Marlowe was the disk jockey emcee at those hops. This marked the beginning of the attacks on rock and roll disk jockeys as well as the music. The jockey quickly came to be viewed as little more than a pimp for rock music, the prostitute of the industry. This image would help pave the way for the downfall of Alan Freed and would help establish a base for attacking the jockeys through the payola hearings. It would require all the clean wholesomeness of a Dick Clark to rehabilitate the image of disk jockeys at the end of the decade and into the first couple of years of the 1960s.

Immediately after the Cambridge incident Mayor Edward J. Sullivan recommended to the city manager that the city prohibit events in which disk jockeys conducted such entertainment. He was joined in his recommendation by former mayor Joseph DeGuglielma. A day later the city council unanimously banned from their city entertainment by "disc jockeys who feature 'rock and roll' music." A committee appointed to study the music labelled jockeys "social pariahs."

Judge John Connelly from Juvenile Court added that the "leadership of the disk jockey had dangerously supplanted the leadership of the good elements in the community among these impressionable teen-agers." Richard J. Linehan, the acting police chief in the town commented: "These record hops are bad things. It is from them that we get a lot of our trouble today with the teenagers."[4] All of this appeared in the local paper under the headline, "Rock and Roll and Hoodlumism." Mayor Sullivan felt that rock shows "incite something that causes a lot of trouble with kids."[5]

The furor spread to Boston where both the music and the jockey came under attack from newspapers, radio commentators, and school and city officials. Boston City Council called on its school committee to appoint area clergy as advisers in the drafting of a list of approved jockeys. Other members of the school committee spent hours listening to records that had recently been played at area record hops. The Boston Catholic paper, *The Pilot*, wanted a blacklist of all jocks who misbehaved, and commented: "The last few weeks have substantiated the worst fears of observers. And it is clear now that the disk jockey-ed dance is in notable instances, a menace to life, limb, decency and morals."[6]

The Boston School Committee was also in the process of setting up a set of rules for the use of school buildings for dances. An applicant would be required to fill out a form stating what type of music was to be played and name the individual in charge of playing it. The chairman of the Boston Licensing Board, Mary Driscoll, said that some rock and roll was "very acceptable" to her but "its exciting tempos could endanger the morals of our youth. . . . Teenagers have no business listening to disc jockeys at 12 o'clock at night. The way they're going, they'll have high blood pressure before they're twenty."[7]

In Hartford, Connecticut police tried to revoke the license of the State Theatre because they were getting what they felt were too many "riot" calls to the building which played mostly rock and roll shows. Eleven people were arrested at one show. The theater owner claimed police were exaggerating and hurled charges of censorship at the police, and their action ultimately failed. It was said that in Hartford the State was known as the "House of Three R's (Rock, Roll, Riot)."[8] It was certainly common during this period to link the three R's together, and newspaper and magazine articles frequently used this phrase.

In Atlanta, Georgia police banned public dances at the City Auditorium and prohibited youths under the age of eighteen from attending public dances at other locations unless they were accompanied by a parent or guardian, or unless they had written permission from the parent or guardian. The city also had a midnight curfew for those under the age of eighteen.[9]

Variety treated the rock and roll shows ambivalently, being enraptured by the large grosses such shows were racking up, but warning, on the other hand, that the music may have gotten too hot to handle and that "its Svengali grip on the teenagers has produced a staggering wave of juvenile violence and mayhem."[10] It was box office dynamite; and it created an explosive situation for the police. A warning was issued by the paper that the situation had deteriorated to the extent that some of the theaters and cinemas were wary of booking rock bands due to "anticipated hooligan capers." Those that weren't scared off were hiring special cops to control the concerts.

The Alan Freed show had just finished a ten-day stand at Brooklyn's Paramount Theatre and achieved an all-time high gross of $204,000 for the house. It was admitted that the house had suffered no damage other than the normal wear and tear expected from such a gross. Moreover, the squads of police and Pinkerton guards stationed inside kept a tight rein on the audience. Yet the connection with violence was still made by pointing out that after one concert part of the audience went out and promptly trashed a subway car.

Less than a month after the MIT disturbance mentioned earlier, Boston radio station WMEX changed its music format by cutting rock and substituting two new programs called "Theatre of Beautiful Music." The station's managing director, William Pote, said they had been playing pop music for a short time hoping the fad would be short-lived and the music would fall from favor. WMEX, choosing not to wait any more, had decided to do something about it immediately.[11] In Portsmouth, New Hampshire the city's recreation director banned all rock and roll dancing at the community center except for "organized" record hops held with "strict supervision."

An appearance in June 1956 of a rock show at the National Guard Armory in Washington, D.C., headlined by Bill Haley and the Comets, attracted five thousand fans. Once again kids started dancing in the aisles and once again police chased them back into their seats. Scuffles broke out inside the arena and spilled over into the street. The manager of the Armory, Arthur Bereman, blamed the music: "it's the jungle strain that gets 'em all worked up." An unnamed sociologist was reported to claim that rock fever was "caused by the same virus which induces panty raids and goldfish swallowing."[12]

A few weeks later city officials in Jersey City, New Jersey banned a Bill Haley concert that had been slated for city-owned Roosevelt Stadium, citing previous rock riots as the reason for the ban. Even though the establishment bandleader Paul Whiteman was scheduled as master of ceremonies, the show could not be saved. A couple of days later Asbury Park, New Jersey followed suit and banned rock and roll shows. They claimed it was for the teens' own good since twenty-five "vibrating teenagers" had been hospitalized following a record hop. A third community in that state, Pompton Lakes, gave conditional approval for a concert. A show which had been slated for midnight was axed but the 7:00 P.M. and 9:00 P.M. shows were allowed. The borough council, however, planned to load the place with cops and members of the city's public safety committee planned to be on hand. This committee was prepared to cancel the second show at the first sign of trouble during the first.[13]

A "riot" during a concert in San Jose, California prompted neighboring Santa Cruz to ban all such events from civic buildings. The Pennsylvania Chiefs of Police Association happened to be meeting in Pittsburgh during another rock concert incident and had a few comments. The group branded the music as "an incentive to teenage unrest." Fred Good of the Pittsburgh force, who did not claim to be a music critic or to have a technical under-standing of rhythm and beats, was convinced nevertheless that wherever there was teenage trouble, rock and roll was in the background. He added that the songs were "more suggestive than those sung in burlesque houses and the rhythm seems to have some special hypnotic effect."[14]

In San Antonio, Texas the Parks Department banned rock and roll records from the jukeboxes located at the various city swimming pools. The move was made in response to "undesirable incidents" which were blamed on the music. An assistant to the parks director, Joe Neel, said teenagers were dancing to the rock music in their bathing suits, a practice frowned on by the city police. Neel added further, "The music attracted a lot of undesirable people who loitered around the pools with no intention of going in swimming."[15]

In Burbank, California a scheduled show by the Platters was can-celled by the city for fear of a riot. The city then changed their minds and reinstated the show provided the Platters did not perform "I Wanna," a song the city fathers termed "too jumpy, hot stuff" for teens. After all that the Platters cancelled out, pleading prior commitments. Station WMIN in Minneapolis dropped their rock and roll music format citing the numerous riots "incited" by rock dances and the "mounting nationwide opposition to this type of music." A fight at a rock dance held in St. Paul led to a police report that stated, "The general brand of people and type of behavior at the dance were not conducive or beneficial in any respect to the proper environment of juveniles."[16]

Fats Domino headlined a rock concert at the enlisted men's club at the naval station at Newport, Rhode Island. It turned into a disturbance; the club was damaged, a number of sailors were injured, and nine were arrested. An investigation was conducted by Rear Admiral Ralph D. Earle, Jr., the base commanding officer. Although the audience contained both whites and blacks, and both sailors and marines, Earle determined that racial tensions and/or service branch rivalry played no part in the riot. He placed full blame on "the excitement accompanying the fever-pitched 'Rock 'n' Roll.'"[17]

Two disk jockeys in Chicago tried to open a rock and roll dance hall there. While they had paid the $100 fee for a license application, the police refused to accept the receipt as adequate. Further protests by a total of twenty-two different area church and parent-teacher groups effectively killed the idea.

The first rock and roll film was the 1956 Columbia release *Rock around the Clock*, starring Bill Haley and the Comets, the Platters, and Alan Freed. It was a seventy-six-minute feature that was largely a showcase for various groups to perform their rock and roll songs. What little story line there was concerned the discovery of rock and roll and its subsequent spread around the country.

When the *New York Times* reviewed the film they gave it thumbs down, more because of rock than any other reason. The dance band manager was played by Johnny Johnson, apparently a real life ballad singer, and the paper commented that he "must have cringed at having to depict enthusiasm over the crudities on the soundtrack." While the *Times* admitted the lyrics were not of the "more suggestive" rock variety they noted there was "a full measure of hip-swinging dancing." The *Times* was upset to see apparently competent musicians "mechanically grinding out this raucous rhythmic commodity that is so far from the jazz with which it is sometimes unfortunately confused."[18]

First released in April in the United States, *Rock around the Clock* didn't cause much of a stir. There were a few complaints about excessive hand clapping and foot stomping at some screenings. At a showing in Minneapolis a group of teenagers snake danced down a major street at the film's end and broke some store windows, causing the police to disperse the crowd. In La Crosse, Wisconsin police were also called out to quell disorderly teens. Generally, though, the film was received very quietly in the United States.

The same was not true for Great Britain where the film was released in the summer of 1956 and which was the scene, in September, of numerous disturbances and arrests. The different audience responses in the two countries could be largely attributed to the relative dearth of live rock shows in Britian. Rock and roll was then the preserve of American stars and they were not yet touring Britain in live shows in anywhere near the number of such shows in the United States. Britain had not yet produced any homegrown rockers and the teens wanted to see the American stars. For them the film was the closest most would get to live rock and roll and accordingly most British "riots" took place at screenings of the film. In America most kids had the opportunity to see live concerts during the period of the film's release and did their "rioting" there.

At one London area cinema the crowd was milling about on the sidewalk after a screening of the film, singing rock and roll songs. Police, who described the singing as "ranting and raving," attempted to disperse the crowd. A couple of youths jeered at the police and were arrested and charged with "insulting behavior." They received sentences of discharge, conditional on good behavior for one year. Seven youths were arrested under similar circumstances after a screening at another London cinema. They were each fined twenty shillings. At a West Ham theater over one hundred teens were ejected during the film; they too were noisy and created a disturbance outside. When the police arrived all left but one who was subsequently fined two pounds for insulting behavior.[19]

Since the initial disturbances in the north and northwest parts of London had taken place on Sunday nights, the Gaumont theater chain decided not to show the film anywhere in South London on Sunday nights, but did screen it the other six nights. At one cinema, the Trocadero, the last-minute substitute on Sunday night was something called *Gun Fury*.[20] The English city of Blackpool banned the film completely from their city. They were worried about all the reports of "noisy behavior" by teens in other cities that had screened the film.

Disturbances continued around the country. In Manchester a showing of the film was stopped in the middle while police ejected about fifty unruly teens. In South London the Sunday night ban proved useless as a disturbance broke out at the first Monday evening screening of *Rock aroud the Clock* after the Sunday ban had been in effect. Trouble started when a few couples started dancing in the cinema aisles. Police were called in and about fifty teens were ejected.[21]

What happened in most cases was police overreaction. The teen offenses were mostly of those dancing in theater aisles and milling about on the street after the film concluded. If the police had not stepped in so quickly the dancing may have led to nothing and the millers may have dispersed and left quietly and quickly enough on their own. The situation escalated only after the police had arrived. The *New York Times*, reporting on the British situation, said, in exaggerated fashion, "After listening to the rock 'n' roll rhythm to which the picture is devoted, teenagers have wrecked motion picture houses, assaulted policemen and danced in wild mobs through the streets."[22]

More towns took action as Preston and Blackburn banned the film, while in Manchester the theater manager turned away from his cinema any youth he felt looked like a troublemaker. In a London court two youths were fined ten shillings each in costs when evidence showed they had brought traffic to a standstill by continuously running back and forth across a street after seeing the film. Another youth was dancing in the theater aisle with his girl and refused to return to his seat when requested to do so by police. As he was being ejected he kicked the cop and was subsequently charged and fined twenty shillings. In Woolwich a crowd of youths blocked the sidewalk while singing and dancing in front of a cinema after it had closed. Five of them were arrested and four were fined one pound for insulting behavior. The fifth was fined an additional five pounds for assaulting a constable.

In Manchester court fourteen teens appeared as a result of a disturbance. After a screening of the film a group of about two hundred left the cinema and walked along, en masse, singing rock and roll songs, or, as the police described it, "shouting and screaming and bawling things." According to police the group was a "noisy and unruly mob" that blocked traffic and "terrorized pedestrians." Fourteen were arrested with most being fined thirty or forty shillings by the judge who termed their behavior "organized hooliganism." He further added that it would have been better "if the police were allowed to deal with you in the way which would give you something to rock and roll about for a bit."[23] Birmingham, Britain's second largest city, then banned the showing of the film, fearing that "riots" in other parts of the country might spread there. Paradoxically, *Rock around the Clock* had already been shown at one Birmingham cinema with no adverse results.

The list of places where the film was banned continued to grow and included: Birmingham, Belfast, Bristol, Liverpool, Carlisle, Bradford, Blackburn, Preston, Blackpool, Bootle, Brighton, Gateshead, South Shields, Wigan, and Berkshire County. In addition the Rank Organization theater chain was not showing the film on Sundays in any of its cinemas.[24] The mayor of Gateshead, A. Henderson, commented that it was undesirable for the film to be shown in that city since the public

34

shouldn't have to tolerate "this sort of hooliganism." Blackburn's town clerk barred the movie because he felt it contained material "likely to lead to public disorder."[25]

When the film was screened in Aberdeen, Scotland the theater manager turned off the sound at the first sign of trouble. When the film first played Edinburgh no trouble was reported other than clapping and stomping. When rebooked into that city's movie houses police officers were asked to stand by in case of trouble. More and more it became the custom for the theater managers to hire "burly" young men to act as bouncers during the film's screenings and to have extra police handy in case of "possible riots." In other areas before the film was allowed to be screened, exhibitors were asked to guarantee to the local judges that no disorders would take place.

Arrests continued and after one London screening twenty-four people were picked up and charged with disorderly behavior. Another group of eleven were fined one pound for insulting behavior after police broke up a milling crowed after the film. The magistrate, A. L. Stevenson, commented, "You have had your fun and now you have to pay for it. We are getting rather tired of this rowdyism."[26]

All in all the film left an aftermath never matched by any movie shown in Britain. Over one hundred British youths had been arested before the month of September was over. Curiously, the film had been shown in more than three hundred British cinemas before any disturbances broke out. Authorities were perplexed by this atypical British behavior. The Bishop of Woolwich put forward the opinion that "the hypnotic rhythm and wild gestures in the picture had a maddening effect on a rhythm-loving age group."[27] The conductor of the British Broadcasting Corporation's Symphony Orchestra, Sir Malcolm Sargent, condemned the film's music by calling it "nothing more than an exhibition of primitive tom-tom thumping . . . if it is capable of inciting youngsters to riot and fight then quite obviously it is bad."[28] Some movie house managers felt the spread of the disturbances were due to the press and "exaggerated reports" of isolated incidents. Others laid the blame on rock's birthplace claiming that if there "had been no stories from America of rock 'n' roll riots, . . . it is most unlikely that there would have been any disturbances in the cinemas or streets of this country."[29]

By the end of the month the disturbances abated as quickly, and inexplicably, as they had begun, but not before the Queen herself was involved. Queen Elizabeth asked that a copy of *Rock around the Clock* be sent to her estate in Scotland where, Buckingham Palace officials said, it was "very likely" she would watch the film at a private screening. Whether she did, or what she might have thought of the rock movie, remained a mystery.

By the spring of 1958 the furor over rock and roll shows had died down considerably, perhaps because there weren't a whole lot of "riots" to report. This quiet period was abruptly shattered on the evening of May 3, 1958 at the Boston Arena. Alan Freed had brought his traveling "Big Beat" rock show to town. Freed was both the show manager and emcee of the seventeen-act concert which featured Jerry Lee Lewis. The arena held five thousand fans that night, in addition to approximately twenty police. As was now customary for such events, some kids got up and danced in the aisles while others stood up in their seats. The police tried to curb such activity by completely turning up the house lights. Freed then said, allegedly, from the stage, "I guess the police here in Boston don't want you kids to have a good time."[30]

No other trouble or damage was reported inside but outside a total of fifteen people were stabbed, beaten, or robbed by gangs in the area. The Boston Arena was in a rough area of town and had been the site of frequent muggings in the past, but of course this factor was overlooked completely as rock and roll and Alan Freed took the full brunt of the blame. The furor over live rock shows reached new heights and those fateful words uttered onstage by Freed marked the start of a quick fall to oblivion for the jockey, regarded as public enemy number one in some anti-rock circles. "Boston policed blamed Freed and his frenetic fans, but could not prove it, since they nabbed nobody."[31]

Within a few days of the show the Suffolk County grand jury indicted Freed with inciting a riot, charging specifically that he "did advocate, advise, counsel, and incite the unlawful destruction of real, personal property."[32] Suffolk County District Attorney Garret Byrne announced he had made a thorough investigation of the fracas and interviewed scores of witnesses. Byrne "made clear his feeling that the juvenile outbreaks following these shows were induced as much by the attitude of those sponsoring the shows — the adults — as by the music itself."[33] This was a clear reference to, and condemnation of, Alan Freed. Byrne felt that some jockeys had put "emotional TNT on their turntables." Even the manager of the Boston Arena, Paul Brown, felt the disorder was encouraged by Freed.

Those that had licensed the Freed show for Boston in the first place found themselves trying to avoid being labeled responsible for allowing such an event in their city. A license was obtained from both the police department and from the city censor in the mayor's office. The police claimed their only responsibility was to determine how many officers need be stationed at an event. The city censor's office claimed that their granting of a permit always awaited final approval from the police.

Two days after the concert Boston mayor John Hynes banned from public halls all rock and roll shows put on by promoters. He said, "I am not against rock 'n' roll as such . . . and not when it is conducted under the auspices of an established organization. However, I am against rock 'n' roll dances when they are put on by a promoter. This sort of performance attracts the troublemakers and the irresponsible."[34]

Other communities soon followed suit. A performance by Freed's show slated for May 6 in Troy, New York was cancelled by the local sponsors. Authorities in New Jersey cancelled a show scheduled for Newark at the armory drill hall. The ax came from Major General James Cantwell, state chief of defense and head of the New Jersey National Guard. Cantwell broke the armory rental agreement in the "interest of public safety," and at the urging of Newark police officials. Two communities in Connecticut, New Britain and New Haven, both banned all rock and roll "melees" from their cities. Freed already had a scheduled date for New Haven and he went to court to get an injuction to lift the ban. However, the court upheld the New Haven ban. In Washington, D.C. city officials refused to allow a similar show scheduled for June 1 at Griffith Stadium on the grounds that it might lead to a riot. A Massachusetts state senator, William Fleming, went so far as to introduce a bill in the state house to ban rock and roll from all publicly owned buildings such as the Boston Arena.[35] The measure didn't become law.

The print media joined the assault on rock and roll. The *New York Daily News* charged jockeys and record manufacturers with "pandering to the worst juvenile taste." The paper described the music as a "barrage of primitive jungle-beat rhythm set to lyrics which few adults would care to hear."[36] The solution they advocated was a clampdown on the "riotous music" with teens being banned from dancing in public unless they had written consent from their parents. The *Daily News* also wanted a midnight curfew on all those under the age of twenty-one. The editorial department may have been outraged, but while they were venting their spleen the paper's promotion department was busy sponsoring a rock and roll contest.

A bizarre event took place in early 1958 in the state of Tennessee when an individual radio listener brought a suit against a local station for replacing classical music with rock and roll. The judge ordered the station to restore the classical music to the time period from which it had been bumped by rock.[37]

Articles appeared sporadically announcing the imminent demise of rock and roll music, pointing out that the fad was dying, musical tastes were changing, good music was making a comeback, and so on. One such story in *Variety* was headed "Onward 'n' Downward with R 'n' R."[38] Most of these reports were exaggerated and represented wishful thinking on the part of the writers more than they mirrored reality. Others took a more active part in trying to hurry rock into the grave. At Chowan College of Murfreesboro, North Carolina a jukebox was installed in the student center of this Baptist college. Students who listened to the rock records on the box couldn't contain themselves and ended up dancing. This caused the college president to issue a statement that dancing was forbidden by the college and the Baptist State Convention. Still the temptation to dance to rock was considered too great. Faculty members enforcing the edict felt it might be impossible for students to refrain from dancing. The end result was that a new collection of records was ordered for the jukebox: no rock and roll tunes were included.

On January 12, 1958 St. Louis radio station KWK announced the start of its "Record Breaking Week." The station played each of its rock and roll records once, then the disk jockey took the record and broke it over the air, so the listeners could hear the snap. Robert Convey, president of KWK, instituted the action after conferring with his jockeys and finding them in agreement with the proposal. Convey felt rock and roll had "dominated the music field long enough [and had] grown to such proportions as to alienate many adult listeners."[37] He felt the ban he was imposing was not the same as book burning but was just "a weeding out of undesirable music." After two days of record breaking on the air, protests from youth clubs in the area caused the station to cease the destruction and give the remaining rock records away to the teen groups. KWK claimed to have received over two hundred letters, running eight-to-one in favor of its anti-rock stance.[40]

Toward the end of the 1950s the story was much the same in England where one of the leading music journals did a feature on rock concerts under the headline, "Stars, Theatre Staff Scared Stiff of these Rock & Riot Shows." The story detailed various mishaps and injuries sustained by people attending such shows, how established pop stars didn't want to appear with rock acts, and how theaters lost business permanently when they booked rock shows. One pop star, who remained anonymous, said of theaters that booked rock and roll shows, "They book shows expressly designed to appeal to the lowest possible taste — and when the audience behaves like a lot of delinquent morons, they profess surprise and indignation."[41]

4

Combat the Menace

Racism

The most obvious example of racism as a focus of attacks on rock and roll took place in the spring of 1956 when a segregationist leader named Asa Carter delivered a vicious diatribe against rock and roll. Carter was the executive secretary of the North Alabama White Citizens Council which initiated a campaign in the Birmingham and Anniston areas of Alabama to get rock and roll off the jukeboxes. He claimed the records were smutty, had dirty lyrics, and were "sexualistic" and "immoral." He added further that rock and roll was "the basic, heavy-beat music of Negroes. It appeals to the base in man, brings out animalism and vulgarity."[1] Rock music was, according to Carter, a plot by the National Association for the Advancement of Colored People (NAACP) to pull the white man "down to the level of the Negro." And it contributed "to moral degradation of children and serves the cause of integration."[2]

The group claimed to be prepared to contact jukebox owners, to approach the sponsors and promoters of the music, to monitor radio stations, and perhaps institute boycotts of offenders. Carter's plans failed to materialize as, for one of the few times in history, everyone connected with Carter's threats came out and stood squarely behind rock music. Segregationist groups such as this one were still lashing out at the NAACP for its part in the landmark 1954 decision by the Supreme Court which struck down school segregation. When the NAACP executive secretary, Roy Wilkins, was appraised of Carter's statements he commented wryly; "Some people in the South are blaming us for everything from measles to atomic fallout."[3]

41

Things reached an ugly head in Birmingham in April 1956 at a concert given by Nat "King" Cole. The audience of over three thousand was all white and six men rushed onstage while Cole was performing and attacked the singer. Police rescued Cole but not before he had been knocked off his piano stool and mauled. One of those arrested was a director of the White Citizens' Council of Birmingham. The next month this same group picketed a Bill Haley concert in the same city. This concert also had a segregated audience. They carried signs which said, "Christians will not attend this show. Ask your preacher about jungle music."[4] They generally linked rock with communism, degradation, and sin. They were counter-picketed by teens who yelled pro-rock slogans.

The Citizens' Council of Greater New Orleans was also active. They printed and distributed a handbill in which they denounced the "screaming idiotic" lyrics of rock and claimed the music was eroding the morals of American "white youth." The group urged parents not to let their children buy these records, or to listen to them. Parents were also urged to phone advertisers and complain to them if they bought time on any radio stations that played rock and roll.

Another racist group circulated a pamphlet that stated, "Help save the youth of America! . . . Don't let your children buy or listen to these Negro records. The screaming, idiotic words and savage music are undermining the morals of our white American youth."

When black rocker Bo Diddley finally got a booking in 1958 on nationwide television his contract stipulated that he had to perform motionless, "to preserve decency." While he was performing, Bo forgot and just naturally started to move with the music. He was docked his full fee.[5]

While these examples are obvious cases of racist assaults, under the guise of protecting youthful morals from rock and roll, they were the exception. Most anti-rock hysteria contained little that was openly racist. One example of covert racism was the use of the term "jungle music" to refer to rock and roll. At first glance it may have been seen as a put-down of the music because it was more primitive. But the real purpose of using that term was to connect rock with the jungle, or black Africa, and to imply that rock and roll had to be scorned because it was the music of blacks, who were "savages."

Some of this attitude surfaced in 1956 when hearings were held by city officials in El Monte, California to determine whether rock dances should be banned. The dances had been held for a while in the small city at the edge of Los Angeles when police complained about a growing number of problems. The city suspended the dances pending a hearing.

The American Civil Liberties Union (ACLU) appeared at the hearing to argue against what they felt would be a "monstrous denial" of free expression. Those arguing for the ban complained the music was attracting a rowdy crowd.

The ACLU had gotten involved because of the subtler nuances of this rock attack, namely racism. There was "evidence that the objection to the music extends to and may be based upon, the fact that it is largely the product of Negro bands."[6] Despite ACLU intervention the city of El Monte barred the dances. Racism may not have always been evident in many instances. Whether the performer was white or black the roots of the music itself were definitely black. Today racist attacks on rock are no longer popular but there are those who would argue that blacks have more difficulty getting their music aired than whites. In most record stores black rock and roll is segregated under the label "soul."

"Good" Musicians Mourn "Good" Music

Famous musicians were another group that lined up almost solidly against rock and roll, particularly in the early years. Their views ranged from the condescending and patronizing all the way to the openly and viciously hostile. All of them had a vested interest in the music world of pre-rock days. For these musicians the rise of rock was a direct threat to their livelihood. They feared there would be less of a demand for their product and that those raised on rock would never turn back to "good" music. What ultimately happened was that many of the most vociferous of these early critics soon swallowed their principles and jumped on the rock and roll bandwagon. Only a few years after violently denouncing rock, Frank Sinatra and Elvis Presley appeared together on Sintra's television show and did a duet composed of each other's material. Even Mitch Miller would eventually produce "teen numbers" in his distinctive pablum style. In the beginning though, the musicians fought it all the way.

One way some had of dealing with the threat was to pretend that it was just a fad and would soon run its course. One of the first such was bandleader Les Elgart who felt the music would have to run its course, like an "epidemic." He saw rhythm and blues as so limited that he felt kids would get over it in a hurry. Elgart used the term rhythm and blues because he made this pronouncement in March of 1955, before rock and roll had even established itself fully.[7] He was thus writing the obituary almost before the birth. Clarinetist Buddy De France also declared rock close to death. The jazzman had determined that a return to jazz and "good" pop music was underway. He felt rock and roll was not bad, but also dismissed it as not "important."

Singer Tony Bennett worried that all the controversy over rock was self-defeating since these condemnations helped keep it alive and going. He considered it just a temporary phase in music, and teenagers would become bored with it. Bennett felt that as they matured kids would "slow down and require less noise." But Bennett's skills as a prognosticator failed a second time when he said America was more critical of rock than other countries where it was accepted as "crazy American music."[8]

The even more famous singer, Bing Crosby, was able to pronounce in January 1962 that "Rock 'n' Roll seems to have run its course." No fan of the music, he admitted to turning the radio off after hearing a couple of bars of a rock song. He also agreed with Bennett that the criticism had been helpful in keeping it alive. His favorite singers of the time were Frank Sinatra, Perry Como, and Pat Boone. With rock safely in its grave Crosby took a guess at what might replace it. He opted for "slow, pretty ballads."[9]

Percy Faith, then riding high on the charts with his "Theme From A Summer Place," was one of those who regarded rock with a negative, but patronizing manner. Faith admitted rock was here to stay and that it was "elementary music like the A.B.C.'s of grammar." One learned the simple melodies and then moved "upward to better music."[10] Bandleader Paul Whiteman went so far as to say rock was alright "in a pretty simple way." He felt there were only about "two words to a lyric."[11]

Perry Como tried to straddle the fence by saying rock could be both good and bad. He was adamant though that any suggestive lyrics should be thrown out. He felt there was no excuse for anything in a song which might be construed as dirty, although he was also of the opinion that the teens didn't really listen to rock lyrics.

Even a teen girl group, the Poni-Tails, then on the charts with the big ballad hit "Born Too Late," came out to say that they very definitely were not a rock and roll group and had no intention of becoming one, for reasons they never made clear. The group disappeared as quickly as they had arrived, another one-hit wonder.

Strange ideas began to appear. Harry Owens, the bandleader of the Royal Hawaiians from Honolulu, felt that the frenzy of rock and roll music had people looking for an antidote to soothe them rather than jar them further. It was thus only logical, according to Owens, that people would soon turn, in ever-increasing numbers, to "Hawaiian and exotic-island" music for such relief. Songwriter Johnny Green was of the opinion that rock had its place in the music world and he compared it to tarragon seasoning used in cooking. He liked tarragon once in a while, but not on everything and he objected to rock taking over "like an uncontrollable cell."[12]

The jazz magazine, *Down Beat*, sponsored a forum in their May 1956 issue for musicians to argue the values of rock.[13] They approached Benny Goodman for some comments for publication but he refused, giving "only a raised-eyebrows, mouth-turned-down silence." Four musicians did offer comments. One was Billy Taylor who called the music "trite" and "gimmicked-up" with melodies that were repetitious and/or stolen. When asked if the music hadn't brought back the beat he replied whatever it brought back "would have been better discarded." John Lewis, of the Modern Jazz Quartet, condemned most of rock as being "very poor quality musically," although he did admit he hadn't listened to it very much. When asked if the music didn't get the kids back dancing, Lewis claimed that the kids still weren't dancing, or if they were, it was "the worst dancing I've ever seen." He again admitted he hadn't seen much of the dancing. Milt Hinton, a New York bassist, called the music "pretty bad, pretty crude." As a parent he was worried about its effect on kids and he thought musicians had an obligation to educate people to a better type of music.

The fourth musician was tenor Sam Taylor, who, according to *Down Beat*, presented the case in favor of rock music. When asked about the monotony of the rock beat Taylor agreed it was repetitive, but claimed he didn't want a rhythm section that change every eight bars. Overall, about the most favorable comment Taylor could muster was that rock had "different phases, good and bad." So ended *Down Beat's* forum which "objectively" presented both sides of the question with three musicians definitely anti-rock, and one in favor, in a half-hearted and vacillating way.

Other musicians had comments more openly hostile. Bandleader Bob Crosby found it almost impossible to find an individual or striking melodic line in rock. "The so-called 'tunes' are monotonous with a similarity that is often ridiculous."[14] Singer Mel Torme blasted disk jockeys for "pandering to mediocre music." While touring in Britain he claimed only a couple of jockeys were playing good music while the rest put over junk. He urged the English to stop blindly following America and not let "so much rubbish be foisted" on themselves.[15]

Pop singer Jane Morgan laid the blame on payola for damaging the music industry and for setting the stage for the popularizing of bad music. The payola, along with teen influences, brought "exposure to tunes that for the most part are illiterate and meaningless."[16] It was popular, and erroneous, to blame payola for rock and roll as the adult world tried to expunge and erase the evil and look far and wide for causes. Morgan's sentiments were echoed by the pop-singing Andrews Sisters who said that, "the recent payola scandal . . . put a brake on the bribery that helped to promote bad quality discs."[17]

One of the most virulently anti-rock people was Mitch Miller, the chief producer, or artist and repertoire man, at Columbia Records. For him rock music was the "glorification of monotony" and with its "illiterate" lyrics was aimed at the twelve- to fifteen-year-olds. Miller boasted proudly that none of Columbia's hits were rockers and he accepted losing the twelve- to fifteen-year-olds but was ready to welcome them back to Columbia's fold later, when they had developed "taste." He dismissed Presley as a "three-ring circus." His distaste bordered on revulsion, for political and social reasons as well as musical ones. He thought rock was a credo among teens. "They accept almost any form of it, even the lowest and most distasteful. . . . It seems to encourage sloppy clothes that become the accepted uniform. The kids take it all without discrimination. It's one step from fascism."[18] During a 1957 interview with Sammy Davis, Jr., Miller called rock records the "comic books" of music while Davis asserted that if rock and roll were here for good he "might commit suicide."[19] It was, but he didn't.

Even more vitriolic was conductor and composer Meredith Wilson of *The Music Man* fame. He complained that rock stupefied the kids and he laid the blame for this "creeping paralysis" on the doorstep of the record companies that released such material. After this attack Mitch Miller was quick to issue a statement to clarify that the majority of such tunes were turned out by small record companies, and not big ones like his own Columbia — a statement which was correct. Wilson decried the influence rock had on kids and went on to say, "The people of this country do not have any conception of the evil being done by rock 'n' roll; it is a plague as far reaching as any plague we have ever had. . . . My complaint is that it just isn't music. It's utter garbage and it should not be confused in any way with anything related to music or verse."[20]

One of the most famous and hostile comments was delivered by singer Frank Sinatra who damned the music, singers, and composers and tied rock to delinquency, all in one breath. He said, in 1957, that "rock 'n' roll smells phony and false. It is sung, played and written for the most part by cretinous goons and by means of its almost imbecilic reiteration, and sly, lewd, in plain fact, dirty lyrics . . . it manages to be the martial music of every sideburned delinquent on the face of the earth."[21] Not content with that, Sinatra later added that rock and roll was "the most brutal, ugly, desperate, vicious form of expression it has been my misfortune to hear."[22] It wasn't long before Frank had changed his tune.

Comments from musicians outside the United States were similar. The conductor of the Berlin Philharmonic Orchestra, Herbert von Karajan, tried to explain the effects of rock by stating, "Strange things happen in the blood stream when a musical resonance coincides with the beat of the human pulse."[23] In Australia harmonica player Larry Adler was unhappy with the way rock desecrated such standards as "Blue Moon." To him it was like someone painting a moustache on the Mona Lisa. Adler was convinced that rock, which he didn't consider to be music, had a bad effect and helped "keep the IQ down" since it stopped "teenagers thinking."[24] BBC Symphony Orchestra conductor Sir Malcolm Sargent snidely noted that the music was not as new as the teenagers believed since "Rock 'n' Roll has been played in the jungle for centuries."[25]

Others in Britain were equally incensed. Bandleader Vic Lewis called upon the music industry to "stop these insults to teenagers." He felt teens didn't know what they wanted and that "musical worth" never entered their heads. He was joined by Harry Francis of the British Musicians' Union who damned the "rubbish" forced on teens, a rubbish churned out, and controlled, by America. The union was considering more stringent tests before "so-called musicians" would be admitted to membership. Victor Knight of the Songwriters Guild of Great Britain called on parents and teachers to organize and "demand that recording and broadcasting companies stop this poisoning of youth immediately."[26] Much of the British outrage had to do with an increased amount of U. S. rock music being played on the BBC. This meant less British material, which meant less royalties for British musicians.

Venerated musician Pablo Casals was one of those who most hotly damned rock. To him it was a terrible and convulsive sound. He didn't accept the idea that there was no such thing as bad music, comparing that to taking the word of a blind man who swore colors never clashed. A person who said there was no bad music had to be "partially deaf." Youths growing up were subject, according to Casals, to two terrors. One was to have their bodies exposed to continued bombardment from atomic bomb test fallout; the other was to have their souls exposed to rock. Casals called rock and roll an "abomination . . . a disgrace. Poison put to sound . . . the raucous distillation of the ugliness of our times."[27] The editor of the magazine in which Casals's comments appeared, *Music Journal*, felt moved enough to add an editorial note in which he said Casals's reaction "should be assimilated by the entire world of music."

Religion Rocks Rockers

As one might expect, religious figures came forward, particularly during rock's first few years, to voice their displeasure. Their opposition ran the gamut from what might be called the mildly reproving voice of reason to the extremely righteously indignant who favored sweeping the music from the face of the earth, as soon as was humanly possible. Two examples of the former were the Reverend Norman J. O'Connor, a Catholic, and the Reverend Alvin L. Kershaw, a Protestant. Both said they felt there was nothing morally wrong with the music, but it was too commercial. Responding to somebody who was a rock fan O'Connor added, "I do hope you outgrow it."[28] The Reverend Edward J. Hales, a Baptist minister from New Bedford, Massachusetts, delivered an entire sermon on Elvis Presley one Sunday morning. Refraining from attacking the singer, Hales saw the rocker more as a reflection of the turmoil in the lives of youths and contented himself, in 1956, with the thought that Presley would fall from popularity within a year or two.

When New York's Cardinal Spellman appeared before thousands of Roman Catholics at Buffalo's Civic Stadium, he quoted at length from an article by the *New York Times* critic, Jack Gould, who had commented negatively on a recent TV performance by Elvis Presley. Spellman addressed the problem of "today's teen-age craze for suggestive TV performers and performances," by saying that the gravest and greatest challenge facing parents was that of their children. The cardinal laid the blame on the parents, teachers, and clergy, "who do not constantly and actively work and pray to arrest the avalanche of . . . obscene dancing."[29] Monsignor Gonzi, the Roman Catholic Archbishop of Malta, in a circular distributed throughout the churches of Malta, kept his plea short and simple by warning dance organizers "not to burden themselves with the responsibility of ruining souls by rock 'n' roll."[30]

A religious columnist for the *Toronto Telegram* used the old guilt technique. Jan Scott spoke of the three R's, the third being "regret." "Have you ever felt that way after a session of rock 'n' roll? . . . you couldn't [sleep] because deep down in your heart you felt that the whole business of pleasure-seeking and self-indulgence was a mockery and a sham." The minister of the Evangel Temple in Toronto, the Reverend W. G. McPherson, complained that rock music wasn't the same as revivalist music where people were moved by the spirit of the Lord. Rather, rock worked upon man's emotions "like the music of the heathen in Africa."[31]

Moving into the more extreme reaction was that of the Irish Catholic magazine *Redemptionist Record*. In 1954, the magazine was already complaining about the suggestiveness and "blatant vulgarity" of pop songs. They considered that songwriters were deliberately breaking down reticence about sex and that Church "enemies" were using such songs "as an instrument for the propagation of immorality." All of this came under the heading, "Knock the Devil out of Dancing."[32]

In Boston the Very Reverend John P. Carroll, addressing a group of teachers, lashed out at the music and the jockey. He felt that some jockeys were not living up to their responsibilities and that the suggestive lyrics themselves were "a matter for law enforcement agencies." As for the music, Carroll blasted rock for inciting and inflaming youths and "readying warriors for battle." He warned adults to be wary of using such music at teen dances since you can "inject a wrong word or misunderstanding and the whole place blows up."[33]

The Reverend John J. Grant, associate editor of the Catholic paper *The Pilot*, blasted jockeys for serving as substitute parents, advisers, and clergymen to teens while the public allowed itself to be "prostituted" by youth entertainment on radio and TV. Samuel Cardinal Stritch of Chicago decried what he called rock's tribal rhythms and advised that rock and roll not be played in Catholic schools. Stritch's remarks were picked up by daily papers around the nation and he hoped his "word [would] have the effect of banning such things in Catholic recreation."[34] A week after his remarks a survey of record retailers, distributors, disk jockeys, and others showed the Cardinal's word to have had no effect on rock record sales.

Some of the most extreme reactions came from the English clergy. The Reverend J. H. Chamberlain, Vicar of St. Michael's and All Angels, Smethwick, Staffs, claimed to see a sharp dividing line in music with it being "of God or of the devil. It inspires and uplifts, or it poisons and degrades." It goes without saying where he thought rock and roll fell. His solution was to "ban evil music" with the censoring being done by a board of "distinguished musicians." Commenting on all this in the English music magazine, *Melody Maker*, columnist Steve Race was horrified by the censorship idea but shared many of Chamberlain's fears about the effect of rock on the morals of youth. Race felt that some of Presley's records contained "cheap, meretricious lyrics" which crossed the line "between harmless fun and lightly disguised filth."[35] Another clergyman denounced rock as a revival of devil dancing and ominously declared its effects would be to "turn young people into devil worshippers, to stimulate self-expression through sex, to provoke lawlessness and impair nervous stability."[36]

Equally hostile was Dr. Donald Soper, a well-known English Methodist preacher who was appalled by the undue emphasis on sex in so many rock tunes. To him it was a case of "artistic suicide," nothing but "trash," and the market for such trash ranged "from the bright 10-year old to the retarded adult." He had no sympathy for those in the industry who said they were just providing what the public wanted. They were "people foisting rubbish on the public." Soper was adamant that some form of censorship was needed and in the meantime he hoped to see courageous disk jockeys who would reject all such trash since "to set out and deprave young people and to plead prosperity as a justification is shocking."[37]

A Pentacostal evangelist, Jimmie Snow, son of country music's Hank Snow, was himself a minor rock and roll star for a few years, touring a number of times with Elvis Presley. After attending church one Sunday he felt the Lord speaking to him and gave up rock and roll to become an evangelist preacher, speaking at revival meetings to say that the harm rock did to kids wasn't apparent until later. He claimed that hundreds of teens had come to him and told him they got into trouble after rock and roll parties and dances. Snow denounced the music's "evil beat" from the pulpit. The causal connection was plain to him; after teens heard and danced to rock "gangs fight and the beer riots break out. Their grades in school start dropping."[38] He firmly believed the music to be sinful, a corruptor of morals, and a "major contributor" to juvenile delinquency.

All of these reasons for being against rock, especially the religious ones, remain with us today. It was not an isolated phenomenon of the 1950s. Now it tends to be the fundamentalist religious leaders who rail against rock more than the mainstream religions such as Catholicism. But the assault is still carried on with as much fervor and intensity.

"Stimulated" to a "Frenzy"

Rock and roll soon came to be linked with just about every form of delinquent behavior exhibited by the young and just as quickly the music was labeled the cause of such behavior. Statements abounded that rock and roll "stimulated . . . copbaiting and outbursts of vandalism and mayhem,"[39] or "outbursts of violence spurred by the heavy, pulsing beat of this latest derivative of Negro blues, by the moaning suggestiveness of most of its songs, have occurred all over the country. . . . Social workers . . . concede that most trouble can be attributed to the craze for Rock 'n' Roll."[40] The attacks on the music continued to spread and to encompass a wider variety of youthful behavior as rock became a bigger and bigger scapegoat for everything about teenagers that the adult world didn't like. Every time a rock show was held the theater shrieked and rang "like the jungle bird house at the zoo" and anything which could do this to America's youth just had to be bad.

Any number of "experts" were ready, willing, and able to come forward and lend their august opinions to the anti-rock movement. A. D. Buchmueller, a psychiatric social worker and executive director of the Child Study Association, agreed with the idea that rock might be an outlet for teen's sexual aggression or impulsive behavior. He did admit that this was mere speculation and that no thorough studies had ever proved such connections. Adolescent Court Judge Hilda Schwartz said that while rock and roll didn't produce delinquents, any teen who was insecure, hostile, or disturbed would find the "stimulation of the frenzied, abandoned music" to be anything but therapy. Both Buchmueller and Schwartz were of the opinion that rock was just a fad of passing interest.[41]

A psychiatrist by the name of Dr. Francis J. Braceland, chief of the Institute of Living, regarded the music form as "cannibalistic and tribalistic." To him rock and roll was a "communicable disease."[42] A professor of music at the University of Texas, Dr. Archie N. Jones, said he saw nothing wrong with rock music itself and claimed it was impossible for any type of music to be immoral. What Jones found objectionable was the "beer hall atmosphere" and some of the people connected with the music. Immorality in rock only became an issue "when people are involved."[43] He felt many performers were not very good and many were not in "good taste." He too saw rock and roll as a passing fad, a matter of no importance which, when gone, would leave nothing as a memory except for the name. In the meantime he thought some other singer might be able to take Presley's songs "and do them well."

Dr. Howard Hanson had been the director of the Eastman School of Music at the University of Rochester for close to forty years when he tuned in on "cultured Boston" from his summer home near Maine and came face to face "with the most violent and vicious rock and roll." This sudden assault on Hanson caused the doctor to label the music as "acoustical pollution." It took on ever greater significance as he compared it with a civilization gone awry, a civilization that has "lost the way . . . lost its sense of values."[44] A. M. Merrio, an associate professor of psychiatry at Columbia University, was afraid that if we didn't stem the rock and roll tide we were "preparing our downfall in the midst of pandemic funeral dances."[45]

Australian critic Sam Dunn was exaggerating only slightly when he claimed that rock and roll, "a musical weed sold to school children and adolescents," was unique in earning the unanimous contempt of the entire music profession. Describing the music as violent, brutalizing, and crude, he was sure it "must be just as powerful an influence for evoking crude and brutal emotions." His thoughts appeared under the damning title, "The Music of Violence."[46]

Even a man named Charles Pintchman, who was public relations director for *Reader's Digest*, vented his spleen. His music credentials seemed to have been limited to singing in church. Pintchman stretched back in entertainment history to the times when Christians had been thrown to the lions. It seemed that rock had been the only entertainment medium since then that "appealed entirely to man's baser instincts." Rock and its singers were described as "the frustrated bleatings of a bunch of nose-picking teenagers . . . pompadoured pipsqueaks . . . adolescent whinings and pseudosexual retchings." To mention rock with "good" music in the same breath would be like putting "pooltables at the Metropolitan Museum." Pintchman linked it all firmly with juvenile delinquency by claiming rock's banner was "the open switchblade."[47]

Various magazines and newspapers joined in the rock attack through their editorials. To the *New York Times* editors rock was just another craze which they compared with the "frenzies" that swept through medieval Europe such as "St. Vitus Dance." They found a similar parallel in early nineteenth-century America when efforts to bring religion to the frontier through revival meetings resulted in "mass shaking, jerking, babbling, and rhythmic chanting." The only difference in modern crazes, such as rock, was that they were able to spread amongst the masses much more quickly due to more sophisticated communications and advertising. The *Times'* solution was to discourage rock and provide "diversions." To deflate rock required "less talk about it but more unobtrusive supervision."[48]

In April 1956 the mass circulation paper, the *New York Daily News*, ran a two-part series slamming rock as an "inciter of juvenile delinquency," and blasting Alan Freed. The series even then was predicting the death of rock mainly because "disgusted adults were battling the music of delinquents." According to the writer, Jess Stearn, it had taken a lot to set off this adult revolt, "riots and bloodshed, slurs on the national anthem, and slowly gathering public disgust at a barrage of primitive jungle-beat rhythms, which when set to lyrics at all, frequently sound off with double meaning leer-ics few adults would care to hear."[49]

To the editors of *Musical America* this new music was no more than a "passing fad," and there would soon be something else to replace it. With this comforting thought they smugly took the position that rock was so poor in quality that it couldn't move anybody to do anything, "rock 'n' roll music in itself can hardly be an incitement to violence. It just isn't that good."[50]

The editors of *Music Journal* were much more horrified and revolted by the specter of rock and roll. The magazine considered it to be its "duty" to comment on "the most disgraceful blasphemy ever committed in the name of music." They made a quantum leap in generalizations by stating that the Western world was about to crumble because of rock's "definite threat to civilization." The music was savage, illiterate, and vicious and the link between the music and juvenile delinquency was overwhelmingly clear. Teens listening to rock were

> definitely influenced in their lawlessness by this throwback to jungle rhythms. Either it actually stirs them to orgies of sex and violence (as its model did for the savages themselves), or they use it as an excuse for the removal of all inhibitions and the complete disregard of the conventions of decency . . . it has proved itself definitely a menace to youthful morals and an incitement to juvenile delinquency. There is no point in soft-pedaling these facts any longer. The daily papers provide sufficient proof of their existence. . . . It is, however, entirely correct to state that every proved delinquent had been definitely influenced by rock 'n' roll.[51]

Sex and delinquency remained popular complaints over the following years — delinquency in the form of drug addiction as alleged by the Nixon regime, and still later by the Washington wives; and sex as alleged, again by the Washington wives and by Jesse Jackson, to mention just a few examples.

One of the magazines that lobbied hardest against rock in the early years was Britain's *Melody Maker*, led in particular by a columnist named Steve Race. In 1956 Race was urging the BBC to carefully vet the "cheap and nasty lyrics" of rock songs. He too saw a crumbling of the West from the influence of rock. As a social phenomenon he viewed rock as "one of the most terrifying things ever to have happened to popular music." When Judgement Day arrived he felt the music industry would have to answer to St. Peter first and foremost for rock and roll. For Race the music was "a monstrous threat. . . . Let us oppose it to the end."[52] A couple of years later he was still waxing indignantly about this "infantile and often suggestive chanting," which for him was "the bottom of the barrel." He made a list of the items not required for success as a rock singer. The list included: a singing voice, stagecraft, business acumen, ability to sing in tune, experience, good looks, and personality.[53] The editors of *Melody Maker* joined Race when they issued their own call to arms to stop "Pop Rot." They were of the opinion that the public really didn't want rock music and that even those who produced the music all privately deplored it. They urged the profession, the industry, and the public "to rebel against the handful of men who are responsible for this lowering of musical standards," such as agents, managers, and disk jockeys.[54]

Britain's *Dance Teacher*, the official magazine of the Midland Association of Ballroom Instructors, called for "a campaign to discourage rock 'n' roll."[55] Rock had had little effect on them until mid-1957 because "respectable" people didn't dance to rock until that year, when it was discovered that Princess Margaret liked rock and "public taste shifted from civilized dance movements to primitive capers." The magazine added that ballroom dance teachers would be giving Princess Margaret "no bouquets."

Another way of attacking the music was by claiming the singers had absolutely no talent. By knocking these singers one also slammed the music, as well as indirectly ridiculing the tastes and intelligence of those who liked rock and roll. This method was used by John S. Wilson who unfolded the stories of two such singers, Edd Byrnes and Fabian.

In the late 1950s there was a popular television detective series called "77 Sunset Strip," which had a hip, young parking lot attendant named Kookie, a role played by Edd Byrnes. A producer at Warner Brothers Records, George Avakian, saw the character on TV and was claimed to have said, "I was offended that there should be someone who looked like that and talked like that. . . . But in the same instant I was struck by an obvious inspiration — he should make rock 'n' roll records."[56] Trying to turn Byrnes into a singer proved a tortuous process as even Avakian wasn't ready for the "monumental lack of talent" displayed by Byrnes. Kookie had no range, no grasp of rhythm, no sense of pitch, and he couldn't carry a tune. Wilson suggested that the latter fault was so common among rock singers as to be virtually taken for granted. Still, the executive persisted and after adding Connie Stevens to do most of the actual singing, and tailoring a song to Byrnes's image, a hit was produced. It was called, "Kookie, Kookie (Lend Me Your Comb)." (On the TV program Kookie spent a great deal of time engaged in combing his hair.)

Also during the late 50s a fourteen-year-old named Fabian Forte was discovered sitting on his front porch in Philadelphia by Bob Marcucci, the head of a small record company. Struck by the youth's good looks, a cross between Elvis Presley and Ricky Nelson, Marcucci decided to make him a rock singer. Fabian had about as much talent as Byrnes, and when Marcucci sent him to a singing teacher the teacher sent him back with a note saying, "Don't waste your money." A visit to a second teacher produced the same results. Marcucci went to a third teacher and beat this person to the punch by telling the teacher not to tell him to not waste his money, but to do the best that could be done with Fabian, who did go on to become a big rock star, for a time.

The gist of Wilson's article was that people like Fabian and Byrnes became stars thanks to technology, to the use of echo chambers, tape reverberations, and various other engineering feats of near magic, which according to the writer, really came into being after Presley's voice was "so doctored up." While admitting that such a wholly created star as Fabian was "still a rarity," Wilson dismissed virtually all singers and groups who had one hit and then disappeared as "obviously untalented as Fabian." In attempting to equate rock singers with no talent the writer argued that singers who "sing" like Pat Boone and Johnny Mathis produced good sounds without using technological trickery. He contradicted himself and his argument failed when he later stated, "every pop recording made today, even by well established talent, carried some evidence of the use of echo chambers, tape reverberation, equalizing, speeding, overdubbing or splicing."[57]

A writer in England expressed much the same sentiment and claimed it was "cheaper and easier to produce rubbish." Yet if a "no-talent" rock singer had to have so much more technical doctoring done on his records, wouldn't it be cheaper and easier to produce a "good" singer? Those involved in attacking rock did not seem bothered by this kind of contradiction in their arguments. The English writer sadly concluded that "really talented singers are thrown on to the scrap heap if they aren't prepared to duplicate the 'stylistic' rendering of some bawling hog-caller."[58]

The no-talent argument was a particularly silly one. Perhaps Fabian had little talent but if one assessed talent by counting those who voted with their dollars then Fabian had talent. That same argument applied to all popular culture endeavors. The older generation who dumped on Fabian or Byrnes were part of the same generation that paid homage to actors like John Wayne who lent new meaning to the word "non-expressive." Neither Fabian nor Wayne may have been talented in some "artistic" sense but both had a lot of fans who thought they were. Fabian was part of the clean and bland branch of rock and roll at the end of the 1950s and there was nothing for people to complain about. He was neat, he didn't do pelvic thrusts, nor were his lyrics offensive. Opponents desperate to find something to attack had only one thing left—they went for the throat.

The no-talent argument would continue to be used against groups like the Stones, Alice Cooper, and Ozzy Osbourne, to name just a few.

Radio stations and their executives were often opposed to rock, even those that featured the music. The president of the independent Diamond Records, I. R. Gwirtz, conducted a survey of the musical tastes of 450 radio stations across the country. The questionnaire was sent out not to disk jockeys but to station owners, managers, and program directors. He found their preferences for six kinds of music broke down as follows: popular 94%; sweet and ballads, 87%; rhythm and blues, 60%; classics, 51%; rock and roll, 32%; western, 30%.[59] Arnold Shaw, vice-president of E. B. Marks Music, made a field trip through the country and found a "definite opposition" to rock music by independent stations. He also claimed that in the western United States there was a tendency by the radio stations to play down rock and roll programming.[60]

In Seattle, Washington radio station KING conducted a survey of one hundred thousand residents of that state and claimed to have found a divergence between their listeners' preferences and the record best-seller lists. In the major age group, 22–40, results indicated that sixty-six percent either disliked or strongly disliked "raucous" or "screaming" rock as the station chose to identify such songs as Presley's "Big Hunk of Love," the Drifters' "There Goes My Baby," and Fabian's "Tiger." In the same age group fifty-one percent liked or strongly liked the non-rock hits. Even in the 17 to 21 age group rock was said to be disliked or strongly disliked by forty-one percent.[61] Favorite disks from the survey were tunes such as "Secret Love" by Doris Day, "Riders In The Sky" by Vaughn Monroe, and "Marie" by Tommy Dorsey. As a result of this poll, station KING revamped its programming to better reflect results of the survey, deciding that "raucous rock 'n' roll will be completely excluded."

Other stations demonstrated their anti-rock sentiments without the bother or rationale of "scientific surveys." For some the anti-rock posture was a result of their growing distaste for rock and for others it was a result of the growing protest over payola which was being linked to rock and would soon culminate in the payola hearings. Station KSFR in San Francisco kicked off its anti-rock and roll campaign with the slogan, "I Kicked the Junk Music Habit by Listening to KSFR."[62] Listeners could get free window stickers bearing that slogan and owner Al Levitt claimed that while everyone talked about rock music he was finally doing something about it. Critics of the slogan interpreted it as an indirect attempt to tie the music to drug addiction. WISN in Milwaukee, a non-rock station, surprised its listeners by one day playing nothing but rock and roll. The station stopped after a few hours and hundreds of phone protests. WISN did it to dramatize their anti-rock position and to show how much the public hated it when you gave them what they "wanted." When the rock music stopped, disk jockey Charlie Hanson went out into the station courtyard and burned two hundred rock records.

Less destructive was WPIN in St. Petersburg, Florida which had banned rock for months and gave all such records away to a charity which auctioned off the disks. Record companies were in the habit of sending their records free to radio stations in hopes of having them played. In Denver, station KDEN launched a "civic improvement" campaign and most station breaks contained the following spot announcement, "Help stamp out Rock and Roll. Patronize KDEN advertisers and KDEN, Denver's first station now busily engaged in stamping out rock and roll."[63]

A more practical approach was taken by Washington's WWDC where president Ben Strouse tried to balance programming and did play rock. He felt people up to the age of thirty-five liked rock music. His programming was purely pragmatic for Strouse admitted that some rock music "makes me cringe. I don't like them, . . . I hope that some day public taste switches, as it always has in the past, to some other type of music."[64]

Station WAMP in Pittsburgh, WZIP in Cincinnati, and KSEL in Lubbock, Texas all banned rock and roll, concentrating on "good" music. At WKBW in Buffalo, jockey Dick Biondi was fired on the air after playing a Presley record. A disk jockey named Jack Gale started his Baltimore program one morning with a new rock and roll record. The station's program director cut in to inform listeners that "Mr. Gale is no longer with us." And he never returned to the microphone. A more theatrical event was staged by station WLEV of Erie, Pennsylvania in September of 1959. The station rented a hearse and loaded their seven thousand rock records into it and staged a mock funeral procession to the harbor where station personnel dumped all the platters into the water.

Station CJOY in Guelph, Ontario had its own problems with rock. Station program director Don Leblanc played rock on the station but despised "the blatant and cheap masquerade" which passed for music. He found the music irritating, startling, disquieting, and disgusting. After carefully reviewing the "oversimplified melodies, monotonous arrangements, and uninspired lyrics" of the Everly Brothers' "Bye Bye Love" and noting it held the number one spot for six weeks he wondered, "Are we all imbeciles?" One might wonder why Leblanc would program any rock at all. The answer was that he tried other music but failed to draw an audience. The station had "gone to considerable trouble to plan programs by the musical masters — and each program had fallen flat on its face." It seems the station had gotten only two letters of commendation for 163 hours of the musical masters while the station's hit parade program drew at least forty letters a week.

Leblanc was clearly beside himself at this outcome and refused to believe his listeners were really telling him what they wanted. Leblanc was allowed to lay his problem before the Canadian public through Canada's best known magazine. It was essentially a plea for adults to write letters to his station, and to other stations across the country, expressing their listening preferences. He was convinced the problem was that adults were not expressing their wants and thus the radio programming was controlled by teenagers, a minority of the population, who did indeed express their preferences. It went without saying that Leblanc was only interested in adults expressing their preferences if those preferences were not rock and roll. For he hoped " a few well placed wails from the adult population will bring popular music back to its proper perspective."[65]

In England rock music received only limited exposure over the airwaves during the middle 1950s. The BBC was a complete monopoly and had no intention of letting this "cacophony, either on record or in live performance, to pollute the airwaves." For English listeners the only alternative was the English language service of Radio Luxembourg. The BBC ultimately relented and instituted a one hour television program of teen music called "6.5 Special." It was produced by Jack Good who asked his superiors if he could have kids dancing in front of the cameras as they did on "American Bandstand." The idea was vetoed since "the British public wouldn't put up with that sort of person 'bopping' around the floor." Good got around this by designing a special set which could be moved about quickly so the cameras could catch the kids dancing. The BBC wasn't happy but the show became very popular.[66]

5

From the Waist Up

"Beware Elvis Presley" warned the magazine *America* in its June 23, 1956 issue. The warning was concerned with his lewd, suggestive, and "downright obscene" stage mannerisms. The magazine felt he might not be too much of a negative influence on young people if he was confined to records "but unfortunately Presley makes personal appearances."[1] Presley started with Sun Records in 1954, went to RCA in 1955, and attained superstardom in 1956. He was the first rocker to attain such lofty heights and his appeal was based largely on his youthful vigor; the sexuality of his stage performances; and his tough guy, Marlon Brando—James Dean image. Bill Haley reached stardom before Elvis but was too overweight, too cherubic, and too old to pose the sort of personal and image threat that Presley carried. Presley's concert performances and TV appearances drew wrath, ire, and indignation from all quarters. It was the TV spots that enabled millions of people of all ages to see Presley for free, at the same time, that speeded up the anti-Elvis attitudes. This very anti-Elvis reaction was also a major impetus to his popularity. Kids figured if he was despised that much by adults he must be worth listening to. This increased popularity in turn fueled more anti-Elvis hysteria.

Bill Haley might have been damned for playing rock and roll, the "bad" music, but Presley, who soon earned the sobriquent "Elvis the Pelvis," was twice damned. Once for doing rock and roll and once for the way he performed it. While the main focus of the anti-rock forces in 1955 had been on the "obscene" lyrics it shifted away over the following couple of years. One branch led to bans and attempted bans on live rock and roll shows. The second branch was an attack on the performers themselves, and their stage presence.

Song lyrics had been greatly "cleansed" by 1956, particularly by the white artists who were trying to reach a larger mass audience. Those who had attacked lyrics found less to complain about and were forced to zero in on other areas. Performers such as Presley were condemned less for the words they sang and more for the way they sang and delivered those words. Certainly no performer in the early years of rock and roll was subjected to a greater amount of invective and verbal assassination than was Elvis Presley.

Presley would come onstage, spraddle his legs before the microphone, and start shaking both legs at once. He would throw down his arm to pluck his guitar, with his lips curled, or in a sneer, a pained expression on his face. He flailed his legs and then snapped them, knees knocking together while shaking his hips and pelvis. These actions were invariably reported by the newspapers as "bumps and grinds." He also made exentsive use of the mike and its stand during his act, straddling it, shaking it, dragging it around the stage, lowering it to the floor and so on. He dressed, onstage, much like the young toughs from the film *Blackboard Jungle*.

At a concert in San Diego, Elvis played to turn-away crowds with what was described as a style that "embraces sensuous gyrations and a savage beat." Nothing untoward happened except the usual loud and emotional response by the crowd of mainly teen females. Yet afterward the San Diego police were moved to warn the singer that if he wanted to appear in their city again he would have to clean up his act and eliminate the "bumps" which were deemed not a fit sight for the eyes of the young and impressionable citizens of that California city.[2] He once performed in Florida in 1955 and the police had forced him to sing without moving.

After he appeared at La Crosse, Wisconsin the local paper branded Presley as "downright obscene" and his performance as nothing more than a "strip-tease with clothes on." Pressure from citizen groups in La Crosse was intense enough that the local company which had booked Elvis, Lyons Associates, promised they would never bring him, or anybody similar, to town again.

A crowd of far less than capacity greeted the singer in St. Paul, Minnesota, which prompted the local paper to address an editorial his way. After denouncing the rocker as no more than a "male burlesque dancer" editor Bill Diehl went on to say he had asked around and discovered the reason for the small attendance, "Moms and dads had seen you on TV and didn't like your unnecessary bumps-and-grind routine."[3] He speculated further that if more parents had seen him the crowd would have been smaller still. Diehl then admonished Presley to "clean it up" if he wanted to prosper in the entertainment business because "nothing grows in dirt."

Since Presley's lyrics were obviously inoffensive, other aspects of his performance were attacked. Compared to the later gyrations of a Jagger or a Morrison, Elvis was relatively stationary.

Before his appearance in Louisville, the music critic on the *Louisville Times* blasted Elvis on musical grounds and pointed out what he believed to be the link between rock and violence. The critic was Gene Lees who later went on to be a well-known featured columnist with *High Fidelity* magazine. After his column ran, Lees claimed to have received "literally hundreds" of letters from teenage girls. He analyzed these letters and reached the astonishing conclusion that more than sixty percent actually disliked Elvis but wouldn't admit it to their girlfriends for fear of being thought square. Lees claimed further that many of these letter writers "were vaguely troubled by what Elvis did to them emotionally."

Lees attended the concert at which a local disk jockey was emcee and the jockey made a speech about Elvis loving his mother, being a church-goer, and feeling patriotic. This DJ then asked the audience what they thought about somebody who would write a negative article about Elvis. This brought a scream of rage from the eight thousand fans and Elvis came onstage, according to Lees, "borne on wings of hate. It reminded one of nothing so much as movies I had seen of Hitler's rallies in the 1930s."[4]

At a concert in Vancouver, Canada a scuffle broke out after the show and a seaman was charged with assaulting a policeman. When he was arraigned Judge Alexander A. McDonald fined the man $250 and remarked, "These shows are a disgrace and should not be allowed here."[5]

As one of Elvis' biographers has stated, "Elvis was assailed all through his first big year by a chorus of newspaper writers, pulpit preachers, high-school teachers, police officials and local politicians. These folk were . . . quick to identify him as a symptom of the dread problem of juvenile delinquency. Not content just to attack Elvis verbally, some of his assailants demanded that action be taken either to curb Elvis' performances or to run him out of town."[6] This statement does not tell the whole story, for the attacks continued well beyond his first big year and he was seen as a cause of juvenile delinquency by many, not just a symptom. An appearance in Ottawa, Canada resulted in a melee and the next day the press complained that "Elvis provoked the riot."

Two concerts at the Pan Pacific Auditorium in Los Angeles brought about one of the more bizarre charges against the singer. Onstage with Elvis throughout the first show was a dog named Nipper, the same breed as the dog on the RCA label who listened to the gramophone. During his performance Elvis would give the dog a pat once in a while. During his last number, "Hound Dog," Presley exuberantly embraced the dog and rolled around the stage with Nipper a bit, to the crowd's delight, before rushing offstage and making his getaway. Some adults took offense and reported to the Los Angeles police that, as part of his act, Presley had buggered a dog onstage. The police warned the singer to clean up his act or he wouldn't be doing a second show. They installed three motion picture cameras in the auditorium for the second show, just in case.

A *Mirror-News* review of the first concert slammed Presley in more than a dozen paragraphs, blasting him as a "Sexhibitionalist" for giving an obscene performance aimed at arousing the "libidos" of "little girls." His music was termed a "lascivious steaming brew."[7]

Presley made his television debut January 28, 1956 on the Tommy and Jimmy Dorsey half-hour program "Stage Show." The show, on CBS, was produced by Jackie Gleason and preceded his own program, "The Honeymooners." Ratings on "Stage Show" had been low and Gleason had been on a desperate talent search to try and boost the number of viewers when he settled on Presley. When asked about his own opinion of Presley, Gleason has never said more than, "If I booked only the people I like, I'd have nothing but trumpet players on my show."[8]

This TV program marked rock's first, and frontal, attack on the nation's living rooms — and the nation was outraged. The day after Presley appeared, "Stage Show" was "flooded with wires, calls and letters denouncing the show and threatening reprisals."[9]

Elvis's next TV appearances were on "The Milton Berle Show" on April 3 and June 5, which provoked the usual reaction. The *San Francisco Chronicle* called his routine in "appalling taste." Jack Gould, TV critic for the *New York Times* said he had "no discernible singing ability," sang in an "undistinguished whine," and "for the ear he is an utter bore."[10]

Attacking Presley's voice was a particularly inappropriate criticism since the rocker had a good singing voice, better than many of his contemporaries. It only illustrated the ludicrous lengths opponents would go to in order to try and find something objectionable.

Another major New York TV critic was Jack O'Brien who, writing in the *Journal-American*, said, "Elvis Presley wriggled and wiggled with such abdominal gyrations that burlesque bombshell Georgia Sothern really deserves equal time to reply in gyrating kind. . . . He can't sing a lick, makes up for vocal shortcomings with the weirdest and plainly suggestive animation short of an aborigine's mating dance."[11]

Ben Gross, writing in the *New York Daily News*, tried to top his fellow scribes in level of invective that could be thrown at the singer. Gross wrote that "Elvis, who rotates his pelvis, was appalling musically. Also he gave an exhibition that was suggestive and vulgar, tinged with the kind of animalism that should be confined to dives and bordellos."[12]

It was hoped in some quarters that TV programs would stop handling such "nauseating stuff" as Presley and then he and all his peers could disappear into the "oblivion they deserve." However "The Milton Berle Show" got a huge rating increase on the strength of the Presley appearances and since ratings were the name of the game, other programs, reluctantly or not, picked him up.

The attacks continued: in Nashville an effigy of him was hung, in St. Louis he was burned in absentia. Writing in the *Catholic Sun* the Reverend William Shannon complained that "Presley and his voodoo of frustrations and defiance have become symbols in our country." Cardinal Spellman, in a sermon, quoted one of Jack Gould's articles on Presley at length. The Reverend Charles Howard Graff of St. John's Episcopal Church in Greenwich Village, New York, called the singer a "whirling dervish of sex." The evangelist Billy Graham admitted he hadn't met Presley and didn't know much about him, but based on what he'd heard he wasn't "so sure I'd want my children to see him."[13]

That summer Elvis was booked on "The Steve Allen Show" which ran opposite Ed Sullivan's program and was consistently drubbed in the ratings battle between the two. Allen was desperate to boost his ratings, but didn't want the sort of stink that Presley had raised on other programs. Steve Allen's solution was to attempt to stylistically defuse the potential "bomb" that Presley was. Allen had the singer appear in a couple of comic skits and had him sing "Hound Dog" to a real hound dog onstage, without his guitar, without "rocking and rolling," and dressed in formal wear — tie and tails. It was likely the singer's worst and most uncomfortable appearance of his life. Nor were his fans pleased. The next day they picketed NBC studios in New York with signs reading, "We want the real Elvis." The only happy people were Jack Gould who applauded a "much more sedate" Presley and Steve Allen who, for the first time, beat Ed Sullivan in the ratings.

Prior to the appearance on Allen's program Ed Sullivan had refused to book Presley or touch him with the proverbial ten-foot pole. Sullivan had said he "wouldn't consider presenting Presley before a family audience."[14] After being trounced in the rating war by Allen, Sullivan quickly changed his mind and promptly booked Elvis for three shows. Sullivan tried to justify his sudden about face by saying his earlier comments were based just on reports he had heard, but when he actually saw tapes of the singer he said he wondered what all the fuss was about. Nevertheless, when Elvis made his first appearance on September 9, the cameras showed him only from the waist up. A view of the famous pelvis was restricted to those in the studio audience and censored to those at home. That night the Sullivan show captured eighty-two percent of the TV audience.

Jack Gould, the *New York Times* critic, continued to lambast Presley. He called Presley's appearance on the Sullivan show the most unpleasant yet. Deprived of hips and pelvis to fulminate against, the critic assailed the singer because "he injected movements of the tongue and indulged in wordless singing that were singularly distasteful."[15] Even when the hip-shaking was gone this critic stretched credulity to find a physical affront. Gould railed against TV broadcasters for abdicating their responsibility as a public trust by permitting such performances into the living rooms of America. He wanted such displays which "exploited" and "overstimulated" youth to be stopped but he didn't consider the issue as "one of censorship . . . it is one of common sense . . . to ask the broadcaster merely to exercise good sense and display responsibility."[16]

Later that year the singer's agents tried to sell their star to one of the networks in a package of two guest appearances and one special, for a sum of $300,000, but there were no takers. Presley had received $50,000 for his first Sullivan guest spot. An NBC spokesman commented that few sponsors would have the money to afford him and "those that did would be class outfits and most wouldn't want him." *Newsweek* commented on this failure by noting, "The networks showed more taste than Ed Sullivan."[17]

In terms of character assassination and put-downs, few could match these inspired insults hurled at Elvis. A *Time* magazine review of his first film, "Love Me Tender," read like this:

Is it a sausage? It is certainly smooth and damp looking, but who ever heard of a 172–lb. sausage 6 ft. tall? Is it a Walt Disney goldfish? It has the same sort of big, soft, beautiful eyes and long, curly lashes, but who ever heard of a goldfish with sideburns? Is it a corpse? The face just hangs there, limp and white with its little drop-seat mouth, rather like Lord Byron in the wax museum. But suddenly the figure comes to life. The lips part, the eyes half close, the clutched guitar begins to undulate back and forth in an uncomfortably suggestive manner. And wham! The mid-section of the body jolts forward to bump and grind and beat out a low-down rhythm that takes its pace from boogie and hillbilly, rock 'n' roll and something known only to Elvis and his Pelvis. As the belly dance gets wilder, a peculiar sound emerges. A rusty foghorn? A voice? Or merely a noise produced, like the voice of a cricket, by the violent stridulation of the legs? Words occasionally can be made out, like raisins in cornmeal mush.[18]

As with most reviews of Presley, the comments were more anatomical than musical. This review encompassed and articulated every conceivable objection to Elvis and illustrated the objections the opposition would find when casting around for something to attack when the lyrics were clean. These ostensible faults were not the real ones — but merely an excuse to attack youth music.

Reactions to Presley were not limited to the critics. One campaign was the brainchild of two Yale students who had become alarmed when they saw a lot of kids sporting "I Like Elvis" buttons. These two launched a counterattack on behalf of Beethoven and had a thousand "I Like Ludwig" buttons made up. A placard on the counter of a music store in Manhattan read, "Combat the Menace! Get Your Ludwig Button." They sold them all in a matter of hours and within a few weeks claimed to be a national club with twenty thousand members across the country. Those who were seen with "Ludwig" buttons included such famed musicians as Issac Stern, Eugene Ormandy, and Pablo Casals.

It seemed that everybody got in on the act, including one used car dealer in Cincinnati who advertised that he would break fifty Presley records in the presence of anybody who bought one of his cars. He sold five cars in one day. In Toronto, Canada a columnist for the *Toronto Telegram* started a club for those who disliked Elvis and rock. It was called the Elvis Suppresley Club. On Canada's west coast, columnist Jack Wasserman of the *Vancouver Sun* held a contest in which listeners were invited to complete, in fifty words or less, the following sentence: "I hate Elvis Presley because . . ." The winner got a Frank Sinatra record album. In the town of Aylmer, Quebec jukebox operators took Presley songs out of the boxes after the mayor-elect urged the ban on the basis that the songs were too suggestive. At a private school in Ottawa, Canada eight female students were expelled after they disobeyed a school edict to stay away from a Presley concert. The principal of the senior high school in Wichita Falls, Texas, Oren T. Freeman, stated that, "We do not tolerate Elvis Presley records at our dances, or blue jeans or ducktail haircuts."[19] The editors of the *Music Journal* blasted Elvis for his "leering, whining, moaning" and for his "filthy performances."[29] Two female students from a San Francisco high school won a "Why I Love Elvis" contest and were flown to Hollywood to be kissed. The principal expelled them and explained, "We don't need that kind of publicity."[21]

While there was at least one critic who felt Presley might not be too negative an influence if he was limited to records, a number of radio stations didn't agree. A jockey known as the Great Scott, in Nashville, burned six hundred Elvis records in a public park. In Wildwood, New Jersey a jockey claimed he couldn't morally justify playing the disks any more and offered to help start a group to "eliminate certain wreck and ruin artists." When radio station WSPT of Minneapolis banned Presley from their airwaves they brought down the ire of some residents. Several DJs reported receiving threatening calls to "play Elvis Presley or else." A rock was thrown through the outlet's front window and the attached note read, "I am a teenager — you play Elvis Presley or else we tear up this town."[22] The ban stood.

The Presley record which caused the biggest furor was "Elvis's Christmas Album," released in November of 1957. The long play album included all Christmas-oriented songs with standards such as "Here Comes Santa Claus" and "White Christmas." Also on the platter were the carols, "Silent Night" and "O Little Town of Bethlehem." It was these that caused the storm. At station KMPC in Los Angeles jockey Dick Wittinghill said he had received requests to play cuts from the album but refused, claiming it would be "like having Tempest Storm give Christmas gifts to my kids."[23] Station KEX in Portland, Oregon banned the record on the grounds that it was in "extremely bad taste." When night jockey Al Priddy played one cut from the album he was fired, not for playing the album, but for disobeying station policy.

In Canada the response was even more irate. Station CKXL in Calgary banned the album completely as having no place at their station. A spokesman for the station said station officials had listened to the album and "it speaks for itself." The spokesman went on to add that Presley sang the songs the way they had expected he would. "It is one of the most degrading things we have heard in some time." The station claimed he "panted" through the carols.[24] Another station in that city, CFCM, denied they banned the album but did admit it wouldn't be played as it was "in bad taste." At least eight other stations in Canada, from Halifax on the east coast to Vancouver on the west coast, also banned the album.[25]

During his stint in the army from 1958 to 1960 Presley spent parts of 1959 and 1960 stationed in Germany where he aroused just as much of a stir as he did at home. Werner Goetze, a disk jockey in that country had originally broken the singer's records on the air while describing him as "the whiner." Reaction from his listeners caused Goetze to change his mind and play the records. A German archeologist named Ferdinand Anton was heard on the Armed Forces Radio Network where he branded Elvis as "a throwback to the Stone Age."

Most of the flak though came from East Germany. The Communist Party newspaper in East Berlin, *Neues Deutschland,* claimed Presley was an ad for NATO in the West Zone and labeled him a "Cold War Weapon." Another East German paper, *Young World,* saw Presley in the same light, claiming, "Those persons plotting an atomic war are making a fuss about Presley because they know youths dumb enough to become Presley fans are dumb enough to fight in the war." In Leipzig police arrested a gang of youths after they had come under the influence of "NATO ideology." The name of that gang was the "Elvis Presley Hound Dogs." The East Germans even offered some proof, stating that authorities in the city of Halle had arrested the leader of a teen gang who had gone bad after buying several Elvis records.[26]

Little did Presley fans know that the Elvis Presley who emerged from the army in 1960 would bear little resemblance to the Elvis who entered the service in 1958. The change of image was a conscious choice made by his manager, Colonel Tom Parker, who had dominated Elvis in terms of career direction. Presley could have gone into the Special Services branch of the forces and functioned as an entertainer and publicity man. It would have been an easy way to put in his two years; other entertainers had done it. But Parker firmly declined, stating publicly only that Presley didn't want to take the easy way out. Presley served as an ordinary soldier in the army; he was primarily a jeep driver and he received no special treatment. Parker knew that by doing so "the adult acceptance he was picking up would multiply vastly."[27] The army would try from time to time to have Presley perform in some capacity or other during his tour of duty but Parker would always refuse. The colonel was going to make his star acceptable to, and popular with, adults.

It's likely that the tremendous amount of negative reaction to Elvis from 1956 until he entered the army had something to do with Parker's decision to seek adult acceptance. Perhaps no singer before or since has been subjected to such a barrage of invective, bile, and hostile assault as was Presley. The colonel likely feared for the economic viability of his meal ticket a few years down the road if the singer didn't bend to the anti-rock pressures and conform to an image more in keeping with adult expectations.

The first step was to have Elvis serve his time as an ordinary GI. The second was to cancel all live concerts. After emerging from the forces Presley would not do a live concert until 1967, a hiatus of almost a decade. It was the live concerts that had given Presley some of his biggest problems and most hostile attacks. They were difficult affairs since the audience reactions could not be predicted or controlled. A third step was appearance — after leaving the army Presley would not appear again as a greasy hoodlum type.

Presley continued to make TV appearances, but in a more subdued fashion. His first TV show after the army was as a guest on a Frank Sinatra special, one of the most ironic of pairings. Only a scant few years earlier Sinatra had said rock was written, played, and sung by mostly "cretinous goons." But like so many before him Sinatra was desperate. This special was the last of a series of four. The first three had not scored well in the ratings and Sinatra was willing to go to any lengths to prove he could do well on TV. He paid Presley $125,000 for about six minutes of work, a price that galled the older singer. It was agreed that Presley would wear a tux and stand still while he sang. They sang each other's songs that night and joined together in a duet. It was indeed a strange marriage.

Presley's major work after the army was in the recording and film studios. In his records Elvis became more of a balladeer, a crooner of middle-of-the-road pop. His film career saw a softening of his image and the increased use of comedy to give him family appeal. This widening of his appeal, in which Parker was aided by film producer Hal Wallis and the William Morris Agency (Elvis's agents), was all part of a plan "inspired partly by the fear that Elvis's public was too narrow and his stance too controversial; partly by the opportunity, which was offered by his military service, to make a fresh start with a clean, wholesome image."[28]

The tough, hard, and vital rocker named Elvis Presley, who had stirred so much fuss as he helped preside at the birth of rock, would enter the U. S. Army in 1958 and disappear forever. In 1960 a man bearing that name emerged from the army but it couldn't have been the same man. For this namesake was a neat, well-dressed balladeer differing hardly at all from crooners such as Sinatra and Crosby. He was a little younger, that's all. The anti-rock forces had wrought yet another change, rung another concession from rock and roll.

6

Stars Eclipsed

Presley was not the only rocker to take heat over the music, or to have his career affected in some way. Bill Haley, with his group the Comets, became the first white rock star. He had been performing mostly country material with groups that had names like the Four Aces of Western Swing and the Saddlemen. He noticed the white interest in R&B and in 1953 Bill Haley and the Comets released "Crazy, Man, Crazy," which is regarded in some quarters as the first rock song. The next year they released "Shake, Rattle and Roll" which became another million-selling record.[1] Also relased that year, two months before "Shake," was "Rock around the Clock" which didn't do that well. It enjoyed modest success but was not a big hit. After the song appeared on the soundtrack of the 1955 film *Blackboard Jungle*, Decca reissued the record and it enjoyed tremendous success. That year it gained the distinction of being the first rock record to chart number one where it stayed for eight weeks. Bill Haley and the Comets had become the first white stars of rock by the middle of 1955. They were the first white artists to penetrate the black R&B charts that year as well with "Dim, Dim The Lights." The youth of the country seized on him as their leader and mobbed him wherever he went. He may have been mild by black standards but to white youths he was frantic and uninhibited and they had never seen anything like him.

The Comets' version of "Shake, Rattle and Roll" was a cover of a black original by Joe Turner. The furor over the so-called obscene lyrics of many of the black songs was heating up and the results can be seen in Haley's rendition of the song which was considerably "cleansed." Turner's version was openly sexual with the action taking place in the bedroom. Haley moved it into the kitchen. Turner's opening went, "Get out of that bed and wash your face and hands." Haley's opening went, "Get out in the kitchen and rattle those pots and pans." Another Turner line went, "Wearin' those dresses, the sun come shining through." Haley sang: "Wearin' those dresses, your hair done up so nice." The chief A&R man, or producer, at Decca was then Milt Gabler who knew that a lot of the R&B tunes didn't get played because of their lyrics and so, as with the Haley record, Gabler said, "If any of the lyrics were double entendre I would clean them up. I didn't want any censor with the radio station to bar the record from being played on the air."[2]

Throughout his early career Haley struggled to keep the image of himself and his Comets above reproach. Bill kept a tight rein allowing no drinking on the job and no picking up women on the road. He strictly enforced the rules and would fire someone if he caught them with a bottle of beer in their hand. Haley also conducted occasional bedchecks of his Comets.

Onstage Haley took pains that his act not be "suggestive," and maintained that "fun can be clean." The band was very energetic, particularly the drummer and the sax man. The latter would, while playing, arch his back and slowly lower his head to the floor, but they were indeed not suggestive. By 1957, when his career was on the skids, Haley and various members of the Comets tried their hand at songwriting, without success. One of the things that worked against them was that they were trying to write and "record material inoffensive enough to pass by the conservative critics of rock & roll."[3] Haley himself commented that he and his group steered clear of anything "suggestive." He felt it was just as easy to write acceptable words and that he and the Comets took "a lot of care with lyrics because we don't want to offend anybody."[4]

Despite these efforts at image-building Haley got jumped on anyway. In 1956 "Rockin' through the Rye" was banned by the BBC which felt it too close to "Comin' through the Rye." They said that Haley was tampering with traditional British folk music.[5] At one of his live concerts a critic first condemned the whole affair as "complete boredom." Contradicting himself, he admitted that because of the noise he couldn't hear Haley who "mouthed meaninglessly" into the mike, and perhaps his inability to hear was a "good thing." The show was summed up as the "meaningless blast and blare of Mr. Haley and his assistant torturers."[6]

One of Haley's concerts before ten thousand Miami fans drew the wrath of Mrs. Regina McLinden, chairperson of the local board of review. This board was charged with the task of censoring magazines and comic books. She was appalled enough by the "vile gyrations" of rock dancing to step outside her sphere of influence and announce her determination to fight against "this worm wiggle via the pulpit and the schools."[7]

Haley toured Germany in 1958 in a series of concerts which led to clashes between police and concertgoers in nearly every city he played. Seven thousand fans fought with police and trashed the arena to the tune of 30,000 marks damage, during an October 26 concert in West Berlin. One of the Comets was of the opinion that East Berlin youths had been sent over deliberately to create an incident. After the event the director of the arena banned any future such shows from the place while the *Neues Deutschland*, the official Communist paper of East Berlin lashed Haley, on page one, for "turning the youth of the land of Bach and Beethoven into raging beasts."[8]

During this German tour the minister of defense in East Germany, Willi Stoph, offered the opinion that West Germany was encouraging rock music in the country, through the defense ministry, and Haley was promoting nuclear war by subverting the kids. Said Stoph, "It was Haley's mission to engender fanatical, hysterical enthusiasm among German youth and lead them into a mass grave with rock & roll."[9]

By 1958 Haley had passed his peak. The year he had become a superstar, 1955, was also the year he turned thirty years old. Haley hotly denied there was any sex in his group's performances and said, "If we wanted to sell sex or sideburns, we'd have dressed differently."[10] This likely contributed to the quick demise of his popularity. Others came along who would indeed sell sex. In later years Haley and his manager were also not able to get good material. They weren't writers themselves and seemed not to have the business acumen to hire people who could write. Haley continued to tour off and on and do his old numbers over the years, being particularly successful in Europe. During the early rock revival period of 1969 to 1972, he made something of a comeback and toured through the 1970s before he died in 1981.

Chuck Berry hit the big time in 1955 with a long string of hits beginning with "Maybelline." He was a handsome and flamboyant showman and, like Presley, he presented an overtly sexual image. He was most famous onstage for his "duck walk." He would squat down over one heel, keeping his back straight and stiff, with the other leg out in front and then sort of bounce across the stage while holding his head at a strange angle, all the time playing his guitar. It was an instrument which he often wielded like a phallus. He never got anywhere near the press attention that Presley got, and that was because he was black.

A black man that could excite young white girls was most certainly a "menace" to the white racist society that America was in the middle 1950s.

On August 28, 1959 Berry was arrested in Meridian, Mississippi, and jailed "on charges of trying to date a Mississippi twenty-year-old white girl.[11] Berry had performed that evening and after the concert a twenty-year-old white woman and her boyfriend asked the singer for his autograph. According to Berry, "some sort of misunderstanding" took place which resulted in his arrest and jailing. He was held without bail in the county jail but released the next day.

That same year a fourteen-year-old girl who worked as a hat check girl in a club Berry owned in St. Louis turned herself in to the police after some sort of fight with the singer. Berry had picked the girl up in Juarez, Mexico, and brought her back with him to his club. Whether he knew the girl's real age is not known. Berry was charged under the Mann Act, which involved transporting a minor across state lines for "immoral" purposes. The language of the indictment charged the singer with having "compelled, induced and incited her to give herself up to debauchery." This charge was a little heavy in view of the fact the girl had been a prostitute before Berry met her. Nevertheless Berry had made a fatal mistake which the anti-rock forces jumped on. It was more than they needed. The case went on for two years through two trials, both of which resulted in guilty verdicts. The judgment of the first trial was set aside due to the overt prejudice of the judge who, throughout the trial, referred to Berry as "this Negro" or "whatever his name is." The anti-rock forces now had proof that rock and roll was corrupting their children for they had caught a "nigger" with his pants down. A newspaper headline read, 'Rock 'n' Roll Singer Lured Me to St. Louis, Says 14 Year Old."[12]

Chuck Berry served almost two years in jail. When he got out his marriage was over and his career was basically finished. He continued to tour and record but lived as a virtual recluse. He too participated in the rock revival period and had one or two anemic hits but his days as one of rock's superstars and driving forces was over. He owned a small combination amusement park and country club in Missouri and in the late 1960s he let a local high school use the park for free as the site of their spring picnic. Some of the parents were worried, though, about letting their children attend because "he was in jail for a sex crime, you know."[13] That the incident had a profound effect on Berry can be seen from the fact that to this day he often denies, in interviews, that he was ever in prison as a result of the event.

Another early rocker who disappeared quickly from the scene was Gene Vincent who often dressed in leather, cultivated the tough guy image, and played hard rock. His first big hit, and the biggest of his career, was the 1956 release "Be-Bop-A-Lula." This was actually the "B" side of the record, backing "Woman Love," which was banned by the BBC that year in Britain as "too provocative." This tune was about a young man who, moaning and walking around in circles, went to his doctor who took one look at him and told him, "You shore be needin' some Woman Love!" In the United States "Be-Bop-A-Lula" became the hit as American jockeys ignored the "A" side because it "was considered too suggestive." Vincent's biographer notes that Vincent's image helped put the skids on his career, "The strong sensuality of Gene's music aroused the ire of a good many parents, politicians and clergymen who thought that rock 'n' roll was eroding the moral fiber of America's youth and this eventually had a negative effect on Gene's career."[14] He was perhaps more overtly sexual than Presley and based on one of his performances was once found guilty of obscenity and public lewdness by a Virginia state court.

Early rock and roll produced two frantic, screaming balls of energy—Little Richard and Jerry Lee Lewis. Little Richard (Richard Penniman) traded a job washing dishes at the Macon, Georgia bus terminal for rock stardom with a string of hits beginning with 1955's "Tutti-Frutti." Richard had been doing the number for a few years in the various small clubs he had played while trying to get a career going. Like Haley, Richard found the song too raunchy for the bigger and whiter mass audience and consequently "Tutti-Frutti" was considerably cleaned up and censored before being released in the famous version which went on to become a hit. That immortal tag line from the song "Awop-Bop-a-Loo-Mop Alop-Bam-Boom" actually began as "Awop-Bop-a-Loo-Mop a-Good Goddam." Another line expunged was "Tutti-Frutti good booty—if it don't fit don't force it."[15] The song was written originally by Richard but a second writer was called in to help provide the cleaner lyrics.

As the song went up the charts it was covered by white artists, notably Presley, and Pat Boone. The Boone version, anemic compared to the original, actually outsold Little Richard and went gold, partly because "the white radio stations wouldn't play Richard's version of 'Tutti-Frutti' and made Boone's cover number one."[16] Richard decided to increase the tempo on his next offering to a speed which he hoped Boone wouldn't be able to keep up to. "Long Tall Sally" did hit number one for Richard despite the refusal of many white stations to give it airplay. Boone did turn out a cover, more anemic than his first cover, but still went gold with it.

Little Richard was also a wild showman with his hair piled up in a high pompadour, covered in makeup, dressed in gaudy and outrageous clothing, and pounding away on his piano. This wild and bizarre image was no accident. He was well aware of the "terrible things" that could happen to a black who was "seen as sexually attractive to white women." His bizarre image was cultivated specifically to counter that. As Richard said, "I decided that my image should be crazy and way-out so that the adults would think I was harmless."[17] And it did work for him. He was viewed more as a black Liberace than a black Elvis. His image didn't save him all the time, on one tour in 1956 he was briefly arrested in El Paso, Texas because "he had this long hair and he was shakin' about up on the stage."[18]

Richard had his share of inner conflicts stemming from the belief he was being ripped off by a racist society, and his own homosexuality, which was at odds with the fundamentalist religious background that was so much a part of his life. Another conflict was "the clash between religion and the music he was producing which was being denounced as evil."[19] In 1957 he abruptly quit rock and roll and announced he would become a minister. Said Richard, "If you want to live with the Lord . . . you can't rock 'n' roll too. God doesn't like it."[20] While he enrolled at bible college, he never graduated. In the early 1960s he returned to rock, being unable to keep it fully out of his system. For a little while he kept the fact of his return secret from friends and family, "partly because he still could not entirely submerge the thought that Rock 'n' Roll was evil."[21] He never regained his superstar status though. Perhaps his time had passed. The British invasion was then underway. Little Richard continued to perform more bizarrely than ever, being almost a campy parody of himself. Toward the end of the 1970s he would quit entertaining again, as well as "quitting" his homosexuality, to work for the Lord and confine himself to preaching. This time his rejection of, and antipathy toward, rock was more pronounced and vehement than the first time, as he explained, "I believe this kind of music is demonic. I have seen the rock groups and the punk-rock people in this country. And some of their lyrics are demonic. They talk against God. . . . I believe that kind of music is driving people from Christ. It is contagious. I believe God wants people to turn from Rock 'n' Roll to the Rock of Ages."[22]

The other screamer was Jerry Lee Lewis, the wild man of rock whose career as a superstar lasted less than a year and a half when, like Berry, his career came crashing down due to his morality. Like Little Richard he was strongly affected by his fundamentalist religious background and had the same kinds of conflicts about the "devil's music" as Richard.

The rebellious nature of Lewis surfaced early. In 1950, aged about fifteen, he appeared on the Ted Mack program "Amateur Hour." At the audition Jerry's father bragged that his son could play anything on the piano. The staff of the Mack show replied that no, he couldn't since Ted Mack would have no "boogie-woogie" or jazz on the show. Mack wanted only classics or pop. Lewis auditioned with a sedate rendition of "Goodnight Irene" and got a spot on the show. When he appeared, live, he tore into a wild version of "When The Saints Go Marching In" and managed to earn both the $10 prize as audience favorite, and the disgust of Ted Mack.

In 1952 Jerry was in Texas where he had enrolled at the Southwestern Bible Institute with the intention of becoming a preacher. He used to play the piano there at services and early in his stay he played a wild version of "My God Is Real." The dean was outraged, claiming "desecration." Lewis was expelled. Jerry Lee was torn between preaching and piano playing. His first cousin, evangelist Jimmy Lee Swaggart, had dedicated his life to God and tried to convince his cousin to do the same. But Lewis saw the money to be made from playing the "devil's music" and decided to follow that path with the hope that one day he would have enough money to quit and found a church of his own.

His big break, after years of playing roadhouses and assorted dives for peanuts, came with the 1957 Sun Records release of "Whole Lotta Shakin'." The record had been released two years earlier in a version by the Commodores, but had gone nowhere. Sun company executives were aware of potential problems with the disk because the lyrics were "too sexy" and the tune was "too suggestive." Sure enough, problems erupted with the record and it was "banned by most radio stations for being too provocative."[23] Members of the clergy railed against him and some thought Lewis was more lascivious and evil than Presley.

Several stations refused to play the song not because it was "risque" but because they thought it was done by a black. One manager at a Texas radio station told Sam Phillips of Sun that he didn't "play songs by niggers on our stations."[24] When informed that Lewis wasn't black the Texan replied that he sounded like one. Sales of the record slowed and Sun tried to get Lewis booked on national TV. Ed Sullivan curtly refused to book Lewis saying that, after Presley, he didn't want "any more of that crap." Finally a booking was made on Steve Allen's NBC show. The Allen people had apparently never heard the song, nor were aware that it had been blacklisted for supposed obscenity. Lewis's appearance was highly successful and the song went on to be a smash hit.

In the summer of 1957 Jerry Lee cut "Great Balls of Fire" for Sun but not without misgivings on his part. Just before the recording session began Lewis decided the song "was of the devil and that to sing it was to sin."[25] Sam Phillips and Lewis engaged in a lengthy debate before the singer was finally persuaded to record the number.

Onstage Lewis's style had to be seen to be believed. He approached his piano the way the Mongol hordes approached their worst enemy. He didn't play it so much as attack it. He started out seated and pounded away and then abruptly stood, kicking his stool away with his foot while he assaulted the keys from a stiff, standing position, while shouting and screaming his breathless vocals. In between numbers he teased his audience while slowly and deliberately combing his long blonde hair, by then completely dishevelled, back into place. He played the piano at times with his head and with his feet. He jumped up on top of the piano and played it from that position. Sometimes he would rip the keys out of the instrument, toss them to the crowd, and finish off the beast by dancing on its carcass. When he toured with Alan Freed's "Big Beat" show in the spring of 1958 it was not uncommon for him to completely trash a piano during his set. One critic remarked that "Lewis makes parents mourn for the comparative quiet of Presley."[26]

During the spring of 1958 Lewis was riding the height of popularity and had aspirations of becoming the king of rock and roll. Presley had just entered the army, and there was a sense that the throne stood vacant; and Lewis wanted it. He never had a chance though, for he was by then a marked man. The storm against rock and roll was beginning to focus on him as the symbolically evil performer. "Those who look frantically for a scapegoat for all the juvenile ills of our day point to Lewis and others of his school of rock-'n'-roll."[27]

The ammunition to bring down Lewis had been supplied by the singer himself in late 1957 when, at age twenty-two, he had married his thirteen-year-old cousin. It was still a secret in early May of 1958 when Lewis was set for a tour of England. The singer was threatening to release the information since he was tired of keeping it a secret and convinced it wouldn't matter to his fans. Jud Phillips, Sam's brother, of Sun knew better. Lewis had a booking on Dick Clark's program just before leaving for England and Jud made a late night and anonymous phone call to Clark to warn him of the impending trouble. Lewis had threatened to break the news of his marriage on the show. Clark thought the situation over and quickly cancelled the appearance, something that Clark would later admit was a cowardly thing to do. Lewis was surprised by the sudden axing of his spot and didn't know the real reason.

The story broke in England that month when Lewis introduced his wife as fifteen. An enterprising reporter uncovered the full story and the scandal was on. Early marriages were not uncommon in Lewis's part of the world and he really didn't understand the fuss. His own sister had been twice married by the time she was fifteen and Jerry Lee had been twice married before himself, at fourteen and then at sixteen. Complicating Lewis's marital status was the fact that lying about ages had occurred all three times and divorces had either not taken place, or happened only after a subsequent marriage. In any event being married to a thirteen-year-old cousin was more than enough to destroy Jerry Lee's career.

The media jumped all over him in England. *The People,* in a page one editorial, urged all teens to boycott Lewis's concerts and demanded that the Home Secretary deport Lewis and company from the United Kingdom. London's *Evening Star* also editorialized for deportation.[28] Another newspaper ran the huge headline "Clear Out This Gang" with a photo of Jerry Lee captioned "Bigamist." The *Daily Sketch* added its voice to the call for deportation by asserting the Home Office would "have no difficulty in finding grounds for sending the whole outfit back to where they came from."[29] The singer was able to give a few concerts of the scheduled tour but they were poorly attended, the halls being from half to three-quarters empty.

Many of those who had come were openly hostile. From the audience Lewis was greeted with shouts such as, "baby snatcher" and "cradle rob-ber." After a couple such shows Leslie Grade, the agent who had booked the tour, met with officials of the Rank Organization, who owned the theaters in which the concerts were to take place. After that meeting Grade announced the remainder of the tour was cancelled, saying, "If he had gone on, it might have done irrepairable harm to British show busi-ness — and pop music in general."[30] After the ax fell on the tour Lewis and his entourage were on the first available flight out of England, leaving such gleeful newspaper headlines as, "Tour Bosses Sack 'Baby Snatch' Jerry" and "Jerry Lee Lewis and his Malodorous Little Circus Have Been Given the Old Heave-Ho by Britain's Theater Managers."[31]

When he arrived back in the United States he received a reception that was less openly hysterical and hostile than in England but had the same deadly effect on his career. Jerry Lee found himself "the target of an industry blacklist. A boycott was in full effect: No records were played on the radio, no television appearances, no bookings."[32] Desperately, Sun Records tried Dick Clark but Clark wouldn't book him, claiming his net-work would never allow it since Lewis was "too hot to touch" now. A bit-ter Jud Phillips remarked later that parents had wanted to "kill" rock and roll then. They held up the marriage to the world and said, "Look what kind of image you kids are idolizing . . . parents could phone radio sta-tions and say I don't want you to play that record and it'd scare the hell out of the stations."[33]

The boycott may have not been one hundred percent but it was more than enough to end the days of Lewis as a rock superstar. He continued to tour and release singles but his success was minimal. He was forgiven enough in England to make a successful tour there in 1962 after first being denied an entry permit by the Home Office. Lewis, along with many other rock stars, enjoyed a short renaissance in the early rock revival period of about 1969 to 1972. His successes, such as they were, after that were in the field of country music to which he turned after being unable to regain his position as a rock star. Toward the end of the 1970s Jerry Lee Lewis was still toying with the idea of being a preacher and remarked that by entertaining people he had served Satan. When asked to elaborate Lewis explained, "'Cause I'm draggin' the audience to hell with me. How am I gonna get 'em to Heaven with 'Whole Lotta Shakin' Goin' On'? You can't serve two masters; you'll hate one an' love the other."[34]

7

Rock around the World

Rock music was the universal language of youth cutting across culture, race, religion, and politics. Islamic fundamentalists, liberal democracies, fascist dictatorships, or totalitarian communist governments had at least one thing in common—they believed rock was somehow subversive. This perhaps reinforces the idea that rock and roll is a generational conflict. It represents the idealistic, spontaneous, and nihilistic tendencies of youth versus the hypocritical, repressive, and traditional tendencies of adult society.

How could children all over the world be indoctrinated in differing ideologies if they shared the same culture? If nothing else, rock and roll united youth. Russian kids liked it and so did American kids. Most youths in foreign countries could not even understand the English lyrics of the songs they were listening to yet supposedly still "rioted" to the music, putting a lie to the idea that "leerics" had an effect.

The irony was that the United States rarely used rock music as a propaganda item. They would not make much of an issue out of how terrible the Soviet government was for banning rock and roll because the U.S. government did not like it either. Russia and any other anti-American countries could of course use rock for that very purpose, labeling it decadent or degenerate, failing to point out the U.S. establishment disliked it as much as they did.

Foreign governments were not necessarily interested in saving the morals of their children, but they were interested in demarcating their sociopolitical structures. Since rock and roll was essentially American in the 1950s, reaction against it varied according to the degree of identification with Western capitalism. In Britain, Europe, and South America banning, censorship, and police surveillance sufficed. In Soviet-bloc countries jail sentences were an added deterrence.

While the U.S.A. and Great Britain reacted with horror and revulsion to the phenomenon of rock and roll, other countries around the world were equally stunned, and often reacted in an even more heavy-handed manner. In late 1956, as the film *Rock around the Clock* made its way through Europe, a disturbance in the streets of Oslo, Norway after a screening, led to the police using their batons to break up a group of about six hundred "rocking and rolling" teenagers.

When the film opened in Germany exhibitors tried to get anti-riot insurance on their cinemas. They had become nervous after the film's reception in England. After the exhibitors had been turned down by all the German insurance firms, they approached Lloyds of London who informed them that they too would not be interested in providing that type of protection. When the film opened, precautions were taken by having police guards posted throughout the cinemas. In the city of Duisburg police advised the cinema owner to have the leader of the local teen gang, an equivalent to England's teddy boys, make a speech from the stage and ask the audience to stay calm during the film. Columbia Studios had originally planned some rock and roll dance competitions in Germany to coincide with the film's opening, and to provide publicity. But in view of the potential problems Columbia called off all promotions.[1]

In Mons, Belgium, *Rock around the Clock* was banned from that city after a disturbance broke out following a screening there. Police were called to break up an impromptu rock and roll dance in the streets, with the result that teens pelted the local police station with tomatoes and eggs.[2] The following year Iraq banned the showing of *Rock around the Clock* as authorities deemed it "dangerous to youth." Iran banned rock and roll dancing at all public dance halls after terming such dancing "harmful to health." Police warned owners of the halls that if the ban was not observed the owners would be prosecuted and their establishments shut down.

President Sukarno of Indonesia was in the process of trying to gain public support for his "conception" of a more effective government administration. One group of student veterans kidnapped Mrs. Maria Ulfah Santoso, head of Indonesia's film censorship board. Santoso was held for over an hour before being released and "warned not to permit the showing of 'immoral' rock 'n' roll motion pictures that might divert the people's attention from the Sukarno 'conception.'"[3]

Rock and roll music was featured daily over stations in Havana in pre-Castro Cuba and the music became more and more popular with teens. This increased popularity led to increased criticism, especially from teachers and parents. The controversy reached a head when the country's minister of communications, Dr. Ramon Vasconcelos, banned rock and roll programs, describing them as "immoral and profane and offensive to public morals and good customs."[4]

A similar controversy was brewing in Egypt. Several American rock films had been shown within a few months and records by stars such as Elvis Presley were selling out immediately upon arrival in that country, at prices said to be up to four times their cost in New York City. Youths were wearing blue jeans and "strange haircuts." More and more nightclubs and cabarets were featuring the music as age-old Egyptian songs and dances were elbowed out of the way. Rock and roll dance contests were being held and some of the dancers were so "enthusiastic" that city officials in Cairo decreed that female contestants must wear slacks, a radical move for a country that had traditionally frowned upon such garb for women.

The more politically minded in Egypt saw the American import as a sign of "Western degeneracy," a plot to undermine the morals of Egyptian youth, and used the music as more ammunition in the fight against the "imperialist West." The Middle East policies of President Eisenhower were called "the rock 'n' roll doctrine."[5] The furor reached all the way up to President Nasser's cabinet where the pros and cons of banning rock were discussed. While the cabinet was divided, a ban was imposed. The Ministry of the Interior announced, in June 1957, that all nightclubs and other public places were barred from playing rock and roll. As well, all rock and roll films were banned from Egyptian cinemas, the playing of rock music was forbidden, and "newspapers were advised not to mention it any more."[6]

Bill Haley took his traveling rock show to Barcelona, Spain in 1958, but when his first performance led to kids dancing in the aisles and destruction of some furniture, his remaining performances were quickly cancelled. Yugoslavia was trying to rid the country of rock, blue jeans, and pony tail hairdos, all considered to be "manifestations of hooliganism." Toward the end of 1958 a dance and music congress was held in Prague, Czechoslovakia, with delegates from eight communist countries in attendance. They passed a resolution which "called for better jazz from Eastern Europe to combat rock 'n' roll."[7]

France was later than most countries in joining the crusade. It was the summer of 1961 before a number of French legislators tried to get rock shows banned by law. They were prompted to seek such legislation after attending some concerts in and around Paris. The French minister of the interior, Roger Frey, refused to comply, however, and in a classic political reaction, passed the buck. Frey claimed it was the responsibility of Paris police or mayors of provincial towns to ban such concerts if they so wished.[8]

Variety, which was, in the early years of rock, ever hopeful of its demise, spotlighted a story in which it claimed rock was on the rocks in West Germany. One problem was said to be that promoters lost money on the shows since the mostly teenage fans bought out the twenty-five and fifty cent tickets but most of the tickets in the top end of the price scale, $3 to $5, remained unsold. The second reason for this supposed decline was the fear of violence. A final straw for the already nervous hall owners had been the Alan Freed incident in Boston which got "wide coverage" in the press of West Germany.[9]

The *New York Mirror Sunday Magazine* summed up the European situation in a sensationalized and exaggerated fashion. They claimed that "rampaging youths" had been "aroused to an uncontrollable state of frenzy" and had rioted in many European cities causing Europeans to remark that rock and roll was the greatest evil the United States had ever exported. The magazine duly noted that every riot had the same cause, "the insistent beat of rock and roll."[10]

That same theme of rock being an "evil" export gave the U.S. State Department cause for concern in the summer of 1958. At that time a group of ten American disk jockeys were set to depart for Europe where they planned to stage U.S.—style record hops, all of this under the sponsorship of the State Department. Another disk jockey, from WFEA in Manchester, New Hampshire, didn't care for the idea and wrote to several U.S. senators, expressing his misgivings. This jockey felt teen record hops were "powder kegs" and that it would be easy for a "few Communist plants" to set off riots. All this would have dealt a blow to America's already "low prestige" in Europe. Senator Norris Cotton protested the idea and the State Department withdrew its sponsorship. The president of the National Council of Disk Jockeys for Public Service, Murray Kaufman, mollified the State Department by promising no rock and roll records would be played and the hops would be restricted to U.S. army bases, under the supervision of the USO.[11]

In East Germany it was the fans of the music who had the most to worry about. In the city of Leipzig a group of fifteen youths marched through the streets shouting derogatory remarks about East German music and country leader Walter Ulbricht. The youths also chanted "Long Live Elvis Presley." For their efforts the group received jail sentences ranging from six months up to four and a half years.[12]

Presley ran into German troubles again, this time in West Germany in 1961, with his recording of "Wooden Heart." The song was based on an old German classic and the Presley number was banned from the West Berlin and Bavarian government radio stations. The stations objected to the singer commercializing and ruining, in their view, the old national classic. As one radio spokesman put it, "We will fight this invasion with all our strength. . . . We won't let foreigners dictate to us."[13]

Nationalist anti-rock sentiments were raised in South America as well. Argentina underwent what was termed a "crisis of the Tango." The dissemination of foreign music into the country had produced a generation of youths who were not tango enthusiasts, but were hooked on rock and roll, creating a loss of "national physiognomy." An association of Argentine tango conductors, singers, and composers called on the state to enforce native music in all public places. The mayor of Buenos Aires went so far as to ban any dancing, in February 1957, which featured "acrobatics" or "exaggerated contortions" or, in short, rock and roll dancing which the mayor feared "could offend morals and good breeding or degenerate into collective hysteria and cause friction and/or violence."[14] Argentinian parents, who kept a tight rein over their children, were also putting a damper on the music.

In Mexico City rock and rollers came under attack by the Federal District Musicians' Union. The union's leader, Venus Rey, planned to ban the homegrown rock and roll groups from working anywhere in the country such as at nightclubs, on radio, television, and in films, ostensibly because they weren't members of his union, and made no efforts to join. However, some rock groups had tried to join the union but were refused as the union didn't really want them in. "They want the kids to stop playing the rhythms."

A popular rock music program which had aired over local televsion had been cancelled after city authorities ordered the network to do so following a disturbance which took place after one such program. Others in the Mexican music industry condemned the Mexican rockers as merely being carbon copies of U.S. stars such as Presley and plagiarizing U.S. songs, singing them in poorly translated Spanish versions. Rey insisted he would purge the Mexican music business of such "musical hoodlums." Another industry official claimed that public taste in Mexico was "deteriorating with rock and roll combo units finding wide acceptance despite their vulgarity."[15]

In Russia as late as March 1957 *Variety* reported that although the music was heard there, "there is no interest in rock 'n' roll."[16] Moscow authorities soon reacted though, and warned in the newspaper *Pravda* that rock and roll was a sign of "western degeneracy." They banned such records and Western performers from their country. The homegrown variety still provided problems. A fight started at a gathering where a group of students had hired a rock group to perform. The newspaper *Evening Moscow* was quick to condemn the "disgusting music" and brand it as having a bad influence on the nation's young. *Pravda* jumped on the bandwagon in condemning homegrown rockers and describing them as "fifth columnists who are infiltrating the trite and convulsive music of the West by playing and singing its songs."[17]

Banning rock from Russia, or any other country for that matter, proved to be an impossible job. There were always the beams from Voice of America, a variety of short wave radio programs, and a host of ingenious bootleg methods to beat the ban. One such method surfaced in Russia in 1960 when authorities broke up an illegal group specializing in "rock on bones." A group of youths had set up a black market gang which produced rock records by using exposed X-ray film, of organs and bones, and turning them into rock records. The group was thought to have obtained the music by taping short wave radio and/or buying records from tourists. From there they turned out a one-sided, seven-inch record from the x-ray film which was played at 78 rpm and, with care, could last a few months.

A conventional two-sided disk purchased in a Russian store cost five rubles. The one-sided black market items ranged from ten to twenty rubles in price. The bootleg records were sold all over Russia and there was even a mail order service, before police broke up the gang. The two ringleaders were each sentenced to a two-year prison term. According to police this "banal" music had found its way into clubhouses and dance halls with even members of the Young Communist League being active promoters and salesmen. Shortly after this gang was broken up the Russian Communist Party ordered the start of a new, massive indoctrination campaign aimed at those who shirked their responsibilities to do socially useful labor and to counter "alien and bourgeois influences from the West."[18]

8

ASCAP, Payola,
and Alan Freed

The purpose of the payola investigation was ostensibly to determine the extent of corruption in the music industry. Practically speaking though, the focus of the investigation was much more narrow. First, it was another attempt by ASCAP to do away with the rival BMI, a group which had broken ASCAP's monopoly hold on song licensing. Second, it was an attack on rock and roll music itself. While there was much evidence to show payola had been around, in one form or another, for decades, the hearings chose to ignore this fact and gave the impression payola was a recent phenomenon associated with rock. The "bad" rock and roll had spawned payola; payola had bred rock. It was a vicious circle and the anti-rock forces seemed to assume that if they could eradicate one then perhaps the other would disappear.

ASCAP dealt with very few rock tunes while BMI licensed the majority of them. ASCAP members, predominantly white writers and publishers of middle-of-the-road Sinatra and Crosby pop material, Broadway show tunes, and Hollywood film songs, despised rock because it was largely through rock and roll material that BMI had gained such a strong foothold. BMI had broken ASCAP's monopoly and was then weakening ASCAP still further by undercutting the very type of music considered popular by "imposing" this awful form of music on an unsuspecting public.

ASCAP's position can be summarized as follows: BMI broke the monopoly but didn't achieve a great deal at first since all the "best" writers and publishers were still with ASCAP. BMI took the dregs, including "amateur" and "bad" songwriters who turned out junk, namely rock, since that's all the talent they had. This BMI trash was so bad no one would ever play it unless they were paid. Enter payola. People pushed this junk on the air because of bribes and it became popular since the audience heard little else and only that which was heard became popular. The result was the rise of rock fed by, in order, BMI, poor writers, trashy tunes, payola, and corruptible jockeys.

ASCAP's solution was simple enough. Stamp out payola and the whole chain would stop. With no bribes jockeys wouldn't play garbage, which meant both rock and BMI would lose popularity and both would wither away. While this basically reflected ASCAP's position, things didn't work out the way ASCAP had hoped, mainly because the world wasn't arranged quite the way ASCAP thought.

The American Society of Composers, Authors, and Publishers (ASCAP) was formed in 1914 to protect songwriters and composers from exploitation and to afford a measure of protection so that whenever and wherever their songs were performed, in whatever medium, they would be able to collect the revenue that was due them. Getting admitted into the group was so difficult that one critic commented, "ASCAP had admission standards more rigorous than a private club."[1]

Broadcasters decided to fight what they thought was an ASCAP monopoly during a 1941 strike by that group. The networks, NBC, CBS, and ABC, formed an organization of their own, Broadcast Music Incorporated (BMI). This new group was to function in the same fashion as ASCAP, to provide competition against the monopoly, and to give the broadcasters greater control over the music they could air. This move by the broadcasters worked as ASCAP and the radio networks reached a new contract agreement late in 1941 in which ASCAP backed down and settled for an amount substantially less then they had been originally asking for. Their previous five percent take was reduced to 2.1 percent. Despite their concessions, the monopoly had been broken.

The two groups coexisted fairly peacefully for the next decade and a half because ASCAP remained the giant. ASCAP retained all of its name people and it was their material which dominated popularity polls and the airwaves. BMI had to satisfy itself with the leftovers — country music, Latin-American music, and black songs — material that ASCAP didn't touch in the first place. ASCAP collected royalties only for live performances on radio while BMI promised to collect for live and recorded performances, an immediate benefit for black and country performers who had been recorded for years for little or no money.

That ASCAP was a monopoly during that period can be attested to by court desicions. In 1941 the government brought a criminal antitrust action against ASCAP, who had then fixed prices free of restraint. Fines were levied against the organization, its officers and directors, and a corporate reorganization took place.[2] Several years later, in 1948, ASCAP was judged to be a monopoly in two seperate federal courts resulting from two different actions which charged ASCAP with antitrust violations.[3] In none of these cases was BMI involved as an instigator.

By the mid-1950s rock and roll was sweeping the country and BMI grew along with it since the rock writers and publishers did not meet ASCAP membership "standards" and, of necessity, became affiliated with BMI. May Axton, a schooltecher from Jacksonville, Florida, was a cowriter of Presley's first big hit, "Heartbreak Hotel." She had twice written letters to ASCAP to join but both times ASCAP hadn't even bothered to reply to her letters.[4]

Even before rock had fully arrived, ASCAP's loathing for BMI and fear of their draining the market could be seen in their response to an early 1950s tune, "Such A Night," first recorded by the Drifters in 1954. Played originally on the black stations this BMI song drew no ire at all until covered by Johnnie Ray, a move that gave the record considerable airplay on white stations. ASCAP had been unconcerned about the song's suggestiveness but after Ray's cover was released they pressured the networks and had the record banned as offensive to good taste. Strangely, censors in Great Britain, not known as particularly liberal, found nothing to object to, and the Ray record climbed to number two on the charts, remaining a best-seller for months. No complaints were ever launched against "Rock around the Clock," one of the few early rock songs which was actually an ASCAP tune.

The coming of rock didn't sit well with ASCAP. Paul Cunningham, president of ASCAP, announced in 1956, that rock and roll had had it, saying, "we can expect a revival of good music in the style of the Gershwins, the Kerns and the Rombergs."[5] While ASCAP publicly engaged in wishful thinking, behind the scenes they were seeking protection from the government. They were clearly worried that rock had not had it.

In 1956 the House Judiciary Anti-Trust Subcommittee, chaired by Emmanuel Celler (D-N.Y.), was scrutinizing network radio and television practices, specifically charges that the networks, through BMI, controlled the popular songs the public heard over the air and on records. The charges were laid mainly by songwriters, and one such ASCAP writer and showman, Billy Rose, appeared as a witness. Rose lashed out at BMI and claimed they were "responsible for rock-and-roll and the other musical monstrosities which are muddying up the airwaves. . . . It's the current climate on radio and television which makes Elvis Presley and his animal posturings possible . . . it's a set of untalented twitchers and twisters whose appeal is largely to the zoot suiter and the juvenile department."[6]

Rose claimed BMI published seventy-four percent of the "top" songs and went on to detail a trip he had taken that summer. Rose had visited several Communist countries and claimed to have heard orchestras over there playing tunes he no longer heard in the U.S., due to the domination of rock. He concluded, "Our best musical talents seemed to be having an easier time crashing through the Iron Curtain than through the electronic curtain which the broadcasting companies have set up."[7] Rose considered most BMI songs to be "junk" on a level with "dirty comic magazines." BMI executives appeared and defended themselves by saying their company had formed only to compete with ASCAP. Chairman Celler was clearly on ASCAP's side, claiming there was a big difference between the two and ASCAP didn't "have the influence of the big broadcasters behind it."[8]

One of the stranger happenings was a telegram from Frank Sinatra that was read into the record. Sinatra blamed his popularity decline in the early 1950s on BMI and, of all people, Mitch Miller, A&R chief of Columbia. Sinatra claimed that Miller, by design or coincidence, had denied the singer the right to choose his own material, and as a result Sinatra got "many inferior songs" all bearing the BMI label. Columbia Records quickly presented evidence that of fifty-seven songs recorded by Sinatra under Miller's direction, fifty-two were ASCAP. As one commentator noted, "Frank doesn't know his ASCAP from his BMI."[9]

Hopes that the Celler committee might take specific action and recommend dissolution of broadcast ownership of BMI came to naught in June of 1957 when the group simply suggested a thorough investigation of the music industry to be undertaken by the Justice Department. Representative Celler remained a staunch ally of ASCAP even though his hearing had not damaged BMI. He addressed ASCAP's annual dinner in 1958 and used the occasion to blast BMI and the broadcaster link. Celler recalled the legend whereby a swan sings before it dies and paraphrased it thusly, "there are those who should die before they sing."[10] Celler was so frankly in favor of ASCAP that some elements of the group wondered "whether Congressman Celler's ardor unwittingly hadn't gone too far for the occasion. . . . For one thing it was embarrassing."[11]

ASCAP presented its views in March 1958 at another government hearing, held this time by the Senate Interstate and Foreign Commerce Subcommittee on Communications. These hearings were brought about by the lobbying of the Songwriters Protective Association, virtually all of whose members were ASCAP people. A letter presented by ASCAP charged monopolistic practices by the broadcasters saying pressure exerted by BMI was responsible for the "deteriorating quality of music on radio and TV." The letter was signed by many luminaries, including Bing Crosby. This time Senator Smathers introduced a bill into Congress which would have required broadcasters to divest themselves of music publishing and recording interests. But it came to naught.

One witness was Seymour M. Lazar, a Beverly Hills lawyer who specialized in music industry clients. Lazar claimed that BMI paid disk jockeys to play selected records and commented that this was "practically the only way that a song can be exposed." Other comments came from Burton Lane, the president of the American Guild of Authors and Composers (AGAC). Most of this group's people were also ASCAP people. Lane claimed BMI had "achieved control of American popular music through forced feeding of rock 'n' roll music to the public."[12] Author Vance Packard complained that "conniving disc jockeys" along with BMI had foisted "cheap music" on teenagers.

ASCAP got another chance to pressure BMI in 1959 through the Special Subcommittee on Legislative Oversight. This was an offshoot of the Committee on Interstate and Foreign Commerce and was then investigating the TV scandal which involved rigged game shows such as "The $64,000 Question." ASCAP was able to get the committee to move from there to investigate payola, a set of hearings that would have an effect on rock and roll music.

ASCAP had previously failed to make any headway against BMI mainly because their arguments left them without a leg to stand on. A director of ASCAP, noted songwriter Oscar Hammerstein II, expressed the ASCAP position when he stated that BMI and the broadcasters decided what the public would hear and were in the position of "limiting the songs from which the public might select its favorites."[13] Yet the figures did not back him up. Statistics showed that eighty-five percent of copyrighted music played on the radio, and ninety percent on TV, were licensed by ASCAP.[14] These figures were given under oath by the executive in charge of such statistics at ASCAP itself.

Hammerstein could not refute these figures so he lamely argued that BMI dominated in terms of "new" songs being released. This was nothing more than a reflection of current music tastes and ASCAP's reluctance to deal with writers who produced that type of material. The conspiracy theory fell flat as well, when BMI was looked at in terms of stockholding stations and nonstockholding outlets. At that time BMI stock was held by the three networks and 623 of 3,362 stations on the air. The BMI stockholders did not play a higher percentage of BMI material than did the nonstockholding outlets.[15] Most telling of all was the fact that from the time of BMI's founding up to the mid-1950s, ASCAP revenues from broadcasters had increased from under $5 million to over $20 million.[16]

Yet ASCAP was still determined to defeat BMI, and the payola hearings were used as ASCAP's next assault. The word "payola" may have been a new term for corruption in the music industry, but the practice itself was as old as the music business — a fact which the payola hearings chose to largely ignore. Even *New York Times* TV critic Jack Gould admitted as much, and with his aggressive diatribes at Presley he could hardly be considered a friend of rock. Gould stated that the practice of payola or giving commercial gifts had "been part of the entertainment world for years." He was also aware of the real reason for the payola hearing when he mentioned the fight started "with many of the country's foremost composers — the writers of Broadway and Hollywood hit tunes — who have been dismayed to witness the dominance of rock 'n' roll on the nation's airwaves."[17]

Another commentator also noted that payola existed long before the era of the disk jockey when "it was widely known that certain influential vaudeville performers and band leaders were open to persuasive gifts — in some cases 'composer' credits and resultant royalties — in return for featuring certain new songs."[18] Still another writer noted that during the vaudeville era, "song pluggers bribed headliners and acts to 'expose' a song." Also noted was the big band era when "song pluggers romanced the bandleaders, so did the recording companies." During that period the record companies "paid for band arrangements, picked up many a 'tab' and in return got its song played a lot on tour."[19]

During the payola hearings themselves evidence of payola was uncovered with a final tally said to be $263,245 paid by record companies to 207 broadcasting personnel, mostly jockeys, in forty-two cities.[20] These figures were the result of a mail survey taken by the committee. This practice was actually not illegal at the federal level when the hearings were held. A record company could give a disk jockey a record, a sum of money, and a note to play the song "x" times a day for whatever period. The jockey could follow those instructions and no federal law would be violated. One result of the hearings was that in 1960 Congress passed a bill which did make payola illegal. Amendments to the Federal Communications Act prohibited the payment of gifts or cash in exchange for airplay. Radio stations were held responsible for any employee who accepted such gifts.

One of the witnesses at the hearings was Paul Ackerman, music editor of the trade magazine *Billboard*. Ackerman gave a long and detailed statement on the history of payola saying that the practice was "rampant" by the 1930s and was a firmly established part of the business long before the era of the disk jockey and long before the expansion of the record business.[21] It was something which the committee didn't want to hear, however, preferring to find causal links between payola and rock.

The committee members themselves showed a strongly anti-rock bias. John Moss of California complained that the singers couldn't sing, that it was a "raucous" sound that he personally tried to avoid, and that he had heard some "horrible things" on the radio.[22] The chairman of the sub-committee, Oren Harris of Arkansas, claimed that his group was getting loads of mail from people complaining about rock and roll music "sometimes a thousand or more letters a day." Harris offered his own thoughts on rock music later when he said that "when this type of music, if you call it music, that is anything but wholesome is forced onto them at that age, I think it is the worst possible service that the medium could be used for."[23]

Several disk jockeys also came forward at the hearings to cement the link between payola and rock. Alan Dary of WBZ in Boston commented that he never played rock, the "raucous kind of sound that I always associated payola with."[24] Stan Richards, a DJ at various Boston radio stations, claimed that he, like most jockeys, wouldn't have the time to listen to a new rock record unless somebody "gave me a gratuity." He was then coaxed by committee member Peter Mack of Illinois who led Richards with the thought that without gratuities perchance only the "best music" would be played. To which Richards replied, "There is no question about it in my mind."[25]

Another jockey, Norm Prescott, was asked by committee member John Bennett of Michigan if he thought the "junk music, rock and roll stuff" would be played on the air without payola. To which Prescott replied, "Never get on the air." Bennett then asked if he thought payola was responsible for this music. Prescott answered, "Yes, it keeps it on the air."[26] Prescott insisted payola started in 1947.

John Moss revealed his own feelings and biases when a witness demurred after Moss implied that rock wouldn't have happened without payola. Moss told the recalcitrant witness, "Well, we disagree." Chairman Harris unleashed his bias when another witness tried to say that it was the people who ultimately decided what they would listen to and what they would buy. Harris replied, "I wholeheartedly disagree with you, based on the information we have received here. There is no question in my mind but that a lot of these so-called hit tunes and questionable records, insofar as acceptable music is concerned, would never have reached the top had it not been for the various unusual ways of getting them there."[27]

But the payola hearings did seem to have an effect on the music industry. Some radio stations were reported to have abandoned the top forty format "because of the investigations" and several record companies were said to have changed the type of material they released, also as a result of the hearing.[28] While the stations were being scrutinized there was a tendency for them to play more nonrock tunes since it was this material which drew the heat and the inclination of the media to continue to link payola and rock, despite the contrary evidence. Harrassment by the FCC was also a real fear for radio stations, with the threat of licence revocation ever present.

From ASCAP's point of view the payola hearings failed in that neither BMI nor rock and roll faded away. But the hearings were productive from the point of view of the government since its members could point to the committee and state that they were investigating this "terrible" music, thereby keeping in step with public opinion which was largely hostile to the music. The hearings were concluded in the spring of 1960 and there was an election the following November. It was an appropriate time for the government to bash rock.

Nor was rock-bashing a historical accident which occured only at one election. The Reverend Jesse Jackson would later condemn the music to gain media exposure as a preliminary move in his presidential try. President Nixon and his administration would come down hard on the music and try to win votes, and more recently the Washington wives would use their influence to have members of Congress hold a hearing to bash rock. Those seeking elected office were quick to damn anything they thought offended the majority of voters and rock was a particularly nice target. Many of its fans were too young to vote.

The payola hearings did have an effect on rock though. The most obvious was the fall of rock disk jockey Alan Freed and the rise of Dick Clark to fill his place. Clark had more economic clout than Freed since he presided over a show with $12 million in annual advertising while Freed produced only about $250,000. This would work in Clark's favor but the important distinction was what they each represented. These men symbolically stood for different aspects of rock. Freed represented the wild side, the black side, the raunchy side, the sexual side, the carefree side, the anarchical side. Clark represented the mild side, the white side, the quieter side, the nonsexual side, the controlled side, the obedient side. In short, Clark represented the side of rock and roll that adults could tolerate, if they had to put up with rock at all. The hearings did strike down Freed and confirm Clark as acceptable. Not that Clark was free of taint, but adults could live with him because he played their game. Freed didn't and wouldn't. He lined up squarely behind youth.

WABC radio had demanded that Freed sign a statement that he had taken no payola. The same network, ABC, didn't require Clark, also their employee, to sign such a statement. WABC sacked Freed while the ABC network issued a statement in support of Clark. When the payola issue first broke, and before the hearings, Dick Clark revealed he held an interest in thirty-three different companies in the music field — recording companies, publishing companies, and so on. ABC gave Clark a choice of divesting himself of these companies or leaving the network. Clark chose to divest. At that time, 1959, the companies were earning Clark an estimated $500,000 a year. [29] And Clark had by his own admission already become a millionaire through those holdings. At the hearings Clark told the investigators that he had an interest in twenty-seven percent of the plays on his program but that he had divested himself of the thirty-three companies. Between 1958 and 1959 "Bandstand" played eleven records by Duane Eddy a total of 240 times, which was more than Clark programmed Presley. At the time, he managed the guitarist, owned stock in his record company, and held all the publishing rights to the songs.

The following illustrates how one of those companies operated. The song "Sixteen Candles" was first copyrighted in 1953 and later recorded by a group called the Crests. The publishing company was Coronation and the recording company was Coed Records, both owned principally by George Paxton. Toward the end of 1958 "Sixteen Candles" was registered by January Music Corporation. Clark was president, his wife secretary-treasurer, and his mother-in-law was vice-president. About a month after the Crests recorded the song the two companies, Coronation and Coed, "gave the title, copyright, all the mechanical rights, and half of the performing rights to January Music." The song became a hit but not until most of the rights were turned over to the Clark company. Then the song hit sales of six hundred thousand and a share in the royalties to Clark's company of about $10,000. [30] Before acquiring the rights Clark had featured the song on "Bandstand" a total of four times in ten weeks. After January Music got "Sixteen Candles" it was played twenty-seven times in thirteen weeks.

Ultimately, though, Clark came through the payola mudfight without a speck on him, pronounced "a fine young man" by committee chairman Oren Harris, who noted Clark was neither the inventor nor architect of the payola system. Clark's position was vindicated and strengthened.

During the mid-1950s Presley may have been the "King of Rock and Roll" but the "Father" was the flamboyant disk jockey Alan Freed. He was the first disk jockey to emerge as a showman in his own right and his influence on the development of rock was indeed enormous. He was also one of the earliest and most obvious victims of the anti-rock forces of the times. The enemy was able to "slay" the father, but his infant would survive, waxing and waning in health but ultimately reaching a thriving and robust adulthood.

Freed was born in 1921 in the town of Salem, Ohio where he grew up in less than prosperous circumstances as the son of a low-paid clothing store clerk father. He graduated from Ohio State University with a degree in mechanical engineering. While at university he played trombone and led a band called the Sultans of Swing, named after the famed Harlem group. His main ambition was to front a band of his own but this possibility was eliminated by an ear infection. His next two years were spent in the army after which he started his radio career at a station in New Castle, Pennsylvania, WKST, where his program featured classical music.

In 1946 he began working in Akron, Ohio on WAKR where he hosted "Request Review," a program that grew in popularity. He then moved to Cleveland in 1950 where he hoped to place his show on TV. Things didn't work out as he had planned and he wound up being emcee for the late night movie on station WXEL. Finally, in June 1951, he got another radio disk jockey program on a Cleveland independent station, WJW.

At first he played classical music until a conversation with Leo Mintz altered the course of Freed's career, and ultimately that of music. Mintz owned a local record store and was a sponsor of Freed's program. Mintz had noticed the growing trend of whites to buy R&B tunes and suggested Freed might want to feature such music on his program. Freed demurred initially until one day he happened to be in the store and saw firsthand the reaction of whites to this black music. Freed thought about the situation for a week and then approached the station manager and talked him into letting him play some rock and roll after his classical records. Alan Freed later claimed he jumped on the music immediately after the Mintz visit but others said he was more cautious, playing only a little at time until he was swamped with requests.

For his theme music Freed picked a tune called "Blues for Moon Dog" and used part of the title as his stage name, changing his program from

"Record Rendezvous" to "The Moon Dog Rock 'n' Roll House Party." It was at this point that Freed claimed to have invented the phrase "rock and roll." However, the term had been used for sometime in R&B tunes as a euphemism for sexual intercourse. An example was the Dominoes' 1951 release "Sixty Minute Man" which used the phrase "rockin' and rollin.'" While it is not true that Freed invented "rock and roll" it can be said he was the first person to apply this phrase to the new music, to popularize it, and to instill it into the national vocabulary. He used this new phrase rather than the term "rhythm and blues" because he wanted to eliminate the racial stigma associated with R&B.

His personality and jive talk vocabulary made him the ideal super-salesman of the big beat. An operation to remove a polyp on his vocal chords left him with a hoarse and gritty voice which made him sound not unlike a blues shouter himself. By 1952 he had begun staging live concerts and was so effective that eighteen thousand tickets were sold that year for a show at the Cleveland arena, which only held ten thousand people. The inevitable riot resulted and the promoters, including Freed, were charged with fraud in overselling, although the charges were later dropped.

What really upset the establishment was not the sheer numbers who had shown up but that the group was roughly half white and half black at a time when Cleveland was largely a segregated city. Long before his troubles in Boston, and over payola, Alan Freed was damned and subject to harrassment as a "nigger lover,"[31] and was criticized for mixing the races. Freed continued to run nonsegregated dances, often defying local customs, and brought down the wrath of segregationists for his preference for playing black material instead of white covers. The concert was held March 21, 1952, also at the suggestion of Mintz who thought the kids might like to see the acts live. Authorities, perhaps fearing gate crashing, stopped the show part way through because of the crowds outside who couldn't get in. It was the spark which set off rock and roll. The next day Freed apologized over the air and promised nothing like that would happen again. In the future there would be reserved seats only. If one is looking for the date rock and roll started, March 21, 1952 would have to be a major contender.

The following year Freed was seriously hurt in an auto accident. He suffered various internal injuries which left him forever after susceptible to pneumonia and may have played a part in his early death. He also needed plastic surgery on his face. He was left with a pathological fear of cars and during the peak of his career at New York's station WINS he arranged to broadcast from his home in Connecticut so he could avoid driving.

In July 1953 he staged another show in the Cleveland arena and this time the "Moon Dog Ball" was a great success. He held such affairs in other locales such as Akron and New Jersey, always attracting a capacity crowd of thousands while turning away equal numbers. The audiences were mixed, one third or more white, proof of the growing popularity of the big beat.

His popularity grew in Cleveland and his show was syndicated to a few other stations, one of them in New Jersey. The general manager of a New York outlet, WINS, was persuaded to listen to the show and hire Freed, who then billed himself as Moon Dog. Alan Freed joined WINS in August of 1954 and rock took hold of the nation.

In New York there was a blind street musician who for years had called himself Moon Dog and who successfully sued Freed and prevented him from using his professional name. Freed renamed his show "Alan Freed's Rock and Roll Party." The station program director soon found himself called before a group of black community representatives at a meeting held in a Harlem YMCA, who were upset that a white was doing something, playing black music, that should be done by a black jockey. The major complainers were a black jockey on WHOM and a columnist for Harlem's *Amsterdam News*. It was a hard point to counter but the criticism soon died away. From WINS's perspective Freed was able to translate black music into white cash. Both WINS and Freed soared in popularity as rock took hold and spread. At least one WINS staffer from that time argued, "Freed made it happen."[31]

Much of his appeal had to do with his style as a jockey which matched, in vigor and energy, the music he played. He would sit before the mike with a big telephone book on his desk and thump away on it, keeping time to the music while the microphone was on. He would also add his own vocal accompaniments to songs by every now and then yelling in the background phrases such as, "Go, man, go" and "Yeah, yeah, yeah." The kids in the audience couldn't get enough. He quickly moved into pomotion and began to present live rock shows at various big theaters such as the Paramount in New York and various other cities, concentrating the shows during school holidays. At such concerts he would appear in flashy clothes such as checkered sports coats and solid red jackets with silver buttons. He blew kisses to the audience and made his delivery with distorted vowels, in a raspy hoarse voice. He had a somewhat greasy look about him, with slight scarring on his face due to the auto accident. His first live show in New York was held at Manhattan's St. Nicholas Arena just four months after he started at WINS. His two shows drew a capacity crowd of fifteen thousand to hear the all-black bill.

In physical style and appearance he was the complete opposite of his main disk jockey rival, Dick Clark. Clark was clean, wholesome, sedate; Freed was oily, slightly sinister, raucous. The audiences at his rock concerts greeted emcee Freed with ovations and cries of "We want Alan!" He was more popular than many of the singing stars he introduced and "was accorded the same shrieking welcome the Beatles got nearly a decade later."[33]

Freed's show aired over WINS from 6:30 P.M to 11:00 P.M. six nights a week, and was heard over the entire CBS network from 9:00 P.M. to 9:30 P.M. each evening. During this time he had an ill-fated fling with television. He briefly hosted the CBS-TV show "Rock 'n' Roll Dance Party" which was sponsored by Camel cigarettes. Freed, not the sponsor or the station, came under attack for encouraging teens to smoke. But what really did the show in was when the cameras caught the young black singer Frankie Lymon of the Teenagers dancing with a white girl. Freed was cancelled.

Freed was riding high in May of 1958, the undisputed top jockey in rock. Dick Clark, then hosting "American Bandstand," which had gone national the previous year, may have been second, but he was a distant second. As king, Freed was secure on his throne until the "riot" at the Freed rock show in Boston the night of May 3, 1958, as previously mentioned.

As a symbolic figure of rock and roll, a promoter, he was a much disliked figure in anti-rock quarters. As well he was an adult helping to spread and disseminate this "rebellious" music of youth, which made him a traitor to his own "class." He openly promoted the black, original version of songs, refusing to play the white cover versions. Other jockeys and stations would hear a song they liked, by a black, and then demand a white cover to play. This aspect of Freed failed to endear him to some. He was also a friend of the small independent record companies and a foe of the majors, something that wouldn't lend itself to a long career. The so-called Boston riot gave anti-rock and anti-Freed forces their chance to plunge the first knives into him.

After May 3 his position on the throne became shaky and he would be completely dethroned and out of the business within eighteen months. While fifteen people had been beaten, robbed, and so on, after the concert, in separate incidents, no one was ever charged in any of the incidents and there was no proof that the violence was done by those attending the concert. One could just as easily argue the violence was done by people in the area who hadn't attended the show, but set upon the concertgoers. The arena was in a part of the city which experienced muggings. There was no proof either way. Nevertheless the Freed show and rock were quickly branded as the cause.

The *Cleveland Plain Dealer* took a smug, "I told you so" attitude and drew upon their city's experiences with Freed's live shows. The paper editorialized that such sessions were "seductively publicized" over the air and became a draw for hoodlums whose "jungle instincts" were aroused by the "caterwauling and mass hypnotism." The paper concluded that "Clevelanders can be just as happy that Freed moved his disc jockey talents elsewhere."[34] By now it was apparent that rock and roll was not going to quickly disappear on its own. Those who feared and disliked it, and there were many, "went looking for someone to blame. They found . . . Alan Freed."[35]

The Freed show was banned in a number of places after Boston and Freed himself was arrested and charged with inciting to riot by a grand jury. He was actually charged with inciting to riot twice. One charge was under an old antianarchy law, a charge that was later dropped. Even the state realized the futility of trying to prove, as would be necessary under the anarchy provision, that Freed advocated the overthrow of the United States government. Freed and rock were soundly condemned as well by the media and community leaders.

On May 8 the manager at station WINS announced that Freed had resigned from the station in protest over what Freed termed the station's refusal to stand behind him in the face of all the hostile publicity directed toward him. WINS had refused to make any comment on the Boston affair and when newsmen tried to contact station officials about Freed's resignation they received the same no comment.[36] In court on May 16, 1958, Freed pleaded innocent to the two indictments and was released on $2,500 bail.

The first indictment was dropped subsequently by the state. But on November 3, 1958, a superior court judge refused to quash the second indictment. The case dragged on with no trial being held and the charge hanging over Freed's head for a year after that until November 12, 1959. On that date Superior Court Judge Lewis Goldberg allowed Freed to change his plea from not guilty to one of no contest. In return, at the request of Assistant District Attorney Edward M. Sullivan, the case was filed, or "pigeonholed," which basically meant it would be put in a drawer and forgotten. According to Sullivan this was done because witnesses had scattered to different parts of the country, even overseas, and a policeman in charge of the initial investigation had died, which made prosecution difficult.[37] It may have only been a coincidence but just ten days after that action Alan Freed would be blown away totally by the payola storm. That is, Boston could have filed the riot charge since Freed would very shortly be no problem to the music industry.

More than just a man who played rock and roll records on the radio, or the jockey most loved by teenagers, Freed actively and vigorously defended rock, and in the process earned more hate from the opposing forces. He appeared in a few early rock movies, *Rock around the Clock, Rock, Rock, Rock,* and *Don't Knock the Rock.* The latter film in particular was an attempt to show, in its thin plot line and mostly rock songs, that this form of music was perfectly acceptable and harmless. Freed played himself in the story of a rock singer who returned to his home town to be denounced as a menace to the country's youth. Everything turned out alright in the end as rock was vindicated. Sometimes when rock was criticized Freed hurled back the charge of "racial bias" against his tormentors. "Not a word was raised against it until I drew 80,000 persons — mostly all Negroes — to the Cleveland Arena for a musical stage show."[38] This was largely true but an exaggeration of the numbers involved by Freed.

Freed also answered his critics, particularly the New York newspapers, on his WINS program on the air from time to time. In addition Freed appeared on TV programs, such as Eric Sevareid's news program, where he often countered rock attackers and/or presented the pro side of a pro/con debate. One such program was the CBS-TV show "Right Now!" where the program's moderator discussed the "moral responsibilities" of rock artists, a veiled slap at Jerry Lee Lewis whose marriage was then highly controversial. Freed took umbrage and vigorously defended rock and roll musicians. Even as early as April 1956 he was "a primary target for recent anti-r.&r. press blasts."[39] In analyzing his appeal, and unearthing some of the reasons he was feared and hated, a former associate said, "He gives the kids what they want. Maybe that's why kids don't get along with their parents who are always telling them 'no.' They come in, tear his clothes, leave the studio in shambles. He doesn't care at all."[40] Another associate said, "Freed opened up a lot of permissiveness, with very insidious effect, I think. He said, not in actual words but in effect, 'Fight your parents if you don't agree with them!' . . . He stiffened the kids' backbones, but maybe he stiffened them in some bad directions."[41]

In June of 1958 he joined New York radio station WABC as a disk jockey and shortly after that WNEW-TV where he hosted a teen dance show, holding down both jobs at once. But gone were the live rock shows which one critic claimed was like having "an aisle seat for the San Francisco earthquake." His programs were still syndicated to some other stations, in Baltimore, St. Louis, and even Radio Luxembourg, but his days were numbered.

By November of 1959 the U.S. government turned its attention to investigating the charges of payola in the music industry. That month station

WABC demanded all its jockeys sign a statement to the effect they had never taken money or gifts to promote or play a record on their programs. Many other stations followed the same practice. Alan Freed refused to sign the statement on principle and stated that the document was an insult to his integrity. He denied ever taking any such bribes. On November 21 WABC fired Freed. General manager Ben Hoberman claimed the decision had nothing to do with payola but refused to give a specific reason for the dismissal.[42]

At WNEW-TV where Freed produced and hosted the program "Big Beat" which aired from 5:00 P.M. to 6:00 P.M. Mondays through Fridays and 9:00 P.M. to 10:00 P.M. Saturdays, the station terminated Freed on November 23. Freed did sign a statement for WNEW-TV stating he had commited no "improper practices" while working for the station, but it wasn't enough. Vice-president of the station Bennett H. Korn said the outlet wished to "resume control" of popular music programs, that Freed's contract dismissal had been "long in coming," and he was "terminated by mutual consent."[43] When he took his final leave from the TV program, many of the kids were in tears and one girl cried, "Now they've taken away our father."[44]

For all intents and purposes that was the end of Alan Freed's career and his force as an influence for rock. Freed would not be a factor during the payola hearings themselves, which lasted through the spring of 1960, since he had been already removed from the scene. The hearings would concentrate on Dick Clark who had by default taken over the position of top disk jockey. Alan Freed was not the only jockey to be fired that month, based on no facts, but he certainly was the most important and the most influential.

At the end of November, Freed admitted receiving checks from record companies for what he called "consultations" but denied it was payola. Freed personally felt he was being picked on, not without justification, when compared to the treatment Dick Clark was receiving at the hearings. The head of Sun Records, Sam Phillips, revealed he had worked a deal with Clark to promote a 1958 Jerry Lee Lewis record, "Breathless." On his show, "American Bandstand," Clark offered viewers a copy of the record if they sent him fifty cents and five Beechnut Gum wrappers. Clark was then trying to get Beechnut to renew their sponsorship of his dance program. This promotion resulted in the sale of close to forty thousand copies of the record which were supplied at no cost to Clark. Phillips and Clark then split the profits in what the record company owner described as a "legitimate business promotion." Yet Clark was never really tainted by payola.

Finally on May 19, 1960 Alan Freed was arrested and charged under New York state's commercial bribery statute, a misdemeanor in that state, punishable by up to a year in jail and a $500 fine. Seven others, jockeys and record librarians, were similarly charged. The ironic thing to remember about payola was that at the time of the hearings payola was not illegal under any federal statute. The only way to pursue the matter in the courts was under a state's commercial bribery law. If Freed had operated in a state without such a law, and not all of them had such a provision, then he couldn't have been legally prosecuted. Freed's indictment charged him with receiving $30,650 in bribes from seven record companies in 1958 and 1959. Freed pleaded not guilty.

District Attorney Frank Hogan was aware that companies had used such tactics with radio stations in the years before rock but he drew a sort of distinction. While it was cash at the end of the 1950s it had previously been "friendly persuasion." Hogan added that with five hundred rock records being released in New York City each week, sales were based on popularity "however synthetically created for the recordings by disk jockeys in their repeated exposure of records."[46] On December 17, 1962 Freed pleaded guilty to part of the indictment, receiving $2,700 in bribes from two record companies, and was fined $300 and received a six-month suspended jail sentence.

During his last years he had periods of employment as a disk jockey, mostly in California, but he labored in obscurity, no longer an influence. However, the hounding didn't stop. Toward the end of 1964 the government was after him again, this time indicting him for evading income tax on about $40,000 in income which supposedly came his way via payola between 1957 and 1959. Before this case could be settled Alan Freed died on January 20, 1965 from uremia, at age 43. His condition was likely exacerbated by the heavy drinking he had indulged in all of his life.

Alan Freed was no saint. He took payola, but it was common practice. It is important to note that no action of any kind was taken against any of the record companies, yet they flashed the money around. Other jockeys, notably Dick Clark, profited enormously from using their programs to generate other, conflict-of-interest income, yet no action was taken against them. Freed had himself listed as cowriter of a dozen or so hit songs from the era, including, "Sincerely," and Chuck Berry's "Maybelline." Berry would much later say that Freed had nothing to do with writing the song. Dick Clark held copyright to 162 songs but claimed that all but forty-three were given to him. Freed likely profited much less from "extra" income than Clark did, yet it was Freed who was harassed out of the business. While his conduct can't be condoned, in particular ripping off Chuck Berry, Alan Freed, on balance, was no worse than any jockey of the time, and didn't deserve to take the fall for the industry. But down Alan Freed went, and not for payola. He was a marked man because of his uncompromising stance in favor of rock. More than any other music industry source he aided all black artists in getting their material played, and accepted, by white audiences. He genuinely liked rock music and believed it was in the best interests of youth. Freed staunchly defended it and encouraged kids to enjoy the music and to have a good time. He didn't try to control or regiment either the teens or the music. It was these "sins" which were the real reasons that Alan Freed had to go.

While many jockeys took payola, and Freed was not the only one fired, many record companies were also found to have given it out. Nothing happened to any of them. A few were required to sign consent decrees in which they promised to cease and desist from payola, although these decrees carried with them no legal admission that the companies had engaged in the practice in the past nor did the companies admit to any guilt. Rock and roll had become popular and as big as it had not due to payola but to its overwhelming acceptance by the nation's youth, a fact the adult world could not, or would not accept.

During the hearings themselves the public gained the impression that payola was associated with rock and roll and generated by it. Had rock been pleasing to the general popular music audience, to the adult world in general, the payola hearings would probably never have occurred in the first place. The real force behind the hearings was not pay for play, which had been around for decades, but the idea the music was "bad," that it promoted delinquency, that it corrupted morality, and that no one would possibly play such awful stuff unless they were paid under the table. And the real force behind those assumptions was the desire of ASCAP to destroy BMI and regain their monopoly, the racists to get rid of "nigger" music and "nigger" lovers, the desire of crooners like Sinatra and Crosby to drive out competition which threatened their economic position, and most importantly the desire of the adults to curb teenagers and bring them back under their control.

At the end of the 1950s however, little had changed in terms of the music's popularity. A survey done by Ohio State University revealed that among teenagers, aged fourteen to eighteen, eighty-two percent preferred rock over seventeen other categories of music. Among adults, aged nineteen to seventy, rock and roll was disliked more than any of the other categories with thirty-five percent indicating they would change the radio dial if rock were played.[47]

9

1960–1962:
Emasculated Rock

The years 1953 to 1958 had seen rock streak to the top. From 1958 to 1960 rock and roll lost much of its early drive and impetus, due largely to anti-rock pressures. From 1960 to 1962 rock was toned down to suit adult standards of propriety. The controversy continued but the furor was nowhere near as great as it had been. One source of friction was the dance craze resulting from Chubby Checker's hit "The Twist." The Barberry Room and Roseland Dance City in New York City banned the dance as "vulgar" and "offensive." A foreign visitor claimed it was such antics which made Americans seem "vulgar" and "uncultured" in other lands. It was claimed to be a lewd, exhibitionist dance and comedian Bob Hope remarked, "If they turned off the music, they'd be arrested."[1] A Broadway television choreographer, Geoffrey Holder, called it dishonest and dirty, "a sick spectator sport." He could hardly believe that the "oldest hootchy kootchy in the land had become the latest thing."[2]

A hit song in the U.S. during that period, "Tell Laura I Love Her" sung by Ray Peterson, raised a storm of protest in England. The song was about a young man who needed money to get married, entered a stock car race and was then killed in a car crash. Released in the U.S. by Decca, British Decca refused to release it on the ground it was "too tasteless and vulgar." This company changed its mind a few times on the subject before finally deciding not to release it, at which time they had to scrap an estimated twenty thousand copies already pressed.

In the meantime another British company, EMI-Columbia, released a cover version by Ricky Valance which made its way into the top of the charts. This prompted a protest from the British Safety Council. The national

103

director of the group, Leonard Hodge, complained to the police, the Director of Public Prosecutions, asking that an investigation be held into the wording of the "macabre" record since the Council felt the song would "tend to deprave and corrupt impressionable teenagers." Hodge was worried that the record's "nauseating theme" would generate a "glorious death cult" among teens. The council claimed one or two such records were released every week and that they "must dam the stream of horror before it becomes a flood." The council declared it would not stop pressing until something was done since they felt such records were "far more insidious than books such as *Lolita* and *Lady Chatterly's Lover* that had been banned."[3] A few months earlier British jockeys had imposed a ban on "Teen Angel" by Mark Dinning which was about a high school girl's death at a railroad crossing auto crash.

One of the more innocuous and nonthreatening phenomena of this period was the emergence of the "girl groups" — the Crystals, Ronettes, Shirelles, and so on. Even they came in for their share of heat. The Crystals issued a record titled "He Hit Me (And It Felt Like A Kiss)" about unfaithfulness and a sort of sado-masochistic relationship which led to the song line, "He hit me and I was glad." After the record started selling kids started singing it at school and according to lead singer Barbara Alston, "their teachers heard them. They didn't like the title and the lyrics, so the P.T.A. got it banned."[4] Ed Sullivan was said to be "a staunch enemy of the tougher girl groups," which presumably would have been groups like the Shangri-Las, and the Ronettes.[5] The girl groups in general were blasted by the Lutheran Christian Encounter publishing house who centered on these groups in a book they issued attacking pop music, condemning the groups lyrically and musically. To this Lutheran group the girl groups presented an "unhealthy, false and fantasy-oriented way of thinking."[6]

A group call the Kingsmen released a song called "Louie, Louie" which made it to number two on the charts in 1962. It was a song that would be redone by many groups over the coming years and by virtually every amateur, basement rock band in the country, supposedly because it was so easy to play. When released by the Kingsmen it created its own curious storm. The lyrics were indecipherable and this led to speculation that therefore they must be dirty. Incredibly enough the U.S. Congress deemed it a fit subject to investigate. This august body played the record at 78, 45, 33, and 16 revolutions per minute in an effort to get at the truth. But it was still too much for Congress and they had to declare the record "indecipherable at any speed."[7]

The imminent demise of rock was declared again and Frankie Avalon was said to be getting ready for the end by preparing to become a nightclub entertainer, and looking for "difficult" film roles. The supposed death of rock was attributed to payola since for the teens it had become "too much trouble to support their faves in view of the unfavorable headlines."[8] Some radio stations continued to move away from rock and roll programming. In Atlanta station WEST switched over to a "good music" format. Jockey Steve May of WINY in Putnam, Connecticut conducted his own on-the-air survey of listeners and rock lost with the result that WINY devoted a portion of its airtime to playing oldies from prerock times. The Storer Broadcasting Comany, which owned a chain of radio stations, adopted a quality control system for all of its stations. Under the system all programming on all stations was monitored via tape. Company executives could then check the tunes to "improve the quality of programming" at such stations. The setup of this system was "a direct result of the payola scandals."[9]

Some still weren't happy even with this watered-down version of rock and looked around hopefully, and mistakenly, for some sign from above, or anywhere else, that rock and roll would be slain totally and permanently. The director of WABC, ABC's New York flagship station, Roger Coleman, found this hope in FM stations. In the summer of 1961 FM stations were relatively scarce, there being only 159 FM stations in the entire country. Coleman felt FM would be the "antidote" to rock and would feature "good pops, show scores, and longhair music" and thus "knock rock 'n' roll out of the musical box." Coleman was not alone as a number of record industry executives and the Record Industry Association of America agreed that FM would be "a boon to lovers of good music."[10] It was another idea with more fantasy than reality behind it as many FM stations would feature rock album cuts, as opposed to just hit singles, and thus, over the years, allow for an expansion of groups and types of material in rock and roll. FM proved to be more a boon to rock than a bane.

Losses in rock and roll had begun in 1957 when Little Richard suddenly quit rock to become a minister. In 1958 Elvis went into the army and would emerge changed from hard rocker to middle-of-the-road crooner. Jerry Lee Lewis was blacklisted out of the business due to his controversial marriage. Chuck Berry wound up in jail, his career ruined.

Buddy Holly and Eddie Cochran both died in separate accidents in 1959 and 1960, both under the age of twenty-three and both showing great promise and potential. These latter accidents had, of course, nothing to do with anti-rock opposition but added to the music's troubles. The ones gone were the most vital, most innovative, and energetic of the period. February 3, 1959 has been called the "Day the Music Died," for it was then that Holly perished in a tragic air crash along with singers Richie Valens and the Big Bopper. The changes in early rock cannot be said to have started or stopped on one specific day but to the extent that one date is needed or useful as a symbolic date then it should be May 3, 1958, the day of the Boston "riot." To say that the Boston "riot" was the "Day The Music Was Murdered" instead of "Died" would be an exaggeration but certainly the event was devastating, for Alan Freed represented all that was vital about rock while Dick Clark, who would rise in his place, stood for all that was bland. The years 1959 and 1960 saw Alan Freed gone, beaten by payola. As well those payola hearings themselves did a certain amount of damage to rock and roll.

Dick Clark took over hosting "American Bandstand" in 1956 when it was still a local teen dance program in Philadelphia. It went national in 1957 where it ran for many years as Clark became the nation's leading disk jockey. When Clark took over the show he replaced Bob Horn who had been fired due to an arrest for drunk driving. Clark was actually the second choice, getting the position after a disk jockey named Al Jarvis turned down ABC because "the networks wanted no black artists appearing. Clark willingly conformed to the racist network policy."[11] At its peak "American Bandstand" was seen over 105 TV stations and reached at least twenty million viewers.

On the program Clark maintained rigid standards for the teens who were admitted to his program as the studio audience/dancers. First, two lines were formed outside the studio, one male, one female, so equal numbers could be admitted. (There were usually more girls than boys who wanted to get in.) A strict dress code was enforced. Boys had to wear a tie with either a sweater or a jacket. The girls couldn't wear tight sweaters, low necked dresses, or pants. No turned up collars were allowed. Turning up the collar was a teen fad of the era projecting a "tough" image. As the kids entered the studio they were checked out by doormen who made them get rid of items like chewing gum. All this was done, as Clark himself said, to "make the show more acceptable to adults who were frightened by the teen-age world and their music."[12]

"American Bandstand" admitted no one under fourteen since the show considered thirteen-year-olds as "too giddy and difficult to control." No one over eighteen was allowed either, a cutoff that kept soldiers and sailors out since Clark was worried about the image of a sailor dancing with a teenage girl. Clark kept a dress code for himself as well and outfitted himself in a manner that also wouldn't offend. He always wore suits that were "dark and nondescript." "American Bandstand" never had any fights, stabbings, or other problems, said Clark, unlike the image associated with rock fans "during the riots in New York and Boston at Alan Freed's rock shows."[13]

Clark was compared to a teacher overseeing a class or a "pleasant camp counselor" hired to play records on television. Dick Clark provided the perfect rebuttal to the charges that rock and roll led to riots and delinquency and corrupted morals. His increased popularity was due in no small part to the blessings of adults high up in the music industry who didn't want to abandon the music because it was profitable. With Clark in the forefront they could clean it up, water it down, and soften considerably the most vociferous of the rock criticisms.

Despite these precautions the show still got flak. Clark could not use the phrase "going steady" when he talked to the kids and churchgoers were said to be upset about the dancing on the program which they felt to be "lascivious." Girls from a local Catholic high school wore their school uniforms on the show until the nuns at West Catholic High vetoed that and made the girls cover the uniform with a sweater. According to Clark, "Bandstand" was a segregated show for years until it became integrated in 1957, when Clark determined "to make it so." That was the year Clark had the first black on the program, as part of the audience, and he claimed he "had black representation which increased as the years went by."[14] Dick Clark's autobiography contained a number of pictures, sixteen of which showed portions of the "Bandstand" audience. While undated, these pictures likely cover the period from the late 1950s to the early 1960s. They contained in total about 340 faces which could be identified in terms of color. Not one of them was black.[15] Philadelphia then had a black population of twenty-six percent.

This period of rock and roll, symbolically led by Dick Clark, has been described as "Philadelphia rock," or "schlock rock," and has been denigrated by most critics. The major performers were all clones of Clark himself. They were neat, clean, wholesome, and sedate. They included: Fabian, Frankie Avalon, Bobby Vinton, Bobby Vee, and Bobby Rydell. No more slovenly dress, no more performers like Jerry Lee Lewis or Little Richard, who ripped the joint. No more wriggling of the pelvis and no more lewd lyrics. No screamers, no jumpers, no hip shakers. For the most part they were, like Clark, nondescript pretty boys who all basically stood still while they sang.

Mom and Dad could watch from home, along with the clergy, the media, the sexually uptight, and so on, if not with perfect ease, then at least with a great deal less discomfort than before when they had to confront specters like Richard, Lewis, Berry, and Presley. Many, if not most, of the rock opposition would still have preferred the music to go away altogether but if it wouldn't then they might just be able to tolerate it with Clark at the helm as he presided over the changed face of rock, this tamed and emasculated version.

And so it went through the early 1960s as 1962 gave way to 1963. While the anti-rock forces may have been somewhat tolerant and accepting of this development the kids were less so. And as 1963 began a group of young men in another country were working away almost anonymously. They were men with names like Paul McCartney, John Lennon, Keith Richards, and Mick Jagger and they were soon to break out of their anonymity and return some of the life and vigor to the world of rock and roll. The kids would love it. The anti-rock people would hate it as once more the ominous and terrifying Jolly Roger of, sex, drugs, rock, roll, and rebellion would be hoisted high.

PART II
1963-1973

10

Rock Resurrects

Adult society heaved a collective sigh of relief at the end of the 1950s. They believed that rock and roll had been neatly channeled into mainstream culture. They were soon to gasp in horror. The beast was not dead; it was merely sleeping. What woke it up was the powerful jab of the 1960s counter-culture youth.

In the 1950s rock lyrics had taken on the family or school, urging mild rebellion against parents or teachers. In the 1960s rock took on the entire system, calling for an end to the oppressive and hypocritical values of established social structures. In the 1950s parents were reassured by the knowledge that their teen-aged children would soon mature into responsible adults accepting the status quo. In the 1960s there was no such assurance.

The young people of the 1960s questioned every aspect of traditional authority, and it began with something as basic as appearance. Military haircuts and concrete bouffants gave way to long flowing hair. Dark suits and rigid girdles were replaced by colorful T-shirts and blue jeans worn by both sexes. High heels and oxfords were kicked off as youth embraced sandals or even bare feet. Dirty, scruffy, and weird were the words used to describe the new look. Rock musicians became the fashion trend-setters of the day and the establishment viewed them with distaste.

Behind the image a whole new perspective on culture and politics was developing. In the forefront was a sexual revolution. Virginity was no longer worshipped. Females were urged to emerge from behind their facade of purity, and living together, promiscuity, and free love became common experiences of the times. Many rock lyrics represented the expression of sexual permissiveness, and rock performers in their suggestive dancing and gesturing made certain the message was getting through. Adults were shocked. Major efforts were made to censor rock lyrics and force performers to tone down their acts.

As more and more young people joined in the reaction against established political and economic institutions, they began to be known as hippies. Anti-war sentiment was one base of their cohesion as they refused to be cannon fodder in Vietnam. "Make Love Not War" became their battle cry as they lashed out in demonstrations against first the Johnson and then the Nixon administrations. Rock and roll lyrics often took up the cause and again there were efforts at censorship or accusations that rock music was a communist plot.

The military-industrial complex which supported the war was shunned by the hippies, and money became a dirty word. Police became the enemy as they attempted to control the movement for civil rights against racist doctrines. Rock and roll music took up the beat. After all, their music had its roots deep in black culture. And the young white rockers of the 60s blatantly acknowledged their debt to Chuck Berry or Little Richard. Worse yet, in the eyes of the establishment, they encouraged a revival of rhythm and blues, bringing old-timers like B. B. King back into center stage. The liberal attitudes of youth made it possible for labels like Motown to grow and prosper, much to the dismay of reactionaries.

The hippies' interest in Eastern philosophies and distrust of organized religion rocked the church to its very foundations. This was true for the Catholic church but above all for the right-wing Christian fundamentalists. Since rock music was an easily identified voice of youth, fundamentalist opposition was overwhelming. Rock and roll was seen as an instrument of the devil leading youth into a sinful orgy of sex, drugs, and communism. The religious right was to become one of rock's most dangerous adversaries.

Gatherings of young people were becoming common events whether it was at rallies, demonstrations, or rock concerts. The sheer numbers of the young and their exuberant behavior at live rock performances intimidated security police and hall managers. Rock festivals became associated with violence and drugs in the minds of the public as the media exaggerated any disturbances into riots and mayhem. Authorities often provoked fans into confrontations. Gradually the movement to ban rock concerts and festivals gained momentum as officials refused to issue permits for these events.

Crusades against obscene lyrics were organized in the 1960s just as "leerics" had been attacked a decade earlier. But the most intense efforts at banning and censorship culminated in the campaign against drug lyrics by the Nixon administration in the early 1970s. Politically motivated, the anti-drug fervor once again brought rock and roll under severe scrutiny by the Federal Communications Commission and Congress.

In trying to build a case against the music, anti-rock proponents tried to suggest that rock was even a health hazard. It could make you deaf, damage the nerves, or create mass hypnosis.

Above all, rock was attacked for its aesthetics. It wasn't "good" music. It was the work of amateurs, so simple it could be learned in a few hours. Heavy metal was labeled "rot and roll," its loudness and driving beat were abhorred. Rock was considered the "caterwauling of a disturbed generation." During the 1960s rock music was one of the most threatening forms of entertainment around.

By the 1970s however, change was already in the air. Young people were growing up, Beatle songs became Muzak, and yippies turned into yuppies. Once again rock was relegated to the grave. "Mourn the music," said a writer for *Crawdaddy*. "It has died." What he forgot was that there was a new generation evolving, ready to take rock and roll to even greater heights of excess.

With the elitism of youth, every generation thought that their brand of rock and roll was the culmination of the music. It was not uncommon for one group of rockers to despise those who came after them, or before them. For example, in the early 1970s, Presley expressed a loathing for the Beatles. Some of the punk rockers, like the Sex Pistols, rejected virtually all rockers that preceded them. One reason for this seemingly strange turn of events has to do with the fact that rock music is anything but static and it is subject to wide swings in form and content.

The volatile nature of rock can be explained mainly by the way the industry organized itself in the 1960s. The independent companies retained their control over the market until the mid-1960s when they were bought up or merged with the majors. The process had started with Dot Records which was an independent company set up in 1950. It functioned more like a major in that it was a predatory company which made its fortune by covering black songs. Paramount Pictures bought Dot in 1957, making it the first independent to go. Most went in the 1960s; Atlantic for example was swallowed by Warner Brothers. This was the only way the majors could regain the market since they were still run by middle-aged and middle-class white men who had no way of selecting talent that would be successful with teens. They bought up the independents and kept some of their personnel on to spot the talent.

The majors had historically worked through specialization. They had singers who sang and did nothing else. They had songwriters who wrote, and nothing else, and used musicians who solely played. There was no overlap. The majors would then try to match up a combination, songwriter with singers and musicians, to produce a hit.

During rock's first period, specialization had vanished to a large degree. The artists did two or three things. Most played, in addition to singing, and many wrote. Little Richard, Chuck Berry, and Buddy Holly did all three. Jerry Lee Lewis and Bill Haley sang, played and wrote a bit, but not their hits. Presley played and sang but didn't write. During the end of rock's first period from 1960 to 1962, led by Dick Clark's schlock rock, specialization had returned. Artists such as Frankie Avalon, Fabian, Bobby Rydell, and so on, sang, but nothing else. The large number of girl groups around at that time sang, and nothing else. The independents controlled the market but specialization returned nonetheless. Such specialization was not beneficial for rock, or anything else, since it amounted to production by committee and led to a bland, lowest-common-denominator product.

When the majors regained the rock market through the 1960s, though devout believers in specialization, they were forced by the nature of rock to abandon that principle. It was done not by choice but through necessity. It was a difficult enough task for the majors to try and identify and sign talent that would appeal to teens, without also having to find material for them to perform. Imagine Decca signing up Mick Jagger and then finding him songs to sing and musicians to back him up. So what did develop in the 1960s, more completely and more permanently than in the 1950s, was the rise of the self-contained act. The trend started with the Beatles and the Stones and continues today. The rule, then and now, is that in order to be a rock star you have to sing, play, and write your own material (there are exceptions of course).

This development has had advantages and disadvantages for rock. It has kept the music alive and vital as a continually changing crop of young people rise to the top and it has assured that the music would reflect the interests and concerns of the youth of the day. This also helped to explain why rock can eliminate fans as they age. A seventeen-year-old who enjoyed a Presley song and performance in 1956, perhaps for the earthy sexuality which the teen could identify with, may have found himself a thirty-one-year-old accountant in 1970 and completely turned off by the long-haired rockers singing about drugs. Similarly a mellow twenty-year-old grooving to the pot-celebrating Jefferson Airplane in 1967, would perhaps, as a thirty-year-old, have difficulty with the Sex Pistols in 1977.

By leaving rock and roll up to rock and rollers the majors have in a way ensured a continued controversy over the music due to the fact that the young rockers will sing about current teen interests. These interests have often been the very things the adults have been most uptight about at a particular time. Singing about sex in the 1950s was one of the surest ways to rattle an adult. Drugs became the sore point in the late 1960s and early 1970s. In short, the self-contained rock and roll act was almost guaranteed to celebrate something which adults would find offensive, and thus kept the music both under attack by the old and alive for the young.

11

Out of Sight

SHOCKERS! UGLY LOOKS! UGLY SPEECH! UGLY MANNERS!
These were the headlines that greeted the Stones on tour. Like all
celebrities rock stars were scrutinized for their appearance, behavior, and
private lives; and the adult public did not like what it saw. Used to a
young generation that less than a decade before wore army uniforms and
brushcuts, society was appalled by the long hair and hippie love beads of
the 60s youth. Accustomed to genteel "yes sir" and "no sir" politeness from
their progeny, parents were horrified by the "fuck off" attitude of the
flower children. Comfortable with familiar intoxicants like alcohol, the
establishment was unprepared for marijuana, LSD, MDA, peyote, mes-
caline, hashish, cocaine, or heroin. Secure behind their suburban doors,
safe within the nuclear family, the older folk were baffled by communes,
free love, living together, and other manifestations of open sexuality.

As one politician believed, rock bands created "scenes which could
only tend to exalt and influence ridiculous youthful styles, thus
humiliating and certainly not favoring the education and formation of
youthful generations."[1]

PTA magazine, which tried to provide guidelines for parents concerning youth entertainment, blasted the 1965 rock show "Hullabaloo"
because, "Soloists, male and female, moan, groan and grimace in the sick
songs and lyric agonies of frustrated love. . . . Whatever this program
may represent psychologically, sociologically and economically,
esthetically, it is ugly, grotesque and revolting."[2]

The Beatles were one of the first groups in the 60s to meet opposition for
their appearance. Sporting long hair, the four "mop tops" were considered a
bad influence on school boys who were often suspended for wearing

Beatle haircuts. Said one British headmaster, "This ridiculous style brings out the worst in boys physically. It makes them look like morons."[3] On the Beatles' first visit to America the *Washington Post* described them as "asexual and homely." Chet Huntley refused to show film footage of their arrival on the NBC news. Others saw their long hair as effeminate.

Public disdain of the Beatles came to a head in 1965 when they were awarded M.B.E.'s (Members of the Order of the British Empire). Although they had received their medals because of their contribution to the entertainment industry, both financially and as international boosters of British culture, many believed they were undeserving of the award. This attitude was particularly true of those who had also received the honor; they felt it had belittled their own achievements.

At that stage of their career the Beatles were still very much the good, clean, wholesome boys next door, although their hair may have been too long for many people. The furor over the award showed that even such a "good" rock group as the Beatles would never really be accepted by the adult establishment. The Labour government gave the award probably because the Beatles did have such a good image and it thought little furor would be aroused. What the Labour government failed to take into account was that, at the bottom, the Beatles were still a rock group. And rock groups and music were, after all, "bad."

Hundreds returned their medals in protest. One of the men who posted his M.B.E. back to the Queen was a former R.A.F. squadron leader, Paul Peterson, who had received his award for air-sea rescue operations during World War II. Commented Peterson, "I feel that when people like the Beatles are given the M.B.E. the whole thing becomes debased and cheapened. I am making this gesture in the hope that the Queen's position in this situation can be reinforced so that she can resist and control her Ministers."[4]

Another military officer during the war, Richard Pape, returned his M.B.E. stating, "The Beatles' M.B.E. reeks of mawkish, bizarre effrontery to our wartime endeavours."[5] And Dr. Gaetan Jarry, a former lieutenant-commander in the Royal Canadian Navy, renounced his M.B.E. declaring, "For the next war do not count on me — use the Beatles or the Beatniks."[6]

As well as collecting returned medals, the government received scores of letters running two-to-one against the Beatles, as did the newspapers. The *London Times* published one such letter to the editor which asked, "What is the point of serving a country that awards the M.B.E. to a group of young pop singers?"[7] The Beatles were called "vulgar nincompoops."

A retired army officer, Colonel F. W. Wagg not only returned his war medals to the Queen but also said he was resigning from the Labour Party, then in power, and cancelling a £12,000 bequest he was leaving the Party in his will. "I have nothing against the Beatles personally," he claimed. "But I do object to this kind of award. In my opinion an order of public utility — as opposed to an order of chivalry — should be instituted for this type of case."[8]

The Mayor of Poole, Councillor L. Drudge, wanted Parliament to ensure that such a mistake as giving the Beatles M.B.E.s would never occur again. Drudge and his two brothers all had been awarded M.B.E.s. Explained the angry mayor, "One of them won it for combating enemy planes at a height of 20,000 feet in 1917. Giving it to the Beatles is an insult to all of us."[9]

John Lennon, not one to back down from criticism of his group, responded to the brouhaha by noting that army officers got their awards for "killing people. We received ours for entertaining. . . . I'd say we deserve ours more. . . . We were given the MBE for exports, and the citation should have said that. . . . If someone had got an award for exporting millions of dollars worth of manure or machines everyone would have applauded. Why should they knock us?"[10]

Ironically in 1969 John Lennon would return his M.B.E. in protest against the Vietnam war and Biafra, making his statement flippant by also including a protest against one of his songs, "Cold Turkey," slipping in the charts. Papers which blasted him for accepting the award four years earlier now blasted him for returning it.

The early Beatles' image was tame compared to the Rolling Stones. The Stones became the bad boys of rock right from the start. On their British TV debut on "Thank Your Lucky Stars," their long hair and Jagger's sensuality shocked middle-aged viewers, even though the Stones wore suits. The program received letters from outraged parents with sentiments like, "It is disgraceful that long-haired louts such as these should be allowed to appear on television. Their appearance was absolutely disgusting,"[11] or "The whole lot of you should be given a good bath, then all that hair should be cut off. I'm not against pop music when it's sung by a nice clean boy like Cliff Richard, but you are a disgrace. Your filthy appearance is likely to corrupt teenagers all over the country."[12]

Yet in those early years the Beatles and Stones were remarkably similar in appearance. Hair length was the same for both groups and in fact neither group was in need of a bath. Both were "clean." The Stones were hated and the Beatles were liked for other reasons. Those who criticized the Stones for being "unwashed" and for their hair were using this as a smoke screen to hide the gut-level fears the Stones raised. The Beatles smiled a lot, the Stones didn't. The Beatles just wanted to "hold your hand" while the Stones wanted to "spend the night together." Stones' material made them a distinct sexual threat to every father's daughter while the Beatles were cute and innocuous. Onstage the Beatles performed in a remarkably sedate fashion, standing fairly still, while Jagger never stopped moving, mostly in a taunting, sexual manner. The honeymoon with the Beatles ended fairly soon, for no matter how clean and wholesome a rocker might be he was still performing the "devil's music" and would soon find himself the focus of a hostile establishment.

The president of the British National Federation of Hairdressers commented, "The Rolling Stones are the worst. One of them looks as though he has got a yellow feather duster on his head."[13] Brian Jones, who was quite vain about his looks, was very offended. The Stones were called "the ugliest group in Britain" and, ironically, headmasters began urging their students to get their Stones haircuts "neatly" styled like the Beatles. Headlines in *Melody Maker* asked, "WOULD YOU LET YOUR SISTER GO OUT WITH A ROLLING STONE?" or "WHY DO PARENTS HATE US?" A magistrate in Glasgow who was trying a youth for being rowdy after a concert took him to task for liking the Stones. Said the judge, "They wear their hair down to their shoulders, filthy clothing, act like clowns, and you buy a ticket to see morons like that."[14]

The Stones' unrepentant attitude just infuriated adults more. "We know a lot of people don't like us," said Jagger, "'cause they say we're scruffy and don't wash. So what? They don't have to come and look at us do they? If they don't like me, they can keep away."[15] Jagger's early image was mild compared to the persona he would develop over the years. He began to wear makeup, and his effeminate lipstick and eyeshadow gave him an androgynous look. Mick's colorful tight pants and open shirts suggested nudity. Dancing all over the stage, Jagger writhed and stomped as if in sexual torment. He throttled the microphone, snapped his belt around, whipped it on the stage floor, and pouted his lips and pointed his finger to taunt and tease the audience. Jagger described his own performance this way,

> I get a strange feeling onstage. I feel all this energy coming from an audience. They need something from life and are trying to get it from us. I often want to smash the microphone up because I don't feel the same person onstage as I am normally. . . . I entice the

audience, of course, I do. I do it every way I can think of. . . . What I'm doing is a sexual thing. I dance, and all dancing is a replacement for sex. What really upsets people is that I'm a man and not a woman. I don't do anything more than a lot of girl dancers, but they're accepted because it's a man's world. What I do is very much the same as a girl's striptease dance. I take my jacket off, and sometimes I loosen my shirt, but I don't stand in front of a mirror practicing how to be sexy, you know.[16]

Jagger would eventually play up the bisexual image to such an extent that one promo picture showed the Stones in drag. Brian Jones and Bill Wyman were shown in female military uniforms, Keith Richards looked like a blowsy housewife, and Jagger sported a tea-dance hat. It was antics such as these that created headlines like, "HAVE THE STONES GONE TOO FAR?"

They were to go even further, however. When the Stones dabbled in the occult, Jagger was accused of practicing black magic and ultimately of being Satan himself. He was totally flattered by this. After all, it was the next best thing to being labeled a god. The Stones used demonic metaphors in some of their songs, and got as much mileage as possible out of their menacing image. Their actions perpetuated the old image of a causal connection between rock and delinquency or violence. One observer said they looked like "five unfolding switchblades."

The press had a field day insulting the Stones. *Newsweek* called them "slightly simian," described Jagger as "liver-lipped," and said they dressed like "carnival coxcombs."[17] The *London Times* reported, "There is no doubt that, in any poll for the best-hated man in Britain taken among people over forty, Mr. Jagger would be near the top." A nonplussed Mick jauntily replied to this type of criticism, "Everytime somebody curses me, I think, 'Remember, that's what makes me very rich.'"

The Stones' personal behavior was objectionable as well. In 1965 they pulled into a British service station to use the washroom. It was late at night when no other customers were around. Bill Wyman, a "shaggy-haired monster," according to the garage attendant, Charles Keeley, asked "in disgusting language" if he could use the toilet. Keeley told him the public one was out of order (it wasn't) and refused to allow him to use the staff lavatory. At one point some of the other Stones got out of the car. Jagger "pushed" Keeley aside saying, "We piss anywhere man." The others took up the chant and Jagger, Jones, and Wyman pissed against the wall. Keeley pressed charges and the Stones were convicted of "insulting behavior" and were fined three pounds each and fifteen guineas for court costs. Said the magistrate, "Because you have reached exalted heights in your profession, it does not mean you can behave in this manner."[18]

The Stones were often hassled by police and even their most minute traffic offenses were blown up out of all proportion by newspapers. When Jagger appeared in court for one of these minor charges, his lawyer believed that the court was so hostile to longhairs that he felt obliged to remind the judge that Britain's illustrious war hero, the Duke of Marlborough, had had hair longer than Mick Jagger.

Rock stars in the first rush of fame and big money sometimes got a little reckless on tour. They were often noisy in hotel rooms, smoked dope, or vandalized furniture. The Stones were no exception. In 1966, fourteen hotels refused to book them. The Stones finally had to file suit, claiming their civil rights were violated.

Another aspect of the Stones' life that upset the adult public was their sexual freedom. When Mick was living with Marianne Faithfull and she became pregnant, society was shocked. Jagger was invited on the David Frost television show to debate the defender of British morals, Mrs. Mary Whitehouse, head of the National Viewers' and Listeners' Association. The staunch Mrs. Whitehouse had a difficult time with quick-thinking Jagger. When she insisted a Christian marriage was based on vows that kept people together through rough times, Jagger replied, "Your church accepts divorce. . . . I don't see how you can talk about this bond which is inseparable when the Christian Church itself accepts divorce."[19] The more the Stones upset the establishment values, the more they were criticized. Their flagrant disregard for conventions, transvestite posturings, and worst of all, enormous popularity among youth were barely tolerated.

One American father expressed the indignation of many parents when he exploded: "It's time we exorcised this demonic influence over our children!" He apparently believed in going eye-to-eye with the Devil for he hoped that Jagger would come to the States more often to perform since he did the country a service by forcing the people to confront the question of where they had failed. He felt that American parents and the establishment had clearly failed youth since they had elevated Mick Jagger, a "pimple-faced disciple of dirt," to the status of "hero." To this observer the Stones delivered a performance which was a blitzkrieg, a "packaged excess of four-letter words and tacky smut." The group "bombarded" American kids with filth. He felt the blame, however, didn't lie with the teens, but rather with the adults. The adults had lost their way in a rapidly changing world and in their efforts to keep up and be modern they had forgotten to tell the teens about important values, the timeless ones that had made America great. This failure had allowed atrocities like the Stones to slip through and it was clearly time to return to such values. "Things that have a lot to do with God, a flag and a country."[20]

The most scathing attack on the Stones came from Albert Goldman who compared Jagger to Hitler. In a 1968 *New York Times* article, he described their L. A. Forum concert as a Nazi rally. Goldman claimed to have seen every person and "love-child" at the concert stand up on his chair, raise his right arm and hold it high over his head whereupon they each made a big, black, hard fist. As Goldman then enthused, "What a climax! What a gesture! What pure Nuremburg! . . . Ja wohl, Mein friends, dot's right! Dat good ole rock 'n' roll could warm the cockles of a storm trooper's heart. . . . You can. . . . fasten eye, ears, soul on the Leader. . . . Der Fuhrer would have been gassed out of his kugel by the scene at the Forum. . . . Actually the idea that rock is Fascism spelled Fashion is as familiar as the fact that smoking causes cancer."[21]

Jagger as Hitler? Why not. It made sense to a lot of rock's enemies. There was no real logic to it though. Goldman himself practically called Jagger a "nigger-lover" something that Hitler was never accused of. In fact, Jagger shared the stage at the L. A. Forum with several black performers. As Goldman disapprovingly noted, "The bill was black-heavy, with people like B. B. King, the regnant blues belter, and Ike and Tina Turner, the belle and beau of the ball-'n'-sock'it circuit. Two hours of diathermy by these deep-fat fryers."[22]

Calling the Stones' style "sado-homosexual-junkie-diabolic-sarcastic-nigger-evil" Goldman showed himself to be more in tune with Hitler's antipathies than Jagger was.[23] It was a vicious and irresponsible accusation for Goldman to make against an entertainer.

Although the Stones got the lion's share of bad press for their image and behavior, many other rockers came under fire at one time or another. Jim Morrison of the Doors built a reputation for outrageous actions, on and off stage. Morrison, who had been known for his use of obscenities, went too far at a concert in Miami in 1969. He made the ultimate faux pas by exposing his penis on stage. Because of his action, six warrants for his arrest were filed. One of the charges was a felony for "lewd and lascivious behavior in public by exposing his private parts and by simulating masturbation and oral copulation."[24]

An outraged public held a "Rally for Decency" at Miami's Orange Bowl. It was organized by Mike Levesque, a nineteen-year-old high school football hero. President Nixon sent him a letter of support. Thirty thousand people, including teens and adults, turned up. Basing the rally around "five virtues," participants demonstrated for "Belief in God and that he loves us; love of the planet and country; love of our family; reverence of one's sexuality; and equality of all men."[25] Among the celebrities attending the rally were Kate Smith, Anita Bryant, and Jackie Gleason who said, "I believe this kind of movement will snowball across the world."[26]

Organizers of the rally tried to exlude anyone with long hair or weird clothing, but doing so would have violated regulations pertaining to the city-owned stadium so everyone was allowed entry. Numerous religious groups backed the event and the Miami Drum and Bugle Corps was on hand to entertain the troops. The American Legion distributed ten thousand small American flags. Many held aloft signs reading "Down With Obscenity." A local reporter in Miami commented about the reaction against Morrison, "They'd crucify him if they could, they're so worked up."[27]

Many subsequent Doors concerts that spring were cancelled. After the Miami incident whenever the Doors appeared in concert, authorities were excessively vigilant, so Morrison was careful not to wear leather or use obscenities. In Minneapolis, the hall manager and the police stood in the wings in case of "indecent exposure." The mayor of Philadelphia tried to stop a Doors concert by unearthing an 1879 law which gave him the right to prohibit a performance that could be "immoral in nature or unpleasant and harmful to the community." The promoters fought the ruling and won.

A Pittsburgh show was halted when the stage was rushed by hundreds of teens. A sheriff came to the Las Vegas concert with blank arrest warrants for each of the Doors which could be filled in on the spot if the band did anything offensive. Morrison tried to behave, but by the time the Doors hit Boston, Jim lost his cool. When the concert ran overtime to 2 A.M., the hall manager turned off the power to the amps. The microphone was still working though when Morrison yelled "cocksuckers." Because of this the next night's show in Salt Lake City was cancelled.

A Grateful Dead concert scheduled for a city-owned Miami auditorium a few weeks after the Morrison incident was banned. Concert promoters had to find another venue. Said a civic spokesman about the Grateful Dead, "They're the same type of people as the Doors. . . . It's this underground pop music. . . . I don't think our community could stand another affair such as that."[28] For some reason Morrison's exhibitionism created more of a stir than the shocking action of an MC5 musician who crapped on stage in Seattle.[29]

The FBI had a big file on Morrison. He had been arrested ten times between 1963 and 1969 on charges ranging from battery and drunk driving to lewd and obscene performance. The FBI memo describing the Miami incident concluded that Morrison "pulled all stops in an effort to provoke chaos among a huge crowd of people. Morrison's program lasted one hour during which he grunted, groaned, gyrated and gestured along with inflammatory remarks. He screamed obscenities and exposed himself which resulted in a number of the people on stage being hit and slugged and thrown to the floor."[30] Among the obscenities he used were fuck, shit, and bullshit.

What outraged the establishment was different in 1970 than in the 1950s. Plain old hip shaking was too common by then and too mild. Raunchier acts were needed to shock and rock was always ready to oblige. Morrison was openly challenging and based much of his act on charged sexuality and open rebellion in a more obvious way than many others. Jagger walked on the edge of the line while Morrison slipped right over to the other side. Morrison's act flowed from the same continuum as Presley's and the reaction was parallel in the 1970s to that of the 1950s.

Morrison was tried in the Dade County Court in 1970 and found guilty of profanity and exposure. When the prosecutor asked Morrison if he had actually exposed himself, Morrison said he had been too drunk to remember. His lawyer, Max Fink, had defended him by using the freedom of expression credo and argued that Morrison had done nothing that wasn't already described and shown in plays, bestselling books, and films and was entitled to the same protection of the law. He used the same arguments for the obscenites and said to the court, "If Mr. Morrison used slang expressions which you as an individual considered crude — some four-letter words — and those same expressions verbally and physically are part of the dissenting scene in this country, as evidenced by plays, books, and the young people of this country, would you be shocked?"[31]

The answer was apparently yes, for Morrison was found guilty, almost a foregone conclusion, and was fined $500 for profanity and sentenced to six months in jail for indecent exposure. He was freed on a $50,000 bond pending an appeal. The Doors never had the same success after this publicity. They had trouble getting bookings and Morrison died soon after of a heart attack in 1971. All sorts of rumors circulated after his death. Some said he had overdosed. Others claimed he was poisoned by an irate mistress. It was even suggested that the FBI had done him in as part of a conspiracy to eliminate leftist elements. (This latter theory had also circulated after the deaths of Janis Joplin and Jimi Hendrix.)

Alice Cooper was another rocker who scandalized society. Cooper's schtick involved looking and acting bizarre. With eyes ringed in black make-up, a live boa wrapped around his neck, legs clad in leotards, and hair springing wildly from his androgynous head, Alice did his thing. And what an act it was! He hacked baby dolls to pieces on stage, feigned the decapitation of chickens with a guillotine, and his coup de grace was to pretend to hang himself from an onstage gallows. Cooper's act prompted phrases like "cult of the ugly," "freak rock," "transvestite rock," or "decadent rock." British parliamentarians wanted to ban Cooper from entering the country, objecting to images of sadism and necrophilia in his songs. Accusing Cooper of peddling "the culture of the concentration camp" one M.P. said, "These are evil attempts to teach our children to find their identity in hate and not love."[32]

More destructive behavior was seen when Keith Emerson of Emerson, Lake, and Palmer hurled knives into his Moog synthesizer. But Peter Townshend of the Who carried violent theatricals further by smashing his guitar to pieces on stage. To a background of smoke bombs going off, Townshend threw his guitar into the air, caught it, smashed it several times against the floor, jabbed it into the amps, and crushed it to smithereens. Many people, including fans and other musicians, were horrified by this kind of wasteful destructiveness. But few realized that the trashing of assembly-line guitars was basically a reflection of their own disposable society. After watching a guitar being destroyed by Townshend, someone irately asked the artist if he would trash a Stradivarius the same way. Peter replied that of course he wouldn't. Pointing to the remains of his guitar Townshend noted it was one of identical and countless thousands which came out of a factory. This kind of ritual destruction of objects was also often more offensive to the establishment than the mass murder officially sanctioned in Vietnam.

Not to be outdone, Jimi Hendrix set fire to his guitar by dousing it with lighter fluid and setting a match to it. The first time he did it an astounded crowd thought the twelve-foot flames were actually burning Hendrix himself. Hendrix raised the hackles of society partly because he was black, and press reaction to him revealed the underlying racism that was apparent in some of the anti-rock sentiment. In 1966 British papers called him "The Wild Man from Borneo" and a "Mau-Mau." He was most detested for his aggressively sexual performance, where he moved "the guitar across his body, standing straight up from his haunches panning the instrument before him like a machine gun cock emitting staccatobursts: humping his ax as it rumbles into low-pitched feedback, and then letting it all out as he falls back to his knees, and then over backward, feedback splitting white-hot noise all over him."[33]

126

Other instances of straightforward sexuality were demonstrated by Grace Slick of the Jefferson Airplane who sometimes displayed her bare breasts on stage. This was topped by Ruby of Ruby and the Rednecks who used her breasts as maracas.

Mick Jagger, borrowing from Little Richard, had set the pace for the transvestite image among rockers and several more popped up in the early 70s. David Bowie and Rod Stewart in their glitter clothes and makeup had people wondering about their gender, as did the Dolls in their lipstick and hot pants. During a 1971 tour of Texas, Bowie was threatened by a redneck who didn't care for Bowie's dress. The transvestite phenomenon was to become a tradition in rock with the likes of Elton John.

If the world thought rock had reached the ultimate in hideous images and behavior, they hadn't seen anything yet. Waiting in the wings were Sid Vicious and the rest of the punk crew. They would not be received kindly.

Stones concert where Jagger was "gyrating wildly" at the front of the stage. Klein thought musicians and their managers were actually encouraging fans to stay away by inciting rowdy behavior. But Klein was wrong about this. It was the hall manangers themselves who were keeping audiences away simply by not booking rock and roll groups. As Klein himself noted, "more and more cities and civic arenas are banning the performers thereby reducing further playdates for these groups."[11]

Eventually the Civic Center put an "indefinite ban" on all rock concerts which was in effect until 1970. University campuses took up some of the slack in Baltimore by booking rock groups, but they usually had auditoriums that could seat less than the civic halls. No problems had been reported at any of the concerts with the exception of a Grand Funk Railroad concert held in 1970 at the University of Maryland, where some windows were broken after the event.

Some of the most notorious out-of-control behavior occurred at Rolling Stone concerts. In 1964 eight thousand fans in the Empire Pool, Wembley rioted. Thirty were arrested. In Manchester and Liverpool kids crashed through stage barriers and in New Brighton two hundred fainted and fifty were thrown out for fighting. One girl pulled a switchblade on two guards who were ejecting her friends, and she had to be disarmed and carried out bodily.

A concert at the Winter Gardens in Blackpool attracted a crowd of drunken Scots. Some of them started spitting at Brian Jones, offended by his fete image. Keith Richards came over and told them to leave off. When they spat at Richards too, he stomped on their fingers which were grabbing the edge of the stage, and kicked one of them in the nose. When cries of "Scotland, Scotland" filled the Gardens, the Stones made a quick exit. The stage was rushed, instruments smashed, and the auditorium trashed. An upcoming concert in Belfast was cancelled because of this incident.

European audiences also went wild at the Stones' performances. In Helsingborg, Sweden fans were bitten by police dogs and struck by batons when they threw bottles, chairs and fireworks. Over 154 brawling fans were incarcerated in Vienna's city hall during a Stones concert. Not enough seats were available in Warsaw's Palace of Culture, and many Stones admirers were turned away. Only the Party elite and their children were assured of getting in. Two thousand fans lingered outside and Jagger decided they deserved free albums. When someone went outside to distribute them the crowd grew frantic trying to get the albums, and police used tear gas, water cannons, and nightsticks to subdue them.

A 1965 North American tour resulted in similar chaos, much of it due to police paranoia. The opening concert in Lynn, Massachusetts was stopped

12

Ban the Beat

As rock and roll increased in popularity among the young in the 1960s, overenthusiastic audiences became more of a perceived threat by authorities. Excited fans rushing the stage and large crowds of teenagers dancing in the aisles or milling about outside concert halls made police and hall managers nervous. It was a replay of furor over live shows in the 1950s. The only difference was that the audiences were much larger. Rock concerts had pretty well died out by the end of the 1950s as the music reeled under the cumulated effects of persecution and "schlock rock" cooled the ardor of the fans. Concerts came back as strong as ever with the British invasion.

For the first time an entertainment form besides sports was filling stadiums with fans. The rock and roll music of the 60s symbolized more than just a few hours of fun. The reaction of youth against repressive governments, morals, and values saw its outlet at rock concerts. They were a place to let loose. There were often violent clashes between crowds and police. Many times it was the police who provoked the mob. Contrary to what rock critics believed, it was not the music that caused violence at concerts. Unruly behavior was rather a reflection of youth's natural rebellion and the 60s generation's deep discontent with society's structures. Rock concerts merely provided a place to express that resentment.

When it was suggested that rock groups play at New York's Radio City Music Hall there was an outcry that the place would be downgraded. Stadiums that tolerated drunken sports fans had no patience with exuberant pot-smoking teenagers. Concert hall managers who were used to booking cheerful musical theater or staid symphonies, were appalled by the rock groups and their boisterous fans. Rock audiences were encouraged to participate — to dance, move, sing, scream, clap, and get high. There were no Perry Comos or Pat Boones on the rock scene to lull the audience into a passive stupor.

A backlash against rock and roll developed when many venues refused to book rock acts. Nevertheless, thousands of rock concerts took place all over the world. Between 1967 and 1970 more than 2.5 million people attended some thirty rock festivals.[1] Eighteen others that had been announced and planned were cancelled.

In 1963 the Beatles gave a concert at Glasgow Concert Hall where thirty-five hundred attendees damaged one-hundred seats, and made the balcony shake "with stamping, jumping customers." Glasgow City Treasurer Richard Buchanan, in a fit of overreaction, exclaimed, "This type of semi-savage conduct cannot be tolerated. There were 100 seats damaged after the show, and it took 50 stewards and 40 policemen to keep the audience under control."[2]

City councillors decided to cancel an upcoming concert by Gerry and the Pacemakers, and Buchanan stated, "Our committee will have to consider seriously all future applications for the lease of city halls by groups of this type."[3] Apparently future applications were indeed considered seriously. By 1965 rock groups with "a large and disorderly following" were banned from performing in civic-owned halls in Glasgow. Bruce Lumsden, manager of the civic theatres department, claimed that the ban did not apply to all "beat" groups, but he felt that rock and roll musicians encouraged their audiences to misbehave. Although Lumsden agreed that it was up to the tenant who was leasing the hall to maintain order, he felt that observing such conditions went completely against the grain and was not in the interests of a "successful" beat group. In case a riot did break out Lumsden feared the "damage could be quite substantial . . . and there could be no guarantee that the manager of a successful beat group would have the financial resources to meet the cost of such damage."[4]

Not all reports of riots at rock concerts could be believed. One had to take media reports with a grain of salt. In 1963 when the Beatles appeared at the London Palladium, every mass circulation British newspaper carried front page headlines and pictures the next morning of a "riot" outside the Palladium involving Beatle fans. The *Daily Mirror* exclaimed, "Police fought to hold back 1,000 squealing teenagers . . . the fans went wild, breaking through a cordon of more than sixty policemen."[5] Other papers reported that the crowd numbered five hundred and that twenty policemen held them back. In reality the newspapers had cropped photos of

the scene so closely that only about three or four teenagers could be [...] Apparently there weren't many more than that hanging around. Sai[...] observer, "There were no riots. . . . I was there. Eight girls we saw — [...] less than eight."[6] The only real damage that was done was to the re[...] tion of rock and rollers accused of causing hysteria.

This kind of erroneous media coverage may be more commo[...] than previously realized. Reporters are less likely to report any pol[...] tivity that may have led up to the "rioting" since the reporters [...] police cooperation for many of their stories. Also, in many cas[...] mainstream press is the mouthpiece of the establishment and refle[...] attitudes, in this case anti-rock. In some of these following acco[...] so-called riotous behavior of teens may very well have been dis[...]

A two-show concert in 1964 by the Dave Clark Five caused [...] to report, "A serious warning must be sounded that the rock 'n' [...] certs at New York's Carnegie Hall are turning into maniac demon[...] that are seriously endangering the lives and limbs of the teenage [...] A near-capacity house of teen girls, well-dressed and well-be[...] they took their seats, were transformed into an hysterical mob [...] show got under way."[7]

The girls shrieked and rushed down to the front of the stag[...] admitted that police overreacted and treated the girls like "h[...] which only inflamed the crowd, "and could have easily precipit[...] riot by the crudity of their (the police) tactics." Yet *Variety* con[...] the police were only doing their job "even if badly," and that t[...] the "frenzied outbreak" went "deep into contemporary cultur[...]

Variety also blamed concert organizers for stirring up t[...] cording to the paper, New York disk jockey Murray Kau[...] emceed the shows, turned "the children into a howling mob [...] garb, which was unspeakably cute, and his secret signals an[...] which only the teenagers are privy." Although Kaufman [...] down the kids' behavior after having "teased, titillated and [...] them, *Variety* reported it was too late to cool down the "in[...] mosphere."[9]

Baltimore was one of the first cities that decided to ban[...] at municipal halls after disruptions at their Civic Center. [...] director of the Center, believed that "agents and managers [...] these acts seem to think that headlines about riots and dis[...] the box-office."[10] Klein felt musicians egged on audience [...] with them, removing clothing, or lying down on stage. He [...]

by police only minutes after starting. The exuberant fans turned into rioting fans because of this action. In Montreal police controlled overzealous kids by ramming their heads against a wooden fence. In Ottawa, the thirty policemen on duty were intimidated by the size of the crowd, which numbered four thousand, so they unplugged the amplifiers and told the Stones never to come back. In London, Ontario the police stopped the show after fifteen minutes by turning up the house lights and disconnecting the amps. The furious Stones yelled abuse at the cops. The headlines in the next day's paper read, "CRUDE AND RUDE ROLLING STONES HURL INSULTS AT POLICE."[12]

At the Community War Memorial Auditorium in Rochester, police brought down the curtain four times during the Stones' first six songs. The thirty officers on duty were overly uneasy about the thirty-five hundred fans in the auditorium. Keith Richards, enraged by police interference, announced, "This is a hick town. They were twice as wild in Montreal. They won't get hurt. You're too rough with them."[13]

Rock concerts were banned in Cleveland after a Stones performance. Said Mayor Ralph S. Locher, "Such groups do not add to the community's culture or entertainment."[14] Keith Richards summed up the negative official attitudes when he told an interviewer about a letter the mayor of Denver had sent the Stones. The mayor said he would be pleased to see them if they came in quietly, did the show quietly, and left town that same night. "That's what the mayors wanted to do with us," Richards said. "They wanted to kick us out of town."[15]

When the Rolling Stones appeared in Vancouver in July 1966, thirty-six teenagers were ejected from the Pacific National Exhibition Forum and several policemen were injured. Police Inspector F. C. Errington stated that controlling the audience was the "most prolonged demand of physical endurance I have ever seen police confronted with during my 33 years of service."[16] The Stones were taken to task for shouting rude remarks at the cops when they shut off the sound system in mid-concert. As a result of this incident, Vancouver City Council gave police full control of curtain, lighting, and sound equipment for future concerts. Promoters of rock bands had to post security bonds to cover damage or injury to policemen and ensure that proper safety and security measures were in force.

In 1969 Dave Rupp, who had promoted a Stones concert in Florida at the Palm Beach Pop Festival, was harrassed for associating with them. "Since the festival," said Rupp, "my business has been firebombed and burned down. My fire insurance has been cancelled, the John Birch Society have been calling me and saying they're going to kill my wife and child."[17] That same year the Stones were banned from playing Albert Hall in London because of their reputation. Nor were they allowed to appear in Tokyo in 1973. Promoters had to refund the money of fifty-five thousand disappointed Japanese fans.

Mick Jagger was philosophical about audience reaction, "People talk about the riots that happen when we play. Of course, there is a certain violent element, and to a certain extent, the kids are conforming to what is expected of them." Jagger saw much more to it than that. As an entertainer he had witnessed the same type of wild behavior in many countries and always with the same pattern. To the Stones' lead singer it was always a symptom of frustration, a frustration that was common to kids of all types of environments. It was a problem that Jagger felt couldn't be solved just by locking them up, but would have to be dealt with by finding out why the kids were discontented. "They are not all morons just spoiling for a fight with the police."[18] On the contrary, it was sometimes the police who were spoiling for a fight with the kids. Some cops had a bad attitude towards rock and rollers. Sometimes they came backstage after a Stones concert carrying an album and saying in effect, "Sign this, ya long-haired sissy pervert, or i'll bust ya goddamned head open."[19]

There were times when police demanded bribes for protecting rock groups. This happened to the Stones when crowds formed outside the theater during their Ed Sullivan appearance. Said Bill Wyman, "Hundreds of girls were screaming and yelling outside the theatre. The police came and told us that if we wanted protection, we'd have to pay them off. Every hour they came back and told us we'd have to give them more money or they'd go away."[20]

When the Jefferson Airplane played Bakersfield, California they kept the concert going for three hours with jamming. Police, who felt the performance had gone on long enough, turned off the stage lights. The rock groups continued playing and led the audience in a chant of "Fat pig, fat pig." The Airplane was banned from playing Bakersfield again by the chief of police.

The Airplane had similar problems with police wherever they played. As soon as kids got up to dance in the aisles the cops would disconnect the amps. In Dallas police went a step further and fined rock stars $500 every time they said an obscenity on stage. As Paul Kantner commented, "With Grace's mouth it could get real expensive." An altercation with the police during a 1972 concert in Akron, Ohio ended with Slick, Kantner, and stagehand Chick Casady in jail. Casady had seen some cops beating up kids who were dancing in the aisles. He yelled out,

"Why don't you pigs leave these people alone?" The police had him hand-cuffed within minutes. When Grace noticed this she started forward. A cop pushed her back and to keep from falling she grabbed his whistle. He gave her a black eye. In 1970 Kantner said "bullshit" on stage and the Airplane lost their $1,000 bond. That year Joe McDonald of Country Joe and the Fish was fined $500 in Worcester, Massachusetts for being a "lewd, lascivious and wanton person in speech and behavior." His crime —encouraging the use of the word "fuck."

The reaction against rock concerts grew by leaps and bounds. A Kansas City performance turned ugly when police tried to stop a James Brown show because of alleged obscene dancing on stage. Brown also encouraged girls to come up and rip off his jacket. Police received minor cuts; some were pelted with rocks; one woman was stabbed; twenty people from the audience of eight thousand were arrested. A police spokesman stated that, "most of the trouble at the auditorium was cleaned up in about 20 minutes."[21]

Jimi Hendrix was kicked off the bill of a 1967 tour with the Monkees also because of alleged obscenity. The squeaky clean Monkees appealed to suburban thirteen- and fourteen-year-old white girls. Apparently the idea of teaming up the Jimi Hendrix Experience with this group was a publicity gimmick dreamed up by Jimi's manager. He knew that Hendrix's sexuality would be unacceptable to the parents of young girls, and felt the protests would attract media attention. He was right. Hendrix all but fucked his guitar. This was how one writer described his performance, "He had lapped and nuzzled his guitar with his lips and tongue, caressed it with his inner thighs, jabbed at it with a series of powerful pelvic thrusts. Even the little girls who'd come to see the Monkees understood what this was all about."[22]

Jim Morrison of the Doors had several run-ins with police during concerts. In 1968 before a show in New Haven, Connecticut, Morrison was backstage in a shower room making out with a girl. A policeman came by, and not recognizing Morrison as the performer about to go on, told them to get out as nobody was allowed backstage. Instead of identifying himself, Morrison got belligerent and told the cop to "eat it." The policeman sprayed mace into Jim's face. Morrison's roadie, Bill Siddons, came on the scene and doused his eyes with water. The cop, realizing his error, apologized. But Morrison had become incensed by the police harassment. During the concert he began to bait the cordon of police guarding the stage, repeating the story of the macing in a "dumb Southerner's voice" and talking about "this little man in a little blue suit and a little blue cap." The audience began laughing at the cops. Suddenly the house lights went on. Jim screamed to turn the lights off again but a police lieutenant told Morrison he was under arrest. Two cops dragged Morrison to a patrol car where they kicked him before throwing him into the back seat. He was booked for "indecent and immoral exhibition," breach of the peace, and resisting arrest.

When the Doors appeared at the Coliseum in Phoenix the concert was headlined as a "near-riot" by the *Phoenix Gazette* describing it as a "war between kids and cops." "Blame it on the Doors," said the newspaper, "possibly the most controversial group in the world. Lead singer Jim Morrison appeared in shabby clothes and behaved belligerently. The crowd ate up Morrison's antics which included hurling objects from the stage to the audience, cussing, and making rude gestures."[23]

Morrison was once asked about the disturbances at his concerts and explained,

> We have fun, the kids have fun, the cops have fun. It's kind of a weird triangle . . . you have to look at it logically. If there were no cops there, would anybody try to get onstage? Because what are they going to do when they get there? When they get onstage, they're just very peaceful. They're not going to do anything. The only incentive to charge the stage is because there's a barrier. I firmly believe that. It's interesting though, because the kids get a chance to test the cops. You see cops today, walking around with their guns and uniforms and everyone's curious about exactly what would happen if you challenged them. I think it's a good thing, because it gives the kids a chance to test authority.[24]

Morrison's viewpoints revealed the naive, almost romantic, notions of the sixties counterculture. To flaunt authority and get a kick out of taunting police was sheer adolescent adventurism. It created the kind of drama young people crave. Morrison in his fantasy of brotherly love, felt that rock stars didn't need protection from the crowd. Yet Morrison's ideas were not out of step with the thinking of the 1960s flower children. Police provocation, overreaction, and tactics such as turning lights on to halt concerts, making kids sit quietly, or beating them with clubs was the kind of behavior that compelled fans to resist.

But Morrison's behavior was counterproductive; there was no excuse for cop-baiting. Morrison's audience ate it up, however, goading him on much as a crowd urges someone threatening suicide to jump off a ledge.

The charges against Morrison were not unreasonable and only emphasized how police reacted to much milder behavior in similar ways. By often not differentiating between youthful exuberance and criminality, the authorities maximized the former and minimized the latter.

Chuck Berry and Bill Haley were not allowed to play Albert Hall in London, England in 1969 because of rowdy crowds at their previous concerts. Hall managers claimed the ban was not permanent but felt it was the only way to stop "the hardcore of hooligans buying tickets and demonstrating their disapproval of non-rock acts by slashing seats and throwing coins on to the stage."[25] The question of why the rockers had to share a bill with non-rock acts was not brought up.

Promoters of the Berry-Haley tour believed that the Albert Hall action paved the way for hall managers to ban other rockers. Albert Hall, with its large seating capacity, was vital to make a tour financially viable. The promoters also felt there was "renewed prejudice against rock 'n' roll . . . similar to the early 50s, when knocking the rock was the rule."[26] Ironically, the same week of the Albert Hall ban, fans were commended in the British House of Commons for their orderly behavior at recent Hyde Park rock concerts, and the government recommended that more be held.

Parts of the American South displayed their hostility toward rock festivals in 1970 when public officials tried to ban these events. Church and civic groups tried to stop the Atlanta International Pop Festival from taking place just outside Macon, Georgia. Citizens feared an influx of drug pushers, and a group called "Save Our Youth From Drug Abuse" was formed to oppose the festival. Police felt they wouldn't have enough reinforcements for a large crowd and foresaw traffic problems. The Bibb County Medical Society declined to provide volunteers for any medical emergencies at the event.

In Louisiana, state legislators agreed to block the "Man and Earth" rock festival scheduled for June 1970. It came too late, however. Festival organizers hurriedly opened the concert before voting was finalized. In Jacksonville, Florida a city ordinance prohibited outdoor rock festivals. A 1970 rock extravaganza called the "Festival Express Train" was banned by the city of Montreal, Canada when authorities decided that earlier concerts at the civic auditorium had caused trouble, even though tension arose only when police showed up in full riot gear for no reason.

Chicago was yet another city that imposed bans on rock music. Hard rock groups, or any musicians that "get the audience on the seats," were blacklisted from the city's McCormick Place exposition hall. A concert there in September 1972 by Humble Pie resulted in torn seats, carpet burns, and vomit stains. Damage figures totalled $1,560. John Sevcik, manager of McCormick Place stated that any groups "with a history of undisciplined crowds in other cities" would not be permitted to perform.[27]

The Chicago park's board also banned rock concerts on its property when a crowd at Grant park rioted prior to a Sly and the Family Stone show in July 1970. Rocks, bottles, and chairs were thrown at the stage. Three fans were shot, 165 arrested, and twenty-six fans and thirty police were injured. Four other scheduled rock concerts were cancelled that summer. As of at least October 1972 the ban was still in effect.

The Grant Park violence created government resistance to other concerts planned for Illinois. Janis Joplin was one of the rock singers who felt the backlash. Known for her raucous, raunchy style and for whipping up excitement in the audience, Janis had a bad reputation. She had been busted for onstage profanity at a 1969 concert in Tampa, Florida when police tried to get the audience, which was dancing in the aisles, to sit down. Infuriated by police meddling, Janis screamed: "If we don't hurt nothin,' they can't say shit."[28] For using this word, she was indicted for "vulgar and indecent language." Joplin had to pay a fine and the publicity hurt her bookings. The FBI also started a file on her.

Janis was due to perform at Ravinia in the Highland Park suburb of Chicago in August 1970. Fearing a repeat of Grant Park, the FBI suggested a police patrol of two hundred officers. This turned out to be overly cautious since the concert went off without problems of any sort. But Joplin's reputation remained threatening. Promoters and hall managers were anxious about booking her even though no real trouble had ever occurred at her shows. Houston, Texas was one city that banned Joplin simply "for her attitude in general."[29]

Perhaps the best known rock event of all time was the Woodstock Music and Arts Festival of August 1969 which drew a huge crowd of close to half a million people. Although generally reputed to be a peaceful and successful festival, the event generated extensive regulations on health and safety drafted by the Public Health Council of the State of New York. The legislation applied to mass gatherings of five thousand or more people for more than twenty-four hours. The act gave "the issuing permit officer wide powers in his review of applications."[30] No doubt the rigid standards in the regulations, combined with the authority of the permit officer, would effectively curb any future rock events of that size.

Pop festivals in Britain ran into opposition when an Isle of Wight County Council committee tried to stop an event there. One member of the committee declared, "I am determined to smash the festival. Unfortunately, local governments are powerless to prevent this sort of thing taking place. However, what we can do is to make the requirements for toilets, water supplies and so on extremely tough."[31] Promoters decided to proceed without approval of the council.

Elsewhere in Britain in 1970 the city council of Edinburgh imposed a complete ban on rock concerts at the city's three thousand seat Usher Hall. Calling fans "uncontrollable" and complaining of damage, city and police officials supported the ban. Only one council member, Peter Wilson, felt "the decision was unjust to the majority of young people who enjoyed such entertainment."[32]

In 1973 an "Indecent Displays Bill" was introduced in British Parliament which could seriously curtail rock concerts if passed. Anybody witnessing anything offensive at a concert would be able to file a private action against the individual who was considered vulgar. For example, if a prudish parent saw an Alice Cooper concert and found it objectionable, the parent could file a complaint. The National Council for Civil Liberties was fighting hard against the bill.

In the United States the bias against rock was showing in Indiana. In 1970 the Montgomery County Festival was cancelled due to a temporary restraining order that prevented organizers from preparing the site. A permanent injunction against a proposed rock festival near Versailles, Indiana was issued by a judge on the circuit court, and another injunction was issued in Madison Circuit Court banning a festival in that county.

Two rock festivals in Tucson, Arizona were cancelled when public opinion found the events objectionable. One of the festivals, planned for an outdoor stadium, won approval from the city manager and the police department, but the decision was reversed when citizens complained. The application for the second festival was accepted but never processed because of the backlash accorded the first festival. Explained Superior Court Judge Ben J. Birdsall, "We called Woodstock and were told that there was so much trouble with stranded hippies that the welfare people there just threw up their hands and hid in the bushes until the trouble blew over."[33]

The negative impression people had about rock festivals was confirmed in the minds of the public by a tragedy at Altamont in California in 1969. Among those appearing at the event were the Jefferson Airplane; Crosby, Stills, and Nash; the Grateful Dead; and the Rolling Stones. The concert was supposed to have taken place in Golden Gate Park but at the last moment officials refused to issue a permit. A fateful decision was made to hire members of the Hells Angels motorcycle gang to act as security around the stage. As the concert progressed, the Angels became more and more aggressive toward the audience, beating up several youths who came forward. By this time the stage was virtually swarming with Hells Angels. Jagger was blamed for not cluing into the enormous tension created by the Angels, and for launching into one of his more provocative songs, "Sympathy for the Devil." Describing the situation, one biographer, Philip Norman, admonished, "Mick Jagger's intuition deserted him or his vanity became overmastering. Either way the result was incredible stupidity. Folding his cloak around him, he stepped forward in the mincing gait he had evolved for this most presumptuous of all his masquerades. 'Please allow me to introduce myself' . . . sang Satan, in his trendy orange satin, across a landscape whose authentic hellishness he could not, or would not see."[34]

According to Norman this song caused the Angels to embark on a frenzy of violence. At this point Jagger tried to calm everything down by pleading with the Angels to cool it. Jagger's band launched into a soothing instrumental. Suddenly a black teenager moved toward the stage. Brandishing a gun, he was stabbed to death by one of the Hells Angels bodyguards.

A lot of the blame for the murder was directed towards Jagger and the Rolling Stones' song, even though Jagger had nothing to do with hiring the Angels, and even though he had sung this song countless times before. In a scathing attack, rock's own mouthpiece, *Rolling Stone* magazine, accused the group of conceitedness and carelessness. In a later 1972 interview with Jerry Garcia of the Grateful Dead, Jann Wenner, editor of *Rolling Stone*, noted, "People used Altamont as an attack point on rock and roll, to prove by it that rock and roll was no good."[35] Yet Wenner himself felt that Altamont had destroyed the myth that rock and roll could liberate people. "Rock and roll," he said, "obviously will not 'save the world,' nor is it for everbody 'the music that will set you free.'"[36]

And even Garcia suggested that it was something in the music that resulted in violence at Altamont, "Yeah, but it was the music that generated it. I think that the music knew, it was known in the music. I realized when the Rolling Stones were playing at the crowd and the fighting was going on and the Rolling Stones were playing 'Sympathy for the Devil.'"[37] One has to wonder if the music wasn't an easy scapegoat for Garcia to nail, however. Some sources said it was the Grateful Dead who okayed the idea of hiring the Angels in the first place. John Lennon, too, blamed the music for Altamont, saying it was the image and mood the Stones created.

If musicians or critics considered rock and roll a catalyst for violence, many fans had no doubts about this matter, as reflected in letters to *Rolling Stone* magazine after Altamont. Some believed the Stones were practicing black magic and that Jagger was the devil (a persona that Jagger, of course, had loved to play up). Wrote one convinced fan, "To those who know, it's been obvious that the Stones, or at least some of them, have been involved in the practice of magic ever since the Satanic Majesties Request album. . . . At Altamont he appeared in his full majesty with his full consort of demons, the Hell's Angels."[38]

After the attention created by Woodstock, Altamont, and other festivals, was it any wonder that the small town of Wadena (population 231) in Iowa was terrorized in 1970 by the fact that a rock festival capable of attracting thirty thousand people was going to be held in a nearby field? Town officials and citizens felt their very lives were threatened, and took extreme precautions in order to protect themselves. Explained Mayor Knox,

the very first thing I thought of was the traffic problem and — based on what we read about other festivals — the chances of vandalism, looting, property destruction. Nothing like this had ever happened in our town. The whole thing is still unbelievable . . . we had to prepare for the worst and hope for the best. We decided to hire eight deputies: local men armed with loaded revolvers. Most of these boys know how to handle guns . . . we got an injunction against the festival. Sound Storm the promoters appealed it. Actually, we feared that if the injunction were upheld, and enforced, Wadena was going to be burned out. A lot of people felt that way. Families began leaving to stay with relatives out of the area.[39]

Harold Halverson, fire chief of the town, described his reaction to the news of the festival,

Our biggest fear was that the crowds would get out of hand. People were scared about doped-up kids taking over this section of the county. At least 90 percent of the people in town had guns. Some others went out to buy guns for protection. I had a 12-gauge shotgun and an automatic .22 rifle within arm's reach of my pillow. . . . The neighboring farmers were worried to death. One farmer sold his livestock. He was afraid if the kids got doped-up they would shoot his cattle. . . . The State sent about 120 of their 410 highway partolmen here.[40]

The rock festival in Wadena took place without incident. Many of the townspeople expressed surprise at the politeness and orderly behavior of the youth. Halverson noted, "But the kids didn't cause a bit of trouble when they came to town. There was no violence, no vandalism."[41]

Wadena's reaction to rock festivals indicated the kind of anxiety that had been manufactured about rock music and its fans. And the anxiety did not abate. The Merriweather Post Pavilion near Washington, D.C. banned all future rock concerts after fans created a disturbance during a Who performance. Most other Washington venues were off limits to rock groups also. The American University banned rock music after a crowd crashed an Allman Brothers show. The same thing happened at George Washington University during a Traffic concert. Constitution Hall, owned by the ultraconservative Daughters of the American Revolution, banned rock and roll after a concert by Sly Stone where he encouraged dancing in the aisles and on the seats. As one observer concluded, "This virtually kills the last available site for rock concerts in this area – and this is just one aspect of a blackout of concerts and festivals that is taking place all over the country."[42]

While a few concerts had gone bad the vast majority took place without incident. The police often adopted a confrontational presence by appearing in massed numbers, by turning on the house lights, and by trying to make kids sit down. Given such a posture it was not surprising that confrontations sometimes took place. Some of it was a self-fulfilling prophecy whereby kids were expected to "riot" and then lived up to the image in a kind of game between kids and cops. Opponents were quick to seize any evidence – even flimsy and distorted facts – to damn all rockers and all fans.

Along the west coast of the United States, efforts to ban rock festivals were multiplying. The California State Legislature was considering two bills in 1970 to halt these events. Assembly Bill 148 would have required festival promoters to put no limit on the amount of front money that could be demanded. The American Civil Liberties Union (ACLU) was leading the fight to kill the bills. According to ACLU lobbyist Chuck Marson, "The bills are in part an election gambit. They're anti-kid bills introduced to satisfy the law and order people."[43]

The County Board of Supervisors in Los Angeles passed a thirty-one-page ordinance requiring front money for security, which promoters said would make it "economically impossible to put on a rock festival." Any event expected to attract more than five thousand people was to undergo a public hearing before a license would be granted. The ordinance forbade booze, drugs, and "unreasonable" noise. A requirement that each person have a ticket to enter effectively banned free festivals.

Further up the coast, San Luis Obispo placed unmeetable rules on assemblies of over five hundred people for example, requiring that ten gallons of water be available for each person attending. In the Pacific Northwest, church groups in Clark County, Washington influenced county commissioners to pass a strict ordinance making a proposed rock festival impossible. In a letter-writing campaign to the local newspaper, the religious groups complained of "naked communist" fans of "killer rock music" which was "the invention of the devil" and "against all the teachings of the Gospel of Jesus Christ."[44]

Some of the restrictions proposed in the ordinance were a traffic control system employing four thousand licensed patrolmen, and a full-scale drawing of parking facilities for twenty-five thousand cars; a $750.00 permit fee; $27,500 for penal and indemnity bonds; liability insurance of $100,00 per person attending for bodily injury; $300,000 for bodily injury per occurrence and $100,000 property damage; a limit of seventy decibels on the music; and no liquor. Permit applicants would be fingerprinted, photographed, and investigated as to "character and reputation." The ordinance included these conditions plus many more, putting a damper on things.

In Portland, Oregon two of the largest halls, the Masonic Temple and the Portland Civic Auditorium, banned rock music outright. Portland's Coliseum allowed rock concerts, but manager Don Jewell had stopped shows by the Jefferson Airplane, Jimi Hendrix, and Blind Faith by turning the power off. A proposed rock concert series at Kezar Stadium in San Francisco was banned by the Recreation and Park Commission after residents and property owners in the area protested. As one policeman explained, the concerts would attract "a real poor element of howling idiots."[45]

When tens of thousands are killed each year in traffic accidents, no one mentions banning automobiles. Drinking and violence resulting in death had occurred at sporting events but nobody has tried to ban football or soccer games. But when it came to rock and roll, hardly a lethal form of entertainment, plenty of people were eager to prohibit concerts and festivals at the first sign of a torn seat. This newspaper item of 1970 summed up the attitude of many citizens.

> Those rock "festivals" are really death traps. . . . Isn't it about time we normal Americans outlawed these damnable "rock festivals"?

. . . These deafening, dope-ridden, degenerate mob scenes have no more place in our America than would a publicly promoted gang rape or a legally sanctioned performance of the Black Mass. . . . A few bewildered sheriff's deputies are assigned to police tens of thousands of hopped-up sex maniacs, and wind up stunned by the decibel level, daunted by dire threats against their lives and discouraged by the sheer magnitude of the problem which confronts them. Results: the laws end up unenforced. . . . This is an absolutely intolerable and dastardly situation.[46]

13

Against the Groove

In the 1960s rockers were still having difficulty gaining recognition as legitimate musicians. The music was a decade old but still far from being accepted by the musical establishment or by television. Rockers were often milked dry by their agents and careers tended to be very short. In their quest for ratings, television shows booked rock musicians more easily than in the 1950s but gave them short shrift. "Legitimate" musicians continued to rail against rockers not unlike they had in the previous decade. The few years of peaceful rock from 1960 to 1962 had lulled much of the establishment into the hope that they would have to deal with no rock and rollers more offensive than Fabian or Frankie Avalon. The coming of the Stones and others was an unhappy shock and the musical establishment set up a howl similar to the one ten years earlier.

One way the bias against rock became apparent was over the "Invasion" of British groups in the mid-60s. Under an agreement with the British Musicians Union (BMU), the American Federation of Musicians (AFM) allowed any musicians of "cultural value" into the U.S.[1] This appellation did not apply to rock and roll groups. For the "non-cultural" musicians the AFM had a one-for-one reciprocal trade deal with the BMU, which effectively limited their performance venues.

This kind of cultural snobbery continued to affect rock and roll. In 1969 Jimi Hendrix was the first rocker to play at Philharmonic Hall in Lincoln Center in New York City. The hall officials booked him on condition that the event "emphasize symphonic or an otherwise classical approach to music."[2] Promoter Ron Delsner lined up harpsichordist Fernando Valenti and the New York Brass Quintet. Hendrix was supposed to accompany them, but actually had no intention of doing so on the night of the concert. When the curtain came up Jimi's drummer Mitch Mitchell, dressed in white tie and tails, was sitting at his instruments.

Another way the anti-rock bias was discernible was with regard to television. TV sound studios had been set up to record the likes of Andy Williams or Eydie Gorme and didn't upgrade their facilities to handle the electronic sophistication of amplified music. Several record producers interviewed by *Variety* in 1968 complained that sound technicians in TV studios tended to be older men who "ruined" the quality of the music, and lacked respect for rock and roll.

Television producers wanted the benefits of high ratings that rock groups provided, but had an attitude of "let 'em on, prepare for the next act, get 'em off."[3] (About fifty percent of the viewing audience was under thirty in the late 1960s.) Sometimes rock groups weren't allowed to rehearse on the set or with the technicians, and other times they were not given access to dressing rooms because "what they looked like didn't matter."[4]

When the Rolling Stones had their debut on American television's "Hollywood Palace" in June 1964, host Dean Martin got some cheap laughs at their expense. Mocking their appearances he said, "Their hair is not long. It's just smaller foreheads and higher eyebrows." Between songs and commercials Martin quipped, "Now don't go away anybody. You wouldn't want to leave me with these Rolling Stones, would you?" And when a trampoline artist did his act, Dean pointed out, "That's the father of the Rolling Stones. He's been trying to kill himself ever since."[5]

Later that year the Stones appeared on "The Ed Sullivan Show." Fans inside and outside the theater caused such a ruckus and the Stones looked so freaky to the adults, in their flamboyant clothes and hairstyles, that Sullivan tried to distance himself from the whole situation by issuing a statement in which he denied responsibility for booking them. He promised they would never be back on his program again. Sullivan had become so uptight that he contemplated never booking any more rock acts, and even banning teenagers from the theater. He did have a few good words for one group, the Dave Clark Five, who he felt performed well, and were nice gentlemen. Sullivan commented, "Frankly, I didn't see the Rolling Stones until the day before the broadcast. They were recommended by my scouts in England. I was shocked when I saw them. . . . It took me seventeen years to build this show. I'm not going to have it destroyed in a matter of weeks."[6]

In less than a year Sullivan ate his words. The Stones became one of the hottest groups around, their records topping the charts, and Sullivan knew his ratings would soar if he had them on his show again. They had to spruce up their look a bit, and be in the studio eight hours before transmission time, but their second appearance was a huge success.

In a telegram congratulating the Stones after the show Sullivan said, "Received hundreds of calls from parents complaining about you but thousands from teenagers praising you. Best of luck on your tour."[7]

The Stones clashed with television producers in 1967 in Britain when they appeared on "Sunday Night at the London Palladium." It was the most popular variety program in the coutry at the time. At the end of each show all the performers were supposed to stand on a revolving platform and wave good-bye to the audience. Jagger took exception to this schmaltzy bit of show biz, and refused to let the Stones take part in the finale, insisting they were not "part of a circus." A furious argument between the Stones, their managers, and the television people ensued. But the Stones wouldn't agree to revolve.

The Palladium's director complained, "They are insulting me and everyone else." When the story got out, the Stones were viciously attacked on a TV talk show by comedian Terry Scott and singer Susan Maughan. Several people wrote angry letters to the editor of the *Daily Mail* with sentiments such as, "Who do they think they are?"

Jagger added fuel to the fire when he defiantly told reporters, "The only reason we did the show was because it was a good national plug — anyone who thought we were changing our image to suit a family audience was mistaken. It was a mediocre show, and it made us the same. It was all terrible. I'm not saying we were any better than the other acts — it was just too depressing . . . we will never do a program there again."[8]

Things hadn't improved much by 1969 when musician Howard Kaflan of the Turtles said that rockers were treated like a bunch of "stepchildren." He declared flatly that TV "execs are still hung up on rituals, with video in an even more deplorable state by having it run by a bunch of old fogies."[9] Kaflan insisted that there "should be a more tasteful presentation of the rock bands, not just a token guesting. . . . We're as much a part of show business as anybody."[10]

As late as 1972, complaints about TV production were heard from rock musicians. John Denver felt the networks were incompetent and unsympathetic. He believed that most TV rock shows failed because the presentations weren't honest. "Contemporary artists just aren't treated well," said Denver. "They have to do the lip sync thing. They don't give us a chance to set up, to get in tune, to get comfortable. They just rush us out there between a commercial."[11]

There were other ways in which rock was excluded from the established music world. Music educators questioned whether rock and roll was appropriate in schools. Some felt that since students already listened to rock at home, there was no need for it in music appreciation courses. Others thought it a passing phase, with no artistic merit, that would only lower the standards of musical education if brought into the classroom.

A music professor at the University of Texas, Morris Beachy, was concerned that pop music would not "provide a broad enough exposure to the vocal textures."[12] Beachy felt that if choral students relied on amplifiers, they would never learn to sing out or develop voices of "strength, focus and resonance."[13]

One educator who supported rock and roll in the curriculum was Harris Danziger, of the Third Street Music School Settlement, in New York City. Danziger noted that some viewed rock as "the death-knell of serious music education."[14] The Third Street school had introduced rock music into its program and Danziger joked, "the building still stands." But Danziger quickly modified his "positive" comments, and let slip his own bias when he noted that adding rock music to the program was not at all like adding just any course, "The introduction of Rock will have a most profound and disturbing effect on the rest of the curriculum."[15]

Danziger was talking about the teacher-student relationship which he believed would be radically altered. Traditionally, music teachers have been perceived as masters whose students obey without question. Rock lends itself more to a group effort where there is a leader among equals. Said Danziger, the "ideal of a teacher imposing rules is completely foreign in Rock."[16] No wonder then that certain teachers resisted rock's inclusion in their programs. They perceived it as a threat to their authority.

In Britain the bias against rock was manifested by BBC policy. The BBC controlled all radio licensing in that country and had only one pop music service, the Light Programme. No rock and roll was played, only music hall or show tunes. Some rock was leaked into Britain via Radio Luxembourg or the U.S. Armed Forces Network.

It took a pirate radio station, Radio Caroline, set up in 1964, to get rock and roll onto British airwaves. The station transmitted from a ship set up in international waters, three miles off from England's shores, so that it wouldn't be illegal. Radio Caroline was soon joined by Radio Atlanta and they merged to form Caroline South and North. Soon Radio London and fifteen other smaller pirates were added. Sales of rock records began soaring in England, but it had required this back-door approach to fully bring the music to the British.

Perhaps the most treacherous bias against rock came from some of the record producing companies themselves. Eager to sign up rock groups because of their tremendous profit potential, many of the established companies had no admiration for the music. MGM signed up progressive acts like the Velvet Underground, but then tried to dull their creativity. For example, they censored lyrics on Mothers of Invention songs without consulting them and released a John Sebastian album that was recorded off a single speaker at a concert.

RCA was another company that often handled rock groups poorly in the late 1960s. Joe Di Imperial, A&R man at RCA who signed up the Jefferson Airplane, really had no insight into rock music. He was more interested in selling power and reportedly said, "a person didn't need to hear any of these new groups to tell which were worth signing, he had only to look outside the clubs where they were playing to see if there were lines."[17]

The Youngbloods, who had put out the million-selling single "Get Together" for RCA, were discontented with that label. The Youngbloods defected for Warner-Reprise claiming that RCA limited their recording style and used album covers that the Youngbloods disliked. Stu Kuchins, their manager, explained the problem with RCA when he told an interviewer, "Their company policies are set up for an older industry. Their style is old and their ideas are old. . . . It's a very stale company. Lately, they've been making some efforts, but mostly what they've done is to update their vocabulary. They have a basic lack of comprehension of what the music's about and what the people who enjoy it are like."[18]

One young agent, Frank Barsalona of Premier Talent, said that many agencies felt that rock performers could not have a long career, that their fame was just a flash in the pan. They would promise their clients film or TV deals, but not really take these promises seriously. It was generally believed that a rocker's career lasted eighteen months "since anyone vulgar enough to sing rock had already ruined his image as far as the mainstream show business moguls were concerned. (Elvis was a fluke, the Beatles an exception)."[19] This meant agents milked their clients for everything they could get, sending them out on tour after tour, having them at the beck and call of influential disk jockeys, and making them work for peanuts just for exposure. As Barsalona put it, "If you were young and had a hit record, to them you had no talent, you were just lucky and manufactured. . . . There was no chance of growth for a new performer. . . . Rock was the asshole, it really was."[20]

Even those who were pop singers themselves sometimes objected to the "long-haired, dirty-looking, sloppily dressed groups." One such singer was Len Barry who complained that the Beatles and Rolling Stones were "appealing to the lowest common denominator in their appearance, performance and in some cases their material. I know dozens of artists," said Barry, "who feel just the way I do and I hope that my speaking up will encourage them to do the same."[21]

Singer Jo Stafford was one of the entertainers who did speak up. Calling the dominance of rock and roll music on the airwaves, "sad," Stafford lamented the passing of lyrical ballads. Jazz musician Moe Koffman complained that rock music was "dull" and made him fall asleep. "Too many rock musicians," he said, "have very limited talents—they're just kids, after all."[22] He noted that background music on many albums was played by skilled studio musicians and that was why they sounded so good. But Koffman realized that at live performances this kind of "professional" backup wasn't available, and kids seemed to like the music anyway. Koffman therefore decided that young audiences didn't know much about music and that heavy amplification covered the lack of talent.

Koffman held out hope for rock though. He felt it was headed for a change, and only a matter of time before it would become more like Koffman's own music—jazz. He concluded, "And I think rock musicians are realizing that they've reached a saturation point with their guitars."[23]

If rock could not transform itself into some "higher" form of music like jazz perhaps it could coexist or even share the stage with classical and other musical genres. This was partially the case when rock musicians began to use symphonic scores as backup on albums. At other times the mix caused friction. Mel Powell, who composed "serious" new music, was one musician who was adamant about keeping rock in its place. In 1970 he was part of an event organized by the Los Angeles Philharmonic as a fund raiser. Contempo '70 included rock and "modern classical" music. Powell was to present a piece for orchestra led by Zubin Mehta, supplemented by a tape. The tape machine failed so Powell agreed to let Frank Zappa and the Mothers of Invention go on. Humiliated by the tape break-down, and angry because Mehta introduced Zappa's band as "the main attraction, what you've all really come here for," Powell walked out of the concert in a rage. Powell subsequently delivered a scathing attack on rock music which was printed in the *Los Angeles Times* and *High Fidelity*. Powell expressed his "revulsion at the wretched debasement of new music," "exploitation of pop mobs," and "mockery of art."

Calling rock the music of amateurs and claiming that "art" music and rock didn't mix, Powell concluded, "Minimal music awareness informs us that there isn't an instrumental, vocal or compositional entity presented nowadays by the majority of rock groups to their millions of devotees that is so much an inch beyond the reach of an utterly accomplished amateur. . . . The perennial Kitsch about the 'fusion' of such stuff with art music exposes a bad transplant of a good democratic notion. The idea of egalitarianism, lovely and humane within the world of political and social structures, becomes foolish in connection with the high art of music."[24]

14

Rockers Go Home

Rock and roll music was still not welcomed in various countries because of certain ideologies. Accused of being immoral, and either too communistic or too bourgeois, rock was looked upon with scorn. During the 50s a number of countries had attacked the music simply by banning it outright. It was a first response to a new music and it was not successful since the music could slip into a country in a number of different ways. By the 1960s this approach was used much less often as countries engaged more in condemnatory blasts and fulminating speeches against rock, perhaps hoping their influence would cause people to voluntarily turn away from the "big beat." While in the 1950s the countries attacking rock varied widely along the political spectrum, the range had narrowed considerably by the 1960s when the hostile countries were mainly from the communist camp, and the far right such as Spain or Greece.

Presumably many of the countries had given up the fight because they had more important things to do and had learned in any event that the spread of rock wouldn't topple their country. But many countries were obviously not convinced. Musicians toured more frequently than in the past and they became a prime focus of attacks as countries sought to keep them out. Rock music is not necessarily inherently political. But, because of the way governments respond to it, it becomes a political symbol. This is true of most art forms. It is how people or institutions react to rock music that gives it definition. If it is perceived as a threat it becomes one.

South Vietnam was one of the countries to condemn rock in 1963. American G.I.'s had introduced Western styles and culture to this Asian nation, including a song called "The Twist." The reason given for banning twist music was that "it was not compatible with the country's morality law and its anti-Communist struggle."[1]

Two years later, the American army itself was banning pop music at European army bases because of the anti-nuclear and anti-Vietnam war messages in some of the songs.

Although South Vietnam objected to the twist, East Germany relented in 1963 and allowed Petra Boettcher, a young recording star in that country, to release a version of the music. At first the twist was banned and viewed by the communist government as "an American secret weapon brought to us via the ether waves."[2] However, twist records from the West were being smuggled in at an alarming rate, and perhaps the Soviets couldn't resist the chance to put some of the bucks in their own pocket. Hence the East German version of the twist. The government tried to save face by classifying the music as a fox-trot.

Three years later East German authorities felt that rock music was getting out of control. Although no records were being produced there, live rock groups were springing up everywhere, and were said to number in the thousands. Communist officials were concerned that rock concerts were subversive, "Is a beat music riot merely in response to the music or is it a camouflaged demonstration aimed at the government?"[3]

The regime decided to impose rigid controls over the musicians. Anyone with long hair, who played "too exuberantly" or caused riots in dance halls would be subject to fines ranging from ten to five hundred marks. Groups were told to stop imitating the Beatles. Any groups that wished to perform had to obtain licenses that were issued only if the cultural commission was convinced they had "social qualifications and talent." In protest, five hundred rock fans in Leipzig marched to the city hall demanding the right to have long hair, and to play whatever music they pleased.

Licenses to perform also applied to American groups who wished to perform in East Germany. A spokeman for the East German Minstry of Culture assured that "American groups will be welcomed to the German Democratic Republic (East Germany) as long as they conform to our laws. We have nothing against the music. It is the unkempt dress and the use of the music as a license for excesses to which we object. Any American organization that cuts its hair and wears proper and reasonably clean dress will be welcome in our country."[4] Of course, such stipulations ostensibly disqualified the majority of American rock groups.

East Germany was still fighting to keep "contaminating" Western rock music, especially those with "provocative" titles, off the airwaves in 1973. Deejays were told to conform to regulations "aimed at meeting youthful demand for 'dance and entertainment' while maintaining the 'principles of socialist cultural policy.'"[5] They were required to program East German or Soviet recordings.

The Chinese communists weren't too thrilled by rock and roll either. In 1965 a Peking newspaper described the Beatles as "monsters," saying they produced "an unpleasant noise to satisfy the Western world's need for crazy and rotten music. . . . Great Britain needs the Beatles. But even if more Beatles come, it is difficult to save Great Britain from decline. . . . It is this sort of monster who has big chances in Britain."[6]

Although Cuba tolerated pop songs if the lyrics were in Spanish, American rock music was banned from all radio stations. Raul Castro, brother of Fidel, described Western music as creating "cultural alienation."[7]

One of the most virulent backlashes against rock and roll occurred in Japan. Concerts by the Beach Boys and the Astronauts were cancelled in 1965 because amplified music was banned in city-owned auditoriums. Certain moralistic groups felt that rock concerts contributed to juvenile delinquency and that "rock-beat rhythms inflame passions, stimulate the desire for additional spending money and generally breed corruption among the country's youngsters."[8]

In 1968 Japan's largest television network, NHK, banned rock and roll music. The network, funded entirely by monthly fees paid by viewers, was supported in its decision by Japanese parents. They claimed it was not the music or musicians they objected to, but rather the unruly crowds of teenagers who caused damage to studios and who jumped in front of the cameras.

The Beatles were allowed to perform in Tokyo in the late 1960s, but their presence in Japan caused a great deal of tension. A kamikaze squad of right-wing militant students accused the Beatles of perverting Japanese culture and threatened to kill them. The students were particularly angry that the Beatles would be playing at a national shrine to dead war heroes. Thousands of armed troops escorted the Beatles to and from the shrine, and the famous group was never allowed to leave their hotel room for sight-seeing.

The dictator Francisco Franco of Spain clamped down on rock music in 1969. Worker and student demonstrations against the government were felt to be a consequence of excessive foreign pop music on radio and TV. The government declared that radio stations allocate fifty percent of airtime to Spanish or South American composers, twenty-five percent to foreign material recorded in Spanish, and twenty-five percent to other foreign music.[9] The head of the Spanish broadcasting system declared that the goal of the quotas was to stop "the growing foreignism of music in both media. Spanish-speaking artists will be able to impose a style that is closer to our customs."[10] Disk jockeys retaliated by packing their foreign quota into peak listening hours and playing Spanish music in off-hours.

The ruling military junta in Greece was also opposed to rock and roll. Colonel Ladas, secretary of the Interior Ministry, said that any Greek artists that imitated the decadent imported music "composed by drug-addicted hippies" would be disciplined. Claiming the ancient Greeks had invented music to satisfy the "sensitive requirements" of the human soul, Ladas urged all Greek artists to fight against rock "decadence," music he considered a sign of "decay, senility and decomposition" which suggested "whatever sensual rot exists." Ladas added, "If some people do not want to consider the education of society as the aim of art, then the state cannot allow them to set as its aim the corruption of society. . . . It will stop them and stamp them out to protect both society and art."[11]

Accusing rock music of polluting society, Ladas encouraged a return to Greek folk music to satisfy those sensitive needs of the soul. Rock and roll, he concluded, was degenerate music that aroused sexuality and corrupted youth.

A rock cruise to Bermuda aboard the Greek liner *Queen Anna Maria* was cancelled in 1970 when the Greek government refused to allow one of their ships to be used for such purposes. The cruise was to be a "Festival of Life" celebration for one thousand young people. Bermuda also got into rock-bashing by complaining that promotion for the cruise was "alien to the way in which Bermuda has been promoted over the years."[12]

In 1971 Peru exposed itself as yet one more country where rock and roll was unacceptable. The rock group Santana had been welcomed, at first, to play benefits for earthquake refugees. The group was met at the Lima airport by a crowd of three thousand including the mayor. The mood turned ugly when leaders of the Communist San Marcos University Student Federation opposed the concert, calling it "imperialist penetration."[13] The stage that Santana was to perform on was burned. The government then did an about-face and charged the rock group with acting "contrary to good taste and the moralizing objectives of the revolutionary government."[14] Santana was forced to leave the country after having been questioned for several hours, and were not allowed to take their expensive equipment and clothing with them.

15

The Communist Plot

The anti-authoritarian politics of the sixties youth generation with its stance against the Vietnam War and call for social revolution was often mirrored in rock and roll lyrics. Certain reactionary organizations viewed rock musicians as subversive. The Christian right jumped on the rock-and-communism bandwagon. Reverend David Noebel, a member of the fundamentalist Christian Crusade, published a tract in 1965 called "Communism, Hypnotism and The Beatles: An Analysis of the Communist Use of Music." The gist of this pamphlet was that rock music was a Soviet plot to undermine the characters of American youth, and weaken them in their struggle against communism. Noebel wrote, "Cybernetic warfare is the ultimate weapon and we can't afford one nerve-jammed child. Throw your Beatle and rock and roll records in the city dump. We have been unashamed of being labeled a Christian nation, let's make sure four mop-headed anti-Christ beatniks don't destroy our children's emotional and mental stability and ultimately our nation."[1] Billy James Hargis, founder of the Christian Crusade, echoed Noebel's thoughts, "The beatnik crowd, represented by the Beatles, is the Communist crowd."[2]

In 1966 a recorded telephone message called "Let Freedom Ring" was instituted statewide in Indiana. The message, which was sponsored by the John Birch Society among others, warned that rock music was communistic. It fulminated against the fact that American teenagers were being continuously bombarded by a "potentially destructive process, harmonic dissonance and discord in the form of Beatle-type music." The message went on to explain that scientists in Communist countries had made the discovery that music which had a "broken meter in the treble" and had an insistently regular beat produced dire consequences in the young. Rock music stirred youth to a frenzy and caused hysterics. The Birchers then offered the conclusion that it was no surprise to find Communist countries banning Beatles music while at the same time promoting it with vigor in the United States. While the Birchers and their message denounced all rock music, they had a special place in their heart for the Beatles, about whom the message said, "The Beatles and thousands like them have loosed a veritable flood of musical trash on a generation of young Americans. . . . Most parents seem blissfully unaware of this musical turn to insanity. But other parents have been shocked to see their daughters charged in a state of hypnotic frenzy, clutching at the long-haired slobs who twang, screech and thump in a mixture of unrelated noise that would insult the ear of any self-respecting orangutan."[3] When the "Let Freedom Ring" message went too far and tried to portray the National Parent-Teacher Association as a Communist front, the Indiana Public Service Commission and Bell Telephone were deluged with calls of protest.

Indiana wasn't the only place where rock music was being touted as a red plot. In Seattle, Joseph R. Crow, a former sideman with the Stan Kenton Band, declared in 1970 that rock groups like the Beatles, Jefferson Airplane, Lovin' Spoonful, the Doors, and Small Faces were "part of a Communist movement to incite revolution throughout the world."[4] Addressing a suburban chapter of MOTOREDE (Movement to Restore Decency), Crow called rock music "propaganda with a beat" producing "radical and social political change" and glorifying "drugs, destructiveness, revolution and sexual promiscuity."[5]

Songs such as the Beatle's Beach Boys spoof, "Back in the U.S.S.R." or the Lovin' Spoonful's "Revolution '69" were considered by reactionaries as sure proof of a plot. Folk rockers like Bob Dylan had been influenced by "communists" like Woody Guthrie and Pete Seeger. Paul McCartney was rumored to be a member of the Young Communist League!

As Eric Bentley noted in the *New York Times* in 1970, rock music was accused of being revolutionary in more cases than were warranted. At most, rock represented a spirit of rebellion within the dominant culture. Said Bentley, "If we are to talk, not of the impulse that created the rock beat but of those who manage the whole rock scene, we are talking of people who are exactly as revolutionary, or even dissident, as the Directors of General Motors. . . . The System is an ocean that can absorb these tiny counter-currents quite comfortably."[6]

This was not to say that rock musicians did not sing about political issues. Of course, some did. And certain songs were considered enough of a threat to be banned or censored. In 1970 Neil Young's song "Ohio," about the four students who were shot and killed at Kent State University by U.S. National Guardsmen, was banned on many radio stations. Vice-President Spiro Agnew was prompted by this to call rock music anti-American.[7]

Bob Dylan's 1971 single "George Jackson," about a black American militant, was not banned in England, but was banned on several U.S. radio stations ostensibly because the word "shit" was used in the lyrics. Paul McCartney caused a stir in 1972 with his song "Give Ireland Back to the Irish." The song was banned on the BBC.

One rock musician whose politics were highly visible, especially concerning the peace movement, was John Lennon. In a brief flirtation with American radicals Abbie Hoffman, Jerry Rubin, Rennie Davis, and John Sinclair, Lennon discussed the idea of holding political rallies using rock concerts as the bait. Word of this got through to the Nixon administration and they threatened to expel Lennon from the United States.

In January 1972, the Senate Internal Security Subcommittee of the Judiciary Committee produced a report on Lennon and Yoko Ono. The memo described Lennon's activist causes and his association with radicals, concluding that, 'This group has been strong advocates of the program to 'dump Nixon.'" This subcommittee determined that the radicals had come up with a plan to hold rock concerts in some of the states where primary elections were due to be held. The purpose was to agitate on the college campuses to urge eighteen-year-olds to vote, to push for legislation to legalize marijuana, to generate funds to continue their political activites, and to recruit people to attend the Republican National Convention in August 1972. The radicals were going to feature John Lennon as the major drawing card for this campaign, and the authorities were worried the campaign would produce large sums of money for the "New Left" and that a clash between law enforcement personnel and the radicals' "controlled mob" might take place at the convention. To bring a halt to such possibilities it was suggested that "if Lennon's visa [for his U.S. residency] is terminated it would be a strategy counter-measure."[8] This measure worked since Lennon never did appear at any rock rallies during the 1972 campaign, and he was denied extension of his visa and classified as an "undesirable alien," ostensibly for his 1968 pot bust in London. Lennon lived with the threat of deportation hanging over his head for years.

Lennon and Yoko Ono did bring out a political album in 1972 called "Some Time in New York City." There were songs about Angela Davis (the black militant), and John Sinclair (leader of the White Panther

Party); songs about prison politics ("Attica State" and "Born in a Prison") and songs about nationalism as in "The Luck of the Irish" and "Sunday Bloody Sunday."

The FBI kept a file on Lennon but by the end of 1972 they concluded he was no real political threat, "In view of subject's inactivity in Revolutionary Activities and his seemingly rejection by NY Radicals, [he failed to appear at their rallies] case is being closed in the NY Division."[9]

However, it was not until several years later, after many appeals, that Lennon was legally allowed to remain in the United States. No doubt Watergate and the downfall of Nixon had something to do with Lennon's success. Moreover, by that time the British law under which Lennon had been convicted of his drug offense had been wiped from the statutes.

The Rolling Stones, who came under attack for almost everything they did, were rarely taken to task for their politics. Always alert to trends among the young, the Stones liked to convey the idea that they were political radicals, and many of their fans perceived them as such. Their 1968 song "Street Fighting Man" which recognized a need for revolution, quickly tempered this with the claim that singing rock and roll songs was all a musician could do to help the cause. For the Stones words and music spoke louder than action. Nevertheless, the song was interpreted as a call to arms, by both the left and right.

Since the song was released near the time of the 1968 U.S. Democratic National Convention, some radio stations banned it for fear it would provoke riots. Because of this censorship it only reached number forty-eight on the charts, although it did well on FM and underground stations.

On the basis of "Street Fighting Man" one group of militants in California welcomed the Stones during their 1969 American tour with leaflets that proclaimed, "The revolutionary youth of the world hears your music and is inspired to even more deadly acts. . . . We will play your music in rock-'n'-roll marching bands as we tear down the jails and free the prisoners. . . . Comrades you will return to this country when it is free from the tyranny of the State and you will play your splendid music in factories run by the workers, in the domes of emptied city halls, on the rubble of police stations, under the hanging corpses of priests, under a million red flags waving over a million anarchist communes. . . . THE ROLLING STONES ARE THAT WHICH SHALL BE! . . . ROLLING STONES – THE YOUTH OF CALIFORNIA HEARS YOUR MESSAGE! LONG LIVE THE REVOLUTION."[10]

Their enthusiasm for the Stones as the vanguard of the revolutionary movement was ridiculous. The truth about where the Stones really stood politically came out during the 1969 tour. When the Black Panthers asked Mick Jagger to publicly announce his support for them, he refused. He received several death threats from them as a result of this.

If radicals thought any other rock and roll groups would back their politics, they were wrong again. When Abbie Hoffman tried to deliver his YIPPIE message onstage at Woodstock, Peter Townshend of the Who whacked him over the head with his guitar. Said one rock writer, "Down dear Abbie went, and with him any fantasies about rock as revolution."[11]

The Stones did come under attack for their sexual politics. Feminist Judy Parker wrote in the *Los Angeles Free Press*, "I blame rock culture for opting for chauvinism and patriarchy in one of the only important alternative cultures that this generation has come up with."[12] And of course only a handful of rockers were female. Rolling Stone songs such as "Under My Thumb" ("It's down to me, the way she does just what she's told"), or "Stupid Girl" ("She's the worst thing in the world"), and "Yesterday's Papers" where women are equated with old newspapers, were considered sexist. "Midnight Rambler" even supposedly gave tribute to a rapist. And in "Brown Sugar" Jagger equated his conquest of black women with female slaves who were exploited by their masters. The Stones have "repeatedly and consistently defied what is a central taboo of the social system: mention of sexual inequality. They have done so in the most radical and unacceptable way possible: by celebrating it."[13] Perhaps Jagger's most notorious sexist statement was about his girlfriend Marianne Faithfull: "Q: Mick, what's your favorite shoe polish? A: Here in America, I prefer Kiwi, but at home it's Marianne's tongue."[14]

Whether this was said in the context of a joke or not, the sentiment was obvious. Women themselves had to take some of the responsibility for Jagger's chauvinism, however. If groupies were willing to throw themselves at him or if females adopted a worshipful attitude to fame, power, and wealth, certainly it would be difficult for any man not to take advantage of this kind of subservience.

John Lennon also came under attack by feminists in 1972 with the song "Woman is the Nigger of the World." Although he discussed the ways in which women were oppressed by man, the lyrics were didactic and suggested women lacked "guts and confidence." The use of the pejorative word "nigger" also created controversy. Many radio stations banned the song. Only five AM stations had it on their playlist. When John and Yoko wanted to sing the tune on ABC-TV's "Dick Cavett Show," Cavett and Lennon had to make qualifying statements explaining that no racism was intended.

Only two rock groups had been formed with political mandates. One was the MC5 managed by White Panther John Sinclair. Using slogans like "Revolution for the Hell of it," and "Armed Love," the MC5 declared in their manifesto that everything was free for everybody; that everything sucked — school, leaders, money, even underwear. The MC5 declared itself ready to do anything they could to move people out of their heads and into their bodies. Rock and roll was felt to be the spearhead of this attack because it was "effective and so much fun." The MC5 claimed to "have developed organic, high-energy guerrilla bands who are infiltrating the popular culture and destroying millions of minds in the process. . . . With our music and our economic genius we plunder the unsuspecting straight world for money and the means to carry out our program, and revoutionize its children at the same time."[15]

When the MC5 got into a fight with a major chain of record stores, they took out an ad telling their fans to knock down the walls of the store. This offended Elektra Records who dropped the group. In 1969 Sinclair was sentenced to ten years in prison for selling two marijuana cigarettes to an undercover policeman. In 1970 the U.S. Senate Internal Security Subcommittee investigated the White Panther Party, targeting rock music as the method used to recruit people. But rock music did not turn out to be a potent force for revolution. The MC5 broke with the White Panthers and went commercial, and failed to draw a mass audience. Chicago was the second group created on a political premise, advocating an end to the Vietnam war and revolution in the streets. The group was a huge financial success and soon dropped their political posture.

Those who feared rock music as a revolutionary force leading to communism were reacting against rock and roll for no good reason. Many rockers were millionaires, with no intention of sharing the wealth. Most of the mass audience of young fans did not even understand or could not make out the political allusions in rock songs, and certain sociologists agreed that rock did not cause political activism among the young for that reason.

Using the 1965 P. F. Sloan song "Eve of Destruction" sung by Barry McGuire, R. Serge Denisoff sampled 180 students on their response to the lyrics. Only thirty-six percent had any idea what the lyrics were about. Among other findings Denisoff concluded, "It would appear that the protest song is primarily seen as an entertainment item rather than one of political significance."[16]

Executives in the music industry did not react as lightly to "Eve of Destruction." The message in the song that change was needed or the world would continue on its suicidal way toward nuclear war, violence, and hatred, did not sit well with establishment values.

When the song made it into the top ten of the charts, many radio stations banned it, as did ABC and its affiliates. The BBC refused to play it, calling it "unsuitable for pop shows." Some broadcasters wondered if "an entertainment medium should be used for propagandistic purposes?"[17] Media personality Bob Eubanks asked, "How do you think the enemy will feel with a tune like that No. 1 in America?"[18]

Concerned citizens began a letter-writing campaign to the broadcasting industry, threatening economic boycotts. The Citizens for Conservative Action and the Young Republicans for a Return to Conservatism, both in California, complained to the Federal Communications Commission that the song violated the "fairness doctrine." An attempt was made to release a "reply song" called "The Dawn of Correction" but it never made it out of the studio. In actual fact the "fairness doctrine" in the FCC code did not apply to popular music anyway. It only applied to the controversial statements that were made to ensure that both sides of an issue were presented.[19]

"Eve of Destruction" inspired Christian crusader David Noebel to crank out another pamphlet on rock as a tool of communism. Titled *Rhythm, Riots and Revolution,* the document concluded that the lyrics in "Eve of Destruction" were "obviously aimed at instilling fear in our teenagers as well as a sense of hopelessness. 'Thermonuclear holocaust,' 'the button,' 'the end of the world,' and similar expressions are constantly being used to induce the American public to surrender to atheistic international communism."[20]

16

A Deafening Noise

New ammunition against rock began appearing in the later 1960s which linked rock and roll music with physical problems. Damage to hearing became the most prevalent health issue to be associated with rock. The issue arose at that time as a response to the increased use of amplification by rock groups as the technology developed and as groups of the time, such as the Beatles and the Rolling Stones, began to perform before huge crowds, often in excess of fifty thousand people and needed high-powered amplification to reach such audiences.

Rock and roll annoyed adults in many, many ways and one of them was the high volume level at which fans like to play and hear the music. The adult world quickly held the specter of deafness up in front of the young hoping to "kill" the noise. Adults continued to belabor the point despite the lack of hard evidence of hearing impairment. Youths ignored it all, while long-term rockers such as the Stones rolled on, decade after decade, still apparently not deaf. To hear the adults tell it, or to listen to their evidence, the Stones most certainly must be deaf. Raising the issue of hearing loss resulting from rock music was like tossing a pebble in front of a speeding train, it could not derail or delay the rock and roll express.

In 1967 the medical profession warned that loud rock music could cause hearing loss. In November of that year Dr. Charles F. Lebo presented a paper on the subject to the California Medical Association. The highlights of his speech were summarized in the magazine *High Fidelity* by a reporter whose negative bias was apparent in his statement, "the very sounds of this amplified art form may present as great a trauma to the inner ear as the general quality of the music often does to the inner man."[1]

Lebo made sound level measurements of rock music in two San Francisco establishments. He found that the noise levels "were capable of producing both temporary and permanent inner ear damage in the musicians and audience."[2] He recorded levels of between 100 and 119 decibels at the rock joints. Lebo admitted that noise had different effects on different people but concluded that ten percent of the people in such a building would escape with no effect on their hearing, eighty percent would have their hearing threshold increased from 5 to 30 decibels, and the other ten percent would see their threshold temporarily shifted by 40 decibels. "Essentially the aging process accelerates so that 20-year olds have 60-year old ears."[3] Lebo concluded, "Since inner ear damage of the type produced by noise exposure is cumulative and permanent, the desirability of lower levels of amplification for this type of live music is apparent."[4]

What *High Fidelity* neglected to mention was that Lebo did not actually test anyone's hearing.[5] Where he got his specific damage breakdown is a good question. He only measured the decibel levels in two rock establishments, and *predicted* what the damage *might* be. Lebo was willing to make some very strong statements based on very little evidence and *High Fidelity* was willing to publish them. He did not mention that a temporary shift is just that, it is neither permanent nor cumulative.

According to a 1968 article in *Consumer Reports*, the American Medical Association defined a continuous sound level of about 85 to 90 decibels as a potential danger point.[6] (Conversation generally registers at 60 decibels, a vacuum cleaner at 70).

Even those who made the equipment were ready to believe the worst, as one major manufacturer of audio equipment commented, "The sound pressure levels reached and sustained by rock groups who perform routinely now at high school and college dances, as well as discotheques, are simply incredible. You can have no conception of how loud these sounds are until you experience them yourself. . . . I can't believe [the performers] don't suffer irreversible hearing loss."[7]

Consumer Reports also advised against listening to loud rock music with earphones, listing pain, buzzing, tickling sensations, and tinnitus (a ringing sound in the ears), as warning signals for ear damage. This magazine is taken seriously and regarded as bias-free. The fact that *Consumer Reports* was pushing this fatuous nonsense that rock caused deafness indicated how pervasive and successful were the views of those who defended the position.

In August 1968, Dr. David Lipscomb, director of audio clinical services at the University of Tennessee, conducted an experiment to see if rock music played at 120 decibels damaged hearing. Lipscomb claimed to have measured levels of up to 138 decibels in discotheques, only 2 decibels below the pain threshold. Lipscomb played tapes of this rock music for 88 hours and 30 minutes to one guinea pig in several sessions over a three-month-period. Both ears were exposed for the first forty-four hours, after which the left ear was plugged. The cochlear cells of the guinea pig's ears were then photographed through a microscope. Cells in the left ear were normal. But many in the right ear were destroyed and had "shriveled up like peas," said Dr. Lipscomb. Buoyed by this "success" the investigator moved on to people.

The hearing of 2,768 freshmen between the ages of sixteen and twenty-one "who had experienced less than five years of loud rock played on low output stereo systems in the early years behind them "was tested in 1968 at the University of Tennessee.[8] Thirty-three percent failed the hearing test. The next year 1,410 freshmen were tested "with rock more available live and recorded at higher output levels . . . and 60.7 percent showed high frequency hearing impariment."[9]

Lipscomb admitted that the hearing loss of the freshmen tested was "not serious." Most had failed by a slight degree and were unaware of their impediment. Nevertheless, Lipscomb concluded, "It appears that a generation is entering its vocational life with retirement-age ears."[10] It must be noted that Lipscomb used no control groups for his experiments, such as testing a group who had listened to no rock, and did not take into account any variables such as other sources of noise besides rock that might have caused hearing loss, nor were the hours of exposure reported.

There were other strange results from this study which Lipscomb wrenched and twisted around in an effort to fit his idea that rock damaged hearing. By his own admission the hearing loss in the 1969 group was small but he could at least claim a failure rate of sixty percent. The previous year's group had only a failure rate of thirty-three percent and coupled with the admitted weak hearing loss would have left the investigator with not much evidence to buttress his position. Lipscomb tried to get out of this by arguing that kids in 1968 listened to rock on "low-output" systems, and had for years, while those in 1969 listened to rock on "higher output" systems, while presenting no evidence at all for the great technological advance which seemingly took place that year.

Some skepticism among rock industry members was voiced over Lipscomb's "experiment." David Rubinson, a producer of rock albums for Columbia Records commented, "I don't know any group that plays loud enough to hurt anybody. . . . Not in public, and certainly not on records."[11] He called Lipscomb's guinea pig study "naive" and noted, "They considered the volume of sound, but they didn't consider the volume of the guinea pig. . . . In the same way a hamster in a sawmill might die from breathing in an amount of sawdust that wouldn't disturb a normal man at all."[12] This point is particularly cogent. To draw conclusions based on testing one guinea pig which weighed perhaps a pound or so and extrapolating to 150-pound humans had no scientific basis. This producer said he objected to overly loud playing as much as anybody else but he doubted that even that would result in any permanent ear damage. Rubinson did concede that rock performers might suffer from temporary "ear fatigue." He had himself spent as many as fifty hours a week working with rock groups and suffered no hearing impairment of any kind.

Stan Wegryn, a guitarist with the group Sirocco, felt his sense of pitch was impaired after an evening of playing rock, but he felt the same thing happened even when he was playing quiet music. However, John Nash, a guitarist with a group called Eros, felt he had lost some of his hearing, and had trouble catching what a person said in a soft voice if that person was "across the room." Joe Caballaro, manager of the New York club Cheetah, was concerned about the hearing damage controversy, and planned to measure decibel levels at his establishment. Dennis Wright, assistant manager of New York's The Electric Circus, took a much lighter view of the matter, joking, "We could post the decibel count outside, like the temperature-humidity discomfort index."[13] And Steve Paul, owner of The Scene, mocked, "Should a major increase in guinea pig attendance occur at The Scene we'll certainly bear their comfort in mind."[14]

Further debunking the hearing damage theory was a 1969 study carried out by Doctors William Rintlemann and Judith Borus, auditory scientists at Michigan State University. They tested forty-two rock musicians who had been exposed for an average of 2.9 years to 11.4 hours a week of 105-decibel music.[15]

Forty of the forty-two musicians had normal hearing. The doctors concluded, "Since rock and roll musicians generally have more exposure to this type of music than any other single group, one would expect that if this music does not cause hearing loss in these musicians, it probably does not cause hearing loss in any other group."[16]

Rintlemann and Borus's findings were largely ignored, picked up nationally only by *Rolling Stone* — arguing this position was tantamount to heresy, as more and more people chose to believe that rock and roll was a hearing hazard. Even Ralph Nader got involved in the issue. In 1969 he proposed that amplified rock should be regulated by state and local governments. In letters to Senator Warren Magnuson, chairman of the Senate Appropriations Subcommittee for Labor and Health, Education and Welfare, and to Senator Philip Hart, chairman of the Senate Subcommittee on Environment, Nader wanted Congress to classify rock music above certain prescribed decibels as a "public nuisance." He also wanted mandatory ear protectors for musicians as well as soundproofing of rock clubs. Nader concluded ominously that "acoustic trauma from rock 'n' roll music is emerging as a very real threat to the hearing quality of young people who expose themselves to substantial durations of this music by live rock groups with high amplification. . . . This country may be producing a new generation of young Americans with impaired hearing before they reach the age of 21."[17] Statements such as this, with no supporting evidence, were picked up nationally by the *New York Times* and other publications.

Government regulation was also called for in Britain in 1973. Lord Kennet wanted to introduce a bill which would limit decibel levels on amplified equipment. If sound exceeded 110 decibels the amplifier should be made to shut off. Kennet felt it was necessary to protect young people, explaining, "One may say it would be sacrificing the enjoyment of the fans to save their hearing later. The situation is analogous to poisons and dangerous drugs — people do like them, but they do harm."[18]

Leeds City Council was one group that regulated a 96-decibel level for rock music in their community. They made their decision after Ronald Fearn, a Leeds Polytech lecturer, measured sound levels in discos and found readings between 105 and 118 decibels. Fearn reported, "My work had shown quite directly there is a hearing loss caused by pop music."[19] Although the 96-decibel regulation had originally been aimed at clubs, the offshoot was that it also affected concerts. At least one artist who took exception to the 96-decibel limited imposed by Leeds was Elton John, who said he would never perform there unless the level went up to a minimum of 110 decibels.

The hearing controversy was definitely making an impact. John Coletta, manager of the rock group Deep Purple, which was listed in the *Guiness Book of World Records* as the loudest group in the world, conceded, "Basically, there must be some control otherwise people's ears are going to be shattered."[20]

The case against rock and roll as a threat to hearing continued to mount. Dr. Ralph Rupp, an audiologist at the University of Michigan Speech Clinic felt people should take precautions against rock music. He suggested that musicians should wear ear protectors, reduce the sound intensity of their music by 20 to 30 decibels, and have periodic examinations by an audiologist. Rupp agreed with Nader that local governments should enforce a 100-decibel level on rock played in clubs. He also warned against headphones, "Unfettered by parental monitoring, they may pulse to the rock ritual with such abandon that permanent damage to the inner ear is almost assured."[21] Rupp's disapproving tone came across loud and clear.

Yet another physician, Dr. Frederick Dey of New London, Connecticut, declared that rock music resulted in "acoustic trauma." Funded by a grant from the National Institute of Neurological Diseases and Blindness, Dey exposed fifteen males, aged eighteen to twenty-five years with normal hearing, to rock music of 110 decibels, an average level for rock music. He claimed that the hearing of sixteen percent of listeners to such music would probably be permanently damaged from two hours of rock music.[22] Yet his own test subjects didn't suffer permanent hearing damage. A strong conclusion certainly, and one that, if generalized, should almost produce Nader's deaf generation. Where are they?

So prevalent was the notion that rock damaged hearing that a high school in California installed a device for measuring decibel output. And bands exceeding a level of 92 decibels were not paid. Richard Jackson, the assistant principal noted, "The bands have generally agreed with us that contrary to the concept that the louder they play the better they are, loudness is most often a cover-up for mediocre quality."[23]

Another attempt to defend rock and roll was made in 1970 by D. N. Brooks, M.Sc. of the Manchester, England Audio Clinic. Allowing for some temporary hearing loss, he reasoned that permanent damage to audiences would not result. "Exposure to such a [rock and roll] group for one-and-a half hours is likely to cause a temporary reduction in the standard of hearing [but] no permanent loss will accrue from repeated exposure, providing that recovery from one exposure is complete, before the next one begins."[24]

Brooks' findings were published in *Melody Maker*, a British music journal which had once been virulently anti-rock but which gradually came to support it. *Melody Maker*, in a burst of insight, recognized the obvious and suggested that all the hearing damage warnings about rock were "possibly an attack on pop and beat."[25]

Dr. Charles Lebo, who had first studied the effect of rock music on hearing in 1967, did another experiment with colleague Rayford Rydell. The results were published in 1973. They tested the hearing of forty-three rock musicians whose mean age was twenty-two and who had been exposed to rock music over a period of between one and six years. The last exposure before the testing was from twelve to seventy-two hours, apparently to allow subjects to recover from auditory fatigue. Lebo felt, as he stated before, that rock was capable of causing permanent damage. Despite this bias he was forced to conclude from this study only that temporary threshold shifts "were found in evidence in all subjects . . . the conclusion that permanent hearing loss is probable is implicit in the findings."[26]

Temporary threshold shift (TTS) is defined as "a relatively short-term effect in which exposure to loud sounds raises the threshold of hearing. It temporarily reduces the ear's ability to hear faint sounds. The higher the level of sound and the longer the exposure, the greater the shift in threshold."[27] This doesn't sound like the irreversible inner ear damage reported by Lebo. Moreover, in a 1983 medical text called *Terminology of Communication Disorders*, TTS is defined as "transient hearing loss occuring for a relatively brief period of time following exposure to noise."[28] This doesn't sound like irreversible inner ear damage either.

But the hysteria over rock and roll continued. According to a 1973 article in *Today's Health*, researchers have "proposed" that vibrating rhythms can be harmful in addition to decibel levels and may "throw the protective middle-ear muscles 'off-balance' and thus increase the propensity for damage."[29] The name of the researchers and dates of their experiments were not given. *Today's Health* also decribed a test where young people listened to rock music for one hour at 110 decibels with both continuous and intermittent exposure. The magazine failed to mention who the researchers were, how many young people were involved, and how long they meant by "continuous" or "intermittent." The results published were just as amorphous, "Some [how many?] showed very little temporary threshold shift and others [how many?] had more than a 30 decibel loss."[30] *Today's Health* then concluded that the government should regulate decibel levels in rock establishments and on stereo components.

Calling loud music potentially damaging both physically and psychologically, the journal *Popular Electronics* deserted its prior cautious approach to the controversy and explained how amplified live rock had noise levels equivalent to a team of jackhammers. The music from the amplifiers was reinforced by public address systems, thus pumping totals of "more than 1000 watts of electrical power" through the equipment.[31] For outdoor concerts more than two thousand watts were pushed through massive horn speakers.[32] *Popular Electronics* considered the output generated by these devices to be "unsafe for prolonged exposure," and noted that equipment manufacturers put the following warning on their products, "Caution: Repeated exposure to high sound levels (more than 80 dB) may cause permanent impairment of hearing."[33]

The same *Popular Electronics* article reported that the Public Health Service had been measuring decibel levels at sample rock music concerts (the number of concerts was not given). Decibel levels averaged 112 throughout the hall. The hearing level of both the musicians and the audience were measured before and after the three-hour rock concerts (numbers of musicians and listeners were not given). The Public Health Service found "significant temporary threshold shifts" in both cases, with the musicians having "a greater average hearing loss."[34]

Ninety is the specified decibel level as federally regulated for industrial noise exposure during an eight-hour work day. "The interval of exposure can be increased by 5dB for each halving of the duration of exposure without increasing the risk of noise-induced hearing loss."[35] This meant, for example, that exposure to 95 decibels must not exceed four hours per day or that exposure to 115 decibels not exceed fifteen minutes per day. Concluded *Popular Electronics*, "Clearly, the sound levels generated at live rock concerts are well above the hearing conservation limits set for industry."[36]

To illustrate the casual nature of some of the reported experiments involving hearing damage and rock music, it is worthwhile quoting from a study published in 1973 in *Radio-Electronics*. Merino Coronado, the author of the article, organized a party for forty of his students. Before the start of the event he tested their hearing. He then played three hours of rock music at levels between 100 to 120 decibels. Immediately after the party he tested their hearing again with the following results, "Boys showed an average hearing loss of about 10dB, while girls showed a loss of only about 6db. Of course, these preliminary results are in no way conclusive."[37] Coronado never did any follow-up testing the next day to find out what the recovery rates were. The fact that this kind of trivial experiment was published at all showed the willingness of the media to sensationalize the effects of rock music.

A more scientific study was carried out in 1970 by three researchers in the Department of Otolaryngology at the University of Minnesota. They tested the hearing of twenty-five rock and roll musicians before and twenty to forty minutes after their concerts where music ranged between 105 and 120 decibels. Six of the musicians were found to have some degree of permanent hearing loss but as the study recognized, "Rock-and-roll music cannot be implicated as the sole cause in the absence of other evidence. In each instance, those musicians who evidenced a substantial hearing loss also had engaged repeatedly in hunting, trap shooting, or had served in the artillery of the armed services."[39]

Another six showed evidence of temporary threshold shift. Rock music, the researchers said, could be "potentially hazardous . . . but such a conclusion must be tempered by a realization that the music . . . is intermittent, not continuous."[39] They advised caution about over-exposure, suggesting rock musicians wear earplugs, but concluded, "Until more evidence becomes available, it is unwise to say that music *is* hazardous and will cause a hearing loss."[40]

A point to be remembered is that when intense musical sounds are broken up the ear is able to rest and recover from any effects. Because most live rock music is intermittent in nature the risk of hearing damage is lessened since these periodic breaks, including intermissions, allow the ear to tolerate the sound for a longer period and undergo a partial recovery from any temporary threshold shift.

Sensationalist articles continued to be published, nevertheless. In 1971 *Health Digest* published an account of a mother warning her son about the results of his hearing test.[41] Apparently he had some hearing loss and was told that if he continued to listen to loud music he would need a hearing aid in the near future.

From time to time someone would try to dispel the exaggerated affect of rock music on hearing. Don Hagness was one writer who attempted to present a balanced view of the issue. Commenting on the various experiments that had been carried out, Hagness noted the differing results which had been obtained from the various studies which investigated the problem. He felt these contradictory results were due to the interaction of a set of variables which made it difficult to establish standards to measure rock music. Those variables included: noise levels, length of exposure, frequency of noise, health, age and susceptibility of the listener, and continuity of exposure.

Hagness, after studying all the reports, concluded a number of things. First, the average intensity of music performed by an average rock and roll band was much less than estimates given in magazine articles and newspapers. Second, rock music could produce temporary shifts in hearing but it had not been proven to what degree, if any, such chronic exposures produced permanent threshold shifts. Third, even though an average rock concert might produce a decibel level which exceeded the level set by the federal government it didn't necessarily mean hearing loss would occur. Fourth, such damage would be dependent upon the variables he had cited. Summing up, he said, "Although scientific investigation has provided only a limited number of answers concerning the ultimate effects of rock music upon hearing, enough information has been provided to allow the public in general and parents in particular to realize that the youth involved with rock music are not doomed to deafness."[42]

Music professor Roderick Gordon of Southern Illinois University, a specialist in acoustics, felt that prolonged noise, including the music of loud rock bands, damaged the nervous system. But it was only the musicians themselves who were in danger. Said Gordon, "The audience gets the brunt of the damaging sound, but for shorter periods of time, so probably little if any damage will result."[43] The debate about hearing damage and rock and roll would continue to rage, and those who advocated turning down the volume would shout the loudest.

The hearing issue was not the only problem raised to discourage rock and roll musicians. Another was the possibility of voice damage. A 1973 article in *Science Digest*, by Arthur Snider, suggested that "the tendency to sing loudly for long periods, plus the emotional frenzy that impels even greater output, is creating an abuse of vocal cords."[44]

Snider interviewed Dr. Eugene Batza of the Cleveland Clinic's otolaryngology department. Batza had examined the vocal cords of one rock group consisting of five musicians who had been singing together for five years. He found that they all had "traumatic laryngitis, bilateral vocal cord nodules and a horny growth on the vocal cords."[45] Batza concluded, "The risk of permanent degenerative change is present."[46]Vocal cord ailments affect many singers of all types of music, and is not specific to rock and roll. But how many opera singers, for example, would be described as being in an "emotional frenzy" when performing? Clearly this article displayed a disapproving tone when it came to rock music.

If this was not enough to dampen one's enthusiam for rock and roll, a case could be made concerning, of all things, sexuality. For years, rock opponents had been blaming the music for overstimulating the libido. However, in 1974 *Rolling Stone* ran the following lurid headline, "Loud Rock Linked to Loss of Lust." Quoting from a report by Dr. Maurice Schiff, who studied the effect of noise, finding that it caused reduced sexual activity, the magazine warned, "Loud rock & roll may be hazardous to your sex appeal."[47]

Why a magazine devoted to the rock industry would publish an item like this is anyone's guess. Perhaps just the words "lust" and "sex" were enough of an attention-grabber to boost sales, no matter what the content. Or perhaps a bit of reverse psychology was at work. Many teenagers find it hard to resist anything that is so-called "bad" for them. Perhaps the article was included as a joke. If so, it wasn't obvious and rock certainly

174

didn't need its friends to provide anything remotely resembling assistance to the opponents.

Religious fundamentalists joined the throng which warned that rock music could damage health. They determined that if rock music didn't kill people outright, it had terrible effects on the body, including the brain. One of their tracts claimed that "under the influence of the jungle rhythms and melodies their normal body functions have been 'nerve-jammed' so that they cease to operate."[48] Moreover, the repetition of rock music chord patterns, words, and beats hypnotized audiences. Hypnosis led to brain damage, mental breakdown, and ultimately suicide, since in this state all sorts of words were poured into the minds of rock and roll fans as they were virtualy helpless.[49]

A testimony by a Mrs. Dorothy Retallack was reproduced in a fundamentalist pamphlet. Apparently Mrs. Retallack of Denver, Ohio had played rock music to her plants. Within a month all the plants died.[50] If rock had such a disastrous effect on plants, what might it be doing to teenagers?

17

Holy Rollers

Rock and roll continued to be perceived as a problem by certain religious groups. In 1965 Pope Paul VI censured teenagers for admiring rock and roll singers. At a special mass in St. Peter's Basilica for ten thousand schoolgirls, members of the Italian Catholic Action movement, the Pope warned against "frenzied agitation over some foolish entertainment."[1] By the next year the Church of Rome had made some uneasy concessions towards rock and roll with a "Mass for Young People" and weekly "beat" masses were held every Saturday commencing in 1968. Though the masses were popular and well-attended, critics were quick to complain. The Rome newspaper *Il Messaggero* called for an end to the "experiment which is turning into a habit" and which it described as "a challenge to God and the most sacred temples." Father Bruno of St. Alessio, who initiated the contentious mass, defended it on the basis of the excellent attendance. He countered criticism that he was encouraging a "discotheque" in church, promoting "profane" music, letting the congregation get "carried away," and allowing priests to sway to "fiery beat rhythms."[3]

Other religious denominations were also having difficulty coming to terms with rock-and-roll-styled music in church. Charles Cleall, a writer for the *Methodist Recorder* in the 1970s noted that certain church leaders felt that "Christians should be willing to expose themselves to what pop music is saying; to share the vitality of its movement, and — who knows? — unexpectedly find the Lord of the Dance."[4] But Cleall questioned the type of movement inspired by rock, fearing it would create "states of mind frequently stronger than man's will."[5] The "thrusting movement of the hips" associated with the rock beat reminded him too strongly of the sexual act or masturbation. Cleall realized that some "modern" Christians were of the opinion that God meant sex to be enjoyable, but he felt that rock's erotic overtones were out of place in church.

Although Cleall noted that young people did not actually make these suggestive movements in church, he nevertheless felt the music posed a danger anyway. He was worried that while some rhythms might invigorate the brain's normal activity, others, such as rock rhythms, worked to dissipate or suspend this activity. Cleall cited educator Rudolf Laban and Doctors W. Grey Walter and Ian Oswald who all apparently shared the opinion that rock music was hypnotic and that it maintained a consistent pattern of "mild titillation" upon the body. This stimulus was excitatory yet not "formative" and the implications were dark, "Heaven only knows what mutations this titillation may in time promote." In a contradictory vein he noted that, despite this constant excitatory and titillating stimulus, rock music helped people escape into a dream world; a world where they no longer had to be awake. This seemed to come about because he felt people breathed in time to the music and in the case of rock and roll "people can breathe too fast and too hard. Over-breathing greatly reduces the blood-flow to the brain, and can seriously impair a person's consciousness."[6]

Cleall commented that although pop music was "smart, slick, and alluring" and brought crowds out to church services, he wondered if the music was worth it. "Do we want its effect?," he asked. "If we do, which Lord is it whom we have come to church to find? Which Lord have we chosen this day to serve?"[7] In a subtly racist statement, Cleall concluded that rock and roll was a form of music not indigenous to Europe nor was it an accident that "(1) the communities in which it is have never built a city nor invented a form of handwriting, and (2) that those of our young people who permit pops to reign over them are remarkable chiefly for their tendency to worsen themselves."[8]

The greatest religious furor in this period arose over a remark made by John Lennon of the Beatles. In 1966 pop journalist Maureen Cleave profiled Lennon in the *London Evening Standard*. Musing on organized religion, John commented, "Christianity will go. It will vanish and shrink. I needn't argue about that. I'm right and I will be proved right. We are more popular than Jesus now. I don't know which will go first — rock and roll or Christianity. Jesus was all right, but his disciples were thick and ordinary."[9]

In Britain Lennon's remarks were ignored. But when, several months later, his statements appeared in a U.S. teen magazine called *Datebook*, some of the American public, especially in the southern Bible Belt, were outraged. Two disk jockeys in Birmingham, Alabama, Thomas Charles and Douglas Layton, from station WAQY called Lennon's comments "absurd and sacrilegious."[10] They encouraged listeners to send Beatle records, pictures, and other memorabilia to the station which they planned to burn in a bonfire when the Beatles played in Memphis in August. The fire plan was eventually abandoned when the enthusiasm of irate ex-Beatle fans got out of control. WREB program manager Wayne Dennis announced his station would "discontinue to play all records past, present and future released by the Beatles."[11]

In Cameron, Texas a KMIL station spokesman said, "We're through with them, period." Station KZEE in Weatherford, Texas, which played thirty percent gospel music, announced they were banning the Beatles "eternally."[12] Several radio stations conducted listener surveys to see if fans wanted to continue hearing Beatle music. Many favored the bans. In Longview, Texas eleven hundred calls came into the station with ninty-seven percent supporting a boycott. In San Angelo, Texas KTEO axed the Beatles saying, "We don't care if they come out with 10,000 apologies —we'll not play the Beatles again."[13]

Although only a total of about thirty-five radio stations in the U.S. banned Beatle music, overt media attention to the bans magnified the issue. Records and memorabilia were burned or trashed. Certain record stores refused to stock Beatle albums. Reverend Thurman H. Babbs, a pastor of the New Haven Baptist Church in Cleveland, threatened members of his congregation with excommunication if they attended a Beatles concert. The Grand Dragon of the Ku Klux Klan in South Carolina burned Beatle albums on crosses. One community provided garbage cans with signs reading, "Place Beatle Trash Here;" another used a tree-crushing machine to smash albums. Promoters threatened to cancel Beatle concerts.

The frenzy in America began to spread to other countries. L' Osservatore Romano, the Vatican newspaper, responding to Lennon's remarks, admonished, "some subjects must not be dealt with profanely, even in the world of beatniks."[14]

In Mexico, a strongly Catholic country, the sale of Beatle records was down. In Monterrey and Guanajuato priests burned Beatle records in the central squares. Students vandalized stores selling Beatles albums. The South African government also banned all sales and radio programming of Beatle music. This remained in effect until 1971, after the group had safely disbanded. A representative of the South African Broadcasting Corporation said, "Since the Beatles no longer exist as a group, the corporation has decided that records made by individual members and recordings previously made by the group may be broadcast, subject to the normal criteria of decency and good taste."[15]

The Beatles' manager, Brian Epstein, concerned about the upcoming American tour of the group, urged Lennon to apologize. John was reluctant to do so, having spoken in all sincerity. However, when the Beatles landed in Chicago for their tour on August 11, 1966, Lennon made a statement to the press in which he tried to skirt the whole issue, "If I said television was more popular than Jesus, I might have got away with it. . . . I'm not saying that we're better or greater or comparing us with Jesus as a person, or God as a thing, or whatever it is. I just said what I said and it was wrong, or it was taken wrong, and now there's all this. . . . I believe in God, but not as one thing, not as an old man in the sky. I believe what people call God is something in all of us. . . . I wasn't saying the Beatles are better than God or Jesus. I used 'Beatles' because it was easy for me to talk about Beatles."[16]

Reporters weren't satisfied, or sure that was an apology, and persisted in asking if he apologized for his remark. Lennon boxed into a corner and under the gun from Epstein conceded, "I'm sorry I said it, really. I never meant it to be a lousy antireligious thing. . . . I apologize, if that will make you happy. . . . Okay, I'm sorry."[17] This half-hearted apology did cool some of the hostility toward the Beatles but not entirely. About twenty of the over two hundred radio stations in Texas continued to ban Beatle music, apparently at listeners' urgings.[18] In Brownwood, Texas the president of KEAN radio station said, "We have been amazed at the reaction of teenagers in favor of our action."[19] The fifteen-hundred-member Beatle Booster Fan Club in that town was also disbanded. KEEE in Nacogdoches, Texas got five hundred phone calls after Lennon's apology, the majority in favor of continuing the ban. Said station owner, J. S. Stallings, "Our listeners don't believe there was any sincerity in Lennon's apology."[20]

The Beatles' tour of America that August came off without incident. The only close call came on August 14 at the Memphis Coliseum in Tennessee. The Ku Klux Klan picketed the stadium, and midway through the performance someone threw a firecracker on stage. When it exploded, band members had a moment of terror, thinking it was a gunshot.

John Lennon managed to arouse the ire of the religious community once again, in 1969. His song, "The Ballad of John and Yoko," included the refrain, "Christ you know it ain't easy, you know how hard it will be, the way things are going, they're going to crucify me." Considered blasphemous, the song was banned on the BBC and on several American radio stations including WABC and WMCA in New York and WLS in Chicago. The operations chief for WABI in Bangor, Maine commented, "The new Beatles record violates every rule of fair play and decency and is below the bounds of good taste."[21] WABC's program director, Rick Sklar, said the song was banned "because I'd be talking to more monsignors in two minutes than I've talked to all year."[22]

Some of the most virulent objections to rock and roll came from Christian fundamentalists. After all, each rock fan spending money on an album was one less contributor to the collection plate. Bob Larson, a young musician who became a fundamentalist, published a book in 1967 called, *Rock and Roll: The Devil's Diversion*. He described his experiences as a rock musician and said he was forced by record company executives to write immoral lyrics to songs. At the end of his book Larson included the following:

> Anti-Rock Pledge: CONFESSING my faith in Christ and desiring to communicate his love and truth to my generation, and RECOGNIZING that many of the songs and singers of rock music express and promote a morality and life-style contrary to the highest of Christian principles, I HEREBY PLEDGE MYSELF TO THE FOLLOWING: 1. I will abstain from voluntarily listening to rock music so that I may adhere to the admonition of the Apostle Paul to "Think upon those things which are pure, honest, just, lovely, and of good report!" (Philippians 4:8) 2. I will destroy all rock records and tapes in my possession as an outward, symbolic act of signifying my inner dedication to conscientiously discriminate as to the records I buy and listen to. (I John 5:21).[23]

Readers of this tract were advised to fill in the blanks at the bottom of the page with their name, address and so on and send the pledge in to Bob Larson himself at a post office box in Denver.

A pamphlet published by Bob Jones University in Greenville, South Carolina in 1971, and authored by Frank Garlock, was a virtual litany against rock and roll music. Garlock, a former professor at Bob Jones, insisted that rock music was the root of all evil. He believed that any churches that did not speak out against rock and roll had lost their "spiritual power." Those who incorporated rock hymns into their services as a way of reaching teenagers were using a "cheap substitute" for spirituality.

The extreme reaction by the fundamentalists was similar to the intensity of hatred leveled at rock by the more mainstream religions a decade or so earlier. The mainstream religions had reached a sort of uneasy truce. They didn't like rock but for the most part were prepared to live with it. Nor were the ravings of the fundamentalists much different from those of the authorities in Communist countries. This similarity was no coincidence since both groups established a great variety of dos and don'ts and demanded total subservience to their respective ideologies. Larson and Garlock had laid the groundwork for continuing fundamentalist attacks into the future and people such as the Washington wives would be more than a little influenced by such ramblings.

Garlock quoted a disk jockey who remorsefully admitted, "I feel like a prostitute. I have sold my body and soul to play this music. I know what it's doing to the kids." Garlock concluded, "How much more guilty are 'Christian' leaders who are promoting rock music as a way of life for their teenage 'converts?'"[24] Describing Bob Dylan as the "filthy-minded 'king of pop'" Garlock felt that Dylan's song about John the Baptist contributed to a generation of godless young people. The rock opera *Jesus Christ Superstar* was, he said, "obviously an assault on the deity of our Savior."

The Christian crusaders in their weekly paper also denounced rock musicals. *Jesus Christ Superstar* was labeled a "satanic production" and *Godspell* was considered "blasphemous."[25]

Calling the Jefferson Airplane "as filthy a group as can be found anywhere," Garlock decried their obscenity. Quoting from a concert review that reported the Airplane as a vulgar and crude group that advocated free sex and drug use, Garlock demanded, "These rock 'n' roll performers are not the kind of people who should be influencing our teenagers. But many Christian parents who are too spineless, weakkneed, and timid to control their children will let their youngsters play the sensual, filthy, suggestive music of the devil's disciples by the hour without even knowing what these records are actually about."[26] Claiming that rock music leads to rebellion, crime, and promiscuity, Garlock blamed rock for being "against Christ." "Adherence to the standards of the Bible, and devotion to decency — is about to be inundated by animal behavior unless we can root out the corruption that is associated with and inherent in rock 'n' roll."[27] Bringing racism into his attack, Garlock noted that rock had its roots in the music of Africa, South America, and India, places he said where voodoo, sex orgies, human sacrifices, and devil worship abounded.

Garlock linked some rock performers with Satan, especially Mick Jagger, the Beatles, Frank Zappa, and Jim Morrison. He believed they had the desire to become the anti-Christ. In a plea to young people Garlock declared, "I challenge any Christian teenager! Subject yourself to an hour's worth of rock music and then try having your personal devotions. Your heart and soul will be so numbed by the music that the Word of God will seem dull and uninteresting. . . . I do not know of one person that I consider to be spiritual — that is one who loves the Word of God, had his prayers answered and wins others to Christ — who likes rock 'n roll music. Not one!"[28]

Rock's "satanic" links would also continue to be pointed out in the future and would reach new heights in the 1980s when they culminated in an attempt to link an alleged mass murderer to rock music through satanism without any evidence.

Summing up the evil nature of rock and roll, Garlock continued that rock and roll had shown itself time and time again to be an enemy of Christ. It was an instrument the devil employed to gain control over people's lives and then dragged them down into spiritual wickedness. It was a battle in which there were two sides, and only two, and the author wondered which side the reader was on. Moving on to the sexual side of rock, Garlock said the movement and gyration that went with the music, were not "becoming to a Christian." Explaining that a "Christian's body belongs to Jesus Christ," Garlock preached against giving into lust as promoted by rock music. Sexual freedom was a sham, according to the fundamentalists, and the only way that a Christian teenager, or any teenager, could have real freedom was to submit to the restraints and rules laid down in the "Word of God" and to conform to God's will. "Rock music will only bring slavery to the devil and to his deceitful laws."[29]

Garlock even had a theory about why teenagers like to play rock music so loud. They did this to "drown out" the guilt of their own sinfulness including stealing, rebelling against their parents, and other immoral acts.

It is tempting to reproduce the Garlock pamphlet in its entirety here, since it really was a paragon of evangelistic hype. But the following few phrases will indicate the tone of fundamentalist objections to rock:

It will completely engulf him with its loud, driving beat, its repeated chords and phrases, its wild, sensuous sound and its sadistic, neurotic, sensual, and even obscene words: and it will bend his mind and body until he no longer has any control over any of his actions or thoughts. . . . Rock 'n roll is one of the "weapons" that . . . revolutionaries are using to tear down everything that Christianity has built up in the United States of

America. . . . Rock music is the devil's masterpiece for enslaving his own children. By the grace of God, let's keep him from also using it as a tool to weaken the children of God so that they are powerless to win this generation to Christ.[30]

It is easy to dismiss the ravings of these right-wing evangelists as harmless. Yet they had a profound influence on those very young people they were so afraid were being ruined by rock and roll. This type of fundamentalist hyperbole would not seem so amusing after Lennon's assassination, as we shall see in a later chapter.

18

See No Evil,
Hear No Evil

Dirty lyrics were on the scene again by the mid-1960s and would generate heat through the rest of the decade. Dirty lyrics were the good old "leerics" of a previous time. Opposition followed a remarkably similar pattern with record companies cutting objectionable words, stations banning songs, and the government getting involved through the FCC. It was the 1950s all over again, and more. Toward the end of the 60s an unsuccessful campaign was mounted to have lyrics printed on the record. Some fifteen years later Washington wives would finally succeed with this tactic. The conflict even moved to the innocuous area of album covers.

Album cover hassles were new to the rock scene. The 1960s saw the rise of a different breed of rock and roller. These musicians demanded a say in all aspects of their work. They not only wrote their own songs and played their own instruments, but they were also much more involved in defining their own images. Seeing their music less as a product and more as an art, the 60s rockers wanted their album covers to reflect their concerns. Not interested in pretty packaging, the outspoken young musicians of the hippie era wanted control over their entire output.

Many groups had no control over their covers but the superstars did and considered them important as part of a packaged "concept." Attacks on album covers represented a broadening of the anti-rock assault and harassment: the lyrics were obscene, rockers' physical appearances disgusting, stage behavior lewd, and album covers shocking. This came from a society which fulminated over album covers far more than they did over the legion of porn magazines found in neighborhood magazine stores. Opponents of rock found every facet of the rock and roll scene wanting.

It was the Rolling Stones again who made waves with controversial album covers. Their 1965 LP, "Rolling Stones No. 2" had this message printed on it: "Cast deep into your pockets for loot to buy this disc of groovies and fancy words. If you don't have bread, see that blind man, knock him on the head, steal his wallet and lo and behold, you have the loot. If you put in the boot, good. Another one sold."[1]

The Stones used their own brand of humor and pretended to urge teenagers to beat and rob blind people. The Decca Record Company explained that the cover statement was meant to be a joke, a "giggle." A spokesman for Decca apologized, and explained that the Stones meant no harm, but the public wasn't ready for that kind of black humor and cynicism. The issue reached the British Parliament. Lord Conesford wanted the cover withdrawn and wondered if publication of such material could be deemed a criminal offense. Lord Stonham, Joint Parliamentary Under-Secretary, did not find grounds for prosecution but reassured Conesford, "If it is any consolation to the noble Lord, research I made at the weekend supports the view that even when they are intelligible the words of a pop song are not considered important and teenagers have even less regard for the blurb on the envelope."[2]

The Stones' actions raised controversy again in 1968. Their "Beggar's Banquet" album cover became an issue of contention between the Stones and their record companies, Decca (in Britain), and London (in the U.S.). The offending cover showed a toilet with graffiti written all over the wall behind it. Slogans included "Lyndon Loves Mao," "John Loves Yoko," and "God Rolls His Own." A drawing of a nude girl sliding down a drainpipe was one of the illustrations. The record companies called the cover "in poor taste" even though it had no swear words or actual obscenities. They felt that wholesalers would object to stocking it in retail outlets. Mick Jagger's suggestion that the album be shrouded in brown paper bags marked "Unfit for Children," was not accepted. The Stones, however, would not give up the fight to retain the cover. Said Jagger, "We don't find it at all offensive, so we must stand by it. . . . If we allow them to dictate to us what we can and cannot do in the way of packaging, next they are going to try to tell us what to sing."[3] He also pointed out that a Tom Jones album called "A-Tomic Jones" showed a picture of an atomic bomb exploding and nobody minded seeing that weapon of total annihilation. A writer for *Time* magazine wryly commented, "At last the music of the Rolling Stones has been enshrined where some of their less charitable listeners have always felt it belonged: on a lavatory wall."[4] The LP was finally released in December 1968. But the Stones lost out. The cover was plain with only the title on it.

"Sticky Fingers," the Stones' 1971 album had one of the most provocative covers around. Showing a close-up of a male crotch with a real zipper on the pants which could be opened or closed, the cover was allowed to be distributed without problems. Only the Spanish branch of Atlantic Records refused to handle the album. They insisted that a different photo be substituted.

David Bowie was another entertainer with album cover trouble in 1971. His LP, "The Man Who Sold the World," showed Bowie wearing a dress. The U.S. release substituted a cartoon drawing of a cowboy on the cover.

The Beatles first ran up against album cover censorship in 1966 with their "Yesterdy and Today" recording. The sleeve showed the Beatles wearing white butcher smocks, surrounded by dismembered and decapitated toy dolls and bloody joints of meat. The design was apparently conceived by John Lennon. Capitol Records printed 750,00 record sleeves before they began hearing from outraged disk jockeys and record-rack jobbers. The covers were withdrawn and many were discarded. Others were pasted over. A $250,000 advertising blitz was cancelled. Attempting to justify the cover, Lennon stated that it was "as relevant as Vietnam."

Another Beatle cover that provoked opposition was the sleeve for "Sergeant Pepper" in 1967. The graphics were not so much offensive as they were unorthodox and legally complicated. The Beatles were shown surrounded by famous faces such as Bob Dylan, Karl Marx, Laurel and Hardy, Marlon Brando, and W. C. Fields. EMI feared that those celebrities still alive would sue the record company, and stipulated that the Beatles had to idemnify them for some twenty million pounds against possible legal problems.[5] Permission to use the photos was to be obtained from as many celebrities as possible. The cover was finally allowed to proceed with only one person omitted. Gandhi was taken out. Producers felt the Indian market would be offended if their hero was equated with personalities like Sonny Liston or Diana Dors. EMI's lawyers missed one controversial item, however. A neat row of marijuana plants remained clearly visible in the garden where Sergeant Pepper's Band stood.

Nothing imagined or created so far equaled the horror caused by the jacket photo of John Lennon and Yoko Ono's 1968 album "Two Virgins." One side of the album showed the pair in full frontal nudity. The reverse showed them nude with their backs to the camera. EMI refused to distribute the LP unless the sleeves were changed. Sir Joseph Lockwood, head of the company, asked John and Yoko, "What on earth do you want to do it for?" When Yoko replied, "It's art." Lockwood said then, "Why not show Paul in the nude? He's so much better-looking. Or why not use a statue from one of the parks?"[6] Ken East, managing editor of EMI explained company policy stating, "There is nothing indecent about the human body but standards and morals don't necessarily accept these things in record shops or in homes with young children."[7]

Track Records ended up distributing the album in Britain and Tetragrammaton in America, but each copy was enclosed in a brown paper envelope. Thirty thousand copies shipped to a Newark warehouse were confiscated by New Jersey police. Several British newspapers cropped photos of the album when reporting on the subject, and British music trade papers refused to run an Apple ad for the LP which showed the nude couple. Part of the ad justified the cover by throwing in biblical bits and saying, "It is not a trend and it is not a trick. It is just two of God's children sounding and looking as much as they did when they were born, only a little older. . . . And they were both naked, the man and his wife, and they were not ashamed."[8]

Some of the objections to the nudity seemed to have been aesthetic as well as moral. One biographer described Yoko's breasts as "sagging toward the floor," and Lennon's penis as "shriveled."[9] Even the FBI got involved in the "Two Virgins" album cover controversy. J. Edgar Hoover, who was appalled by the "moral depravity" of the New Left, hoped to suppress the cover. The FBI and the Justice Department concluded, however, that the album cover did "not meet the existing criteria of obscenity from a legal standpoint."[10]

That same year a Jimi Hendrix LP, "Electric Lady," was issued with a photograph on the cover of twenty nude girls. The cover created a fuss in Britain for its "vulgarity." The secretary of the Gramaphone Retailers' Committee, Christopher Foss, angrily predicted, "This type of album sleeve is almost certain to reduce the sale of records."[11] Foss was proved wrong, however. The LP sold over thirty-five thousand copies in Britain within four days of its release.

The cover of the LP "I Think We're Alone Now" by Tommy James and the Shondells was objected to because it depicted two sets of footprints (one small and one large) walking side by side together. The two sets of prints eventually turned to face each other.

The sixties generation was characterized by their liberal attitude towards sexuality and their political radicalism. This attitude extended to dress and behavior, but it also encompassed words. What was considered obscene, vulgar, crude, or controversial among the older population, was incorporated into the daily vocabulary of the young. Words like "fuck" or "shit" rolled off the tongues of youths without a second thought. Since rock and roll music was youth music, it was natural that salty language was going to crop up in their songs.

Moreover, since anti-war sentiment, class-consciousness, and racism were political concerns of the young, it was inevitable that these topics would be discussed in rock and roll lyrics. And finally, since drug use was the focus of adolescent experimentation it was certain that drug experiences would be described in song. It is interesting to survey a cross-section of words, phrases, or lines that were banned in the sixties and early seventies. Many seem innocuous today which merely emphasizes how relative and subjective the label "obscene" or "distasteful" or "damaging" can be.

In 1965 the line "tryin' to make some girl" was bleeped from the Stones' song "Satisfaction" on "The Ed Sullivan Show." The Who song "Pictures of Lily" was banned on many American radio stations because it mentioned masturbation. That year Frank Zappa was fired from the Whiskey a Go Go for saying "fuck" on stage. MGM censored his song "Money," deleting the word "balling" from the phrase "I'm not going to do any publicity balling for you." Zappa's song "Dirty Love" wasn't given any airplay because it dealt with lust and a "nymphomaniac-voyeur-sister act." Retail outlets refused to stock his LP "Ruben and the Jets," considering it too hot to handle.

Janis Joplin had to change her album cover title from "Sex, Dope and Cheap Thrills" to simply "Cheap Thrills." The BBC banned the Beatle song "I Am The Walrus" because it referred to "knickers" and "yellow-matter custard." The Doors were fired from the Whiskey for the Oedipal lines in "The End," "Father . . . I want to kill you. Mother . . . I want to fuck you." The phrase "Sunday trucker/Christian motherfucker" was deleted from the Doors' song "Build Me A Woman," by their recording company.

In 1967 the Stones were not allowed to say "night" in the song "Let's Spend the Night Together" when they performed it on the Ed Sullivan TV show. Jagger just mumbled the word inaudibly. The song had also been banned on some stations including WMCA and WABC in New York. WABC program director Rick Sklar said his staff liked the Stones' music but playing "Let's Spend the Night Together" would jeopardize the station's broadcasting license. A disk jockey at WQXI in Atlanta, Bob Todd, solved the "night" problem by playing an edited version of the song. Said Todd, "Our license is safe this way because we're not broadcasting anything 'obscene.'"[12]

Many of the Stones' lyrics had graphic sexual images that offended people. Their song "King Bee" had lines like "Buzzin' 'round your hive, together we can make honey. . . . Let me come inside." In "I'm All Right" Jagger urged, "do you feel it, do you FEEL it" and "c'mon c'mon BABY!" Some were perturbed with the way rock and roll songs associated sex with violence, as in the Beatles' "Happiness is a Warm Gun," or the Stones' "Midnight Rambler" ("I'm gonna stick my knife right down your throat.")

In 1973 Atlantic censored the Stones song "Starfucker" which alluded to the vagina, and a groupie giving head to Steve McQueen. The title was changed to "Star Star!" The word "pussy" was overdubbed on the U.S. release, and Steve McQueen agreed not to sue for using his name.

A 1965 *Newsweek* article betrayed the adult bias against rock by noting that sexual innuendo was nothing new in popular music.[13] Cole Porter's "Let's Do It," for example, or "All of You" were suggestive. But, said *Newsweek*, rock and roll's sexual lyrics "had no wit" and were "tasteless." Above all they were aimed at adolescents rather than "sophisticated" Broadway audiences.

Even J. Edgar Hoover, head of the FBI, had an opinion on rock and roll lyrics. A private citizen wrote to him saying, "Certainly the great majority of decent Americans will applaud any efforts to make record racks and newstands refrain from peddling such filth." Hoover replied, "I too share your concern regarding this type of recording which is being distributed throughout the country and certainly appreciate your bringing it to my attention. It is repulsive to right-thinking people and can have serious effects on our young people"[14]

Objections to sex were only part of the reaction against lyrics. In 1965 Jimi Hendrix's song "How Would You Feel" was given no airplay because it dealt with how blacks were mistreated in America. Lines about not being served in restaurants and having to sit at the back of the bus were thought to be controversial, even though the music trade papers called it "important, timely and a song that should be heard."

The Who song "Substitute" was censored for the U.S. market by Atlantic. The phrase "I look all white but my Dad was black" was changed to "I try walking forward, but my feet walk back."

Some adults were offended by lyrics that urged teenagers to leave home — songs such as the Beatles' "She's Leaving Home" or Scott McKenzie's "What's the Difference" ("Pick up a toothbrush, sneak down the stairway, You've got no reason you should stay"). They felt these songs encouraged disrespect for elders and widened the generation gap.

The Who's 1965 song "My Generation" was also resisted for this reason with sentiments like "Hope I die before I get old." The BBC temporarily banned it, ostensibly because it mocked stutterers, but after if became a big seller, they relented. The BBC also disapproved of the Who's "Pinball Wizard" because it was about a "deaf, dumb and blind kid." Yet if one bothered to study the lyrics, the song was not derogatory. Their LP "The Who Sell Out" was boycotted in the U.S. because its spoof on advertising jingles was considered "vulgar."

In 1968 the Doors' song "Unknown Soldier" was banned from airplay because of it's anti-war theme. That same year the MC5's debut album "Kick Out the Jams" was censored when the words "brothers and sisters" were subtituted for "motherfucker." Yet the Jefferson Airplane were allowed to use the line "the human name doesn't mean shit to a tree" in their song "Eskimo Blue Day," and RCA agreed to release "Up Against the Wall, Motherfucker."

Why the inconsistency? Apparently there were no hard and fast rules for determining what was obscene or inappropriate. This made the whole censorship issue ridiculously arbitrary. It was left to the FCC, broadcast executives, radio program directors, record company managers, and adult opinion to decide what could or could not be used.

The FCC avoided legal battles over whether lyrics were pornographic or discordant with their vague regulations concerning "community standards," because the courts would undoubtedly argue that the music had "artistic merit." But the FCC exercised their power in no less a heavy-handed manner. Through warnings, short-term license renewals, fines, and bureaucratic red tape the FCC could pressure a station into economic collapse. Rather than provoke the FCC, therefore, almost every station owner and program director toed the line, or in other words, practiced self-censorship. That was why the FCC rarely had to actually shut down a radio station.

AM chains were tightly controlled by executives in their national headquarters. They censored any sexually explicit or drug-promoting references. As one RKO-General spokesman said, if a word or phrase was objectionable in a song "we take it out, or we'll go back to the record company and ask them to take it out before we play it, and we won't be playing that record until they do."[15]

Record companies usually complied with AM demands, even shortening songs if required, because AM airplay meant between fifty to several hundred thousand additional sales. In 1965 Gene Williams, program director of WLS in Chicago, said, "The record studios know they won't get onto the big stations with off-color songs. . . . We screen all the music up here before we play it, and we're pretty careful."[16]

191

Although FM stations had more latitude, they, too, were under constant surveillance by the FCC and broadcasting executives. During their 1966 convention the National Association of Broadcasters (NAB) discussed the kind of control that radio station managers and program directors should exercise so that "dirty" lyrics would not be heard by young listeners.

In 1970 John Lennon's song "Working Class Hero" contained both obscenity and political controversy. One of the offensive lines was "You think you're so clever and classless and free, but you're still fucking peasants as far as I can see." Most progressive FM stations were too scared to play it. As Jim Smith of WBBM-FM Chicago (owned by CBS) said, "Either you have the balls to play it unedited or you don't play it at all. We don't have the balls."[17]

WUHY-FM in Philadelphia was fined by the FCC when Jerry Garcia of the Grateful Dead said "shit" on the air, even though no one had complained to the station or the FCC. Nicholas Johnson, a commissioner at the FCC, realized that his organization had been heavy-handed in the WUHY fine and even commented that he "found it pathetic that we always seem to pick upon the small community service stations. . . . It is ironic that of the public complaints about broadcasters' taste received in my office, there are probably 100 or more about network television for every one about stations of this kind. Surely if anyone were genuinely concerned about the impact of broadcasting upon the moral values of this nation, he ought to consider the ABC, CBS and NBC networks, before picking on little educational FM radio stations that can scarcely afford the postage to answer our letters, let alone lawyers."[18] This was pleasant liberal rhetoric on Johnson's part, but in actuality the big networks were so careful about what they aired that the FCC knew they had nothing to worry about.

Other industry members involved in trying to censor lyrics were jukebox executives and programming services. In 1967 David J. Solish, a jukebox supplier, condemned labels for producing "inflammatory" material that incited "ethnics" (i.e., blacks) to riot. Solish, whose territory included the black Watts area of Los Angeles, felt that the riots there in 1967 had been spurred on by certain rock songs. He refused to list the titles, believing such publicity would only promote the records.

Solish thought that some of the independent labels should be "squeezed out of business. . . . What good does it do and what does it accomplish to play 'dirty music'?"[19] he asked. Solish suggested that jukebox operators should join with record industry officials, DJs, and retail outlets to censor the inflammatory music.

In 1970 Ted Randal Enterprises, which serviced some fifty-five radio stations in North America and Australia, providing weekly record programming of about twenty recommended tunes, imposed a rating system on each song. Categories included drugs (D), sex (S), language (L), and general (G), with subcategories acceptable (A), marginal (M), or unacceptable (X).[20] Randal hoped this would help station managers avoid controversial subject matter. Fifteen years later the idea to use this type of labeling would obtain a ground swell of support.

In Britain most decisions over radio censorship were made by the BBC, which had taken over the broadcasting of rock music in 1967 when the pirate radio stations were outlawed by Parliament. Of course the BBC had always had a reputation for being anti-rock. Each record was judged individually. As Mark White, head of BBC Radio One, noted, there was no specific definition of obscenity. Most censorship issues were decided personally by program producers. For those that needed further discussion, meetings were held with Douglas Muggeridge, controller of Radio One and Two, or with Mark White. Artists could not appeal a ban directly since it was the record companies who gave permission for the BBC to use a song. Any protest would have to come from the record executives.

White was unenthusiastic about having a late-night spot for politically controversial records, explaining, "We couldn't involve ourselves in any of these political records. We are simply not allowed to present a one-sided case in the form of lyrics."[21] Of course by banning any controversial material White was, in effect, not allowing the other side to have their say.

In 1972 the British music journal *Melody Maker* interviewed seventeen artists about their views on censorship. Only four felt the BBC was fully or partially justified in banning or censoring certain disks. Tom McGuiness called censorship a necessary evil needed to "protect" people. George Melly believed that since radio was often left on for long periods during the day, and it was impossible to know what was coming on next, people shouldn't have to be assaulted by four-letter-words. John Mumford thought some "editing" was required. Victor Brox first declared he was totally opposed to censorship but then qualified his statement by agreeing that political content was inappropriate in radio song lyrics.

Many of the artists, like Elton John and Al Stewart, believed that censorship of any kind was wrong. Les Holroyd noted that a right-wing song like "Green Berets" was sanctioned by the establishment while the left-wing views were often censored. Holroyd called it undemocratic that artists could not appeal bans and pointed out that even though the BBC was a public corporation, private citizens were not given a chance to vote on whether or not to play controversial lyrics.

In the United States there were two organized efforts to censor lyrics in the late 1960s. These efforts were independent of the FCC or the NAB. One was localized at the state level while the other was more national in scope.

In 1967 Edwin Mullinax, a Georgia state representative and owner of the La Grange Broadcasting Co., introduced a bill in the state legislature that would make it a felony to sell records or tapes without having the lyrics, the name and address of the copyright owner, and the name and address of the licensing society printed on the album cover. Mullinax was hoping to warn radio programmers and prospective buyers about songs containing obscenities, drug promotion, or "disrespect for law and order." He said he had received forty-seven pledges for the bill. Mullinax also suggested that first offenders be fined $1,000 to $5,000; second offenders would pay $5,000 to $10,000 or be sentenced to one year in prison.

A few months later, due to opposition from the Georgia Chamber of Commerce, the State Retailers' Association, and the Record Industry Association of America, Mullinax met with industry officials to discuss the proposed legislation. These officials included two distributors, a music publisher, a radio station manager, and a retailer. They persuaded Mullinax to tone down the bill, explaining that it would disrupt the recording industry. Mullinax agreed to eliminate the clause calling for printed lyrics on the record jackets, but he inserted a condition whereby record companies would have to provide printed lyrics of any song within thirty days if so requested by a parent. First time violation would be a misdemeanor carrying a small fine.

Jack Geldbart, one of the distributors at the meeting, felt most people could live with the new bill and even thought it a "model" for others to follow. The Country Music Association (CMA) was firmly behind Mullinax and issued a statement that the young people of Georgia were "subjected to a constant barrage of recorded music with lyrics dealing in sex, liquor, narcotics, and profane and disrespectful language. The effect of such music, along with the effect of other media of communications, on the rapidly deteriorating moral climate of the rest of the nation are to be seen in almost every daily newspaper."[22]

The CMA also suggested setting up a review board to screen records. This board would consist of church members, broadcasting representatives, industry officials, and educational, parent, and youth groups. It was difficult to determine who the CMA thought they would be protecting since the Georgia House of Representatives had already enacted a bill making it a misdemeanor to sell records or tapes with obscene lyrics to minors.

194

Mullinax surfaced again in 1970, lashing out at the words "hell" and "goddamned" in record lyrics. In a letter to the FCC, Mullinax wrote that he was sorry the "music license people are so money hungry as to license such profanity for broadcast. The time is long overdue," he said, "when some federal agency should take action to halt such profane utterances by the means of recordings (some of which are broadcast)."[23]

When Mullinax had begun his statewide campaign against rock lyrics in 1967, another broadcaster was lobbying for censorship on a wider level. Gordon McLendon of Dallas, Texas owned thirteen AM and FM radio stations from Philadelphia to San Francisco. One of McLendon's employees had found his nine-year-old daughter listening to the Stones' "Let's Spend the Night Together." He slashed the record with a can opener and then convinced his boss to start a morality crusade against dirty lyrics. McLendon took out full-page ads in the trade journals against recordings "rife with raunchy lyrics" and urged other broadcasters to join his campaign against "intonations or nuances" that "either innocently or intentionally offended public morals, dignity or taste."[24]

Six of McLendon's stations banned songs such as the Beatles' "Penny Lane" and "Sock It To Me Baby" by Mitch Ryder and the Detroit Wheels because of their sexuality, and "Candy Man" by the Nitty Gritty Dirt Band because of a "casual" reference to God. A few Pennsylvania stations also backed the boycott. The program director of McLendon's KILT in Houston commented, "The hippies know what they're saying on these records. But ole John Q. Public doesn't. We're tired of them putting it over on ole John Q."[25]

A spokesman for Capitol Records described McLendon's stance as "ridiculous." He noted that "Penny Lane" was ordered by a million kids even before it was released, but McLendon was undaunted. He enlisted the aid of parents when he addressed the national convention of the American Mothers' Committee in New York City. McLendon listed some of the songs he felt most offensive. These included "Rhapsody in the Rain" which containted the line, "I can't stop together, together," and described a couple making love in a car to the rhythm of the windshield wipers; "Try It" by the Standells; "Day Tripper" about one-night stands; "Running Around the World" considered to be about LSD; and "Straight Shooter" supposedly about heroin.

McLendon told the mothers, "we've had all we can stand of the record industry's glorifying marijuana, LSD, and sexual activity," and asked, "Is this what you want your children to listen to?"[26] He blamed "filthy and smutty" lyrics on a "maverick few" in the American recording industry, and felt that the majority of record companies were run by "men and women of conscience."

Blaming British music as one of the worst influences on children, McLendon called for an updated version of the Boston Tea Party which he named the "Wax Party," implying that English records be dumped. Finally McLendon urged the mothers to go back to their own communites and let radio stations know they were behind the censorship campaign. "Your support at the grass-roots level," he said, "will go a very long way toward arresting the cancerous growth of that irresponsible minority in the record and music industry which unconscionably countenances subtle or downright salacious lyrics."[27] The American Mothers' Committee immediately endorsed McLendon's policy as did 125 other of the 4,200 AM radio stations in the United States, including the American Broadcasting Company.

Appearing on the Mike Wallace TV show, McLendon revealed his paranoia when he alluded to what he felt were the underhanded tactics of rock promoters. "I think we're going to get badly hurt by this stand because we're never going to know from what direction the attacks will be coming. It's unfortunate that a great deal of the opposition will be like germ warfare, because you could scarcely expect the people to come out and insist they be given the right to continue recording filth."[28]

McLendon reiterated his objections to lyrics during interviews with *Time* and *Billboard*. He said he was against songs "that glorify dope addiction, homosexuality, and immorality in general. Some absolutely make permissible, if not encourage, fornication and all varieties of things that would have been called immoral 20 years ago."[29]

Claiming that he couldn't live with himself, because as a broadcaster he had not been "policing the music satisfactorily," McLendon insisted, "I've got to ban these records."[30] He felt that smutty records were the first step toward immorality in teens, just as marijuana smoking led to harder drugs. It was up to broadcasters to control what music teens listened to or "we've been just as guilty as those who do the pushing of drugs."[31]

McLendon realized that most radio stations would continue to play offensive songs, but he was willing to suffer business losses. "Being a practical businessman," he commented, "I had to think of this. But I said, 'Let her rip!' . . . Some elements of the standards we've so pragmatically set will have to change, but I think this is, at least, the beginning of what could be something very, very good."[32]

McLendon's next idea was to set up a panel of five to seven people consisting of prostitutes, ex-prostitutes, junkies, and addicts to screen suggestive lyrics. If any words or phrases appeared questionable to broadcasters, they could phone one of the panel members who would be hip to street lingo. McLendon felt a dictionary of slang could not fill the same purpose as a panel, since teen lingo changed "almost by the week." But as one McLendon opponent noted, were prostitutes and junkies the best judge of moral content? Nothing ever came of the panel. Nor did the majority of people in the music industry support McLendon. Only three record companies sent lyric sheets to McLendon's stations. Most called his demands "outrageous" and felt he wouldn't have time to read 150 lyric sheets a week anyway. "If McLendon thinks that a record is in bad taste," said one record company executive, "he doesn't have to play it. We screen our material and we don't want him to be our a&r department."[33]

Others were angry that McLendon was a "self-appointed" critic and wondered what gave him the right to think he could decide what was objectionable. Said a record company spokesman, "The 18–25 year-old generation has come to embrace rock 'n' roll because it has something to say. If broadcasters let their personal viewpoints guide their choice of songs, the music will be set back."[34]

RCA issued a formal statement against McLendon saying, "We are in full accord with the avowed objectives of radio stations to maintain high standards which we believe are fully compatible with the broadcasters' requirements. Because of this, we feel that a shotgun approach which requires copies of lyrics on all records is particularly onerous. We would hope that a less cumbersome and less costly procedure can be worked out."[35]

Yet there were those who did back McLendon, especially in his home state of Texas. Bert Henry, president of KNEL in Brady banned six of the top forty tunes, and collected a petition of 2,708 names protesting "the insult toward common decency, flaunted by those who release today's records of popular music, filled with innuendos, double meanings and outright tunes of immorality."[36] The petition was sent to the FCC.

KKUB in Brownfield banned "Society's Child" which approved of interracial love, and KEEE in Nacodgoches banned "When I Was Young" and "Let's Live for Today." KEAN in Brownwood banned eight songs including Aretha Franklin's "Respect," "Rhapsody in the Rain," Petula Clark's "Don't Sleep in the Subway," "Eight Miles High" by the Byrds, "Soul Finger" and "Let's Spend the Night Together." Moreover, as a result of McLendon's campaign, Representative John D. Dingell (D-Mich.) introduced a federal bill in 1968 and again in 1969 trying to require printed copies of lyrics for recorded music.[37]

19

Turn On, Tune In, Drop Out

Drugs were nothing new in the music business but until the 1960s drug use was kept as secret as possible. For example, drugs were associated with black jazz when jazz was considered subversive and radical. British rockers were using drugs in the early 60s, and in 1963 the Rolling Stones had to substitute a cover of "Not Fade Away" for one of their songs, "Stoned." In America drug used was most rampant during the mid-sixties and Haight-Ashbury in San Francisco became the center of the drug culture.

The music of bands like the Byrds, Grateful Dead, and Quicksilver Messenger Service was known as acid rock. The Doors chose their name from the title of an Aldous Huxley book, *The Doors of Perception*, about peyote and mescalin. What angered society about these drug-taking rock musicians was the fact that they were so open about what they were doing. When Grace Slick of the Jefferson Airplane was invited to tea at the White House she boasted that she planned to lace Nixon's drink with LSD. Word got through to security and she wasn't allowed in.

Eric Clapton expressed the attitude of many rock musicians when he explained, "Ours is a universal problem; how to find peace in a society which we feel to be hostile. We want to express that search in our music since that is our most eloquent voice. We need the drugs to help us, to free our minds and our imaginations from the prejudices and snobbery that have been bred into us."[1]

Before LSD became illegal in 1966, Paul McCartney admitted in a *Life* magazine interview that he had tried the drug. "It opened my eyes. We only use one-tenth of our brains," he commented. "Just think what we could accomplish if we could tap that hidden part."[2] Reaction was immediate. The *Daily Mail* called McCartney "an irresponsible idiot," and Billy Graham said a prayer for him. The pressure on Paul was so great from the media that he said to a reporter, "It's you who've got responsibility not to spread this. If you'll shut up about it, I will."[3]

But the blame for drug use among the young was laid squarely on rock and roll music. In 1967 Nicholas Von Hoffman wrote a series on Haight-Ashbury for the *Washington Post*. Calling the area Hashbury, and the hippie movement the Neo-American Church, Hoffman said their mandate was to propagate dope by infiltrating and taking over the communications and entertainment industries. Hoffman accused radio station KMPX in San Francisco of being the pusher of the airwaves and criticized "sinister-faced" program director Tom Donahue for playing "mostly dope music."

Constructive Action, Inc. of Whittier, California distributed a thirty-minute color film called *Pied Pipers* which warned that rock groups were leading youth to drug addiction. Yet when one follower of the drug scene drew up a list of rock drug songs he only came up with twenty-eight. This was "considerably less than one-half of the singles material released in one average week in the record industry."[4] The list of twenty-eight, however, was "derived from a four-year time span, which renders an infinitesimally small portion of one percentile."[5]

Nevertheless, the establishment saw a drug conspiracy in rock music and were out to get the musicians. Mick Jagger and Keith Richards were busted in 1967. Jagger was nailed for four amphetamine tablets, bought legally in Italy, but illegal in Britain. Richards was found with cannabis resin and heroin, but this had no legal bearing on Jagger since they weren't in his possession. Jagger's doctor testified that he would have prescribed the drugs for Mick if he had requested them. Yet Jagger was sentenced to three months in prison. He spent one night in prison after being granted bail and an appeal hearing.

As even the staid *Times* of London noted, the sentence had been far too severe for a first-time offender. Jagger's four pills hardly constituted an amount for a pusher or addict. The *Times* felt that it was only because Jagger was who he was — a rock star — that public opinion determined he "got what was coming to him."

Keith Richards was sentenced to one year in prison but also only spent a night in jail, being released on bail. The Appeal Court quashed Richard's twelve-month conviciton and Jagger got a conditional discharge.

A few months before Jagger's bust, the *News of the World* had printed a libelous article on Mick making up false stories about his drug use. Jagger threatened to sue, but didn't. Some people felt that the bust had been set up by *News of the World* so that Jagger would be a proven doper. Commenting on possible *News of the World* involvmement, Keith Richards said, "They knew Mick had an airtight case against them, and the damages would probably have cost them about three quarters of a million dollars."[6]

Around the same time that year Brian Jones, also of the Rolling Stones, was busted. Jones, who did have a serious drug problem, was fined and put on three years probation. Leslie Block, the judge who tried Brian's case, revealed his hostility toward the rock musicians when he gave a speech to the Horsham Ploughing and Agricultural Society, "We did our best . . . I, and my fellow magistrates, to cut those Stones down to size, but alas, it was not to be, because the Court of Criminal Appeal let them roll free."[7]

In 1968 John Lennon and Yoko Ono were busted in London for possession of cannabis. "The thing was set up," John claimed, by Detective Sergeant Norman Pilcher who "went around and busted every pop star he could get his hands on. . . . Some of the pop stars had dope in their houses, and some didn't. It didn't matter to him. He planted it. That's what he did to me."[8]

George Harrison was busted by the intrepid Pilcher in 1969, reportedly another set-up. A 1969 *Rolling Stone* magazine commentary on the Harrison bust noted that the Beatles had lost their image as the nice boys of rock and were now being hassled by the cops. Apparently when they had been in favor with the British public, Scotland Yard considered them "untouchable."

It wasn't until 1966 that some of the first attacks in the press against drug lyrics in rock songs began to appear. "Eight Miles High," a tune by the Byrds, was singled out as a drug song by the *Gavin Report*, an American programming guide used by more than a thousand radio stations to select the music they played. Many banned the song, and it dropped in the charts. The flak was so intense that Byrd member Jim McGuinn tried to insist that the words were about an airplane trip to London. Bob Dylan's "Rainy Day Women," with its chorus "everybody must get stoned," was also listed in the *Gavin Report* as a drug song.

Explained Bill Gavin of his classifications, "In our opinion, these records imply encouragement and/or approval of the use of marijuana or LSD. We cannot conscientiously recommend such records for airplay, despite their acknowledged sales. We reserve the future right to distinguish between records that simply mention such drugs and those that imply approval of their use."⁹

The fact that neither the Byrds' nor Dylan's drug songs were banned on the BBC illustrated the subjective nature of Gavin's judgments. But the BBC did ban the Beatles' "A Day in the Life" because of lines like "he blew his mind out in a car" and Paul McCartney's "Hi, Hi, Hi."

When the Doors appeared on "The Ed Sullivan Show" in 1967 they chose to do "Light My Fire." CBS executives didn't want them to use the word "higher" as in the line "Girl we couldn't get much higher." Bob Precht, Sullivan's son-in-law and the show's director, extracted a promise from the Doors that they would alter the line for the broadcast. The Doors agreed and sang the new line in rehearsal. During the actual broadcast, however, they sang the original line using the word "higher." Precht was furious and told the Doors, "You guys are dead on this show! You'll never do this show again."¹⁰

The Nixon administration's campaign against rock and roll began in December 1969 when Nixon, Vice-President Agnew, and forty American governors assembled one morning to listen to rock music. The lyrics were flashed on a screen so the politicians could follow what they were listening to. It was the first step the government would take in blaming drug use on rock music.

The second step was a speech given by Agnew in 1970 in Las Vegas, Nevada during a Republican fund-raising dinner. Agnew claimed that rock lyrics "brainwashed" young people into taking drugs. "We may be accused of advocating song censorship for pointing this out," Agnew noted, "but have you really heard the words of some of these songs? The Beatles have a song which includes the words, 'I get by with a little help from my friends, I get high with a little help from my friends.' . . . Until it was pointed out to me, I never realized that the 'friends' were assorted drugs."¹¹ Agnew urged the rejection of "creeping permissiveness" and a vote for "square" Republicans.

The government had stated its position in no uncertain terms, and it was time for the music industry to respond. The first reaction came from FCC Commissioner Nicholas Johnson.

Johnson, a liberal Democrat, saw exactly what Agnew was up to. In a speech to the U.S. Information Agency during a symposium called "Rock Music: Underground Radio and Television," the commissioner blasted the vice-president for hypocrisy and political posturing. Johnson explained that there were many rock songs which warned against drugs — songs like

"Amphetamine Annie," "The Pusher," or "Mother's Little Helper." He wondered why Agnew exclusively targeted rock music for promoting the drug culture when advertisers had also picked up the jargon. For example, Ford was using the phrase "blow your mind," TWA's slogan was "up, up and away," and a motor bike company was advertising "a trip on this one was legal." Perhaps the critical point, said Johnson, was the fact that young rock and rollers were not contributing funds or lending support to Nixon. Johnson felt that television ads were much more insidious than rock lyrics with their promises of quick solutions or fast relief if a certain product was ingested.

He also pointed out the irony of Agnew giving an anti-drug speech in Las Vegas where "the only thing that flows faster than gambler's money . . . is alcohol."[12] Johnson added there were more alcoholics in San Francisco than narcotic addicts in the entire country.

Tobacco company executives, whose advertising reached millions of young people and whose product could cause death from lung cancer, were not denounced by Agnew. On the contrary, speaking at a $100-a-plate dinner in Louisville, Kentucky, Agnew took the opportunity to counterattack Johnson. He described Johnson's type of thinking as "the kind of radical-liberal philosophy of permissiveness and self-flagellation that has encouraged so many of our young people to turn to pot or worse."[13]

Not missing a chance for a rejoinder, Johnson said, "Perhaps it is obvious why Vice President Agnew defends big campaign contributors who are urging our gradeschool children to take up cigarette smoking. . . . But I doubt his rhetoric will provide much satisfaction to the dependents who are left behind by the 300,000 Americans who will die from cigarette-related diseases this year."[14]

Returning to the issue of rock and roll lyrics Johnson warned, "The forces of censorship are subtle. This Administration repeats and repeats that it is not censoring . . . [but] the radio station owners get the message: the Administration's listening to them."[15]

Johnson's remarks had no effect on Nixon's determination to use rock and roll as a scapegoat for drug problems. In October 1970, about seventy radio broadcasters attended a day-long drug abuse conference at the White House. Nixon wanted to enlist their aid in screening rock and roll lyrics that promoted drugs. Nixon assured the broadcasters that he had no intention of telling what to program, but he would "appreciate" their cooperation. Other speakers included Dean Burch, chairman of the FCC; John Finlator, deputy director of the Narcotics Bureau; Myles Ambrose,

Customs Bureau commissioner; John Broger, director of the Armed Forces Office of Information; John D. Ehrlichman, assistant to the President for domestic affairs; Elliot Richardson, secretary of the Department of Health, Education and Welfare; Dr. Bert Brown, director of the National Institute of Mental Health; and Attorney General John N. Mitchell. If this seemed like a weighty line-up of speakers, it was. And this fact was not lost on the seventy broadcasters. There would be no coercion for them to censor drug lyrics, but the FCC, a government organization, did issue broadcast licenses.

Also attending the White House conference were members of Day-Top, a New York drug rehabilitation center. When one of the broadcasters asked the Day-Top group if anyone could trace their initial use of drugs to rock lyrics, their spokesman "seemed amazed at the question, and replied there was no connection whatsoever between rock lyrics and becoming a drug user. He said he found he enjoyed listening to rock while under the influence, but that the music was not responsible for introducing him to drugs."[15]

Many people were convinced however, that drug songs caused drug use. One of these was journalist and long-time rock enemy Gene Lees. "I cannot prove this," he admitted, "but if you asked me whether rock music had been a symptom or a cause of America's terrible problems with its young people, I would be inclined to say, 'Both — but primarily a cause.' Rock music has widened the inevitable and normal gap between generations, turned it from something healthy — and absolutely necessary to forward movement — into something negative, destructive, nihilistic."[17]

Even *Billboard* magazine published an editorial "The Call to Action Against Drugs," claiming it was up to the music industry to stop drug problems.[18]

Helen Keane, a record producer for companies like MGM, Verve, and Polydor also blamed rock for drug problems. Saying that she knew acid rock would lead to trouble, Keane said, "Well, the record companies and the rock groups accomplished their purpose: they got rich killing kids."[19]

Art Linkletter also spoke out against rock and roll after his daughter tragically died during an LSD trip. Linkletter had originally spoken out against rock late in 1969 when he testified before a Congressional commission on drug abuse. He called the Beatles the "leading missionaries of acid society," and blamed top forty radio for playing songs that were "secret messages" to teens to "drop out, turn on, and groove with chemicals and light shows at discotheques."[20] Describing terms like "acid rock" as "easy, familiar, non-shockable," Linkletter noted that people like John Lennon could get busted and it didn't harm their careers. "I have nothing against rock music as such — I personally don't like it — but I do object to a music that sells kids on drugs," said Linkletter.[21]

Some radio programmers became immediately wary of playing songs with drug lyrics. In June 1970, when six hundred people petitioned station WFAA in Dallas, threatening to boycott sponsors, Charlie Van, director of programming, withdrew any songs with pro-drug lyrics. Said Rick Sklar, program director of WABC in New York, "We will not play songs dealing with drugs because even if the song is supposedly anti-drug, it tends to glorify the subject."[22]

Yet some tried to defend rock and roll saying it only reflected, but did not cause the drug culture. Dr. David E. Smith, an authority on drug abuse, and founder and director of the Haight-Ashbury Medical Clinic, had treated more than fifty thousand drug cases. He felt that rock music was a political scapegoat and that listening to drug lyrics did not make an addict. "Youth like rock music. Drug-using youth like rock music. Non-drug using youth like rock music. There is no causal relationship between the two. . . . Music — particularly pop music — tends to be a reflection of the times. It is very questionable what comes first: Does rock music influence drug taking, or do people who are participating in drug use like to listen to the music? . . . To say that contemporary music is causative in the current wave of drug abuse, is a very questionable judgment."[23]

Dr. Smith felt that Agnew attacked rock lyrics because it was "politically safe." "A person doesn't become an alcoholic because he hears a pro-alcohol song, such as 'One for My Baby,' and there are many others," noted Smith. "The person with alcoholic tendencies hears the same pro-alcohol songs as does the social drinker, or the non-alcohol user. Whether a person becomes a drug user is not determined by the music he hears but primarily by personality characteristics."

"If we do accept political censorship — and it may come to that," Smith continued, "then we should demand that songs dealing with alcohol similarly should be banned. Alcoholism is a far bigger problem than marijuana. There are 7 million alcoholics in this country and 80 million users. Without a balanced approach, censorship would widen the generation gap. It would demonstrate the hypocrisy behind such a move where the dominant culture takes its social drug and whitewashes it, and then takes a politically safe target such as marijuana and blasts it."[24]

Smith noted that many in the rock and roll industry helped campaign against drug abuse. The Monterey Pop Festival donated $5,000 to Smith's clinic. Rock promoter Bill Graham, the rock band Creedence Clearwater Revival, and rock radio station KSAN in San Francisco sponsored an information program warning about the dangers of heroin. This resulted in San Francisco's board of supervisors setting aside funds for methadone maintenance treatment. Janis Joplin had given three benefit performances to raise funds for the Haight-Ashbury clinic. Frank Zappa and Grace Slick, among others, did anti-drug commercials on FM radio using slogans like "Speed Kills."

While many of these rockers were reported users themselves, these gestures were more genuine than hypocritical. What opponents failed to note was that when fans elevated musicians to stardom one consideration was that the musicians reflected the values and ideals of the fans. Sonny and Cher had been hugely popular in 1965 and then faded quickly away. They used no drugs and came out openly against them and Cher later remarked that the kids thought them square. It was the end of their careers as youth icons (later they successfully returned recycled more as comics and appealing to an older crowd) and their drug stance may have played a part. Any rocker who took such an anti-drug stance had to be sincere since he had nothing to gain and potentially had a lot to lose.

One person who tried to use the anti-drug campaign to his advantage was Mike Curb, the twenty-five-year-old president of MGM records. Curb said he was dropping eighteen rock acts because of drug lyrics in their songs. At no point did Curb ever list the eighteen groups he was dumping. Saying only that the bands were LP chart groups, Curb claimed to be sacrificing sales in order to rid the airwaves of drug messages. Curb also made appointments with major broadcasters hoping to persuade them to join the ban. Curb complained that groups using drugs were abusive to secretaries and promotion people, wasted the time of record company staff, and were careless with studio equipment. "I'm not looking to go on a witchhunt," he said, "and we are not asking any acts to roll up their sleeves."[25] But he did feel a morals clause in MGM contracts could be used to terminate groups that didn't meet his standards.

Only a few people commended Curb for his morality crusade. One was Bill Drake, a national radio programming consultant who recommended songs to nine AM and over fifty FM stations. Drake said that he had alway advised against songs glorifying drug use, even though he had been ridiculed for doing so. Of course, broadcaster Gordon McLendon, who had started his own clean-up campaign in 1967, was all for Curb's position. "Mike Curb and MGM's decision is bold and unprecedented. MGM is the first major record company to take a giant step in joining broadcasters who have steadfastly refused to air drug-oriented songs," said McLendon.[26]

Mike Maitland of MCA records said his company would not deal with "wacked out" groups in the first place since they were undependable. Curb said he also received support from Bill Gallagher, president of Paramount Records; Jules Malamud, executive director of the National Association of Record Merchandisers; and producer Jeff Barry.

Curb was also supported by Morality in Media, Inc. Some three hundred members paid $25 each to honor Curb and others at their fifth annual dinner in the Metropolitan Club of New York, in December 1970. Curb was presented with a plaque for speaking out against drug lyrics.

Several representatives of the music industry, however, felt that Curb was grandstanding. They mentioned his love of publicity and felt there was no substance behind his announcement of sacrificing "chart groups." *Rolling Stone* checked out the number of MGM songs on the Billboard rock charts shortly after Curb's remarks, and found that only five of MGM's albums were charted. Of these, two were safe because they were soundtracks. Two were by musicians that Curb said he hadn't dropped which left only one possible target, Ritchie Havens' "Mixed Bag." But Curb had said nothing at that time about dropping Havens.

Moreover, one of the MGM musicians who had a song in the charts, Eric Burdon, was a known drug user and had put out songs under the MGM label like "Sky Pilot" and "Sandoz" (the name of a Swiss company that manufactured LSD). Yet Curb was keeping Burdon on, no doubt because he had million-selling hits like "Spill the Wine." Burdon's manager, Steve Gold, said of Curb's announcement, "Isn't that the sickest pile of bullshit you ever heard? That man is crazy for publicity. . . . There's these 18 groups trying to make it, and now they're going to have to find a new label when in effect Curb had black-listed them as junkies. That's McCarthyism at its best."[27]

Clive Davis, president of Columbia Records, blasted Curb, suggesting that Curb was only using the drug issue to get rid of groups that weren't pulling in big money. The drug problem, Davis felt, should not be dealt with "by means of artistic witch hunts." The charge that rock music "supports and encourages drug experimentation which leads to addiction is, at the least, erroneous, and, at the most, a complete reversal of a cultural process," said Davis.[28]

According to San Francisco attorney Brian Rohan, who had negotiated many rock contracts, the MGM morals clause left the company open to a libel suit. They would have to have absolute proof a musician was using drugs, which would mean invasion of privacy.

One rock group that left MGM of their own accord was A. B. Skhy. Jim Marocotte, bass player for the band, called MGM an "absurd company that didn't like long hairs." Another rock musician then recording for MGM, Simon Stokes, joked that he was insulted that his group wasn't one of the ones let go. "Who wants to be on a label where the president quotes Spiro Agnew to you?" asked Stokes.

As of December 1970 Curb still had not announced which groups he was dropping and distributors hadn't been told to pull any MGM albums from their stock. Then Mike Viner, head of MGM's Special Projects Division, issued a statement saying Curb had been misquoted in *Billboard* over the dumping of the eighteen groups, "It wasn't 18 groups, he was misquoted. The cuts were made partly to do with the drug scene — like maybe a third of them had to do with drug reasons. The others were dropped because they weren't selling."[29] At last part of the truth was out. The cuts were economic. Drugs were used as a smoke screen.

When asked about the chart LPs Curb said he was dropping, Viner offered this explanation, "Well he might have meant a group who'd had a hit more than a year ago and since then have been putting out bad stuff possibly because of drugs."[30] This remark made the financial motive transparent. A group that didn't have a hit for over a year wasn't bringing in big money for the company. Drugs had nothing to do with it. Mike Curb went on to be elected lieutenant governor of California as a Ronald Reagan protégé.

One of the stranger offshoots of the drug lyric controversy involved Elvis Presley. Presley had sold out rock music and turned to middle-of-the-road schlock. Elvis became friends with John O'Grady, of the narcotics squad of the Los Angeles Police Department.

Even though O'Grady knew that Elvis was a reported drug user, he realized that Elvis had a respect for law and order and felt that if he could involve Presley in drug busts, the singer would give up his own habit. Elvis hated the Beatles and their drug songs and fell for the communist plot theories. This was a classic case of an older entertainer not understanding the young rock generation. Also Elvis used different substances than the current rockers.

Presley's interest in fighting drug abuse reached the ears of Richard Nixon who invited him to the White House and issued him with the badge of a full-fledged narcotics agent. Ten days later, Elvis got a tour of the FBI building in Washington where he met with Assistant Director Thomas E. Bishop. In a follow-up memo Bishop said that Presley talked about entertainers "whose motives and goals he is convinced are not in the best interests of this country" and offered "to make such information available to the Bureau on a confidential basis whenever it came to his attention."[31]

Elvis then fervently wished to meet sometime with the man he considered "the greatest living American" — J. Edgar Hoover. The meeting never took place because Bishop's memo also stated, "Presley's sincerity and good intentions notwithstanding he is certainly not the type of individual the Director would wish to meet. It is noted at present that he is wearing his hair down to his shoulders and indulges in the wearing of all sorts of exotic dress."[32]

The drug lyric controversy continued to rage, without Presley's help. In Illinois a state crime commission hearing on drug abuse had people like William C. O'Donnell testifying. O'Donnell, vice-president of CBS, represented the Illinois Broadcasters Association. He equated disk jockeys with pushers.

Meanwhile, back in Washington, the Federal Communications Commission was carrying out government policy. In March 1971 the FCC notified commerical broadcasters that they had a responsibility not to promote or glorify illegal drug use in their record programming. Their edict, titled "Licensee Responsible to Review Records Before Their Broadcast," said the FCC had received a number of complaints, and maintained that broadcasters must know if lyrics were pro-drugs and make a judgment regarding airplay. Violations, the FCC pointed out, would raise "serious questions as to whether continued operation of the station is in the public interest. In short, we expect licensees to ascertain, before broadcast, the words or lyrics of recorded musical or spoken selection played on their station."[33]

The FCC voted five-to-one to issue the notice. Commissioner Nicholas Johnson was the lone dissenter. One of the commissioners who voted for the action was Robert E. Lee, a one-time member of the McCarthy inner circle and a former FBI agent. Although the FCC was not actually banning drug songs, the threat to broadcasters would make them wary of playing anything remotely associated with drugs. Johnson made several statements concerning the FCC decision, saying it was a way of controlling the broadcast medium "by fear, by coercion, by ambiguity and by threats." "This public notice," said Johnson, "is an unsuccessfully disguised effort by the Federal Communications Commission to censor song lyrics. . . . It is an attempt by a group of establishmentarians to determine what youth can say and hear; it is an unconstitutional action."[34]

Noting that the effort to censor drug lyrics was "in reality an effort to harass the youth culture," Johnson doubted that the FCC was really concerned about drug abuse. What alarmed Johnson the most was the fact that the briefing for the FCC notice came from the Pentagon. They listed twenty-four songs they felt were pro–drugs. Johnson felt it could be a first step toward more widespread political censorship in song lyrics. "If the FCC is going to be used by the Administration to frighten broadcasters to carry only stuff favorable to it, this country is in a lot more danger than any of us had imagined," Johnson warned.[35] Worse yet, the Pentagon briefing made Johnson realize that the government didn't understand what it was objecting to. For example, the Pentagon viewed a song about how evil it was to push drugs as glorifying drug use. Reaction from the radio and recording industry was mixed. Some deplored the FCC notice while others thought it fell in line with their own self-censorship policies anyway. One of the more extreme examples of resistance came from Steve Leon, program director of WDAS-AM and FM in Philadelphia. Steve was fired by his own father, Max Leon, the station owner, for challenging the FCC warning. Steve had intended to file suit against the FCC claiming violation of the First Amendment's protection of free speech. His father, on the other hand, believed, "As a licensee we must go along with the majority of the Commission until their rulings are upset by somebody else. And that's not going to be us. . . . I'm not going to let pot ruin me."[36]

Alan Shaw, president of special projects for the ABC-FM network, found the FCC notice "neither shocking nor drastic." Shaw commented that ABC had always had a policy of being cautious about drug lyrics. "The ruling basically word for word is reasonable," said Shaw, "although it will not solve the drug problem."[37]

Norman Wayne of WIXY in Cleveland also felt censoring lyrics would not alter drug use. Saying that the FCC was "treating a symptom" not a problem, Wayne commented, "The music we play at a radio station is a reflection of the problem, not the cause."[38] Even Bill Gavin, who basically approved the FCC action, criticized "the veiled allusions by government, by the vice-president that "You better be careful or Big Brother will come after you."[39]

But program manager Pat Whitley of WNBC radio banned Brewer and Shipley's song "One Toke Over the Line" because it referred to puffing a marijuana cigarette. The song was also banned on stations in Buffalo, Miami, Houston, Washington, Chicago, Dallas, and New York. Yet the song actually warns about smoking too much dope.

Other radio personnel were worried about how to interpret the FCC notice. Terry Smith of KIOI-FM in San Francisco said he was "scared" by the "vague" wording in the edict. In fact, the FCC notice opened a whole can of worms about how to interpret song lyrics. In a song like "Joy to the World," what did the songwriters mean by "Joy." "Mary" was a code word for marijuana. Did that mean any song with the name Mary in it was to be banned?

The Grateful Dead's "Casey Jones" had a line "high on cocaine," but Casey sufferd the consequences of using the drug and came to a bad end. Was this pro- or anti-drugs then? WHMC in Maryland chose the former interpretation and banned it. Some disk jockeys noted that golden oldies, songs like "I've Got You Under My Skin," "You're Getting To Be a Habit With Me," or "I Get a Kick Out of You," could be construed as drug-related. Was the Beatle song "Yellow Submarine" really about barbituates? Were the first letters in the title "Lucy in the Sky with Diamonds" an acronym for LSD? Did the Beatles' song "Fixing a Hole" refer to repairing a roof or shooting heroin?

So confusing was the FCC's intent that they issued a formal clarification of their original notice. As is often the case with government directives, the "clarification" just resulted in more confusion and anxiety. The new announcement shifted some of the responsibility for screening lyrics from the broadcast executives to the disk jockeys, much to the dismay of the latter. "Disc jockeys could be instructed that where there is a question as to whether a record promotes the illegal drug usage, a responsible management official should be notified so he can exercise his judgment."[40] Station managers wondered how they would have the time to screen the 140 singles and eighty new albums released each week.

The FCC also scolded broadcasters for over-caution, "Some licensees have dropped all records referring to drugs — in erroneous reaction to our notice."[41] But then they immediately tightened the screws again by stressing, "the broadcaster could jeopardize his license by failing to exercise licensee responsibility in this area."[42] Most broadcasters did not want to challenge the FCC document for fear of losing their licenses. But there were certain groups who began to fight the FCC action. Neil Bogart of Buddah Records circulated a petition against the FCC, and it was signed by a number of FM programmers. Bogart explained, "No one ever got addicted to drugs by way of a phonograph needle." The Recording Industry Association of America petitioned the FCC to rescind the notice, claiming it had become "a rallying cry for arbitrary action by censors and vigilantes."[43]

Steve Leon went ahead and brought suit against the FCC action in U.S. District Court in Washington, as did a number of radio announcers who were fired for non-compliance, eight broadcasters, two college radio stations (Yale and University of the Pacific in California), and the ACLU. The National Coordinating Council on Drug Abuse and Information joined the suit. The council, headed by Dr. Thomas E. Price, was a private, non-profit agency that coordinated the activities of close to one hundred organizations.

Said Dr. Price of the Council's decision to sue, "To single out record lyrics, without facts, is not a constructive approach to solving the drug abuse problem."[44]

The suit held that the FCC was violating the First Amendment. The case was dismissed on April 14, 1971, when the judge ruled he lacked jurisdiction. Assistant U.S. Attorney Gil Zimmerman argued the plaintiffs had not tried all administrative channels to the agency and should have filed suit with the Appeals rather than the District Court.

The quashing of the suit was a direct blow to rock and roll. Young musicians and songwriters were put on the defensive as were record companies, broadcasters, disk jockeys, and all other media personnel. Some rock groups were blacklisted. As Lou Reed, of the "suspect" Velvet Underground put it, "All we need is a hit single, but nobody will play our songs."[45]

A *Rolling Stone* editorial asked in 1971 where the courageous and responsible men were who had become rich broadcasting rock and roll. Why were Metromedia and ABC executives not challenging the FCC when each had at least five FM "underground" rock stations in major U.S. cities.

It was left to the small group of original plaintiffs to carry on with their suit. In January 1973, the FCC anti-drug policy was upheld in an Appeals Court ruling. A further appeal to the Supreme Court was defeated in October by a seven-to-two vote. One of the dissenting judges, William O. Douglas commented, "The government cannot, consistent with the First Amendment, require a broadcaster to censor its music." But this is exactly what the government was doing. The court ruling came shortly after Vice-President Agnew's resignation for tax evasion.

This didn't put an end to the rock and roll drug lyric witch-hunt, however. In April 1972 the National Commission on Marijuana and Drug Abuse held a three-day hearing in Los Angeles. Several recording industry officials were called in to testify on the relation between rock music and drug use. Some made strong statements defending rock. Stanley M. Gortikov, president of the Recording Industry Association of America, lamented that rock music became "victim of distorted, stereotyped thinking, and critics sweepingly presume . . . that recordings purvey an evil influence on helpless and impressionable youthful listeners."[46] This commission came to no definite conclusion concerning the effects of rock music.

A last-ditch attempt to discredit rock and roll came from Senator James Buckley (R-N.Y.). In the summer of 1973, Buckley, with the aid of a two-man team, did some research on drug lyrics and reported his findings to Congress in November. Buckley's aim was to remind legislators that rock songs promoted drugs and to compel record companies to clean up lyrics or the government would have to do it for them. "I cannot help but feel," Buckley said, "that the recording of lyrics and the promoting of rock acts extolling the use of drugs, either directly or through code words, must have had their effect on the predominantly young audiences who listened to the records and flocked to rock concerts during the late 1960s."[47]

Buckley then quoted various music industry executives and associates who agreed that rock music caused drug use — people like Mike Curb. He continued, "Just because there is no clinically provable link between drug usage and drug-oriented rock music does not mean that we must discard the conclusions or intuitions of dozens of observers both in and out of the industry."[48]

Buckley insisted he wasn't blaming rock for the entire drug problem, but he felt it was a definite factor. Nor did he think music merely reflected society. He was certain that music was a "culture-former." Yet he admitted that "the majority of rock acts and songs did not deal with drugs."[49]

Buckley realized that the drug controversy "has become somewhat academic insofar as lyrics are concerned. Approving references to drugs have virtually disappeared from popular songs."[50] Nevertheless, Buckley wanted to see "appropriate measures and standards adopted to preclude a continuation or repetition of such abuses in the future."[51]

Unfortunately for Buckley, Congress was now to be preoccupied with weightier issues than rock and roll lyrics. The Watergate scandal was in full force, and nobody would have the time for an issue that had actually peaked two years previously. Rock and roll was left in peace by the government — at least for awhile.

Although government and industry pressure had played a part in the demise of drug songs, the end of the hippie era was the major factor. When the drug counterculture died out so did the drug lyrics which reflected this period.

From 1974 on the music would see a number of trends including glitter rock, disco, punk, and heavy metal. All would come under attack by the anti-rock establishment. By 1985 rock opposition would come full circle as "leerics" again became the target of a puritan crusade, just as they were in 1954–1955. The anti-rock forces would try their best to suppress the music, as they could not accept the obvious: do what they may, rock and roll was here to stay.

PART III
1974-1986

20

New Tunes, Old Fears

The 1970s and 1980s in America were characterized by a shift to the right. "Neo-conservatives" became the political in-crowd, there was a resurgent interest in traditional religion, and patriotism took on a certain glamor that had not been seen in the United States since the Second World War. This did not bode well for a rebellious music like rock and roll. The transition in music from 1973 to 1974 was marked by the final end of drug lyrics, that had faded away along with the entire hippie era. Drug lyrics would be close to nonexistent over the following dozen years even though critics would sometimes continue to damn the music in general terms for promoting violence, sexual promiscuity, and drug abuse. Such critics obviously didn't listen to much of the music.

Rock music itself saw various fads come and go, various genres wax and wane in popularity. In the fifties it was all just plain rock and roll. In the 1960s some slightly different names were added such as acid rock and psychedelic rock. In the 1970s and 1980s even more nomenclature came into vogue, such as punk rock, disco, heavy metal, glitter rock, androgynous rock, new wave, no wave, shock rock, and so on. The period began with the glitter rock of Elton John, the androgynous rock of David Bowie, and the shock rock of Alice Cooper. Then came disco, punk, and heavy metal, which reached its peak in the 1980s. Glitter rock came back with the likes of Michael Jackson, and androgyny resurfaced in the guise of Boy George and Prince. Straight old, garden variety rock continued also. The Who thundered on for most of the period, the Beach Boys continued to surf along, and the Rolling Stones rolled on, still bumping over everybody's toes as they went. New rockers like Bruce Springsteen hit superstar status in the mid-1980s.

The Rolling Stones had become a longstanding institution by the 70s and 80s. They showed no signs whatsoever of fading away, despite the hopes of their critics. A self-styled feminist writing in *Ms.* magazine declared her love for the Stones, something which aroused suspicion and wrath from her feminist friends. After noting all that was macho, evil, and misogynist in the Stones she decided that yes, a feminist could love them.[1] A writer for the *Christian Science Monitor* declared the group provided wrong answers to the questions about life which fans brought with them to Rolling Stones concerts. This writer felt the Stones had to take the responsibility for kids who imitated their stage personalities. The group didn't just play music, "they promote debauchery."[2] The religious magazine *Christianity Today* viewed them from that perspective and stated that no other rock group had so "consistently cultivated a more adolescent anti-Christian image than the Rolling Stones."[3] The writer wondered, in 1978, how long they could survive into middle age. The answer would seem to be indefinitely.

The Stones were, and are, all things to all people. Evil things that is. This may help to explain their enormous success. The Stones are the group everybody loves to hate. To the religious they represented the Devil, the anti-Christ. To feminists they were the ultimate demeaners of women. To the sexually uptight they were leering, carnal beasts out to ravish everyone's daughters. To those who regarded the youth drug scene with revulsion, the group was mainly perceived as an ensemble which smoked, drank, sniffed, snorted, and injected every substance known to man.

One of the high points of the thunderously evil influence of the Stones came in 1977 in Canada when the group, if not quite able to topple a government, was at least able to shake it. In March of that year Margaret Trudeau, wife of Canadian Liberal Prime Minister Pierre Trudeau cancelled some official engagements in Ottawa and flew to Toronto to attend a couple of Rolling Stones shows at a downtown nightclub over a period of two days. She and the Stones then flew, on separate planes, to New York, where she continued to associate with the group for a short time. She apparently had an affair with the Stones' Ron Wood.

An inteviewer for the Canadian Broadcasting Corporation asked her point blank if she was having an affair with either Wood or Jagger. Margaret said no but the CBC decided the whole bit was too risque and never showed it on the air. In general the Canadian press ignored the story or downplayed it, in deference to the prime minister. However, the British papers played it up in lurid detail. Prime Minister Trudeau said only that his wife's life was her own, even if "she loses me a couple of votes." Other politicians from the Liberal Party were less cool. Said one, "The nation's at stake here. . . . You can't have the PM's wife hanging out with the Stones, for crissakes."[4] Another commented that the whole episode didn't damage the Stones, but it did damage Pierre Trudeau. The Stones' Charlie Watts commented, tongue in cheek, "I wouldn't want my wife associatin' with us."

It was the clothes and physical appearance of the metal types, and others, which outraged many. These were groups like Kiss and Twisted Sister who were into leather, studs, semi-nudity, long wild hair, and lots of stage makeup. These aspects of a rock and roll group took on more and more importance. In the 1950s many stars like Presley and Gene Vincent adopted a tough image and wore the same type of clothes as their audiences. Others, such as Jerry Lee Lewis, Bill Haley, and Buddy Holly, dressed neatly, and more or less conservatively, in suits. Even the Beatles and the Stones dressed this way to start with. The Stones dropped that image quickly, and the Beatles followed. However, dress style was one of the last aspects of rock and roll to give up any trace of adult influence. From the mid-1960s onward rockers generally adopted the hippie uniform of long hair and bizarre clothing. They dressed like their audience and both the audience and the rockers had totally rejected adult norms and standards in terms of dress.

By 1974, however, the hippie uniform was virtually gone. From that point the clothing of youth and adults would tend to have more similarities than differences. Blue jeans, for example, were quickly adopted by adults for all kinds of leisure activities and teens moved completely away from bizarre clothing, with the exception of the punk faction. That musical genre represented, once again, a union of performer and audience, in terms of dress. Most teens though, had no specific discernible uniform. The costumes adopted by the heavy metal types were not likely to be seen in the streets as they were too outrageous for most to wear. With no leads to follow from the audience the groups struck out on their own to incorporate dress styles as an integral part of their act, not just an incidental. Because they were not getting much radio airplay, metal groups relied more on touring but it also left them less time to write and record new material. More effort went into making the concert a total event with sound, light, physical appearance. The 1970s and 1980s marked the first time for rock that musicians could not adopt a teen dress style which presented a distinct image. Thus, rockers from this period developed a wider variety of clothing styles to set themselves up as unique.

To illustrate the kind of effect that the appearance of these groups had on parents one only had to look at how Dick Clark would introduce the heavy metal group Kiss on one of his TV specials in 1978. Said Clark to the parents, "I say to the generation who wouldn't go to see Kiss in a trillion years, here's something interesting. This is what a portion of the audience — primarily your youngsters — is into. Don't be afraid, it's going to go away in three minutes. But look at it and try to understand it. This is what they look like in concert."[5]

Whatever was going on and whatever it was called, the adult establishment remained opposed. Educators continued to frown upon rock music through the 1980s despite the lack of evidence that it did any harm. A doctoral thesis was written by a student at the University of Iowa in 1976 which compared test scores of three groups of eighth grade students on a reading comprehension test. One group studied with loud rock music in the background, a second had quieter rock music in the background, while a third group had no music at all. The results found no difference between the groups in the scores they achieved on the test.[6]

In England, Professor Moelwyn Merchant, emeritus professor of English at Exeter University, accused disk jockeys of being the media's pornographers by debasing the emotion of love for youth, through the rock music they played. He refused to name any specific songs, or jockeys, but claimed that explicit sex was much less dangerous for teens than "the playing of pop records that lower the whole tone of human relationships."[7] This opinion was delivered at an education conference at Oxford University.

America's learned men were equally horrified. Allan Bloom, a professor at the University of Chicago, considered rock music to be a more important formative force on youth than home, school, or church, and then damned the music by saying, "The children have as their heroes banal, drug and sex-ridden guttersnipes who foment rebellion not only against parents but against all noble sentiments. This is the emotional nourishment they inject in these precious years. It is the real junk food."[8] Dr. John Parikhal was a social scientist and a consultant to a firm which in turn was a consultant to radio stations. Dr. Parikhal came up with the idea that rock music was aimed at young men who were afraid of sex. "The violent sex rhythm of rock reflects their frustration. Women can't relate to this."[9] He seemed to suggest that females didn't like rock music. Obviously the good doctor had never attended a Beatles concert or a Rolling Stones show.

The educators' fear of rock even extended to the elementary school level. Pupils who were bussed back and forth to H. L. Cottrell Elementary

School in Monmouth, Maine heard rock and roll music in the buses which turned to an area rock station. Parents began to complain to school officials about the lyrics of some of the songs, Madonna being one of the major culprits. In January of 1985 the school's principal denied the kids access to the "evil" music by ordering the bus driver to tune to another station, a middle-of-the-road one. John Seiler, the principal, claimed he "never banned rock 'n' roll."[10]

Many in the media continued to write about rock with all the scorn shown to it in the mid-50s. The comments displayed an ignorant mindlessness paralleling earlier periods. The prestigious periodical, *Atlantic Monthly* featured an article in 1977 in which the writer suggested it was time to put rock aside and move on to something that didn't involve "mass concerts attracting roving motorcycle gangs, and bottle throwing hoodlums." The author believed there was no reason a rock songwriter couldn't turn out three hundred songs in an afternoon, if he tried. She then declared, "I loathe rock music, . . . I detest the mindless lyrics, and I am repelled by the entire rock scene. I can't recall any comparable example of sustained and uniform nonsense in this century."[11]

In 1985 a large number of rock superstars staged charity concerts which were seen around the globe. The effort was called Live Aid and was to raise money for starving Africans. The rockers all donated their services. One might think this was the kind of activity that would redeem rock and roll. But it wasn't so. A syndicated columnist named Edgar Berman, writing for the Gannett News Service, was not impressed. He felt the sixteen-hour concert proved only that we had reached a new low on the evolutionary ladder. "For 160,000 rockers on two continents to pay $35 a ticket indicates that the taste and mentality of our adolescents are below the Neanderthal level." For Berman it was just "a cacophony of weird sounds and gestures" and he was alarmed that perhaps half of the world's population had tuned in to watch. "With rock addiction reaching epidemic proportions, if survival of the fittest really worked, only a cretinous society could evolve. This is probably the only state of affairs that could justify extinction of the species by nuclear war."[12]

Radio airplay has always been rock's mainstay and a survey by *Billboard* magazine in 1981 came to the conclusion that it was getting harder to get rock music played on the radio as many top forty stations moved to a middle-of-the-road format and were disinclined to play hard rock, or rock music with any kind of an edge. The situation was summed up by the remarks of Burt Stein, a vice president of Elektra/Asylum records. Stein said, "There is more reluctance on the top 40 level to play rock 'n' roll than I've seen in the 10 years I've been in the business."[13]

21

Punk Perverts,
Disco Sucks, Metal Menaces

Punk hit the rock scene like a rock though a plate glass window. Johnny Rotten and the Sex Pistols arrived in 1976, a time when opposition forces were fairly quiet. However, the arrival of punk rock quickly stirred the dozing critics and managed to arouse wrath and indignation almost everywhere. The anti-rock forces were moved to heights of bile and invective not reached since the first emergence of rock some twenty years before.

While punk was modelled on a couple of New York groups, it was in Britain that the movement flourished. A London man named Malcolm McLaren owned a Chelsea shop called "Let It Rock" where he sold 50s revival clothes. The New York Dolls, an American neo-punk transvestite group, came into the shop in 1974. One thing led to another and he became their manager and returned to New York with them. While in that city he was influenced by Richard Hell, a member of a group called Television. Hell wore spiky hair and ragged clothes deliberately held together with safety pins.

This managing adventure was short-lived as the Dolls broke up in the middle of a gig and McLaren returned to London in 1975. He renamed his store "Sex" and began dealing in "punk"-style clothes and was soon doing a thriving business. McLaren next formed a band that adopted the punk image. They were called the Sex Pistols. The lead singer was John Lydon, renamed Johnny Rotten in honor of his particularly bad teeth. McLaren singled out Lydon, who often hung around "Sex," for his "imbecilic screaming and obnoxious behavior." At first the group performed old Who and Small Faces tunes, but they quickly turned to writing their own material such as, "I'm a Lazy Sod" and "Pretty Vacant."

The Pistols played gigs all over London in late 1975 and into 1976 and soon came to be known as "the most vile and unmusical group ever to set foot on stage."[1] The Pistols' first concert was in November 1975 at a British art school. The school's social secretary found himself offended by the band's "caterwauling" and pulled the plug on the group after only five minutes. Onstage Rotten did nothing to dispel his image as he swore, spat, and butted out cigarettes on his arm. He also screamed "I hate you" at the audience and scratched his face with needles. The Pistols were a disorderly group. They were loud and arrogant, and they challenged authority. They did it all on a shoestring budget since they eschewed fancy equipment such as synthesizers and powerful wattage systems. They showed that almost anybody could form a band.

Punk music was a drastic change from a rock and roll scene that was in the doldrums. In America the top five best-selling album artists were: Abba, Beach Boys, Slim Whitman, Demis Roussos, and Glen Campbell.[2] The Sex Pistols were a force that could no longer be ignored. EMI, one of the largest and most prestigious record companies in England, signed them to a long-term lucrative contract in October 1976. While the rest of the industry shuddered, the Sex Pistols catapulted to worldwide notoriety almost immediately.

On December 1, 1976 they appeared on a Thames TV talk show program "Today." The Pistols had imbibed freely in the hospitality room while waiting to go on. Once on the air, the host, Bill Grundy, decided to goad them into living up to their hoodlum image. Grundy suggested they say something outrageous and Rotten obliged by calling Grundy "a dirty fucker" and a "fucking rotter." That was more than enough to have the TV station switchboard light up with angry callers and the furor was on. What was particularly galling to viewers was that the program aired at "teatime" which meant kids were watching. For his part in provoking the incident host Bill Grundy was suspended for two weeks without pay.

Media reaction was swift and horrified. The *Daily Mirror* wondered "who are these punks" and labeled them as "obnoxious, arrogant, outrageous." In the *Daily Mail* writer Shaun Usher wasn't concerned whether the Pistols had deliberately uttered dirty words, or been maneuvered into it. What mattered to Usher was that "by accident or design, millions of young people have been given a garish, malodorous beacon around which to rally."[3] The editor of *Music Week*, Brian Mulligan, saw a parallel between the Pistols and the early days of the Rolling Stones. But where the Stones went on to become legends based on their musical skills, Mulligan felt that punk rock was "unconcerned with musical competence."[4]

Even the prestigious London *Times*, which rarely dealt with such puerile pursuits as rock, felt compelled to run a long article on the subject of this "nasty and loutish" group and what they did in front of a television audience. The Pistols' behavior was considered so vile that a father was driven to actually kick his television set in while watching with his eight-year-old son, an impulse the *Times* found difficult not to sympathize with. In their article the paper refused to mention the Sex Pistols by name, calling them only "this pop group," so as not to give them anything that could be construed as free advertising. The paper mildly chastised Grundy, claiming they didn't like what he did but wondered who had decided to give air time to a group whose specialty was "not musical talent but outrage, anarchy and behavior calculated to disgust and shock."[5]

The paper also damned EMI and called on them, indirectly, to censor the Pistols' material. The *Times* was irate that as late as December 3, EMI was still issuing statements whereby, while they apologized for the TV show, they still basically claimed to be one hundred percent behind the Pistols. McLaren was quoted as saying that people didn't like punk because they felt threatened by it and that it was a movement which could not be stopped. The paper smugly felt it could indeed be stopped if EMI, public opinion, TV, record companies, hall owners, and so on all got together to make punk "the kind of rubbish that is not viable without their promotion, sink like a stone."[6]

In reality, virtually all these forces, and more, did align themselves against punk, but it did not sink. In the face of tremendous hostility it survived. The Sex Pistols clawed their way to the top, undeterred by all the pressures, at least initally. The *Times* failed to realize there was more to punk than the "grubby mass promotion" which they felt was the only reason for its being and success. The *Times* was probably wise in not writing much about rock since they knew very little of the subject.

Punks themselves fueled the controversy with quotes such as, "Razors are to punks what flowers were to hippies." *Variety* considered punk fans to be responding to "the concept of mindless violence, gutter language and crass excesses."[7] For them it was yet another pop "menace." Johnny Rotten scorned the established rock stars like the Who and the Stones, claiming they had sold out and were a part of the elitist establishment. The Pistols fanned the flames by refusing to apologize for the TV appearance. Of the record industry, Rotten commented, "The old are scared of us. . . . They don't want the change. It makes them irrelevant to what's going on now, and they know it."[8]

Punk was very much a political music, a music of despair and hopelessness. It flourished and spread in a country with a high youth unemployment rate. Britain was a country in decline and many youths saw no hope and no future. For the first time it seemed likely that a young person could grow up, grow old, and never be able to have a job. Many of the punkers came from lower classes — Rotten himself had been on welfare — and they were expressing their feelings through their music, as youth had done since rock began. This time it was a bitterness, an anger, a frustration and despair at a system which had no place for them, and apparently never would. It was this virulently anti-system attitude, this mocking and scorning of bourgeois societal values that brought down the wrath of the system on them. The system came to quickly portray them as a mindlessly violent group with little intelligence. This tactic masked the true political nature of the punkers.

After the TV fiasco other troubles plagued the Pistols. They had a nineteen-date tour set for December but suddenly received a rash of cancellations. One stop was to have been Darby but city officials in that town demanded the group perform privately for them before permission for the concert would be granted. The Pistols refused and the concert was cancelled. The concert tour was ultimately reduced to only three dates. The group had released just one single with EMI, "Anarchy in the U.K.," around the time of the TV show, and it too came under pressure. It had lyrics like, "I am an anti-Christ, I am an anarchist, Don't know what I want, but I know how to get it — I wanna destroy." Workers at the EMI pressing plant staged a wildcat strike, refusing to pack the Sex Pistols' record into sleeves, as a protest after the TV program. EMI persuaded the workers to end the strike after twenty-four hours.

Airplay was difficult to receive. The BBC wouldn't play the single nor would London's commercial station, Capitol. The Independent Broadcasting Authority reminded all stations to carefully consider what should be played in view of the section of the Broadcasting Act concerning material which might be offensive to the public. At the retail level most stores stocked the record but not all were happy. Laurie Kreiger, head of the Harlequin Records chain, said she was stocking the record but would rather not. She commented, "I think EMI ought to set some sort of standard and ban records like this. That is up to the record company and not the retailer."[9] Despite the difficulties it faced, "Anarchy in the U.K." made it into the top forty.

While EMI initally did come out in support of the Pistols, that quickly changed. Company officer Sir John Read spoke at the EMI shareholders meeting only a week or two after the TV incident and was clearly distancing the company from the punkers. Read remarked that EMI would have to carefully consider whether to release any more of the group's records and would try to control the Pistols' behavior. Read claimed EMI did not wish to be a censor, just to encourage restraint, and that "we should seek to discourage records that are likely to give offence to the majority of people."[10] The ax was poised to fall, and fall it did a few days into 1977 when EMI announced that the Pistols' contract had been terminated by mutual consent. EMI said they could no longer promote the group due to the publicity.

The final straw was reported to be a scene at London's Heathrow Airport where members of the Pistols engaged in "abusive and shocking behavior." There was said to be a public display of spitting and vomiting. EMI added that the "Anarchy" disk had been withdrawn from all markets, no more copies would be distributed, and all those in the warehouse would be recycled. Manager McLaren denied the termination was by mutual consent, but financially the group came away with an estimated twenty thousand pounds in severance pay.

In March of 1977 A&M Records signed the Pistols and announced a new single would be released. Other A&M artists complained about the Pistols being on the same label as them and Sex Pistol Sid Vicious got into a few fistfights which made the headlines. The company also found itself pressured by jockeys, distributors, and its own employees. A&M terminated the group within a week, never releasing any records. As A&M gave McLaren a severance check for twenty-five thousand pounds the manager commented the Sex Pistols were "like some contagious disease —untouchable."[11]

In May the punkers signed with Virgin Records and released "God Save the Queen." The record was released in time for Queen Elizabeth's Silver Jubilee and with lines like, "God save the Queen, she ain't no human being" it expressed less than admiration for the regent, and did not sit too well with the majority of Britons. An almost total ban was placed on the record. The BBC and the Independent Broadcasting Authority refused to play it on the grounds of "gross bad taste." Radio stations would not even carry ads for the record. BBC-TV's "Top of the Pops" termed the song "quite unsuitable." Major retail outlets such as Woolworth and Boots all refused to stock the record. At Virgin Records, press officer Al Clarke said: "There is an unanimity of bans. Every conceivable outlet for the disk is now closed for us and our only chance is to push it via press advertising and a poster campaign, but quite a few posters have been ripped down by supporters of royalty."[12] Despite the bans the record worked its way to the top of the charts. "Top of the Pops" had a top twenty board on its program and it marked the rise of the Pistols' tune by leaving a blank space wherever the song stood.

The backlash against punk continued that summer as members of four different punk groups were assaulted in the streets, in different incidents, including a knife attack on Johnny Rotten and another assault on Pistol member Paul Cook. Hugh Cornwell, member of the punk group the Stranglers, expressed the punk philosophy when he noted that angry music was being produced because people felt numbed and without purpose. Bernard Rhodes of the Clash commented, "There's no way Britain can take a turn for the better, and that's the information we're passing on, in everything we do — clothing, concerts backdrops, attitudes. All [the kids] are fit for is the rubbish jobs and they know it."[13]

The furor reached the House of Commons where British MP Marcus Lipton stated that if punk "was going to be used to destroy Britain's established institutions then it ought to be destroyed first."[14] Rotten once said that while playing a gig at Caerphilly a priest shouted at him that God could forgive anyone "but not punk rockers, they were the devil's children."[15] The media added to the storm with their own distortions. The *Sunday Mirror*, the *Daily Mirror*, and the *Sun* all claimed the record called the Queen a moron, when the line actually went "A fascist regime made you a moron." The newspaper *Sunday People* termed punk "sick, dangerous and sinister" and claimed the punk creed glorified "violence, filth, sadism and rebellion. It defies all authority, despises family loyalties, revels in sexual freedom and even calls for a 'Hitler' in Britain."[16]

Rolling Stone did a long piece on the Pistols under the heading, "Rock is sick and living in London."[17] The Pistols had been banned from performing at almost all of the major rock venues and most other punk groups had suffered similar bans. The Greater London Council had established such stringent rules as to prevent free concerts scheduled separately by the Jam and Johnny Thunder and the Heartbreakers. The council, however, denied there was any blacklist against punkers.

Later that year the group released an album called "Never Mind the Bollocks — Here's the Sex Pistols." As with all their other material it found itself banned from airplay. Nevertheless, it was a commercial success and was charted at number one four weeks after its release. The media even refused to carry ads for the album. These commercials were designed specifically to give no offense but were barred from commercial radio and television. According to Virgin Records the ban was imposed by the Independent Broadcasting Authority (IBA) after being initially approved. A spokesman for the IBA confirmed they had "no technical objection" to the ads but felt that advertising the album might give offense. The IBA advised both the Independent Television Companies Association (ITCA) and the Association of Independent Radio

Contractors to "consider carefully" whether they wanted to advertise the album. Not surprisingly, both these bodies decided they didn't want to. The ITCA's deputy head of copy clearance, Stuart Ruttledge, also said he had no objection to the ad, "It was the record itself we objected to. . . . Some parts of the lyric are unspeakable."[18]

The poster which advertised the album in record shops also came under attack. Several record stores displaying the poster were charged with an "indecent display." The offending word was "bollocks." However, in the first case to come to trial an English professor defined the word as meaning "nonsense," and the case was dismissed.[19]

Early in 1978 the Pistols made their first U.S. tour. Initially they were denied visas by the American Embassy in London, ostensibly on the grounds of minor criminal records. The State Department in Washington later overruled the Embassy and granted the visas. During the tour Sid Vicious was assaulted a couple of times, once in San Antonio, Texas by a non-fan who called the group "sewer rats with guitars." The *New York Times* was not happy, particularly with the wide media coverage extended to a group whose sole claim to fame was "bad taste" and sensationalism. The *Times* felt the media, both U.S. and British, had failed in its ethical responsibility and had devoted too much media attention to the Pistols. Of the American tour the paper noted, "Unfortunately the sick violence and obscenity the group employs . . . has come to the United States. And almost as objectionable as the group's raunchy remarks and performances is the wide public exposure the news media have lavished on the punk rock musicians."[20] This editorial was an example of the attention which the *Times* decried so loudly. The tour itself drew the expected bad reviews and not very big crowds.

From that point on things came undone for the Pistols. Johnny Rotten split from the group in January 1978, claiming he'd had enough. He formed a couple of other bands but with no real success. In the fall of 1978 Sid Vicious was accused of murdering his girlfriend. Released on bail he was dead on February 2, 1979, the result of a heroin overdose. It marked the end of the Sex Pistols, at least as any kind of controversial force. Punk rock disrupted the rock industry but didn't really alter it. Groups like the Pistols found themselves thrown against their anti-materialistic philosophy if they became successful. And if they didn't become successful they couldn't get their message delivered. With its more class-conscious and structured society, punk made a bigger impact in Britain than in the United States. Another factor was the much higher unemployment rate in Britain. Punk remained a distinct part of the rock scene through the mid-1980s but in a peripheral and underground role. U.S. punks didn't display the same kind of angry rage as the British groups and have been largely ignored, except by their fans, always a minority in the universe of rock and roll listeners.

When EMI first signed the Sex Pistols the A&R manager remarked, "Here at last is a group with a bit of guts for younger people to identify with, a group that parents actually won't tolerate. And it's not just parents that need a little shaking up, it's the music business itself."[21] In the case of the Sex Pistols the statement was all too true, and brought about the downfall of the band.

Compared to the Pistols other controversies seemed mild, but there were others. The disco craze, which reached the peak of its short-lived popularity in the late 1970s was the subject of considerable bile for a time. Columnist Russell Baker of the *New York Times* called the music "chloroform on a 12-band record."[22] Others called it monotonous, predictable, repetitive, and muzak for the trendy. One of those who despised disco the most of all was a Chicago disk jockey named Steve Dahl who quit his job with that city's WDAI-FM late in 1978 when the outlet switched to an all-disco format. Dahl resigned in disgust at this turn of events and he soon turned up as a jockey on Chicago's WLUP-FM, an all-rock station which specialized in new wave, as punk was then being called.

Dahl staged a joint promotion with the American League baseball team, the Chicago White Sox, whereby a fan was admitted to a ball game for just ninety-eight cents if he brought along a disco record. For a few months during his WLUP show Dahl had happily been scraping a needle across disco records, cuing in the sound of an explosion, and then smashing the record over the air. The joint promotion by the radio station and the ball team took place July 12, 1979 at Comiskey Park and was billed as a "disco demolition" rally. Between ten and twenty thousand disco records were collected at the turnstiles. In between games (it was a twinight doubleheader between the White Sox and the Detroit Tigers) the records were placed in a container in the middle of the field and blown up. This got the crowd excited and massive numbers invaded the field, lit bonfires, and tore up lumps of ground, all the while chanting "disco sucks." About fifty thousand fans attended the game and applauded those on the field. More than an hour after the second game had been scheduled to start, thousands of people were still roaming around the playing field and the second game had to be postponed because the field was deemed unplayable. Numerous fights broke out and police made a number of arrests.

Dahl called the whole trend "disco dystrophy" and admitted hating disco with a passion. He had recruited ten thousand like-minded souls, by his count, into a "disco destruction army" whose members regularly went to local discos and demanded that other styles of rock and roll be played. When the Village People played Chicago, Dahl got the winners of a contest giving away one hundred tickets to write "Disco Sucks" on marshmallows and take them to the show and throw them at the Village People. Dahl hoped his own campaign of smashing disco records would spread and he had discussed the idea with a radio programming consultant "about doing a national hookup, to blow up disco records all over the country."[23]

Dahl was not alone in his hatred of disco. Commenting on the ballpark promotion, Greg Gillespie, program director of Denver's KAZY considered it "great, as long as no one was killed or brutally beaten."[24] His own station was continuing its campaign whereby listeners called the station to vote for their least favorite disco record. The "winning" record was then destroyed on the air. In Pasadena, California jockey Darryl Wayne of KROQ had as his show's motto "Abolish Disco in our Lifetime." A daily feature on his program was taking calls from the audience about the best ways to destroy disco. Suggestions ranged from "total pacifism to total violence" and included "cut off the Bee Gees' estrogen supply."[25] Another idea called for the records to be buried at the beach. New York's station WXLO held a "no disco weekend." This was after a successful "no Bee Gees weekend" where the station claimed seventy percent of their callers supported the campaign.

Racism made up some of the disco hostility and in many ways was a repeat of the racist sentiments which surfaced against rock and roll in the middle 1950s. This attitude can be best seen in the comments of Harvey Ward, a director-general of the Rhodesian Broadcasting Company. Rhodesia didn't allow disco on its airwaves and Ward commented: "I'm not a fan of disco. I find it mindbending. . . . It's a contributing factor to epilepsy. It's the biggest destructor in history to education. It's a jungle cult. It's what the Watusis do to whip up a war. What I've seen in the discos with people jogging away is just what I've seen in the bush."[26]

By the end of 1982 disco was dead but anti-black sentiments were not. Many felt that album-oriented radio stations (AOR) had "bleached" the air and refused to play most black music. It was a problem felt to be leftover from the disco backlash. AOR programmers admitted their material was almost all white but claimed it wasn't racism at all, that it was what its listeners wanted. Chuck DuCoty of WIYY in Baltimore said his audience wouldn't "go for anything funk-oriented." The program director at Pittsburgh's WYDD, Mike Perkins, was more open. He said if he played something like "Sir Duke" by Stevie Wonder he had people calling who said, "Get that nigger music off the air."[27]

Heavy metal had been around since the late 1960s, went into a decline, and then reached new heights of popularity in the mid-1980s. As a musical style it was played loudly and relied mainly on guitars. It featured performers in leather, studs, chains, outrageous clothes, and makeup. To its defenders it was hard rock, the only youth music outside of punk which contained the idea of rebellion, as for example, Twisted Sister's "We're Not Gonna Take It." To its opponents it was a lot of other things, such as sexist, violent, satanic.

The resurgence of metal was due mainly to its exposure on MTV. MTV "discovered" metal in 1984. Metal's market share was eight percent in 1983, and then rose dramatically to twenty percent in 1984.[28] This big surge in heavy metal was attributed to the idea that it was a very visual form of music and thus ideally suited to MTV. It also brought forth a wave of criticism. *Rolling Stone* magazine duly noted the surge in popularity and was appalled that metal had once again reared its "ugly head," its "leather-clad, lipstick smeared image." According to the magazine this new wave of metal trafficked "in some of rock's stupidest and ugliest notions."[29]

Metal had never received much radio play through the 1970s due to its outlaw nature. Bands had relied on massive amounts of touring to keep their fans, so the MTV exposure was a boon to the music. However, after only a year of intense hype for metal, MTV announced, early in 1985, that it would significantly cut back on the number of heavy metal videos they would program. While MTV claimed it wanted to program more music on the "cutting edge" the metal gap was taken up by an increase in old videos, and "pretty boy" top forty videos. The real reason for metal cutbacks, as most of the industry saw it, was that MTV was bowing to the pressure of various conservative watchdog groups who had been complaining. As John Ivany, editor of *Hit Parader* magazine, noted, "Let's get it straight. If MTV owners have concluded that heavy metal is bad for business (advertisers don't like it), and bad for the public image (the church, politicians, and mommy and daddy don't like it), then kill it."[30]

Metal groups were the targets of religious and other civic groups as well. More than one city had tried to ban Ozzy Osbourne concerts and Kiss was accused of "leading kids in service to Satan." When *Billboard* magazine sought opinions from civic groups, both the Moral Majority and the National Federation of Decency refused to speak for the record.

However, Jeff R. Steele, a Baptist minister who toured the country giving seminars on the negative effects of rock and roll, did comment that, "It (heavy metal) is sick and repulsive and horrible and dangerous. . . . It's terrible when one of these groups can sell a million records."[31] Steele didn't like any rock music. In fact he felt the sexual material from such nonmetal rock stars like Marvin Gaye's "Sexual Healing" or Olivia Newton-John's "Physical" did even more damage than all the "Ozzy Osbournes and AC/DCs put together."

The MTV cutback had its effect as the metal share of the record market dropped back to fifteen percent in the first quarter of 1985. Record companies turned to other forms of promotion such as more in-store display material and more ads in metal magazines to counteract the MTV action. As RCA's market research director Alan Grunblatt said, "We've got a situation now where radio doesn't play heavy metal records and MTV has cut back drastically on its heavy metal playlist."[32]

This decline in heavy metal produced no tears for critics, one of whom summed up their attitudes in his definition of the music:

> pimply, prole, putrid, unchic, unsophisticated, antiintellec-
> tual, dismal, abysmal, terrible, horrible and stupid music,
> barely music at all, death music, dead music . . . music made
> by slack-jawed, alpaca-haired, bulbous-inseamed imbeciles in
> jack-boots and leather and chrome for slack-jawed, alpaca-
> haired, downy-mustachioed imbeciles . . . a perversion of the
> rock 'n' roll dream so grotesque that the sixties experienced "sur-
> vivor," no less the thinking and adult, must recoil in complete
> moral disgust, the thought of reading about it more repellent
> perhaps than the utterly repellent thought of listening to it or,
> God forbid, seeing it.[33]

22

The Evil Beat
Will Make You Weak

The idea that rock and roll music produces hearing loss continued through the 1970s, despite the lack of scientific evidence. It was the ongoing manifestation of the intense dislike of the music by the adult establishment and their determination to cast aspersions on rock for one reason or another.

During this period one of the contentions was that the wattage used by groups had increased enormously. Where a band used one thousand watts in 1968, a 1975 group might carry up to eight thousand watts. It was suddenly claimed that bands of the 1960s, like the Who, were actually not very loud and operated at ninety to ninety-five decibels, a level that could be handled.[1] The implication was that the newer groups were certain to damage hearing. One observer felt the only way to keep the myth going, in the face of no deafness, was to credit the newer bands with an awesomely increased level of power. This had the impact of keeping the threat of hearing loss fresh, but it also called for a large dose of revisionist history for the Who have always been considered one of the loudest of the loud, playing real thunder.

Scare tactics continued in the media. Felix J. Darcy, an industrial hygiene consultant with the Washington State Department of Labor and Industries, measured the noise level in some bars and nightclubs. He claimed that rock musicians were exposed to sound levels ranging from two to five times greater than the limits established by the federal government. Darcy tested no one's hearing, but that didn't prevent him from drawing the conclusion that "severe hearing loss could be expected to occur in some band members." All this appeared under the rather daunting headline, "Documentation: rock music is hazard."[2]

At Pennsylvania State University a graduate student in audiology named Cathleen Anne Malatino wrote a master's thesis on the issue. She measured sound levels at indoor and outdoor rock concerts and came to the rather obvious conclusion that indoor concerts were louder than those held outdoors. Malatino was alarmed by her findings of noise levels which exceeded those set by the federal government. She felt rock fans should be warned about the dangers and groups should play more quietly, perhaps even distributing ear plugs to concertgoers. Malatino tested no one's hearing either, but she subscribed to the notion that damage was taking place and her findings led her to just one conclusion, "indoor rock concerts are endangering hearing."[3] The idea of ear plugs was taken up by *Billboard* who declared that "discotheques may be producing many persons with impaired hearing."[4] The article then discussed the various types of ear protectors available and their cost, durability, and so on.

The whole issue was deemed important enough to make it to national TV when a program aired on the CBS television network show "30 Minutes," in November of 1978. Broadcast on a Saturday afternoon and aimed at a youthful audience, the program was a panel discussion on the health hazards of rock, which in this case meant hearing. Included on the panel were members of the rock bands Meat Loaf and Blue Öyster Cult. The rockers limited themselves to comments about rock needing to be played loud to achieve its effect and that audiences expected the music to be loud. Unfortunately they didn't challenge any of the statements from the experts, which were as unfounded as ever.

Panel member Dr. Joseph Nadol of the Massachusetts Eye and Ear Hospital claimed that anything over ninety decibels had a "significant" chance of damaging some people's ears; that amplified noise (rock music) was worse than nonamplified noise, and that the most dangerous amplified instrument was the guitar (an obvious mainstay of rock bands). Dr. Nadol added that of those "hooked" on rock clubs, sixteen percent risked "some degree of permanent hearing loss."[5] The panel moderator, Betsy Aaron, who was anything but neutral, opened the program with the alarmist statement that that "sound of rock may be making you deaf."[6] Nadol backed up his numbers with no evidence and was simply reiterating what others had said before him. To Dr. Nadol and all the others who argued the same point, all one could ask was, where were the multitudes of hearing impaired they had been predicting for over a decade? There weren't any. Dr. Nadol and company would also have to explain how it was that rock musicians had no hearing impairment. He would have to explain how it could be that all four original members of the Rolling Stones had been playing loud, thundering rock for well over twenty years at that point, and not one of them had suffered any hearing damage. Logically no one was at greater risk than the musicians themselves. The louder and longer they have played the higher the risk should be. It was one of the many flaws in the arguments of those who said rock music damages hearing. These flaws destroy the validity of the theory, but they don't make it disappear.

One conversion did take place in the scientific community however, and that was Dr. David Lipscomb who had been among the first to get the ball rolling in the late 1960s. Lipscomb moved from a position that rock and roll music caused hearing damage, to that it probably caused it, to that it probably didn't. The audiology and speech professor at the University of Tennessee in Knoxville outlined his conversion in *Audio* magazine in 1976. He first recapped his earlier experiments including the one with the solitary guinea pig who gave his ear, and life, in the battle against rock. This time Lipscomb noted, of that experiment, that it wasn't possible to generalize these findings to "human response." With regard to his hearing test of university students and the resultant high frequency hearing impairment that he found, Lipscomb suggested that any one or more of loud recreational sound sources such as sport shooting, or motorcycling, plus the increase in "community noise levels" would have to be considered. In those experiments Lispcomb had found more hearing loss in males than in females but claimed to not understand why females had "tougher" ears than the males. This finding itself did not support the idea that rock causes hearing loss since females attended rock concerts, discos, and so on, in at least equal numbers as males. Other loud sports, however, such as shooting and motorcycling, were participated in more by males than females.

What caused Lipscomb to rethink his position was the fact, as he noted, "that rock musicians have suffered surprisingly little hearing loss."[7] He cited the study which showed forty of forty-two rock musicians had normal hearing and commented that while those results were "not a popular concept among their colleagues," the evidence showed rockers "to have an inordinately small degree of hearing loss when compared with other young persons who are engaged in high noise pursuits (industrial workers, etc.)."[8] Lipscomb was drawn to agree with the conclusion from that experiment that rock music likely posed no particular threat to the hearing of rock and rollers.

He remained puzzled by the apparent paradox that while exposure conditions led him to conclude that the musicians should suffer hearing damage, they didn't. To try and explain this anomaly Lipscomb proposed a psychological theory whereby whether noise did any damage depended on how stressful it was to the listener. As an example he suggested two men working side-by-side in a noisy factory. If one hated the job and the noise, he might suffer ear damage, while the coworker might suffer none if he like the job, enjoyed the work, and accepted the noise as part of it. Since rock musicians had created their own music, enjoyed it, and didn't find the situation at all stressful, Lipscomb surmised his theory might explain why they suffered little or no hearing damage, in the face of "common sense." Lipscomb was not ready to totally discard the idea that "some ear damage is occurring" due to rock music, but he was close.[9] Dr. Lipscomb did deserve credit for essentially reversing his position, in the face of no supporting evidence, and trying to rethink the situation in different terms — something that scientists all too frequently were loathe to do.

The 1980s saw a waning of the "rock will make you deaf" notion but the slack was taken up by a number of other examples and theories about the bad effects of rock and roll on an individual's health. If rock wouldn't wreck your hearing then it might turn you into, as a composite picture, a gay, hyperactive, physically weak, juvenile delinquent; someone prone to errors, reduced output, and suffering a nervous breakdown. Richard Sinnot was the last censor of the city of Boston, out of office by 1982. He had censored a variety of media such as films and live theater and had worked for Boston in that capacity since the 50s. He had once tried to close the rock musical "Hair" but was soundly defeated by the courts. Part of his duties as censor required him to attend rock concerts. In 1982 Sinnot applied for a disability pension claiming that attending rock concerts had shattered his nerves. He specifically cited a Who concert at which he said he was "terrified and in constant fear of bodily injury."[10]

A study from the University of Ankara, Turkey came up with the startling conclusion that prolonged exposure to loud noise, such as found in discos, "causes homosexuality in mice and deafness in pigs."[11] The researcher feared that disco music would make no exception for humans and that the music should be banned. Other intriguing questions from this study, such as why pigs retained their sexual identities and why mice didn't go deaf, remained, alas, unanswered. For obvious reasons this theory never really caught on. But the same can't be said for other theories on the harmful effects of rock music which were almost equally "unusual."

One such theory was put forth by Dr. John Diamond, a New York physician. In 1977 he was president-elect of the International Academy of Preventive Medicine and outlined his ideas in a speech to the Dallas Athletic

Association. He claimed that rock music was the most serious form of noise pollution in the country, more destructive than industrial noise pollution. Not all rock was bad, only that which employed an "anapestic" beat, where the last beat was the loudest, such as "da da DA." An example he gave was the Rolling Stones' "Satisfaction." According to Diamond this kind of rock music could "heighten stress and anger, reduce output, increase hyperactivity, weaken muscle strength and could play a role in juvenile delinquency."[12]

Diamond theorized that the music may have worked its evils by causing a breakdown in the synchronization of the two sides of the brain, although he had done no electroencephalograms on subjects. He did a field study in a New York factory which played rock music all day. When the music was switched to non-rock, Diamond claimed plant productivity increased fifteen percent while the number of errors made decreased by the same percentage. Diamond also claimed muscle strength was reduced by rock music. When a waltz or rhumba was played the muscles stayed strong but when the evil rock was played "every muscle in the body can become weakened. It is like the difference of being able to lift 40 pounds or 15 pounds."[13]

In 1980 Dr. Diamond was still promoting an expanded form of his theory and it was incorporated into a book he had written, *Your Body Doesn't Lie*. His ideas were being picked up by the popular press. He claimed that the anapestic beat was disruptive because it was the opposite of a heartbeat and thus set up a stress on the body's normal rhythm. It was this rock rhythm that was bad, volume had no effect. Diamond had had time to do more research and claimed to have defined the history of this evil beat. It was invented by the late Motown studio drummer, Benny Benjamin, and was first heard on the Supremes' 1962 release, "You Can't Hurry Love." He cited the worst offenders, in terms of playing the anapestic beat, as the Rolling Stones, the Doors, the Band, Janis Joplin, Queen, America, Led Zeppelin, and Alice Cooper. The Beatles were absolved as they didn't use the anapestic beat.

Diamond claimed he wasn't against rock music per se but he had tested twenty thousand pieces of music and found this evil rhythm only in rock music, with three exceptions. It appeared at the conclusion of Stravinsky's "Rite of Spring," Ravel's "La Valse," and in a piece of Haitian voodoo drumming.[14]

In his lab Diamond tested the effects of the music by measuring the strength in the deltoid muscle of the arm. A normal man could withstand about forty-five pounds of pressure on the arm, but Diamond claimed this was reduced by a third if the anapestic beat was played in the background. He further warned that the beat was "very seductive and even addictive with those exposed to the beat craving more of it even as it makes them weaker."[15] The doctor claimed he was not seeking a ban on the beat or even warning stickers, only that he felt people should be warned they wouldn't be as "strong and attentive" as normal when the evil rock beat was played. Diamond surmised that, "Rock music is not going to kill anybody, but I really doubt if Mick Jagger is going to live as long as Pablo Casals or Segovia."[16]

In Russia doctors came to the conclusion that rock and roll had a "tremendously harmful psychic effect." Addressing a Young Communist League rally the medical men announced that rock "noise" was "like a series of alarm signals, causing surges of concentrated energy which must be released somewhere."[17] And where it went was clear to Russian doctors who held up Western rock concerts as an example. The energy was chanelled into the brawls and fights which were a feature of almost all such concerts. They claimed that many fans at such concerts went so far as to have convulsions or hysteria. This attack by the Soviet medical establishment fitted in nicely with a general crackdown on rock in that country.

Rock and roll as a health hazard focused on the idea that the music could damage hearing, at least in the early years. As time passed and a generation of deaf fans and musicians simply could not be found, the focus shifted somewhat to other forms of health hazards which may be induced by rock. Equally without foundation, they have nonetheless continued to surface. Rock rolls on and the theories get curiouser and curiouser.

23

The Decadent Music Abroad

Two decades and more of rock music had blunted most official pressures from the rulers of foreign countries to bar the music, at least outside of the communist bloc. A few countries still struggled against the music but most had given up the fight. It was an impossible task to prevent rock from infiltrating a country.

One of the countries not yet ready to cry "uncle" in the face of rock and roll was South Korea. Korean songs had been censored since 1966 but it was 1975 before censors tackled rock and roll. That year the Art and Culture Ethics Committee of the South Korean Federation of Cultural Organizations tried to purge popular music of what they termed "decadent foreign influences." To this end they issued a list of 261 blacklisted songs which were no longer to be played in that country. The songs were mostly American and mostly rock and psychedelic. They were banned on the grounds that they were morally and politically harmful to South Korean youth. The committee was nominally a private group but since most of its budget came from the government its policy could be taken as official.

South Korean president Park Chung Hee stated that the country had to be more selective and discriminating in "absorbing foreign cultural influences." The government campaign went beyond banning objectionable music and included a campaign against other aspects of youth culture such as long hair and marijuana smoking. Police were then arresting any young Korean with long hair and giving them haircuts on the spot.

The chairman of the committee, Cho Yon Hyon, tried to maintain the fiction that his group was independent by claiming his committee's actions had nothing to do with government policy. Cho rationalized his action by saying his country's situation was unique in that it had to live with the ever-present threat of a communist invasion from the north and that South Koreans were involved in a life and death struggle. In the face of this, youth culture was alienating youth from their public duties.

Cho also claimed the country faced an upsurge in youth crimes and that many adults had criticized Seoul radio stations for "saturating" their programs with "mind-numbing" music from the West. He added, "The uninhibited theme of aggressive sexual behavior contained in the banned songs clashes with traditional Confucian mores of South Korean society. What we want is a healthy, refined culture acceptable to all segments of the population."[1] The five radio stations in Seoul previously devoted four or five hours a day to U.S. rock music but found this time cut in half by the ban.

The committee had generated the list of 261 banned songs over a period of two months. Using a team of three translators, some thirty-seven hundred songs were translated into Korean and scrutinzed to see if there were any political or obscene messages. Anything considered subversive, revolutionary, or antisocial by Korean standards was gone. From this group the banned songs were selected. Banned under the subversive and antiwar category were "Sometime in New York City" by John Lennon and Yoko Ono, "The C.I.A." by the Fugs, and a number of songs by Black Sabbath. Barred as leftist was Eric Clapton's "I Shot the Sheriff." Under the obscene label was "Me and Mrs. Jones" by Billy Paul and a number of songs by Elvis Presley. Everything by Alice Cooper was banned, as the committee called him "subversive, decadent, obscene and freaky."

Young people were said to have had little reaction to the ban, perhaps because they could still tune in to the American Armed Forces Radio Network which was not affected by the government's action. According to President Park the country had to reject these "bad" influences and reject them "at their very inception." Adults who had complained about the "music pollution" were said to be delighted with the ban.

The fall of the shah in Iran was followed shortly by the new regime's attack on rock which was termed an "immoral hobby." The campaign was directed against the shops which sold tapes for about $4. These businesses violated all copyright laws as they were bootleg copies of tapes from the United States. Business was said to be booming to such an extent that other entrepreneurs were making low-quality bootlegs from the bootlegs and sold these for $2 at unlicensed stalls which sprang up on city streets.

242

Some of these were disco tapes which featured "pouting blonde" models on the labels. This particularly infuriated the regime which viewed them as "portraits against public and moral chastity." The Islamic fundamentalists cited the Koran as a justification for their anti-rock campaign and through one of their official bodies, the Center for the Campaign Against Sin, had "decreed an end to the selling and reproduction of vulgar music."[2] Sellers of the tapes were given a couple of weeks to find employment that didn't offend Islamic morality.

The group Kiss ran afoul of West German authorities in 1979. For its logo on posters and T-shirts the group used runic letters for *ss* which were close to those used by the Nazis. In May of 1979 a Bavarian politician, running for office, sported a "Stop Strauss" button. Strauss was the Bavarian president and the button also used a runic *ss* at the end of the name. The politician was found guilty of "glorifying Nazi symbols." At the trial the defense lawyer had pointed out that Kiss had toured Germany before using the same runic double *s*. This caused a state attorney in Bremen to confiscate some Kiss records and for the group to alter its logo for their 1980 tour of West Germany.

Politicians in West Germany found themselves upset again in the summer of 1985, this time over music video clips. Some of the members of the Christian Democratic (CDU) Party wanted some kind of crackdown on the clips which were felt likely to "corrupt" young people. Main offenders were those from the United States and Britain and the group urged the federal office which already inspected films on video, to examine these clips and take action. According to one CDU parliamentarian, Roland Sauer, the artists on these clips were "tying to outdo each other with spectacular gags, trespassing the limits of sexual violence."[3] A 1986 release called "Jeanny" by Austrian artist Falco, was banned by eleven major radio stations in West Germany again on the grounds of "tasteless and offensive lyrics." The song dealt with the rape and murder of a young girl.

Czechoslovakia clamped down on rock when fourteen rockers were arrested and charged with "causing a public disturbance and nuisance in an organized manner." The musicians were members of two western style rock bands, the DG 307 and Plastic People of the Universe. The groups had formed during a period of liberalism in that country which came to an end in 1976. Plastic People last performed in February of that year at a wedding which was raided by the police who searched the homes of the Plastic People and confiscated tapes and compositions. Several months later four of the Plastic People were sent to jail with sentences ranging up

·to eighteen months for giving a "grossly vulgar performance."[4] The following year the dissident group Charter 77 claimed that rock musicians had been banned in that country if their hair was too long, if they or their audiences were dressed in "unacceptable" clothing, or if the lyrics of their songs were not approved. Musicians also had to have government approval and had to pass qualifying tests. Those exams tested not just musical theory but political leaning and a lot of the most popular rockers were "unable to pass on either count."[5]

East Germany issued another of its regular warnings about the right wing influences of western rock through the major youth magazine of that country, *Melodie und Rhythm*. The magazine cautioned East German singers not to imitate singers from the West or use their songs, claiming these musicians sought to force attention on right wing political power groups "and to use their influence on mass consciousness in favor of the capitalistic powers."[6] Examples given were "Rasputin" by Boney M, and the Village People's "In The Navy."

The East Germans weren't alone in giving bizarre interpretations to the meaning of rock. Czechoslovakia went a step further when they studied punk rock and decided it had been invented by capitalist manipulators who used it to implant in the minds of young people "the conviction that one should identify with life under capitalism and not revolt."[7]

East Germany did allow West German rock star Udo Lindenberg to appear at an East Berlin concert, a rarity for that country. Lindenberg was not allowed to do his top hit called "Special Train to Pankow" a satire in which East German leader Erich Honecker was portrayed as a closet rock fan who slipped into a leather jacket and locked himself in the bathroom to listen to Western rock music. The West German was allowed to sing three songs at the concert. Presumably that was all he had in his repertoire that was acceptable to the authorities.

Poland's homegrown rockers proved to be more of a nuisance to the state than anything that might be imported. The country's top rock group, Lady Pank, was banned from performing in 1986 after lead singer Jan Borysewicz exposed himself and used vulgarity during a concert attended by forty thousand fans.

By the end of the 1970s China had adopted a more open-door policy with the West and many foreign tapes, records, and television sets came into the country. Western music provided a welcome relief from officially sanctioned music from the days of the Cultural Revolution when the hit parade contained such tunes as, "The Nightsoil Collectors are Descending the Mountain" and "Medical Teams in Tanzania." It also provoked the government to take a harder line against rock. A Communist youth paper, *Quingnian Bao*, attacked the music and particularly criticized the Soviet Union for the prevalence of rock there. The conclusion was that rock and roll, a strange and crazed music, was a "product of decadent Western capitalism" and had "no place in a developing socialist country."[8]

Such advice wasn't sufficient to stem the flow and popularity of rock. In the spring of 1982 the Chinese government moved against this "bourgeois poison" by banning the import and sale of records and prerecorded tapes, with their "decadent and incoherent content," for commerical purposes. Individuals could still buy small quantities of tapes and records for personal use, but only after the authorities had inspected and approved such materials.

While Mozart and Beethoven remained available on the open market, only the most innocuous of Western pop music, such as "Jingle Bells," could be purchased at record stores. People defied the ban by purchasing tapes on the black market and organizing dances in their homes. A baker in Shanghai was sentenced to fifteen days in jail for charging twenty-five cents admission to illegal dances in his home; his tape recorder was also confiscated. Police also raided private disco parties held by the children of government officials. University students were ordered to turn in all of their foreign music tapes.[9]

State-run radio and television had blacked out the Beatles for years, although John Lennon's murder got ample coverage. But the new menace was harder to control. Officials worried that the Western lyrics which often suggested individual freedoms might somehow disrupt the highly regimented and controlled Chinese society. In June 1982 the government issued, through the People's Music Press, a guide titled *How to Distinguish Decadent Music*. The booklet explained the perils of the "quivering" rhythm, its unclear melodies, and its drunken pronunciation. Dancing to the music was called the same as having "nervous convulsions." With regard to rock dances the guide noted that, "rock music mixes with drinking, drug abuse, violence and homosexuality. A rock dance actually is mad chaos at which people riot. For this reason, police are present at every rock dance to prevent an accident."[10] The music was said to have no artistic value and existed to meet "the needs of people's negative spiritual life in capitalist society. . . . It also meets the needs of capitalists who make money."[11] By 1986 top leader Deng Xiaping seemed to be taking a more relaxed attitude to Western culture. Chinese students were dancing to Michael Jackson tunes and rock and roll was slowing becoming acceptable as China's open-door policy escalated.

The Soviet Union continued to be the country most strenuously engaged in the battle against rock and roll. By the early 1970s a small Russian rock industry had taken hold, although rigid controls were maintained. Homegrown rock groups were monitored for their lyricis, politics, movements, and dress and were purged of anything considered "morally, politically or sexually suggestive." They were urged to write and perform songs on topics such as space heroes or economic achievements. On television they weren't allowed to play too loud and were allowed to play no more than fifteen percent Western material at concerts.[12] Not surprisingly, "official" rock didn't really become big.

The black market continued to thrive with bootleg tapes. Russians could also hear rock on the radio through Voice of America and BBC broadcasts. The ambivalent government attitude toward rock resulted in the growth of the number of discos. In 1980 about 260 such dance clubs existed in Moscow alone, compared to none in the country five years before. The Nitty Gritty Dirt Band became the first American rock group to tour Russia, in 1977, followed subsequently by ABBA, Boney M, and Elton John.[13]

The old British rocker Cliff Richard had toured Russia in 1976, giving twenty sold-out performances. No longer a rocker Richard was then doing middle-of-the-road pop material and gospel. His tour was booked through the official state booking agency, Gosconcert, as all tours had to be, and Richard had to submit the song lyrics for each of his proposed numbers to the agency for inspection and approval. Only one number had to be dropped and that was a song which mentioned a number of countries, China among them. This mention of China was the suspected reason for the banning of the song. When Richard was asked why Gosconcert had invited him to tour, the singer speculated it was because he was "safely middle road, with a clean-cut image and no drug rap. They're still miles away from inviting the Rolling Stones."[14]

While the attempt to supplant foreign rockers with the homegrown variety was not successful, the further loosening of restrictions was an attempt to approve some of the less strident foreign rock in hopes of keeping the popularity down of hard and acid rock which most annoyed the government. These "liberalizing" trends were suddenly reversed in the 1980s as authorities decided that a crackdown was necessary. The Swedish group ABBA had long been the most popular foreign group in Russia and its records were pressed, under license, in vast quantities by the state-run record company, something rarely done for a Western group.

In January 1982 President Reagan and his advisers put together a TV special called "Let Poland be Poland" about the military clampdown there and ABBA agreed to tape a contribution. Ultimately the ABBA segment wasn't used on the program but the gesture was more than enough to remove them from the Kremlin's list of benign foreign rockers. A feature-length film with ABBA, then showing in Russian cinemas, was withdrawn and all pressings of the group's records were halted. The group was soundly denounced in newspapers for their commercialism and described as "utterly without talent and a corrupting influence on Soviet youth . . . garnished on stage by the anatomical writhings of the singers."[15]

In the early 1980s official Soviet policy turned sharply against the clubs and discotheques. Authorities had somehow hoped to use the discos to lure youths inside where they could be indoctrinated with party ideologies. Specially trained jockeys were supposed to broadcast propaganda messages in between the songs. It didn't work that way, however, and the discos turned into copies of those found in the West with sound and light shows, rock music, but no propaganda.

The disco scene began to be criticized in 1982 and officials called for the clubs to be run by adult-only committees. It was claimed adults hadn't taken enough interest in the discos and as a result they were largely run by teens themselves. This created shows "full of empty and anti-artistic ideas." The newspaper *Sovetskaya Kulture* called for the discos to be "properly" organized in order to answer "the spiritual demands of the people and include serious conversation on musical themes."[16]

The following year Politburo member Constantin Chernenko gave a speech on culture and struck out at Western culture, including music, claiming the West was trying to exploit "youthful psychology" in Russia. The country's discos werre compared to sleazy dockside bars in Marseilles, France, and dancing in the discos was banned. The number of discos was severely curtailed. Moscow would be allowed sixty-six, two in each of the city's thirty-three districts. The only records played would be from a governmentally approved list, which included virtually no Western rock. Lectures on politics were to be given between records. In his speech Chernenko added that rock music, along with other elements of Western culture, "were part of an arsenal of subversive weapons aimed at undermining the commitment of young Russians to communist ideology."[17]

Also under attack were Russia's homegrown rockers. Local rock groups were required to purge themselves of all Western influences. Many groups were banned outright because they were "ideologically unsound."

Soviet officials wanted their rockers to have a "sober appearance" and to do Russian songs without theatrics or loud guitars. Domestic rock music was lashed as being "akin to the wailings of enraged natives on some distant South Seas island."[18] One example was the Latvian rock group Modo which was banned for causing youths to shout nationalistic slogans. Their music and the disco atmosphere had caused, in Soviet minds, "free association, punk tendencies and the shouting of nationalist slogans."[19]

Russia's official attitudes toward rock and roll have gone back and forth over the years, ranging from mild encouragement to harsh repression. In 1986 the state finally sanctioned the sale of Beatle records. But the Soviet recording company, Melodia, was still producing only two Western-style rock records per year, even though surveys showed that forty percent of young people preferred this music.[20] Soviet leader Mikhail Gorbachev was taking a hard line against liberalization in the arts, and the Moscow press was spreading outrageous propaganda against Western rock stars. Eric Clapton and Rod Stewart were denounced as racist, David Bowie was described as an admirer of Hitler, and Kiss was said to be a Nazi group.

The official measures have had little effect on the music, however. In periods of repression more of it went underground as groups performed privately and tapes were obtained through various illegal and black market methods. In liberal periods more of the music surfaced, as in the middle 1970s in Russia. You can't stop the music, however—a lesson which most countries seem to have learned by now. The long holdouts are mainly the communist countries who continue their three-decade-long war on rock and roll. While there is no chance they will ever purge rock and roll from their countries they seem determined to keep trying.

24

Sex Rock

As the tirade over drug lyrics played itself out in 1973 the storm over the words of rock songs went into a quiet period, but only for a couple of years. In 1975 sexual lyrics came under attack again, an attack that gained momentum over ten years. Critics of rock had moved full circle and like the mid-1950s the outrage was about leerics, and it started with black music.

The opposition to sex rock was similar to that of the 1950s in its knee jerk quality, its rhetoric, and its inanity. The material being criticized was different. Lyrics of the 50s were accepted in mainstream society by the 70s and 80s and were not still a subject of criticism. Subjectively and objectively, those lyrics were mild. Since the music was constantly in flux it sought out lyrics and ways of expression which would offend the current generation of adults. Standards changed over time just as for example *Playboy* changed over time (50s — airbrushed, no genitals; 80s — no airbrush, genitals) to maintain their constant position. Ultimately the attacks on 70s sex rock were as ridiculous and unfounded as attacks on 50s lyrics. It was perhaps more ludicrous in the sense that the complainers in the 70s were of the generation who had enjoyed leerics of the 50s, and probably got hassled by their parents for it.

At the end of 1975 *Time* magazine took note of the rise of what they termed "sex rock," a genre which, according to them, accounted for fifteen percent of the air time on AM radio.[1] It was a movement led by Donna Summer, queen of the burgeoning disco scene, with her song "Love to Love You Baby" with "mostly five words repeated 28 times" and containing a "marathon of 22 orgasms." *Time* mentioned that while the FCC had drawn up guidelines about drug songs, so far the agency had kept "mum on sex rock." This was due to the fact that sex was subjective and the FCC didn't know what standard to use. The *Time* article didn't take a particularly irate or offended stance but it was enough to get the ball rolling.

The following year others felt compelled to speak out on sex rock, a genre that most in the industry agreed was growing by leaps and bounds. Two big hits of 1976, both charting number one, were Johnny Taylor's "Disco Lady" and "Tonight's the Night" by Rod Stewart. Both records were mentioned as among the most suggestive records of that year. The RKO chain wouldn't play the Stewart song until the line "spread your wings and let me come inside" was edited out.

Billboard magazine surveyed a number of industry people and found a growing anxiety over the sex rock trend. Jerry Boulding, the operations manager of station WVON in Chicago, considered suggestive lyrics to be harmful to kids. The vice president of Casablanca Records, Cecil Holmes, felt "that a group should be able to express itself without using a string of four-letter words."[2] Otis Smith, a vice president of ABC Records, was also opposed to overtly suggestive lyrics but claimed the public wanted that type of record and the company was obliged to give the public what it wanted. Warner Brothers Records vice-president Tom Draper also commented that he didn't "want to see the airwaves inundated with lyrics that are explicit and have a negative effect on youth."[3]

Neil McIntyre, the program director at WPIX-FM in New York City, was already censoring sex rock at his station. While he did play a "borderline song like "Disco Lady" his station would not play Elton John's "The Bitch is Back" no matter how popular it was. Dolphin Record chain owner Earl Dolphin saw an upsurge in "suggestive" records because radio stations were then playing them. He said his customers were always open to such records but until recently stations had not played them.

At KGFL in Los Angeles operations manager Lucky Pierre remarked that just eight years earlier if his stations played a song that only hinted at sex, they got all kinds of letters from adults objecting to the tune. But speaking of late 1976 Pierre said, "Now the songs are worse and the objections are less. We try to be cautious. Whenever we can we will bleep out something. We would just rather not play that kind of stuff but it's what audiences want to hear."[4]

At the same time the National Association of Broadcasters (NAB) had noticed the same trend as it watched with a wary eye. It noted, through its Radio Code Board, a rise in sex lyrics and told its membership that the NAB rules discouraged filling the airwaves with that type of song.

It was also noted at that time that sex rock was not "one of Washington's burning issues — either on Capitol Hill or at the FCC."[5]

Leaping into the leeric battle at the end of 1976 came the Reverend Jesse Jackson who was then national president of one of the country's leading civil rights organizations, Operation PUSH (People United to Save Humanity). In December of that year he announced a campaign to remove "sexy songs" from the airwaves. Jackson planned meetings with record company executives, artists, and radio station personnel as well as planning a series of "media-ethic" conferences. Jackson stated that if voluntary compliance could not be obtained then PUSH would be ready to use selective boycotting against offending records. He felt this threat was necessary since without it the industry would not assume the responsibility for the cleanup itself.

Jackson felt that where in the past the church, family, and school had set moral values for children, that function had been taken up by radio and television and they had not assumed the ethical responsibility that went with that power. He was particularly upset with "sex rock" songs like "The More You Do It," and "It's All Right To Make Love On The First Night," and "Shake Your Booty," which adversely affected children's minds.

Jackson cited the increasing number of illegitimate births and abortions in major U.S. cities and placed "the major blame for these figures on songs advocating 'sex without responsibility.'" There is a definite correlation between the two," he said.[6] As further evidence he cited a study from *Jet* magazine which had surveyed one thousand unmarried and pregnant girls at a North Hollywood high school and which claimed that ninety percent of them had had sexual intercourse "to the rhythms of songs with suggestive lyrics and rhythms."[7]

Jackson seemed to point the finger more at the companies and radio stations engaged in their "competition for decadence" over the airwaves. Helping to crystallize his opposition was his attendance at a live show where Jackson "heard kids in the audience singing 'get up off your ass, smoke some grass, shit goddam.' This has gone too far and we must do something about it."[8] So said the outspoken and outraged clergyman as he exercised his group's responsibility as a movement to lash out against such songs and those who put them on the air.

Soon Jackson announced even tougher measures which could be in the works. He proposed the formation of "ethics review boards" in the top dozen radio markets. These boards would be composed of parents, ministers, educators, students, and radio station managers and would assign ratings to the records, in the same manner that films were rated.

PUSH would then put pressure on radio stations to ban X-rated records. If a station ignored this pressure PUSH would then make a complaint at the station's license renewal time.

For 1977 Jackson had tentatively scheduled half a dozen "media ethics" conferences for different cities. Attendance was expected from record industry personnel, radio stations, artists, lyricists, FCC staffers, and so on. The object was to develop a battle plan to combat rock tunes with suggestive lyrics that were, in Jackson's words, "destroying the nation's moral fiber."[9] PUSH already claimed one small victory saying the record "Damn Right, It's Good" had been removed from the air and the market as a result of their campaign.

The first of the conferences was held on January 14 and 15, 1977 in Chicago. Jackson said he would personally try to persuade the music industry to stop producing "this garbage and pollution [which is corrupting] the minds and morals of our youth."[10] The meeting passed a resolution to form review boards in the top twenty radio markets to screen not only "sex-rock" but also "other negative messages" and to develop "no-play lists." PUSH was also prepared to encourage major companies not to advertise on radio when these songs were played, and if necessary, to conduct consumer withdrawal campaigns against this "moral menace." One of those at the conference was Dr. Joseph Cronin, state superintendent of education for Illinois, who also tied the increasing number of illegitimate births to "suggestive pop tunes" and "the increase in venereal disease as well."[11]

Jackson wouldn't name artists who were violating their ethical responsibilities, in his view, but did name some who presented a "more positive image." These included Aretha Franklin, Harry Belafonte, Sammy Davis, Jr., and the Jacksons. Notable by their absence at the meeting were representatives of most of the major record companies, all of whom had been invited by mail and/or phone. Jackson regarded his campaign not as a military attack, but as a "moral appeal" on the sex rock issue. He claimed PUSH was not "aiming at censorship, but hopes to encourage the media to accept a moral obligation to act with responsibility."[12]

The plans for more such media ethics meetings did not materialize, perhaps due to the poor response from the record company officials. Jackson's response was to meet with record company executives in February, first in New York and then Los Angeles. Attendance was not great and consisted of mainly black executives. Many of them complained that Jackson had sidetracked the issue from "ethic" to "ethnic." As a response to that Jackson named a white record which he found "totally offensive." That was Elton John's "The Bitch is Back."

On the surface the PUSH campaign seemed to be having some effect as the record companies which had met with Jackson indicated they would comply with his request to exercise "greater restraint" over their product. The president of Cotillion Records, Henry Allen, said PUSH caused his company to delay for three weeks the release of a Cerrone album. The original cover pictured three women "a little short of being naked." The revamped cover showed four bare hands linked at the wrist.

Larger companies such as RCA, Columbia, and Atlantic were also said to be agreeable to heeding Jackson's request and to use their influence on their artists. The head of New York City's top black radio stations WBLS and WLIB, Pepe Sutton, said his stations would comply. When asked if a record like "More, More, More" would be played on his outlets if it were shipped today he replied, "I don't think so."[13] On the whole, though, the industry was not thought to be overly concerned with PUSH's moralizing.

Jackson tried to maintain the fiction that he was against censorship and only wanted the music business to exercise responsibility. As a rather inane example he cited Aretha Franklin's "Respect," released during the black urban riots of the 1960s and noted, "She could have done 'Burn, Baby Burn' but she didn't."[14] The *New York Times* had been silently watching the whole affair and felt compelled to issue an editorial noting the "exploitive" nature of the rock industry and that Jackson's objectives were admirable; they wished him well.[15]

At that point his campaign began to run out of steam. In reality it had had little effect. Record companies may have expressed agreement, but they largely ignored him. In May 1977 PUSH organized a Chicago conference called "Music and Morality." While he still attacked sex rock Jackson modified his position considerably. He began referring to the fight as a "spiritual matter" and made no mention of censorship, no-play lists, or pressure on advertisers.

At the PUSH annual convention that summer, he responded to the then revealed "severe criticism" from the industry over his hard-line censorship stance and the criticism over turning the matter into a black issue only. On the defensive Jackson claimed again he was never after censorship. He even stated that PUSH accepted "boy meets girl" sex music and only objected when the music became "pornographic" and transmitted a message of "raw sex and drugs." Claiming the issue was of the total market, and not just black, Jackson drew the parallel that the drug scene became glorified from Woodstock, not Harlem, and that punk came out of England, not the ghetto.[16]

Clearly Jackson's crusade was faltering in the summer of 1977. Likely it would have remained dead but for a record released about one year later. It was opportune for Jackson since it was sex rock and, to allay the ethnic label, it was done by some white boys, the dirtiest of the dirty white boys, everybody's villains, the Rolling Stones. Jesse Jackson could not resist and the campaign resumed. All the fuss was about a song called "Some Girls" which contained the lines, "Black girls just want to get fucked all night/I just don't have that much jam." From his Chicago home base Jackson tried to get area radio stations not to play the title track from the album of the same name. Station WVON had never played that cut but, apparently feeling they had to stop playing something, withdrew the Stones' "Miss You." Jackson contacted area church and civic groups to get their support and fired off an angry telegram to Atlantic Records chief Ahmet Ertegun, whose company distributed the Stones' records. Ertegun was asked to stop producing and selling "Some Girls."

This particular furor sufficiently cowed Ertegun into flying to Chicago to personally meet with Jackson. At the meeting Ertegun said the piece was fiction, but that he would recommend to the Atlantic board that the song lyric be changed since "the result is an insult even though I know he (Mick Jagger) didn't mean it."[17] Ertegun relayed that Jagger regarded the song as a parody of clichés, which was supposed to be funny and sarcastic. Under pressure from Jackson Ertegun said he would support the idea of establishing a panel to look at the question of the industry's "moral responsibilities." The Atlantic boss played the supplicant further by claiming he originally asked Jagger to change the lyric but Jagger had refused. The indignant Jackson was not appeased however, and demanded that Jagger personally apologize to him for the song. Ertegun could afford to appear appeasement-minded since Atlantic only distributed the Stones' records. They had absolutely no control over artistic content. In fact, by their agreement they were required to distribute the Stones' products, like them or not.

Once more Jackson's organization had achieved no results and by mid-November of 1978 he announced PUSH would escalate its campaign and launch a national fight for a retailer and consumer boycott of all Rolling Stones' records. The plan was to contact key retailers in major cities and tell them to remove all Rolling Stones records or else face picketers. The first picket lines went up around Atlantic Records' Los Angeles office. PUSH was joined by NOW (National Organization for Women) members who objected to the record on sexist and racist grounds. They also found the term "girls" to be "demeaning."

Jackson was miffed that Atlantic had not gotten the words changed, even though the company had no control over Jagger. PUSH claimed to have sixty other volunteers working in Los Angeles, on street corners, in department stores, and so on, getting petitions signed as well as having ministers speak against the record from the pulpit.[18] A groups of parents from across the country, said to represent more than one million nationwide, called Compensatory Education, announced they had joined forces with PUSH against "Some Girls."

In the face of the boycott he had initiated, Jackson still insisted he wasn't advocating censorship but was determined to rid the industry of this "cultural decadence." Letting the artists police themselves wouldn't work since that was akin to "leaving a hungry dog to guard the meat house."[19] When appraised of the situation Mick Jagger said that Atlantic had tried to get the Stones to drop "Some Girls" but he had refused since, "I've always been opposed to censorship of any kind, especially by conglomerates. I've always said, 'If you can't take a joke, it's too fucking bad.'"[20]

In the end this Jackson campaign failed as did all of his attacks on sex rock. Jesse Jackson was using the whole issue as one way of getting media publicity. It was all part of a bigger Jackson campaign, that of making himself a big enough name to take a run at the presidency, which he did in 1984. That campaign failed too. *Rolling Stone* magazine was one of the few media outlets to recognize, and state, what Jackson was really doing. In an editorial they pointed out how ridiculous it was to believe that the song could "unravel the social fabric." They abhored Jackson's call for censorship and argued that the Stones had as much right to free speech as Jackson did. The magazine pointed out there were more pressing problems for a purported leader to deal with than rock and roll. The editor, in thinly veiled contempt, noted the real reasons for Jackson's sex rock attacks, "Jackson is clearly seeking to regain a lost power base, and he has seized upon a publicity campaign to purify all pop music — both black and white — as the easiest way to get headlines."[21]

Jesse Jackson wasn't waging his battle alone. The Southern Baptist Convention had a radio and television commission which produced a half-hour rock music program used on 950 stations coast-to-coast. The program's producer, Claude Cox, found it more and more difficult to find "acceptable" music for the show. He found only about half of the top forty songs to be usable and cited Carly Simon's "Nobody Does It Better" as a tune he wouldn't play "on a bet."[22] In 1976 the FCC had received over twenty-three hundred complaints about "vulgarity," mainly from songs, and the agency was said to be considering how it might enforce an existing federal ban on "obscene" material. The problem lay in how to meet the Supreme Court's definition of obscenity.

U.S. News & World Report also said the boom in sex rock had occurred only recently and the critics were worried about the long-term effects of such "permissive lyrics" on the young and impressionable. X-rated records, unlike x-rated films, were available to listeners of all ages. One of the items fueling the issue was the emerging punk rock. Not that punk rock was particularly sex rock, and it was limited then to England in terms of its effects. But critics felt that punk, staring across the Atlantic Ocean with its jaundiced and angry eye, might invade at any time. Clamping down then on sex rock would make it easier to clamp down on punk rock, if the beast should dare to invade and become a problem. All in all the record industry was a little worried by late 1977 and some executives believed "that the industry eventually may have to bow to pressures from critics."[23]

The NAB was worried enough to keep looking at the issue and in April 1978 held a panel on the subject at their convention. One of the speakers was Dr. Richard Peterson of Vanderbilt University who said kids didn't interpret lyrics in the same fashion as adults and that he didn't think the kids knew what the lyrics were about, although they did know what the lyrics were. After this somewhat contradictory statement he opined that radio was in an era of "highly critical morality."[24]

Less than six months later the NAB looked at the issue again with a more boldly named panel, "Record Lyrics—Dirty, Dangerous or Dynamite?" One of those on the panel was an industry record producer, Mike Chapman of Chinnichap, who recounted some of his own sex rock censoring. On Blondie's "Heart of Glass" he had changed the line "pain in the ass" to "pain in the grass." From an album by the Knack he had excised lines like "sit on your face" and "get into your pants." Chapman predicted that "lyrics will get 'stronger' and complaints will get worse."[25] By the end of the 1970s the issue seemed to have waned somewhat. For one thing it was then clear that punk rock would not cause the storm in the United States that it had in the British Isles. Not that the issue died completely. Instances of censorship abounded. Rather than lying dormant, sex rock became the focus of a sort of sniper warfare as opposed to an all-out assault by anti-rock forces. It would remain so until such an attack was indeed launched, in 1985.

In England "Love to Love You Baby" ran afoul of the moralists and was banned by the BBC. Actually the BBC never banned a song, they just declined to play it. London's Capital Radio adopted a similar stance toward the tune. The group 10cc was in trouble with "Head Room" a cut from their album "How Dare You!" With a theme of masturbation it received a firm "no" from radio. The National Viewers and Listeners Association had recieved complaints about the Donna Summer song and the group's secretary, Mary Whitehouse, although she hadn't heard the song, thought the BBC ban was appropriate.

The controller of BBC Radio One and Two, Charles McLelland, said the company had no official policy regarding such records but judged each one on its merits. He considered the Summer song "offensive" and "unsuitable for family listening. The sex bit was far too overt."[26] Over at Capitol Radio Aidan Day, the program controller, justified his ban by saying that certain records weren't suitable for the majority of his audience. "Personally, I should be most perturbed if my son heard the Donna Summer record."[27]

Frank Zappa ran afoul of censors in 1976 when Warner Brothers excised a portion from his album "Zappa in New York." The portion had to do with fellatio. Later "Jewish Princess," a cut from "Sheik Yerbouti" dedicated to women who enjoyed anal intercourse, drew heat from the Anti-Defamation League. Zappa had always vociferously defended free speech and the right of the artist to use whatever word he wished. Commenting about four letter words Zappa noted, "The way people fear these words and the length that they go in order to keep these words out of broadcasting is preposterous."[28]

South Africa banned "Physical" by Olivia Newton-John. Initially the South African Broadcasting Corporation had played the song but abruptly withdrew it without explanation. It was then reinstated on the air just prior to a tour of the country by Newton-John. However, the reinstated version excised the lines, "There's nothing left to talk about/ Unless it's horizontally." Speculation was that the singer's record company, EMI, had suggested this as a workable solution to the problem for both parties.[29]

"Physical" provoked wrath in the United States as well. The record was banned at KFMY-FM in Provo, Utah and at KSL-AM, Salt Lake City, Utah. A spokesman for MCA records, Pat Pipolo, stated the tune had generated pockets of resistance, "One station tells me they won't play it because of the lyrics. In the Bible belt, a station says the lyrics are too pubescent."[30]

In February 1983 Frank Scott, the program director of Voice of America (VOA), issued a memo to the staff which emphasized that VOA had to be particularly careful not to present any music which was offensive to any part of their audience. VOA programmed around the world in some forty-two languages. One of the records on Scott's blacklist was Marvin Gaye's "Sexual Healing," a song that would win several Grammies that year. A couple of weeks after the memo Scott had a meeting with several dozen top staffers, most of whom were hostile to the memo and then leaked a transcript of the meeting to the press. In answer to a question about how difficult it was to judge songs as to their degree of offensiveness Scott offered to set up some sort of rating system to aid his staff. Scott later claimed that only a few people at the meeting were hostile and that he, Scott, was only trying to establish a broad policy of good taste.

One astute question managed to trip up Scott. At the meeting the questioner asked whether the song "Ebony and Ivory" (performed by a black artist and a white artist) should be played in South Africa. Scott, who admitted he wasn't familiar with the song, said no. The questioner then pointed out that "Ebony and Ivory" was then number one in South Africa.[31]

"American Bandstand" had banned the 1978 song "Disco Inferno" by the Trampps. The offensive line was "burn the mother down." In 1985 the program refused to let Sheena Easton sing her Prince-written hit "Sugar Walls." The program felt the tune was "suggestive pornography." The producer of the show, Larry Klein, routinely submitted "red flag" songs to ABC censors for judgment. Tom Kersey, the vice president in charge of standards and practices on the west coast (the censors), and Klein both felt, however, that censorship had eased. Kersey said "Sugar Walls" exceeded "any level of acceptance for a sexual fantasy." To show how censorship had relaxed Kersey pointed to the song "Obsession" by Animotion which dealt with a repeated obsession to make love, and was given the green light. When asked about the difference Kersey explained that the latter was about making love to a woman while "Sugar Walls" focused on female anatomical features in an intimate sexual fantasy. "One is beautiful and the other pornographic."[32]

In a particularly silly bit of censorship the BBC banned the tune "Relax" by Frankie Goes to Hollywood from both radio and television in 1984. It was banned from the BBC-TV "Top of the Pops" program the week that it charted number one. When the TV show ran down the charts, as was customary at the end of the program, only the group's name was mentioned, not the song title. The BBC had come to the rather belated conclusion the song was "sexually explicit" and wasn't suitable for a program with a family audience. Frankie Goes to Hollywood wondered, justifiably, why the BBC had taken so long to decide this. The BBC did not respond.[33]

Almost as strange was the case of Joan Jett in America where her albums were removed from stores all over the country because one of the cuts was her version of the Rolling Stones' "Starfucker." Ironically the song was only on the cassette tape, and not on the vinyl album itself, even though it was these that were removed.[34]

Even the thoroughly nonsexual rock tunes sometimes ran into opposition. One such was the October 1985 release "Sun City" which featured a host of performers ranging from Bruce Springsteen, to Bob Dylan, to Miles Davis. It was a record against the South African apartheid system and a pledge by the superstars not to perform there. It was a follow-up to other superstar efforts to raise money for causes such as African famine relief. However, "Sun City" was slow to get full airplay. Some programmers said it was because the record's sound was "abrasive" and "rough."

A Chicago programmer was more honest when he admitted the record's "subject is a little controversial." Airplay was particularly slow in Los Angeles, again due to conservative programmers who felt the material too strong for mainstream stations. This caused Mayor Tom Bradley to publicly urge the stations to give it airplay, claiming that it fit into any radio format and that every station in the country had an obligation to play the song.[35] Needless to say, the South African Broadcasting Corporation announced it was unlikely that "Sun City" would ever be heard on state-controlled radio.

The Scorpions ran into trouble with the cover of their album "Love at First Sting." The original showed a partially clad couple embracing while the man was putting the tattoo of a scorpion on the female's thigh. One of the rack jobbers reported a key account, the 670-store chain, Wal-Mart, refused to handle the album with that cover. A substitute cover was quickly arranged which showed a simple photo of the band. The rack jobber company, Handleman, claimed this was not the only account to complain. The record company, PolyGram, showed the cover to rack jobbers initially, as was the industry custom, to see if any of the rack jobbers found anything to complain about. In turn the jobbers screened the product at their major accounts to see if there were any objections. Mario DeFilippo, vice-president in charge of purchasing for Handleman, commented that objections to album covers and lyrics were a common complaint from his customers and he noted, in 1984, that "there seems to be a rash of complaints lately concerning album cover art and lyrical content."[36]

In 1980 anti-rock forces focused primarily on sex rock but at least one intrepid crusader was still locked in a 1970 time warp. That was Julio Martinez, director of the New York State Division of Substance Abuse

Services, an agency responsible for rehabilitating drug addicts. Martinez called for the imposition of a $1 tax each time a record was heard on the radio, or sold, which advocated drug use. He even compiled an "enemies list" which included the Grateful Dead, Eric Clapton, Bob Dylan, Jefferson Starship, Jackson Browne, Paul Simon, and everybody's favorite, the Rolling Stones. Martinez said, "The Grateful Dead should drop dead."[37]

The election of Ronald Reagan to the presidency in 1980 provoked some uneasy thoughts from the industry on the possible effects of this swing to the right on rock and roll. Steve Leber and David Krebs, who managed acts such as Aerosmith and AC/DC, felt the Moral Majority would be after rock and the greatest threat to the music over the coming ten years would come from the evangelical movement. Mark Spector, an A&R man at A&M Records in New York, and then manager of .38 Special, offered the thought that rock fans were as reactionary as their parents and there was a rise in anti-black music sentiments.[38]

Radio programming consultant Paul Drew thought the number of complaints about "suggestive" lyrics would rise and that the swing to the right, mirrored in broadcaster sensitivity, would cause composers to tone down their material.[39] From KMET-FM in Los Angeles talk show host Mike Harrison noted that rock opponents appeared to be growing in both numbers and vocal strength and he received more and more calls from people citing rock and roll as a destroyer of youth, and calling it the devil's music. Jon Keller of WRKO-AM in Boston noted the same trend. Harrison was worried about the "growing wave of opposition" to rock music.[40]

Most of these fears proved justified as anti-rock opposition intensified during the 1980s. Fundamentalists provided strong opposition and Congress was dragged into the picture yet again. The hit-and-run skirmishes on the suggestive lyrics would erupt into a full-scale war in 1985 as the Parents' Music Resource Center (PMRC) spearheaded an attack on alleged porn rock. The PMRC battle had its roots in the minor skirmishes which took place from 1979 to 1984. These in turn came from the more vociferous attack led by Jesse Jackson from 1976 to 1978. In turn this sprang out of a 1975 article in *Time* magazine which opened the campaign and alerted the public to "sex rock."

25

Stage Fright

In the mid-1970s rock concerts were still beleaguered by bannings, bad press, and censorship. A Led Zeppelin concert was cancelled in February 1975 by Boston's Mayor Kevin White. Three thousand fans (average age, fourteen) who had been let into the Boston Garden in January to buy tickets for the show had caused $30,000 damage to the arena. They vandalized doors and seats, looted concession stands, and damaged the surface of the hockey rink causing the postponement of a Bruins game. In New York that year the Shaeffer Music Festival, which had been an annual event at the Wollman skating rink in Central Park for nine years, was told to look elsewhere for a venue. Edwin L. Weisl, chief of city parks, said the building was in bad repair and that the rock festival had in the past "caused millions of dollars worth of ecological damage."[1] The Hartford Civic Center in Connecticut banned rock concerts in 1975. This came about after a metal roof was damaged during an Alice Cooper concert. Some overzealous crashers had tried to get in by cutting a hole in the ceiling, resulting in several thousand dollars of damage.

Official attitudes toward rock concerts in this period could be surmised from the planning behind an Elton John concert at L.A.'s Dodger Stadium in 1975. John was the first rock act to play the stadium in the nine years since the Beatles' tour in 1966. Peter O'Malley, president of the Dodgers, had refused to allow rock acts to use the venue not, as he said, because he was against the music, but because he didn't like the caliber of the entertainment. "Elton John," he explained, "is a very special act. He also attracts a very special audience. I doubt if we're going to find many who can match his standards. When someone else comes along like the Beatles or Elton John we might do it again. But we want to hold it at that level."[2]

261

Because of O'Malley's positive attitude toward Elton John, police chief Edward Davis planned for "a low-profile enforcement of the law within the stadium. . . . Past experience has shown that the manpower and resources available to police at large rock concerts is insufficient. Therefore, law enforce efforts will be concentrated on the more serious violations of the law."[3]

During the two nights of Elton's concerts the stadium had thirty-five police on duty and each made about one arrest — twenty for drug sales and the rest for marijuana use. A concert the previous spring by Pink Floyd at the L.A. Sports Arena was policed by seventy-five officers who arrested 511 people during five concert evenings. That was almost three times as many arrests per night as at the Elton John concerts.

Was John really an entertainer who attracted more law-abiding audiences or did the supportive attitude of the police and stadium manager have anthing to do with the good behavior of fans? "Low-profile enforcement" and only going after "serious" violations indicated that police intended only minimal interference with the crowd, and had decided this *before* the concert took place.

O'Malley had checked out other Elton John concerts and found that there had been very few narcotic arrests. This was probably what he meant by a "very special act." But either O'Malley had his facts wrong, or Richard Crofoot, a member of the Richfield, Ohio zoning comission, had a faulty nose. Crofoot had attended a 1974 Elton John concert in Ohio and "smelled and saw marijuana being smoked."[4]

As a result of this shocking experience, Crofoot wanted to ban all rock concerts at the Coliseum that served the Cleveland/Akron area. But the trouble that came to Ohio was not in Crofoot's territory. It happened in Cincinnati in 1979.

The Who were slated to play the Riverfront Coliseum in December. The show was scheduled to start at 8 P.M. The hall had festival seating which meant that kids would sit on the floor on a first-come, first-served basis. Of course, everyone would try to get near the front. By 2:15 in the afternoon of the concert, a line-up had formed. At 6:15 most of the eighteen thousand ticket holders were waiting to get in. There was a lot of pushing, shoving, and jostling, but coliseum staff and the promoters, Electric Factory Concerts of Philadelphia, wouldn't open up until 7:00 P.M. even though the police advised opening up earlier. When the crowd was finally let in, they stampeded toward the single entry. Only one door was opened to let in eighteen thousand people. Eleven died in the crush, they were either trampled or suffocated. Seven of the dead were teens; four were adults. Several others were hurt. The Who played their entire show unaware of the deaths as were most audience members. Organizers felt it would only cause more panic if the deaths were announced and the concert cancelled.

After the tragedy, everyone wondered where the blame lay. Most agreed that festival seating was one culprit. The police and coliseum staff had to take responsibility for poor crowd control. But ultimately The Who and rock music took their share of the guilt. The *New York Times* ran an article, "Is Rock the Music of Violence?"[5] The writer made no conclusions about rock as a cause of violence, but he didn't have to, the association was already established in the headline. John G. Fuller, who wrote a book *Are the Kids All Right*, used the Cincinnati deaths to say that rock produced "physiological and emotional changes that seriously damage the will to live and be creative."[6]

Even Dave Marsh, writer of a sympathetic biography of the Who, chastised the groups for the Cincinnati incident. He claimed that the Who were "greedy" to have allowed festival seating where more people could be jammed in a hall. He also felt the Who's onstage guitar-smashing rituals instigated destruction. "In a way, given the band's rowdy image," he said, "it's surprising that some haunting catastrophe hadn't occurred earlier."[7] Marsh also attacked the Who for continuing to allow festival seating at future concerts even though Roger Daltrey had said the band would do "anything we can do to stop it from ever happening again."[8]

Yet how greedy were the Who? According to rock promoter Bill Graham, the financial advantage of festival seating had been reduced "with most promoters compelled by local ordinances to limit the tickets sold to a number no greater than what the space would accommodate with seating."[9] "There have been millions and millions of people at rock concerts over the years," Graham noted, "and nothing like this has happened. I don't condemn anybody for Cincinnati. But sometimes kids are forced to react like cattle."[10]

Surprisingly, Mayor John Blackwell of Cincinnati did not blame rock and roll music for the tragedy. Though he received many angry phone calls demanding that all future rock concerts be banned at the Coliseum, he refused to act on public pressure. The Coliseum had booked 150 rock acts in its four-year history and never before had any serious incidents. The mayor asked the city's legal department to draw up a report outlining measures to prevent such a tragedy from occurring again. Some of the recommendations included a prohibition of festival seating and crowd management plans. Republican State Senator Stanley Aronoff intended to introduce a bill in the Legislature "requiring that all seats be sold on a reserved basis, that patrons be admitted at least an hour before the start of a concert, and that concert halls open enough doors to ensure safe crowd control."[11] The report compiled by the city's legal department concluded that the crowd attempting to enter the Who concert was "not riotous or violent" and that "some risk to public safety is inherent in any activity in any place."[12] Yet the concert incident did have repercussions for rock and roll. Two scheduled rock shows at the Coliseum were postponed indefinitely.

When a man was pushed, or fell, down the stairs and died from a broken neck at an Ozzy Osbourne concert in Long Beach, California in 1986, heavy metal music came under fire again as though the lyrics had something to do with the incident.

In Britain government regulation of rock concerts resulted when a girl was crushed to death at a 1974 David Cassidy concert in Whitsun. The Greater London Council issued a report entitled, "A Code of Practice for Pop Concerts." The document listed rules for outdoor and indoor concerts. One of the recommendations was that crowds be split into "manageable sections by railings and barriers." In addition, one steward would be provided for every thirty fans. For outdoor concerts the ratio was one steward for every one hundred people.[13] The report also prohibited noise from 8:00 P.M. to 7:00 A.M. for indoor concerts and from 11:00 P.M. TO 7:00 A.M. for outdoor venues. Rock promoter Harvey Goldsmith called the barrier concept "prison pens" and said of the noise limitations, "If people want to live on top of Wembley Stadium that's not my problem. They get as much noise from football matches as rock concerts and if they don't like it they should move."[14]

Ironically the music the British were about to hear at rock concerts was related to sports. In 1981 the Oi sound in rock swept the country. "Oi" was London cockney for "hey" and it was chanted at soccer games. Oi was an extreme outgrowth of punk rock. Embraced by white "skinheads" the music was said to exacerbate race and class conflicts. The skinheads, who shaved their hair off and wore heavy work boots, were bitter, unemployed white working-class youths. Oi groups had names like Blitz, Last Resort, Infra-Riot, and Splodge. Their songs were called "Someone's Gonna Die" or "Riot, Riot." In "Nation on Fire" the lyrics went, "The clubs come down around your head/It's war on the streets and they're running red." The Oi were said to have ties with neofascist British organizations like the National Front or the British Movement.

In July 1981 a white Oi band, the 4-Skins, played the Hambrough Tavern in Southall, a predominantly Asian area. Hundreds of skinheads from all over the city converged on the Tavern. Seeking revenge for skinhead attacks in their neighborhood prior to the concert, Asian youths rioted with the skinheads. The Hambrough Tavern was wrecked, and sixty-one police ended up in the hospital.

Reaction against the Oi bands was immediate. All scheduled Oi concerts were cancelled. Retail stores banned the Oi single "One Law For Them," and Decca records suspended sales on the second 4-Skins' album "Strength through Oi" which was a play on the Hitler slogan "Strength through Joy." Twenty thousand records had already been sold. John Preston, manager of Decca Records, explained the decision, "It is obvious that there is an association between some of the music and violence."[15] The "Strength through Oi" album cover showed a picture of skinhead Nicky Crane, once lead singer with the rock group Afflicted. Crane was also a bodyguard for the head of the British Movement and was serving a four-year prison term for conspiracy to assault and incitement to racial hatred. A director of one of Britain's major record companies commented, "There is no doubt in my mind that the National Front and the British Movement view Oi fans as a fertile recruiting ground."[16] The rock music journal *Sounds* was also criticized for advocating violence because it promoted the "Strength through Oi" album. The London *Daily Mail* described *Sounds* as "a vehicle for viciously extremist and fascist views."[17] *Sounds* said it would sue.

On the other hand, some of the Oi groups tried to back down. Drummer John Jacobs of the 4-Skins said of the National Front, "We don't need it . . . it's no good for us."[18] David Long, manager of Splodge said, "We have nothing to do with politics, but you can see three million out of work and this government doesn't give a toss. It's not a threat to the government when the working class are fighting amongst themselves. We're saying to the kids 'why fight each other? We have to get rid of Maggie Thatcher.'"[19] Long believed that the neofascist violence was wrong but would continue whether there was Oi music or not, "because of the government," and its indifference to unemployed youth. Long noted that if kids started to yell "Sieg Heil" at a Splodge concert the singer made a joke of it saying, "I can't see any seagulls."[20] He felt that most of the kids didn't even understand what they were shouting.

The Oi bands weren't the first groups to attract skinheads to their concerts. Punk rockers also had trouble with these fans from the British Movement and National Front. The punk group Sham 69 had to give up live performing in 1979 because they were so threatened by the audiences.

After the Southall riot, some Oi groups were willing to improve their image by giving a joint concert in Sheffield with racially integrated groups. But this was easier said than done. One of these integrated groups, the Specials, composed of two black and five white musicians who had played Rock Against Racism concerts in Britain, had given up touring because of attacks from skinheads. Lynval Golding, the group's twenty-eight-year-old black guitarist, was beaten with lead pipes by three skinheads in 1980. Golding knew that his group's music did not incite violence but it occurred anyway. In their song "Ghost Town," The Specials put the blame for skinhead anger where it belonged, with the government for "leaving the youth on the shelf." Surprisingly, even though he was a victim of violence Golding sympathized, "I know what it's like to be unemployed."[21] Carl Fisher of Blitz felt that Oi was the only music that talks about what's really going on in Britain."[22]

Still it would be hard to convince people after the Southall riots, the picture of Nicky Crane on an album cover, the Seig Heil chanting, that Oi rock music did not incite racism. As one spokesman for a British record company put it, "In the future all bands will be screened; we're not imposing censorship but we don't want to give out contracts and money to fascists."[23]

The United States didn't have any Ois but they did have Ozzy Osbourne. In February 1983 a sold-out Osbourne concert at the Catholic Youth Center in Scranton, Pennsylvania was cancelled because of the rock star's "alleged desecration of a national monument, alleged affiliation with Satanic cults, and alleged abuse of animals."[24] A second concert in Odessa, Texas was cancelled for similar reasons. Osbourne had apparently urinated on a wall at the Alamo, arousing the wrath of the American Legion and Veterans of Foreign Wars groups. He was also said to have bitten off the head of a live bat at one of his performances, creating much consternation at the SPCA.

Makoul Productions, the promoters of the concert in Scranton, tried to get a court injunction to order the youth center to allow the show. Judge Kosik turned Makoul down saying it was "a simple contract matter" and that "no one is denying your client the right to come to this city and shout his lungs out."[25] The Youth Center claimed there was only an oral not a written agreement, but the promoters had negotiated a rental price and reserved a date. Makoul, joined by the ACLU, then appealed to the Pennsylvania State Supreme Court but they also refused to issue an injunction. The promoters had to refund over four thousand tickets, and planned to sue the Youth Center.

In Newark, Ohio rock concerts were banned in 1981 at Legend Valley Park because the shows were considered a public nuisance and crowd control was a problem. Judge Laughlin, who issued the decision said that "hard rock, rock or heavy metal music, is typified by driving, forceful rhythm, crashing chords, predominantly three or four instruments . . . and extreme amplification causing noise levels of 90 decibels or more, as measured from approximately 50 feet."[26] Laughlin ordered that music that fell within the parameters of his definition must be prohibited. Interpretation of Laughlin's definition of rock was not very consistent, however. Bruce Springsteen, for example, was not classified as rock.

Adding to the bad reputation of rock concerts was the three-day US Festival in Devore, California in 1983 which drew three hundred thousand people. Forty-four were injured, eighty-seven were arrested, and a drug dealer was beaten to death. Most charges had to do with drugs or alcohol. County Sheriff Floyd Tidwell described the event as an "absolute zoo" and commented that the crowd seemed more violent than at the festival the previous year.

Alleged obscenity was the problem at an Amarillo, Texas concert by the "mock shock-rock group" Twisted Sister. Band leader Daniel Dee Snider, twenty-nine, who wore a fright wig and dressed like a transvestite, was charged with being obscene by an outraged mother, Sherry Palmer, who had taken her fourteen-year-old daughter to the show. Palmer was horrified when teens sang along to songs like "S.M.F." (I'm a Sick MuthaFucka), and when Snider allegedly screamed something like "Suck my Dick." Commenting on the case, prosecuting attorney Monte May criticized Snider for "recommending, urging and encouraging to defy, rebel and ignore such authority figures as teachers, police and parents in common Anglo-Saxon terms."[27] Twisted Sister offered to issue a warning before each concert, "Attend with caution. Not for the faint-hearted or weak-kneed. The contents contain strong language."[28]

Heavy metal groups were not welcome in at least one Canadian city in 1985. George Depres, manager of the Winnipeg Arena, was shocked by Twisted Sister and found the group "absolutely vulgar." He concluded, "If they ever try to book this city again, I have no hesitation in saying I would recommend that they not be allowed in."[29]

Promoter Tim Mays had trouble staging rock concerts in a San Diego venue, the Adams Avenue Theater, in 1984. He had produced hardcore punk acts like Black Flag, Social Distortion, and Circle Jerks, as well as new wave groups such as Missing Persons and Public Image Ltd. In November a heavy metal concert by Assassin was shut down by police because of alleged noise violations. Mays was then unable to get permits for two scheduled punk and heavy metal concerts, and police licensing officials gave no explanation for the refusal. Mays decided to go ahead with the shows anyway but police arrived shortly before the first concert and threatened arrest if the band went on. Mays had to cancel the concerts and lost $10,000 in expenses. Angry fans vandalized the theater. Mays was finally told by the permit office that neighboring businesses had complained about health and fire code violations in the Adams Avenue Theater. After a thirty-day investigation to determine the safety of the theater, no violations were discovered. Mays believed the police were trying to force him out of business.[30] But Lieutenant Ron Seden of the San Diego Police Department denied they were harrassing the promoter. Seden said that Mays was operating without a permit and creating a "disruption." Seden sidestepped the issue of why Mays couldn't get a permit in the first place.

Nobody stood up for the rights of punks to perform. But it was a different story when Republican Secretary of the Interior James Watt banned rock music from the 1983 Fourth of July celebrations on the Mall in Washington, D.C. Bands such as Grass Roots in 1982 and the Beach Boys in 1980 and 1981 had played the Mall, attracting hundreds of thousands of people. There had been fifty-two arrests at the 1982 event—mostly drug busts. The prohibition was quickly taken to be a ban on the Beach Boys. A spokesman for Watt explained, "Not to hark back to the 1960s days, but I am sure Mr. Watt was avoiding having another Woodstock kind of event."[31] Watt said he wanted the ban because rock groups attracted "the wrong element," described as "drinking and drug-taking youths." "We're trying to have an impact for wholesomeness," Watt explained, "July Fourth will be . . . for the family and solid, clean American lives."[32] Watt couldn't even make the distinction between a rock group which was unaccepted by the establishment and a group like the Beach Boys who were indeed clean, wholesome, and family-oriented. Even President Reagan could see that difference.

Watt planned to replace the rock bands by "military and patriotic people"—so he invited singer Wayne Newton and the Army Blues Band to perform. Newton, a Las Vegas middle-of-the-road crooner, was close to Nevada Senator Paul Laxalt, a confidant of President Reagan. When Newton was called to testify at a grand jury investigation of alleged underworld activities of Guido Penosi, Newton's lawyer was Frank Fahrenkopf, Jr., who became chairman of the Republican National Committee. (Penosi was found not guilty.) Newton campaigned for Reagan and was an inaugural ball host.

But Watt made a mistake when he blackballed the Beach Boys. The group was considered as American as apple pie, and their cheerful surf and sun melodies had never offended anyone. Moreover, the Beach Boys had also been Republican supporters. Vice-President Bush had first invited them to perform at the 1980 Mall celebration. An aide to Bush noted that "the Vice-President thinks highly of the Beach Boys and likes their music . . . He surely would have been happy to recommend them."[33] The Beach Boys had held a fund-raising concert for Bush when he was campaigning and they also played at the 1981 Reagan-Bush inaugural ball. Michael K. Deaver, White House deputy chief of staff, also spoke up for the group commenting, "There are a lot of us who think they are a national institution. Anybody that thinks that the Beach Boys are hard rock must think Mantovani plays jazz."[34]

The Beach Boys issued a statement through their publicist saying they found it "unbelievable" that Watt claimed they attracted a "wrong element." They listed all the concerts they had given in conjunction with state fairs and major league baseball teams that "not only helped increase attendance at these games but projected the all-American and family-oriented aspect of baseball."[35] The group mentioned they had been invited to play in the Soviet Union in 1978 and the statement pointed out that "Obviously the Soviet Union, a much more controlled society than our own, did not feel the group attracted the wrong element."[36]

Clearly James Watt had not done his homework. But apparently such bungling was routine for the Interior Secretary. He had accused environmentalists of demanding a centralized society like Nazi Germany, had called Indian reservations failures of socialism, and said he preferred the terms "liberals and Americans to Democrats and Republicans." As to Watt's choice of Wayne Newton for the July Forth concert, *Washington Post* columnist Richard Cohen noted, "It is Wayne Newton, after all, who performs in saloons before drunks . . . dressed loudly, holding highballs, squeezing women they have rented for the occasion."[37] Realizing his error, Watt admitted, "Obviously, I didn't know anything to start with."[38] Both President Reagan and his wife Nancy said they were fans of the Beach Boys and the president upbraided Watt with a joke gift—a plaster trophy of a foot with a bullet hole in it. The Beach Boys ended up playing in Atlantic City for the July Fourth celebration.

The White House became involved in rock concert controversy again in 1986. First Lady Nancy Reagan was a strong anti-drug crusader. Promoters of a Los Angeles fund-raising concert to prevent drug abuse wanted Nancy's endorsement of the event. The White House asked for an advance list of the performers. Mrs. Reagan objected to six of the twenty-one scheduled acts including Black 'N Blue, Ozzy Osbourne, Sheena Easton, the Fixx, Berlin, and Iron Maiden because of their "offensive lyrics." The promoters refused to ax any of the groups and Reagan withdrew her support.

In San Antonio, Texas another major backlash against rock concerts occurred. Certain fundamentalist religious groups like Community Families In Action, with a watchdog organization called Parents against Subliminal Seduction (PASS) objected to rock lyrics that were obscene, negative, or had satanic associations. The groups pressured the San Antonio City Council to institute measures which would control the type of concerts played in the area. City Attorney Lowell Denton said that outright censorship would be unconstitutional, so the council proposed other means of protecting the innocent. Smoking bans, strict crowd control ordinances, age limits, and noise regulations were considered as possible sanctions. The age factor was taken most seriously by the council. The city hired a child psychiatrist, Dr. Robert Demski, to do a $2,000 study on the effect of rock music on children, especially those under the age of thirteen. He concluded that the "glamorization of suicide, drug abuse, alcohol abuse, incest, rape, dehumanizing sexuality and violence as a way of life are potentially harmful influences on young people growing up."[39] Calling rock "potentially hazardous" Demski felt that if a child were depressed, and added that many were, then rock music could be the last straw which would push the child over the edge. The Texas council was also highly influenced by the Parents' Music Resource Center hearings which were taking place in Washington, D.C. concerning controversial lyrics.

A San Antonio-based promoter, Jack Orbin, planned to sue the council if he suffered business losses due to their actions. "Basically it's become a religious issue down here," he said, "and I think they'll bring about just what they're afraid of — they'll alienate youth here more than ever."[40] Orbin did agree to cooperate with PASS by supplying records, lyric sheets, and biographies of bands, as well as interviews with musicians if possible. PASS would then issue a monthly report evaluating rock groups which would be distributed free to stores and theaters.

But city council member Bob Thompson felt further action had to be taken because minors "deserve special protection in certain circumstances."[41] Hoping to take advantage of U.S. Supreme Court rulings that allowed for "local standards" when defining pornography, Thompson was pushing for legislation concerning age limits at concerts. Mayor Henry Cisneros wanted similar restrictions for minors that were applied to movie attendance. Orbin wondered how he was going to tell the difference between a 13- or 14-year-old since no one that age carried I.D.

The most vocal opposition to the city council's proposals came from the younger generation themselves. Mike Courtney, a twenty-six-year-old construction worker, set up an organization called Rock, Inc. His group operated booths outside San Antonio concert venues and registered voters against the proposed ordinance. RYDER or Rocking Youths Defending Equal Rights had nineteen members, most from school honor rolls, prepared to defend their music. As seventeen-year-old Rita Barrientos explained, "We have goals, we want things, but we listen to heavy metal and it hasn't ruined our minds. . . . I want to tell parents that we hear the foul language every day. We read it in books. There's no way they can protect us from it."[42] Perhaps not; but the good citizens of San Antonio were certainly going to try.

In November 1985 the city council passed a law designed to limit attendance of those under the age of fourteen at "obscene" rock concerts. They had to be accompanied by a parent or legal guardian. Obscene was defined as "vulgar or profane descriptions of sexual relations."[43] Orbin and the American Civil Liberties Union decided to sue the council and some of its members for unconstitutionality. Orbin was worried that he could be sued if anyone over fourteen was mistakenly barred from a concert that he produced. He also believed that he would have trouble attracting rock performers to a city that was so repressive. It was going to be a tough fight. As one councilman reportedly remarked, "the First Amendment should not apply to rock 'n' roll."[44] Still there was a good chance the constitution would prevail. The Supreme Court had recently upheld a suit and fines against Burbank, California municipal council which had tried to prohibit rock concerts in 1979 at the city's Starlight Bowl.

26

Visual Violations

Rock and roll has always been more than just music. Image has played a major role in rock culture right from the start. If teens couldn't see their favorite rock stars live in concert, they could be seen on an album cover or poster. Sometimes rock musicians made it into the movies. More often they appeared on TV on programs like "American Bandstand" or "Don Kirshner's Rock Concert."

In the 1980s another medium for rock visuals was created with the introduction of music videos. Rock videos are three-to-four-minute film clips accompanying a rock song. They can be seen on certain television channels, in clubs or on college campuses, or they can be rented or bought for home video machines.

The largest exposure for rock videos was on MTV, Music Television, Warner-Amex's twenty-four-hour cable network which has an audience of over eighteen million viewers. MTV was launched in 1981. Often a rock song would be aired first on MTV, and if it was popular, radio would pick it up. Thus MTV's main purpose was to promote rock groups and their songs. Record companies sent videos free to MTV and the station ran the name of the band, song, album, and label at the beginning and end of every clip.

In previous eras, visual violations had more to do with the actual performer. The physical gyrations were the biggest shockers in the 50s on TV while the lyrics themselves were inoffensive. Hairstyles and clothing were little criticized. A decade later it was these latter elements which drew greater flak than the gyrations which, having been around so long, had lost the power to shock. Sexual lyrics then came under fire because sexual material had disappeared for a time and its reappearance had more power to offend. The videos of the 80s opened up a whole new area for creative artists, and a whole new area for opponents. Opponents focused more on the peripheral elements, the scenes which depicted the songs. Attacks on sex rock drifted away from lyrics and often centered on scantily clad women or items opponents took to be overtly violent. The attacks, however, maintained a consistency. Rock was offensive and shouldn't be seen or allowed on the air because of lewd gyrations in the 50s, obscene lyrics in the 60s, and visual scenes in the 80s videos. Underlying all these attacks were similar outrages by the anti-rock forces.

Just as the 1950s generation of adults was upset by the sexuality of Elvis Presley and the rebellion and violence in *Blackboard Jungle*, so too were the 1980s parents disturbed by the sex and violence in rock videos. An early rock video to come under attack was Captain Beefheart's 1970 clip for "Lick My Decals Off . . . Baby." It was considered too strange and the title too obscene to be played on television.

Since MTV viewers included families and children, many bands would make two versions of the same video. The censored version was aimed at MTV while the racier version was for adult cable, video clubs, or home videos. But since MTV had the largest rock video viewing audience, most video producers geared their product to the standards of this station. And the standards were explicit. Said Ed Steinberg of the video club RockAmerica, "There are three ways to guarantee MTV rotation, no black faces, pretty women, and athletic guitar solos."[1]

It was ironic that even into its third decade rock and roll was still trying to deny its black roots. In 1983 rock superstar Rick James said a better name for MTV would be "White Rock TV," and Arthur Baker cocomposer of the rap hit "Planet Rock" said of MTV's roster, "They're all white groups playing black music. It's the same old story, racism."[2] It had been much the same in the 1950s with a black like Chuck Berry never getting the media attention of say a Presley because of the color of his skin. MTV did eventually add more black artists, especially after the success of Michael Jackson's videos, but whites dominated.

As well as making sure that rock videos did not offend the white market by showing too many blacks, MTV also censored sex and violence. As Bob Giraldi, a producer for MTV, put it, "we professionals are liable to ruin MTV by . . . taking that wildness out of it."[3] Anything controversial was aired on late-night time slots or edited. For example, the scene where a nubile young girl changes from street clothes into a bathing suit was excised from a Bryan Adam's video "Cuts Like a Knife."

Les Garland, programming vice-president at MTV, claimed to have only rejected "a handful" of videos for being offensive. One of these was Van Halen's "Pretty Woman" which was taken off the air after complaints from viewers about bondage scenes. Duran Duran's "Girls on Film" was only aired on MTV after shots of full-frontal female nudity and ice cubes being rubbed on bare nipples were cut.

John Sykes, another programming executive at MTV, explained that editing or banning of rock videos was necessary in only a few cases because most record companies knew what MTV's "guidelines and limitations" were. "We don't show anything we consider to be gratuitous sex or violence," Sykes explained. "But censorship is a gray area."[4]

Women's groups have complained about sexism in rock videos. Many of the clips treat women as sex objects. Women are often scantily clad and shown in hot pursuit of the male rock star. Jennifer Brown, the executive director of the National Organization for Women (NOW) felt that rock videos were "very destructive" and she was "very distressed to see a new avenue of exploitation opening up. But we can't advocate censorship," Brown said. "There's a First Amendment issue there, for one thing."[5]

Feminist groups were more aggressive about pushing for censorship of album covers, however. In December 1976 the twelve thousand-member California chapter of NOW and WAVAW (Women Against Violence Against Women) threatened a statewide boycott against seven Warner Brothers record labels — Atco, Atlantic, Asylum, Elektra, Nonesuch, Reprise, and Warner Brothers. Their demand was that Warner stop using images of women as victims of sexual or other violence on album covers and other ads for records. WAVAW singled out the Rolling Stones' album cover "Black and Blue" as exploitative. Advertising and billboards for the album showed a bound and beaten woman smiling. The caption said, "I'm black and blue from the Rolling Stones and I love it." The billboard was removed immediately after the complaint was received. NOW and WAVAW said they would widen their campaign in the future to include other record labels. They claimed that after surveying major record retail outlets they found forty-eight albums containing explicit or implied sexual references. They specifically objected to images implying abuse, rape, or bondage.

The Recording Industry Association of America (RIAA) supported the feminists. Stanley Gortikov, head of the RIAA, said he acknowledged a need to seek "more careful reviews and discretion by recording companies in graphics" so that packaging would not demean women. But

Gortikov noted that rock artists, not record companies, usually had a contractual right to choose their own album covers.

Meanwhile the boycott went into effect in Los Angeles, San Francisco, San Diego, and Orange County. By February 1977 two of Warner's labels, Elektra and Asylum, agreed to oppose any album covers depicting women as victims. Joe Smith, chairman of the board of Elektra/Asylum, said that the company would try to influence artists against using images of women that were brutal. "We don't want to put out a product that offends anyone," Smith explained. "And it's not only a matter of sales; it's a question of morality and eithics as well."[6]

The boycott continued, however. The two women's groups said it would remain in effect until the other labels agreed to a similar policy. It wasn't until November 1979, almost three years after the boycott started, that Warner Brothers agreed to NOW and WAVAW's demands. A spokesman for Warners stated that the company opposed "the depiction of violence against women or men on album covers and in related promotional material and . . . the exploitation of violence, sexual or otherwise, in any form."[7] Warners said the agreement took so long to come about because it took time to coordinate the various labels. Bob Rolontz, information director for the corporation, estimated that maybe fifty out of five thousand album covers might be considered "violent."[8]

WAVAW representatives intended to meet with Warner's art department staff to "explain the subtler points of what is and isn't offensive."[9] A spokeswoman for the group felt that since Warners was one of the largest corporations to make a public statement about their policy, "a precedent has been set for the other major record companies which we will be approaching."[10]

Censorship became an issue with a poster enclosure in the Dead Kennedys' 1985 album "Frankenchrist." The poster showed close-ups of ten sets of male and female genitals engaged in sexual acts. Eric Boucher, the twenty-seven-year-old leader of the group, who went by the stage name of Jello Biafra, was charged with distributing harmful matter to minors. He faced a maximum penalty of a year in jail or a $2,000 fine. The complaint was filed by the mother of a teenager. The poster had been created by Swiss surrealist artist H. R. Giger. Giger had previously won an award for special effects in the movie, *Alien*. Again the issue of art versus morality became a rock-related problem.

Video stations were also careful about toning down violence and sex and adhering to "community standards." Cynthia Friedland, programmer for ATV Night Flight, defined these standards as "no frontal or rear nudity and no bloody violence." ATV rejected Trio's "Da Da Da" which showed a woman being stabbed in the back, and Rod Stewart's "Tonight I'm

Yours" because it showed partially clad women. ATV also edited out an explicit sex scene from Blue Öyster Cult's "Joan Crawford Has Risen from the Grave."

Videos were censored according to which countries they would be marketed in. Rod Stewart's "Do Ya Think I'm Sexy" had nudity in the European version but not in the American product. But producing two versions of one video was expensive. In 1983 costs ran in the neighborhood of $25,000 per video. This caused some video producers to practice self-censorship and create a safe version to begin with.

Most pay cable stations were more relaxed about sexy videos. A spokesman for ON-TV explained, "Censorship is not what we're about, we're a pay service."[11] In other words, as long as there were customers for their products ON-TV would not have to exercise caution. But Home Box Office (HBO), the largest subscription pay station in the United States was less willing to take risks. "We stay away from violence and nudity in the music videos that we use," said an HBO official.[12]

The Rolling Stones' 1983 video "Under Cover of the Night" showed Mick Jagger being murdered by terrorists in Central America. BBC-TV's chart show "Top of the Pops" would not screen it. Another British show, "The Tube," used it only after it was edited according to the requirements of the Independent Broadcasting Authority. Explaining the film was about political repression and that there was no "gratuitous violence" in it, Jagger noted that Britain was the only country to ban the video. Julien Temple, who directed the piece, commented, "I don't know what the fuss is about. The average kid in America has, by the time he gets to 21, seen 65,000 killings on television."[13]

In 1984 another Stones video was banned, this time by MTV. The clip called "She Was Hot" was rejected because it showed the brand name on a soft drink can, and because it had a scene where the buttons pop off a bulging male crotch. The Style Council's video "Long Hot Summer" showed two of the male band members tickling each other's ears and smiling. Their record company, Polydor, censored the bit because it might be misinterpreted.

Rock videos became the focus of a censorship issue in Canada in 1984. David Scott, chairman of the Canadian Coalition Against Violent Entertainment said that rock videos averaged eighteen violent acts per hour versus nine per hour on prime time TV.[14] Violent acts or lyrics were defined by the coalition as hostile verbal or physical expression. Scott wanted the Ontario Board of Censors to review videos just as they did movies being shown in public theaters. According to the Canadian coalition's statistics, thirty-eight percent of TV rock videos contained violent acts, eighteen percent suggested violence, and thirty-five percent had sexual violence.[15]

John Martin, producer of a video show "New Music" on Toronto's CITY-TV, said that the majority of rock videos were not "designed as exploitation. Most are just plain fun."[16] The Ontario Censor Board had no jurisdiction over what was shown on TV, as this was the mandate of the Canadian Radio-Television and Telecommunications Commission (CRTC). But the Board did agree to screen rock videos shown in public places such as schools or clubs.

In Vancouver a popular Friday night show on CBC television, "Good Rockin' Tonight," ran into trouble with rock videos in 1985. The popular program was attracting sixty percent of its target group—fifteen to twenty-five-year-old viewers. When CBC executives moved the show to a Thursday time slot, host Terry David Mulligan resigned. The show's producer, Ken Gibson, felt that "someone is really trying to kill the show." He noted that CBC brass were nervous about images of bondage and violence in videos like Power Station's "Some Like It Hot," or Bryan Adams' "Cuts Like a Knife." "We're talking censorship here," said Gibson, "a form of pressure. As a result, we've been playing it a little safer, a little middle-of-the-road."[17]

Violence in rock videos also became an issue in the United States in late 1984. The National Coalition on TV Violence (NCTV), a three thousand-member group consisting primarily of physicians and educators, reported on a monitoring project covering nine hundred music videos. They found high levels of violence especially between men and women. Observing videos shown on MTV and WTBS the coalition said the TV channels averaged 17.9 acts of violence per hour during the month they were monitored.[18] Videos of heavy metal groups contained the most violence, according to the coalition. Dr. Thomas Radecki, a psychiatrist, and director of research for the group, said "The intense sadistic and sexual violence of a large number of rock music videos is overwhelming."[19]

One of the videos that particularly offended Radecki was "Rock School" by a group called Heaven. In the film, high school punk stars dumped their books in the trash, and were chased by a school guard with a rifle and a Doberman pinscher. A sadistic principal wearing a stocking mask threw the kids out of school and the final scene showed the kids and teachers rioting to rock and roll music. Doesn't the story sound familiar? Remember *Blackboard Jungle*? Remember adult reaction to the film in the 1950s? As the saying goes, the more things change—the more they stay the same. Radecki's group also disapproved of the Jacksons' video "Torture" because it showed evil women trying to kill one of the singers, and ended with him falling into the web of a spider woman. Also criticized was "The Curly Shuffle" video by Jump'n the Saddle Band. This film showed old footage of the Three Stooges which was described by the coalition as "endless slapstick violence." One wonders how "endless" a three-to-four-minute clip can be.

The coalition's findings were reinforced by a 1985 study carried out by researchers at the University of Tennessee-Chattanooga. They studied sixty-two MTV videos and found that sixty percent contained sex or violence although only five percent were said to show deviant sex such as sadomasochism or bondage.[20]

But like all censorship issues, the question boiled down to how to decide when violence or sex reached offensive or disturbing levels. For one psychiatrist at a private Connecticut mental hospital, MTV had to be banned for patients, because it was just too excessive. They were allowed, however, to watch the evening news.[21]

27

Thou Shalt Not Rock

Since its inception rock and roll music has often been equated with evil. It has been linked with voodoo, violence, and satanism. On several occasions rock music has even been considered an inspiration for murder. This association was made after the Stones' Altamont concert, and it was brought forward again in connection with the 1969 Tate/LaBianca murders committed by psychopath Charles Manson and his "Family" (members of his commune). Manson had a fixation for the Beatles. He had tried to contact them by phone and letter, but they never responded.

When the "White Album" was released in 1968, Manson felt the lyrics had special messages for him. He interpreted one of the songs "Helter Skelter" (a term for a British amusement park ride), as a sign for him to start killing "pigs" (members of the white establishment).

Many people, including the district attorney in the Manson trial, seized on Manson's Beatlemania as certain proof that rock and roll music brought out an instinct for slaughter. Right-wing religious groups particularly liked to use Manson as an example of a man rendered criminally insane by the music. What they never alluded to was the fact that Manson was equally fixated on the Bible. It was passages from the Bible that Manson read repeatedly, which gave him clues to the Beatle messages, and which directed him toward his murderous plan. He often quoted from Revelations. Manson saw himself as the king whose Latin name in the Catholic Douay Version of Revelations 9:2, was Exterminans.[1] Therefore, if one were to accuse words of inspiring Manson to kill, the words in the Bible would be a prime influence.

Similarly, it was the Bible and Christian fundamentalists which planted the idea of assassinating John Lennon in Mark David Chapman's sick mind. Chapman had also fixated on the Beatles, particularly John Lennon. He taught himself to play guitar and considered Lennon his idol. In his disturbed life, Chapman became a born-again Christian, hoping to find solace in Christ. The fundamentalists, of course, saw John Lennon as a hopeless sinner, and rock and roll music as the devil's work. They particularly despised Lennon for his remarks about being more popular than Jesus. In 1971, Lennon produced the song "Imagine" which idealized a peaceful world. Kids in Chapman's religious group used to joke about it, saying "Imagine, imagine if John Lennon was dead."[2] Chapman did more than imagine Lennon's death. In 1980 he shot and killed him.

Rock music was again targeted as influencing a murderer in 1985. Richard Ramirez, a twenty-five-year-old from the Los Angeles area, stood accused of killing sixteen people and raping or assaulting twenty others. Ramirez was said to be obsessed with the devil. He also listened to the music of a rock group AC/DC, especially their 1979 album, "Highway to Hell." One of the cuts on the LP was "Night Prowler" which had the lines

> I am your night prowler, I sleep in the day./I am your night prowler, get out of my way/ . . . Too scared to turn your light out, 'cuz there is something on your mind./Was that a noise outside the window? Watch that shadow on the blind./And you lie there naked, like a body in a tomb./Suspended animation, as I slip into your room.

Ramirez left a cap with the AC/DC logo on it at the home of one of his victims.

In 1982 Brian Johnson of AC/DC told an interviewer, "I've heard some people say there is some sort of devil worship in the band. It's so silly I'm not going to talk about it anymore. I'm writing about the same things I've always written about: fun."[3] Yet people insisted that AC/DC stood for Anti-Christ, Devil's Child. On the album cover of "Highway to Hell," one of the band members, Bon Scott, had horns on top of his head. When Ramirez was caught several television stations played "Night Prowler" and flashed pictures of the album cover. The *Los Angeles Times* devoted two columns to AC/DC. Ramirez was wearing a T-shirt advertising a whiskey company when he was apprehended. Nobody in the media mentioned the name of the company or blamed alcohol for the killings, even though they were quick to do so with rock.

The band name stood for electricity, as in Alternating Current/Direct Current. Ramirez had no connection with the band and the group was neither more nor less to blame for things done by its fans than is Jesus for misdeeds done by his followers.

Rock music was even blamed for suicide. In 1985 the parents of a California youth sued CBS Records and rock singer Ozzy Osbourne, accusing Osbourne's song "Suicide Solution" of influencing their son to kill himself. They cited the lines, "Where to hide/Suicide is the only way out. Don't you know what it's really about?" Apparently the boy shot himself in the temple while listening to music through headphones. He had also been drinking. The parents felt that because of their son's "psychological background and personality" he was "particularly susceptible to the suggestions of the lyrics found on record albums."[4] Thomas Anderson, their born-again Christian lawyer, explained that it was a felony in California to encourage anyone to commit suicide.

Osbourne defended the song claiming that the word "solution" referred to a liquid. He said the lyrics did not promote suicide but were concerned with the alcohol poisoning death of his friend Bon Scott of AC/DC. "Do you honestly think that, as a married man with six kids, I want to see anyone injured?," he asked.[5] Osbourne hired attorney Howard L Weitzmann to defend him. "Romeo and Juliet cannot be blamed for the many lovers' suicides that have happened over the years," said Weitzmann. "Movies that were seen by millions of people do not result in chain saw massacres,"[6] he noted. As of the writing of this book, the first court decision went against the parents.

The religious right had always been opposed to rock music but never had they been so vocal as in the 1970s and 1980s. Fundamentalism had always been strong among Baptists and Pentecostals but by 1976, forty-eight percent of American Protestants claimed to have had a born-again experience, and forty-two percent believed in the literal and divinely inspired truth of the Bible.[7]

Fundamentalism gained some converts among the young in the 1960s who were known as "Jesus freaks." But when Jimmy Carter, a born-again Christian, became president in 1976, the religious right really came into its own. This was reinforced by the Reagan presidency beginning in 1980 which threw its support behind Jerry Falwell and the Moral Majority. By 1983 thirteen hundred radio stations were Christian-owned and operated. That number represents one out of every seven radio stations.[8] Their listening audience comprised 150 million people. Twenty percent of television viewers or thirteen million households tuned into Christian stations and programs.[9]

Record burnings, anti-rock sermons and lectures, paranoia about backward masking, and several books warning about the evils of rock and roll characterized the fundamentalist crusades against the music. The first major record burning in the 1970s occurred in Tallahassee, Florida in 1976. The Reverend Charles Boykin of Lakewood Baptist Church preached against rockers like Elton John (an admitted bisexual), the Rolling Stones (for onstage debauchery), and John Denver (for smoking marijuana). Boykin claimed that rock music led to "illicit sex, drugs, and homosexuality." In November, he scheduled a record burning where $2,000 worth of records and tapes were destroyed outside the church by youthful members of the congregation. So popular was this idea that people began sending hundreds of records a day to Boykin to be destroyed. A second burning took place in December when Boykin preached a sermon on "The Evils of Rock" at Southside Baptist Church. Five thousand dollars worth of records were set on fire or smashed. When asked why the records weren't just given away, one of the youths explained it would be like giving away dope. Boykin said his record bonfires were unlike the book burnings in Nazi Germany because the record burnings were voluntary.

The most outrageous assertions Boykin made was that a survey had found that of one thousand girls who became pregnant out of wedlock, 984 had been listening to rock music while fornicating.[10] Boykin gave varying sources for his statistical evidence, depending on who he was talking to. He claimed that a professor at Howes-Anderson College in Hammond, Indiana had provided the data. Another time he said he got the figures from a 1968 *Time* magazine article (an article that did not exist). Boykin told Chicago columnist Mike Royko that an evangelist from West Virginia gave him the pregnancy information. When Royko asked, "And you believe his statistics?" Boykin replied, "Oh yes. There's a definite relationship between illicit sex and any music with a syncopated beat."[11]

Perhaps, however, Boykin got the pregnancy theory, if not the actual statistics, from the Population Institute in New York City. In 1975 this organization felt there was a link between rock lyrics and the rise in the number of unwed mothers. The institute started a project to "raise the consciousness of the record industry" even though they admitted there was "no statistical evidence linking any one song to the sharp increase in the number of U.S. teenagers having pregnancies outside wedlock."[12] (Robert Elliot, director of the Planned Parenthood Federation of America listed lack of available contraceptive services and lack of sex education as major causes of teenage pregnancy.)

Norman Fleishman, West Coast director of the Population Institute, claimed that the record industry showed a "great amount of support" for the institute's project to "encourage greater awareness of music's impact on popular sexual mores."[13] However, the Recording Industry Association of America had no comment on the matter.

An individual protest against rock music came from born-again disk jockey Jack Carey of WQUA-AM in Moline, Illinois. Carey quit his job because the station executives would not allow him to choose songs at his own discretion. Carey was particularly opposed to playing the Stones' hit "Miss You" and Exile's "Kiss You All Over." Carey's was the self-righteousness of the newly reformed sinner which is often the most fervent kind of moralism. Carey had been born again after pleading guilty to statutory rape charges in Baltimore. He was given a suspended sentence.

More religious opposition to rock came from the Dade Christian School in Miami in 1984. Students were forbidden to attend a Jackson Brothers concert because rock music would lead to dancing, drinking, drugs and "other unacceptable behavior." Any students who attended would be given fifteen demerits (twenty-five and you were expelled).

Perhaps the most vicious attack on rock and roll was the 1981 crusade by two brothers in their twenties, both ministers ordained by the Jesus People Fellowship in Minnesota. Steve and Jim Peters of the Zion Christian Life Center in St. Paul organized a bonfire and album-smashing event where $500,000 worth of records and tapes were destroyed. About one hundred people attended. Steve described rock as "one of the largest satanic forces in the country." He called through a bullhorn, "Knowing that the life-styles, lyrics, intentions and album covers of many of the rock stars are perverse, immoral, profane and unscriptural, and that they often condone and/or promote indulgence in the same, we rid our lives of them tonight!"[14]

The Peters brothers held about fifty anti-rock lectures in 1980 called "What the Devil's Wrong With Rock Music?" Fourteen record burnings were also organized by the brothers that year. The seminars, which started in 1979, included Bible quotes, slides of album covers and rock stars, and tapes of music. The lectures, which have continued into the present, warned that rock music "will be harmful to your spiritual, emotional and mental health. We recommend gospel and Christian music only."[15]

Some of the "information" the lecturers imparted to their audiences was that the girls on the cover of an Alan Parsons Project album wore veils to cover syphilitic sores; the name of the rock group KISS stood for Kids in Service to Satan; and the song "Hotel California" by the Eagles referred to the church of Satan. Pastor Steve noted that rock music involved more than just a few demons "hiding in a bongo drum over in Africa." But he was quick to explain that he was not condemning rock musicians because after all "Jesus died for them too. They're all on my prayer list."[16]

Steve and Jim credited their mother with instilling them with their keen moral values. She knew right away that the Beach Boys' music wasn't Christian and that Satan was all around them. Mrs. Peters also knew that some people compared the record burnings to the Nazi book bonfires, but this didn't disturb her. "I shouldn't say this," she admitted, "but when we were in high school, we thought Mr. Hitler had some pretty good ideas. He was particularly good in the sciences. But look at what happens without God. If Hitler had accepted Jesus Christ as his personal savior, he wouldn't have done anything wrong."[17]

The brothers sold $8.00 cassettes of their lectures and as of 1981, three thousand had been purchased.[18] Jim and another brother, Dan, also wrote a book on the evils of rock which was published in 1984 by the Bethany Fellowship in Minneapolis. Titled *Why Knock Rock?* the book discussed rock's "four fatal flaws" which were lyrics, lifestyles, goals, and graphics. The authors believed rock and roll fostered despondency, suicide, or escapism; was grossly commercial, rebellious, and violent; encouraged hedonism, occultism and satanism; and promoted drug and alcohol use.

One chapter, called "Dead and Gone: Rock and Roll Obituaries," listed the names of 116 people who had died relatively young, and who had either been rock stars or were somehow associated with rock. Sometimes the link was a loose one. For example, the actor Sal Mineo was included because he had a role in the movie *Rebel Without a Cause*. No doubt this chapter was meant to be a dire warning on two counts. First, rock was murderous and second, rockers got what they deserved for their sinfulness.

The book also warned against rock concerts where "hundreds of people have died," and concerts were discussed under the heading, "Dante's Inferno Is Coming to Your Home Town."[19]

As the authors emphasized, their book was to be seen as a call to action. This was clear in their "Message to Parents" section which urged adults to set a good example for their children. Lest there be any confusion about which groups to boycott, a "Ten Most Wanted List" was published near the end of the book. The names included Angus Young (AC/DC), Rob Halford (Judas Priest), Prince, Joe Elliot (Def Leppard), Gene Simmons (KISS), Mick Jagger (Rolling Stones), David Bowie, Ozzy Osbourne, David Lee Roth (Van Halen), and Steve Perry (Journey).[20]

The authors provided addresses for these rock stars and told their readers to write them, explaining,

In hope that, through prayer and open dialogue, many of rock music's most notorious stars can come to know Christ and thus change their music and their motives, we have compiled a list of Ten Most Wanted. If you would like to change the future of rock music, and of one of American culture's most pervasive influences, please pray for the artists on this list on a daily basis. You might also consider writing to them. Tell them about Jesus and let them know you love them and are praying for them — but also that you cannot tolerate their behavior and recorded material. Give them an opportunity to meet the Lord through you![21]

In case the rock stars did not voluntarily see the light, the book also provided a sample form letter which could be sent to representatives in Congress protesting obscenity or drug lyrics in rock music. Also attached was a petition which could be filled out. The petition, addressed to the president, members of Congress, and the chairman of the F.C.C., called for ratings on record albums similar to motion picture ratings; the banning of all "obscene, indecent, or profane" records from radio and television; and prohibiting sale of such records to those under the age of seventeen.

The idea for anti-rock seminars caught on with other fundamentalists besides the Peterses. Members of the Maranatha Christian Fellowship, headquartered in Gainesville, Florida, were touring the country in 1983 bringing their seminar "Is Rock and Roll a Highway to Hell?" to college campuses. The two-hour lecture presented lyric sheets and examples of backward masking where satanic messages could supposedly be heard if records were played in reverse. In order to hear a recording backwards, a reel-to-reel tape recorder had to be used and then played in reverse. Since the average home did not have such equipment, fundamentalists argued that the backward messages were absorbed subliminally.

Gary Brown, leader of the Maranatha tour group, stressed that "music is either from God or Satan — it's never neutral."[22] Brown claimed that the red ink on the cover of a Marvel Comic about KISS was actually the blood of band members. He also singled out punk rock as being "focused around degradation."

A California evangelist, Reverend Gary Greenwald of Irvine, was another Christian who carried the anti-rock message, this time to Canada in 1982. He told an audience of one thousand in Lethbridge, Alberta that if they wanted to be on the safe side they should destroy all their rock records. Two nights after his sermon, four hundred people gathered to smash three thousand records. Greenwald had been lecturing against rock since 1979. He was also concerned with backward masking. He charged that Led Zeppelin's "Stairway to Heaven," when played backward, contained the phrase "There's no denying it, here's to my sweet Satan."

Greenwald had a heckler at one of his Alberta seminars, however. Peter Raabe, a local radio talk show host on CILA-FM, challenged the preacher's accusations. He claimed that if enough phrases were played backwards some of them would sound meaningful. Raabe reversed some of Greenwald's sermon tapes and said that they too revealed Satanic messages like, "hell on earth divinely greet."[23] Raabe felt that Mr. Greenwald told his audience what to hear, and through the power of suggestion, they did hear it. Raabe tried plugging his ears so as not to hear Greenwald's alleged backwards phrase. "When he played the music," said Raabe, "I couldn't hear anything."[24]

John Vokey, a University of Lethbridge psychology professor studying subliminal messages in music and advertising, agreed that backward masking was mainly myth. "A lot of it's random noise," said Vokey. "People will hear whatever you tell them to when you play it."[25]

But the California Assembly Committee on Consumer Protection and Toxic Materials took backward masking seriously. Assemblyman Phillip D. Wyman (R-Tehachapi) introduced a bill in the state legislature after one of his constituents complained about satanic messages in records. She had heard about these messages at a religious meeting. The bill asked for warning labels on records carrying subliminal information. The assembly committee conducted a hearing in April 1982, and invited consultant William H. Yarroll, II, president of Applied Potentials Institute of Aurora, Colorado, to play records which used backward masking. One member of the committee said that without the printed lyric sheet she would never have made out the inaudible messages.[26]

The committee supplied *Billboard* magazine with a list of some of the songs purported to use backward masking. These included "Revolution" by the Beatles, "Snowblind" by Styx, "Stairway to Heaven" by Led Zeppelin, and "Raunch N' Roll" by Black Oak Arkansas. The committee also supplied *Billboard* with a diagram by Yarroll allegedly showing how the conscious and unconscious portions of the brain interact to create the listener's "self-image." *Billboard* found the diagram "incomprehensible." No record industry officials had been invited to attend the hearing or seemed to show interest in it. Nothing more was heard of the proposed bill and the issue was dropped.

But the California hearing was not completely without effect. Representative Robert K. Dornan (R-California) visited Wyman in May and was spurred to introduce a federal bill which would require warning labels on rock records that had supposed backward demonic messages. The proposed label would say, "Warning: This record contains background masking that makes a verbal statement which is audible when the record is played backwards."[27] Nothing came of this bill either.

Huntington House, a religious publisher in Louisiana, felt there was enough evidence on backward masking to do a book on the subject. Titled *Backward Masking Unmasked*, the publication was written by fundamentalist minister Jacob Aranza, and had an introduction by Louisiana State Senator Bill Keith. Citing William Yarroll of Applied Potentials Institute again, Aranza said that Yarroll described a "check valve" at the base of the brain called the reticular activating system. (There is indeed such a network of nerves.) Aranza explained that, "What Mr. Yarroll is actually saying is that if someone said to you, 'Satan is God,' you would immediately reject it or your 'check valve,' the Recitular Activating System would reject it. But if you heard, 'dog si natas' a number of times, which is 'Satan is God' backwards, it would be 'decoded' by the right part (or creative part) of the brain and stored as fact!"[28] There was no scientific study or experiment cited which proved Mr. Yarroll's thesis. According to Aranza some groups didn't even intentionally put backward messages in their songs they were merely "pawns in the hands of Satan."[29] Not surprisingly, the book gave very few examples of backward masking messages. Most of the chapters rehashed the evils of rock as described in the Peters' book. To get the real story on backward masking readers were advised to send for a ninety-minute cassette to actually hear the messages "for yourself," at the bargain price of just $5.95.

Fundamentalists have not been able to abolish rock and roll, but they have made converts. The most famous was Bob Dylan who was born-again and made two albums with Christian themes, "Slow Train Coming" and "Saved." Disco queen Donna Summer was another rock singer who got religion.

But there must have been an element of the "if you can't beat them, join them" philosophy among fundamentalists, because evangelical rock became a phenomenon in the 1980s. Although Christian pop had been around for a long time, the new Christian "heavy metal" bands like Stryper were recorded on secular labels, sold in secular retail stores, and shared the concert stage with nonreligious bands. The four members of Stryper looked a lot like KISS. They wore tight leather and spandex clothing, used a lot of makeup and chains, and had wild hair. Their name came from Isaiah 53:5 "with HIS stripes we are healed." During their performances Stryper tossed about 500 bibles into the audience. The group wanted to be known as "a metal band for Christ."[30]

Although some audiences were turned off by the Christian message in rock, even fans of Twisted Sister had shown enthusiasm for Stryper. Would rock and roll be infiltrated by sheep in wolves' clothing?

28

Moms Horrified:
Rollers Curl PMRC's Hair

The 1985 attack on rock lyrics began in late 1983 but its roots stretched back to the mid-1950s assault on "leerics" and to Jesse Jackson's late 1970s indignation over "sex rock." As in earlier times the 1985 attack focused on rock and roll's so-called suggestive and obscene content. Since it was a different time, the opposition labeled the beast with a slightly different name, "porn rock."

In October of 1983 Rick Alley, a thirty-year-old junior executive at a machine tool company in Cincinnati dropped into a local record store and purchased a copy of the Prince album "1999." Alley played one side of the record and found no problem as it was basically comprised of top forty hits. When he played the flip side, however, he came face to face with four letter words. As the Alleys listened, along with their eleven-year-old daughter and eight-year-old son, they were particularly offended by one cut, "Let's Pretend We're Married," which contained an "impassioned four-letter invitation to simulate marriage." The Alleys later reread the lyrics from the album sleeve and decided that Prince sang different, and more obscene, lyrics on the record than were actually printed on the sleeve. The Alleys began a crusade against "porn rock," specifically to get accurate lyrics printed on the album. It quickly mushroomed.

Alley first took his complaint to the *Cincinnati Enquirer* where he learned that other parents had similar complaints. A reporter on that paper, Frank Weikel, told Alley to take his complaint to the Parent Teachers Association (PTA) at the school that Alley's children attended, Delshire Elementary. Weikel then persuaded Alley to petition the national PTA. In the summer of 1984 Alley attended the national PTA convention in Las

Vegas where he outlined his story. The delegates of the 5.4 million-member organization applauded Alley and took up the fight themselves.[1] At the convention the national PTA adopted a resolution which called for accurate song lyrics to be printed on all record albums. The group sent out a letter to some twenty-nine record companies and the record company trade organization, the Recording Industry Association of America (RIAA) with these demands as well as a request to rate and label their product.

The RIAA response was not enthusiastic and a spokesman said of the idea, "I find it a dangerous kind of precedent. . . . It's not censorship per se, but it certainly does open up a Pandora's box of unpleasant possibilities."[2] By the end of 1984 the campaign had had no effect. The RIAA washed its hands of the matter and left the rating question up to the individual companies, which simply ignored the PTA. Warner Brothers Records vice-president Bob Merlis said his company would never put warning stickers on its product and noted with insight that the whole issue was just another battle in the thirty-year war on rock and that "one of the functions of rock 'n' roll is to annoy parents. And this just proves that nothing changes."[3]

The PTA's lack of success turned around in the spring of 1985 when a new group formed in May of that year, took up the battle. That group was the Parents' Music Resource Center (PMRC), a grass roots organization composed of Washington, D.C. wives and mothers who were for the most part wives of administration officials or of conservative members of Congress. They quickly became known as the "Washington wives." The cochairs of the group were Susan Baker, wife of James Baker the treasury secretary, and Tipper Gore, spouse of Senator Albert Gore (D-Tennessee). Other founding members were Ethelann Stuckey, wife of former Georgia congressman Williamson Stuckey; Sally Nevius, whose husband John had been a member of the Washington city council; and Pam Howar, married to the head of a large construction firm in Washington. Of the original twenty members of the PMRC, seventeen were married to some of Washington's most powerful politicians and, as one writer noted, half of them "are married to 10% of the Senate."[4]

The PMRC charged that rock music had become sexually explicit and pornographic. Particularly offensive was a Prince cut "Darling Nikki" from the "Purple Rain" album. Prince sang of a girl he met in a hotel lobby "masturbating with a magazine." Pam Howar claimed when she heard that song, "The floodgates opened." Also upsetting to the PMRC was "Sugar Walls" by Sheena Easton and "Eat Me Alive" by Judas Priest. PMRC identified five basic negative themes in rock music: free love/sex, sadomasochism, rebellion, the occult, and drugs.

The music, they felt, had reached an all-time low in terms of gratuitous sex and violence. According to Howar, "Now, it's no holds barred. Anything goes." Rock star Madonna was teaching young girls "how to be a porn queen in heat."[5] The group wanted a rating system for records and had mailed a letter to parents' groups and the media claiming that most parents were not aware of the lyrics their kids were listening to and that rock groups advocated "satanic rituals, the others sing of open rebellion against parental authority, others sing of killing babies."[6]

Explaining how the group came into being, Howar said the members were all friends, "And we thought we'd try to create some public awareness about this."[7] The group held a meeting at a local church on May 13, attended by about four hundred people, to discuss how to combat "porn rock." One speaker was Jeff Ling, a former rock musician who gave it all up to become a youth minister and who presented a slide show documenting the pornographic rock lyrics.

The initial response of the record industry to the idea that it adopt voluntary lyric curbs was a stance of no comment. The National Association of Broadcasters (NAB) did take notice, however, and president Edward Fritts sent a notice to over eight hundred station group owners of this new lobbying effort. Due to the political power behind the PMRC other allies were quickly engaged in the fight and the media offered prime space.

One such ally was Kandy Stroud, described as a singer with the Washington Choral Arts Society, who aired her views under the title "Stop Pornographic Rock" in *Newsweek* magazine on the prestigious guest editor page.[8] That her material came from the PMRC was obvious since she named the same offensive material, Prince's masturbation song, Judas Priest, Madonna, and "Sugar Walls," although nothing was mentioned about the PMRC. Other tunes that got her goat were "Relax" by Frankie Goes to Hollywood, and Mötley Crue's "Ten Seconds to Love," about intercourse on an elevator. She was appalled by the various "orgasmic moans and howls" and "the tasteless, graphic and gratuitous sexuality saturating the airwaves and filtering into our homes."[9] It was all worse than earlier material by artists such as Presley and the Rolling Stones since what had been innuendo had now become overt.

A couple of weeks later David Gergen, a former White House communications director, then a columnist, editorialized in *U.S. News & World Report* on "X-Rated Records."[10] After summarizing the PMRC activities to date, Gergen noted that rock and roll had always pushed at the edge of social responsibility but wondered of the current stuff, "why do we allow this filth?" For him the difference in music from the past to the present was like from "swimming suits in *Sports Illustrated* to the center-fold in *Hustler*."[11] He applauded the efforts of the PMRC in the face of those who said nothing could be done about rock music. He felt there was a growing army of parents who were anxious and willing to join the fight.

The response of the industry to the PTA had been one mainly of silence and studied indifference. In the face of pressure from the PMRC, however, the response changed rather dramatically to that of knuckling under to the pressure, blaming somebody else, and a fear response. It was those politicians standing behind the Washington wives who provoked this sudden turnaround.

The previously mentioned letter Edward Fritts sent out May 13 came about after a meeting with the PMRC. The letter suggested the NAB was not trying to impose censorship but simply to "foster awareness" of the problem with top management people who might not be aware of the type of material their program directors were selecting. The letter quoted the lyrics of the Prince tune, "Darling Nikki," as an example and closed with the thought that it was up to each broadcast licensee to decide how it would carry out "it's programming responsibilities under the Communications Act."[12] This letter marked the first time a broadcast industry leader had gone on record expressing concern over rock lyrics.

On May 31, Fritts sent a second letter, this one to the heads of forty-five record companies. It asked the companies to send printed lyrics to radio stations along with all records so stations could "clearly understand what words are being sung."[13] He claimed this was not censorship, just a decision-making aid for stations. At the companies, only Clive Davis, of Arista Records offered comment. He felt the offensive records accounted for only about one percent of the music and that censoring artists was unfair as they had as much "right to be heard as a novelist or a playwright."[14]

Editorials continued to turn up blasting rock and lionizing the PMRC. One such editorial appeared in the *Washington Post* where writer William Raspberry applauded the wives for taking action while most everyone else was hidebound by apathy and inaction, though all were said to be "sick of the filth that passes for lyrics."[15] Portrayed not as blue-nosed record smashers but mothers saving their children from exposure to "filth, violence, sado-masochism and explicit sex" every time they turned on the radio, the PMRC were almost turned into martyrs, the last line of defense between decency and total degeneracy.

Some members of the industry continued to resist the PMRC-backed pressure but others yielded. One record company MCA, sent a letter to programmers stating that "Let's Talk" by One Way was too suggestive for programming. The company apologized on behalf of itself and the group, and announced the single had been pulled. Willie Davis, the president of the five-station All-Pro Broadcasting, said that Fritts's letter reinforced a policy his company had set a few years earlier. A number of radio stations in New York and Los Angeles dropped from their playlist "Sugar Walls" and Marvin Gaye's album "Dream of a Lifetime."

Even retailers began to feel the effect of the pressure. A large record store chain, Camelot, sent a memo to all its stores warning them not to give "Darling Nikki" any in-store airplay. It was the first such warning ever issued by the chain.[16] At least one outlet of the Record Bar chain, in Columbia, South Carolina, imposed the same ban. Heavy metal lyrics and album covers were under fire in the South where Harold Guilfoil of Disc Jockey at Owensboro, Kentucky, said the chain's executives wondered how long they could "keep shipping albums into the deep Bible belt that depict demons with crosses."[17] In Detroit, albums by Witchfinder General, W.A.S.P., and Impaler were returned to the companies by Harmony House because of unacceptable covers.

In July 1985 the "running scared" had begun in earnest and was beginning to resemble a stampede. At station KAFM in Dallas vice-president William Steding had recently formed a group called the National Music Review Council (NMRC) which was intended to act as a review board. Steding envisioned the board having equal representation from all facets of the music industry and acting to warn consumers and broadcasters about songs with "abusive words or messages." If the board approved a song it would receive "a seal, similar to the Good Housekeeping seal, that is basically a positive statement about what is inside."[18] Steding proposed this board because he feared the PMRC had enough power to push a bill through Congress which would require music to be reviewed by a policing unit which likely wouldn't include music industry members.

The music video television outlet, MTV, also met with the PMRC. Even though the women had directed their attack at records, MTV was sufficiently worried to call the meeting at their own request. MTV feared that if records fell to PMRC pressure, music videos would soon follow. At the meeting MTV emphasized that they had defined programming standards and adhered to, and were sensitive to, public taste. In attempting to save themselves MTV went so far as to claim "that many other music video outlets do not share MTV's high standards."[19]

Meanwhile Stanley Gortikov, president of the Recording Industry of America Association, was working behind the scenes to rally the record companies to make some show of strength to resist the PMRC. Warner Brothers Records, who less than a year before had rejected the PTA's demands out of hand, was having second thoughts. They still claimed they would decide for themselves whether lyrics were offensive but the company had "discussed the possibility of putting a sticker on albums with lyrics that may cause a problem."[20]

Gortikov held meetings with most of the major labels and the point was raised that the RIAA had long been after Congress to do something about the amount of illegal taping of recorded material that was going on. Some of it was organized trading in bootleg tapes but most of it was home taping, or piracy, of material by individuals. What the RIAA was after was some sort of tax applied to each blank tape sold. This money would go to the industry to compensate for revenues lost through home taping. With the PMRC pressure the RIAA found itself between the proverbial rock and a hard place. If they fought the PMRC they feared they might antagonize Congress and lose all hope of compensation for piracy. However, they didn't want to yield to any of the PMRC's demands. It was their product and they wished to control it. Also they didn't really think there was much of a problem. It was a dilemma for the RIAA.

On August 6, 1985, the Senate Commerce Committee announced they would hold a hearing on "porn rock" on September 19, 1985. One of the members of this committee was Senator Albert Gore. The decision to hold a hearing came after more pressure by the PMRC. They had testified before the Justice Department's Commission on Pornography and also made a special presentation to senators which depicted the sins of rock singers. In August, about three months after its formation, it was revealed, ironically, that $5,000 in seed money to help start the PMRC was donated by the Love Foundation, a charitable organization set up by Beach Boy Mike Love after the death of their drummer Dennis Wilson in 1983 from a drug overdose.

On August 5, the long-awaited response by Gortikov was delivered in the form of a letter to the PMRC. In it the RIAA expressed a willingness on the part of the record companies to place warning stickers on albums which the companies deemed to contain "explicit lyrics" of a violent or sexual nature. Gortikov was speaking on behalf of nineteen companies who represented about eighty percent of the prerecorded music business. Under the RIAA's proposal, stickers themselves would be standardized but each company would make its own decision on each of its albums.

While the language of the sticker warning had to be worked out with the PMRC, the RIAA suggested "Parental Guidance: Explicit Lyrics" (PG).

All other demands of the PMRC were rejected. The RIAA claimed a uniform rating system was impracticable since about twenty-five thousand individual songs were released each year, as compared to about 325 films, whose type of rating system the PMRC favored adopting. Gortikov rejected the demand that retailers keep explicit covers hidden or covered since the RIAA had no control over retailing. Also rejected was the PMRC's demand that companies "reassess" artists who displayed explicit or abusive behavior at concerts where minors might attend, since Gortikov considered this role "inappropriate" for the companies.

The PMRC idea of rating video productions got a no from the RIAA as something better left to the broadcaster. The PMRC had asked the companies to "refrain from the use of hidden messages or backward masking (on records)." Gortikov replied that none of the companies used this. The RIAA chief felt music was being singled out unfairly compared to other forms of culture and entertainment and he closed his letter hoping his proposal would be acceptable and that the PMRC would "cease its campaign through the press and government for targeted attacks on recording companies. The industry is being totally maligned under the mass of PMRC's extensive, almost daily media protests."[21]

As might have been expected, the PMRC quickly rejected the RIAA's proposal. Within a couple of days the wives responded that they were still after the uniform standards which would be set by a panel made up of representatives from the music industry in general, and the community at large. Companies would label their own records but by using the very specific guidelines set by the panel.[22] The PMRC wanted specific stickering as well. For example, "X" for profanity and sex, "D/A" for glorification of drugs and/or alcohol, "O" for occult, and "V" for violence. The trade papers had been editorially silent until after the exchange of letters between the RIAA and the PMRC at which point *Variety* stuck out its neck and argued against the women. While stating they felt the PMRC was sincere, the *Variety* editorial warned of right-wing conservative groups and how one erosion of freedom could lead to another. It was time for someone to get mad enough to fight back and *Variety* nominated the record companies as the logical candidates.[23]

On August 13 the RIAA fired off another letter to the PMRC. Gortikov hardened his stance that no panel would pass on lyrics. He told the wives to be satisfied with what he offered or he hinted the companies "might stiffen their attitude and drop their plan to place warning stickers on 'explicit' produce."[24]

Billboard was slower than *Variety* in taking an editorial stance but finally did so at the end of August. They applauded the RIAA's "tough but supportable" decision. They too worried about the warning as a move to censorship and felt this RIAA concession was offered in the spirit of compromise and was more than adequate. The editors urged the record industry to "stand fast in its resistance to further demands that carry an implicit threat to essential rights. Enough ground has been given."[25]

By far the most vocal of all the artists in resisting the PMRC was Frank Zappa. While on the surface Gortikov's proposal seemed to offer the PMRC little of what they wanted, Zappa considered the industry to have "caved in" to the pressure. And indeed the concession offered was greater than appeared on the surface. Placing a warning label on albums was the obvious first step toward censorship and it was possible that radio stations might simply impose a blanket restriction not to play such material and that retailers might also refuse to stock them. This fear was echoed by the owner of the Sausalito Record Shop chain who worried that mall owners might require them not to retail anything with a warning label.[26]

Zappa called the whole campaign nothing but extortion on the part of the PMRC, whom he termed "cultural terrorists." He suggested that no one related to a government official should be allowed to waste the country's time and money "on ill-conceived housewife hobby projects such as this." Zappa urged everyone in the industry to lobby Congress against the PMRC and he concluded, "The PMRC's case is totally without merit, based on a hodge-podge of fundamentalist frogwash and illogical conclusions."[27]

The PMRC continued the pressure by popping up on broadcasting panels, on TV talk shows, and on radio hotline programs, as well as being featured in such magazines as *People*. A standard tactic at these appearances was to display offensive album covers and/or recite some "suggestive" lyrics. PMRC members appeared on over one hundred programs around the country including, "The CBS Morning News," "Today," the BBC, and the Phil Donahue program. After the Donahue show on July 17 the PMRC claimed to have received five thousand letters in a twenty-four hour period. At a "to rate or not to rate" panel held on September 10 by the New York chapter of the National Academy of Recording Arts and Sciences, Tipper Gore appeared and claimed that the explicit lyrics were escalating and "becoming mainstream." Rock singer Wendy Williams cut her down nicely by pointing out that the PMRC had looked at material released over the past couple of years, perhaps fifty thousand songs, and could only find a handful to complain about.[28]

The national PTA finally had its meeting with the PMRC and on September 11 the groups announced they had formed a coalition. New demands were made, and they marked a slight backing down on the PMRC's part. Now they wanted the industry to voluntarily affix an "R" warning on explicit material, instead of the various specific categories they had previously wanted. The groups also demanded full disclosure of lyrics with the words printed on the albums and/or attached to cassettes on cards as part of packaging, or made available in some fashion. They remained opposed to the RIAA's proposal. The coalition wanted to "pressure the music industry to accept responsibility for correcting the excesses that have developed."[29]

The president of Gold Mountain Records, Danny Goldberg, announced the formation of a new group called the Musical Majority. Formed under the auspices of the American Civil Liberties Union, Goldberg hoped to recruit from all segments of the music industry to resist the PMRC. Feeling the RIAA wasn't pushing back hard enough Goldberg said he was tired of "every extremist that wants to get their name in the paper using rock and roll as a whipping boy."

As the hearings on porn neared, the PMRC continued to fulminate and add to their "Rock File" of offensive lyrics. They collected quotes from artists which might support their "rock is evil" position and even kept such things as pictures of rockers drinking onstage. Those on the PMRC's bad list tended to an overrepresentation of heavy metal groups and they appeared to be offended by the way these groups looked, as much as anything. A sample of their baddies included: "Eat Me Alive" by Judas Priest, "Bastard" by Mötley Crue, "Darling Nikki" by Prince, "Sugar Walls" by Sheena Easton, "High 'n' Dry" by Def Leppard, "Dress You Up" by Madonnna, "She Bop" by Cyndi Lauper, "Let Me Put My Love Into You" by AC/DC, "Trashed" by Black Sabbath, "Possessed" by Venom, "Hot For Teacher" by Van Halen, "Ten Seconds To Love" by Mötley Crue, and "We're Not Gonna Take It" by Twisted Sister. Even the inoffensive Michael Jackson was singled out by Susan Baker when she claimed his latest album had a song about sadomasochism on it.

The porn rock hearings were to be chaired by Missouri Republican Senator John Danforth who was no friend of rock, nor objective when he said, before the hearings, that he was "shocked by some of the lyrics."[30] Of her own reaction to the lyrics Tipper Gore said, "I'm a fairly with-it person, but this stuff is curling my hair." PMRC member Sally Nevius said they wanted the industry to police itself but if they didn't "we're going to look into legal ways to stop what we feel is a form of contributing to the delinquency of minors."[31] Susan Baker hoped the group was out of business soon but added "we will be around until there is a satisfactory solution . . . so we can protect our children from harmful messages."[32]

Tipper Gore claimed the PMRC didn't request the hearings and didn't discuss the hearings with anyone on the committee, except her husband. Tipper said it was Senator Danforth who called the hearings, after being alerted by his wife who, according to Tipper, was "connected with" the PMRC. Finally the much-heralded hearing took place on September 19 before the Senate Commerce, Technology and Transportation Committee. It lasted about five hours. The crowd was standing room only with hundreds of others turned away who milled about in the halls.

All the principal players were there to testify, Baker and Gore of the PMRC, the PTA, Gortikov and Fritts for the industry, plus a few other lesser lights. The star performers though, and the ones everybody had come to see were the three singers who defended rock against the critics. An unlikely trio of allies, they were John Denver, Frank Zappa, and Dee Snider, lead singer of the heavy metal group Twisted Sister.

First up to bat were rock's enemies and first to testify was Senator Paula Hawkins (R-Florida), not a committee member, but a friend of the PMRC. She held up enlarged pictures of album covers by artists such as W.A.S.P. and Wendy O. Williams, which Hawkins claimed glorified unacceptable behavior and sexual activity for youth. The senator continued her porn rock demonstration by showing bits from two rock videos, "Hot For Teacher" by Van Halen and "We're Not Gonna Take It" by Twisted Sister. Hawkins then issued printed lyrics to each senator provided "they will promise not to distribute them beyond their own possession." When she had finished Hawkins turned to the chairman and said, "This issue is too hot to cool down. Parents are asking for assistance."[34] Tipper Gore gave a slide show on demonic album cover art, bondage, and sadomasochism and stressed that young minds were "at stake."

In her testimony Susan Baker noted the music had come a long way from "I can't get no satisfaction" to "I'm going to make you eat me at gunpoint." To illustrate she mentioned one song "Animal (Fuck Like a Beast)," but coming to the offensive word the best she could do was wince and spell it out. On a more insidious note Baker disagreed with those who said rock music was no cause for concern. "But we believe it is. Teenage pregnancy and teen-age suicide rates are at epidemic proportions . . . and rape is up . . . it is our contention that pervasive messages aimed at children which promote and glorify suicide, rape and sadomasochism have to be numbered among the contributing factors."[35] She then claimed that only a week before a young man committed suicide in a small Texas town while listening to the group AC/DC, and he wasn't "the first."[36]

Next up was the minister and ex-rocker Jeff Ling who had given a presentation at the PMRC's first meeting the previous May. By the time of the hearing Ling was a "consultant" with the PMRC. He also gave a slide show flashing on the screen album covers by groups such as Twisted Sister, Mötley Crue, KISS, the Rolling Stones, AC/DC, Prince, and W.A.S.P. As he flashed the slides he read out the lyrics in a fast, staccato voice. At one point he reminded the senators of the dangers of listening to rock music in general, and AC/DC in particular, when he mentioned the recently arrested man in Los Angeles charged in a series of murders. "One of their fans I know you're aware of is the alleged Night Stalker."[37] Ling claimed the porn rock lyrics severely affected ten- to twelve-year-olds since they had no frame of reference while for older youth such lyrics reinforced "aberrant behavior."

For the defense John Denver mentioned his own experiences with his song "Rocky Mountain High" which some stations had banned since they thought it had to do with drugs. Denver explained the "high" had to do with clear nights, fresh air, the mountains, and so on. He was opposed to any type of rating system and regarded it as the first step toward "totalitarian regimes." As might be expected Frank Zappa was opposed to any rating system. He said that taken as a whole the PMRC demands read like "an instruction manual for some sinister kind of toilet training program to housebreak all composers and performers because of the lyrics of a few . . . the equivalent of treating dandruff with decapitation."[38] As an alternative, Zappa compromisingly suggested that the printed lyric sheet could be inserted in the album packaging but then wryly suggested that such extra cost be perhaps borne by the government.

Dee Snider appeared in full heavy metal gear, minus his stage makeup and started off by announcing that he was thirty, had a three-year-old son, didn't drink, smoke, or do drugs and was a Christian. One of his songs, "Under the Blade" had been attacked for supposed rape, bondage, and sadomasochistic themes. Snider stated the song had nothing to do with that but was about the anxiety one feels before surgery. The PMRC had also complained about the video for his group's "We're Not Gonna Take It" wherein a teen destroys his father in a number of different ways. Snider explained it was all based on the cartoon characters Roadrunner and Wile E. Coyote from where he took many of his comic video scenes. Like the cartoon, each time the villain was destroyed he entered the next scene unscathed. It was all fantasy. Snider reported that the United Way had asked permission to use segments of that video for a program on the changing American family.[39]

Taking the offensive, Snider claimed his own image, that of his band, and his music had been damaged by the PMRC in an "irresponsible, damaging, and slanderous campaign," citing in particular Tipper Gore who told an interviewer that Twisted Sister used T-shirts which showed a woman spread eagled and in handcuffs. Snider said the group produced no such shirts. Opposed to ratings of any kind, Snider suggested it was the parents' right, and responsibility, to monitor their children, not the government's. When Senator Rockefeller suggested that every parent didn't have the luxury of time to do that, Snider shot back that the average kid could probably buy no more than one album a week and surely it wasn't too much to ask a concerned parent to listen to just one record per week. Snider also suggested that retailers use a "satisfaction guaranteed" policy whereby they would exchange any records which customers found to be objectionable.

Senator Danforth stated the government was not contemplating introducing any legislation on the problem of rock lyrics and the hearing was just to provide a forum to air the issue. Other members of the committee were less temperate. Senator Hollings demanded that somebody "by God, rescue the tender young ears of this nation from this-this ROCK PORN." He said the only redeeming feature of the music was that it was mostly "inaudible" and added "the music does not have any redeeming social value. It's outrageous filth and we've got to do something about it. . . . If I could find some way constitutionally to do away with it, I would. . . . [I've asked] the best constitutional minds around to see if the stuff could be legally outlawed."[40]

The hearings ended with the positions of the parties unchanged. The PMRC and the PTA were after three main items. One was the generic sticker warning on offensive albums. The "PG" suggested by the RIAA was not considered strong enough and the PMRC was in favor of an "R." They also wanted printed lyrics made available to the customer before purchase and they wanted a one-time panel set up which would set up guidelines which would determine whether or not a record got an "R" sticker. The RIAA was willing only to use a PG label but the rating would be done by the individual record companies. They were prepared to grant no other concessions.

At the conclusion of the hearings it was clear the senators felt the industry had been negligent and had offered too little, too late. Some were not above threatening the industry with legislation to impose the PMRC's will even though Danforth himself admitted the chances of passing any legislation would be nil, due to First Amendment protections. By the end of the day the PMRC felt they had dispelled the notion they were after censorship and planned to continue their fight until they had won labeling and then move on to their other demands such as changes on MTV and plain brown wrappers at stores for some album covers. Mr. Gortikov, they said, would be hearing from them.

The executive director of the National Academy of Songwriters (NAS), Kevin Odegard, was a vocal opponent of record rating and had appeared on various newscasts, talk shows, and so on. He complained about media bias. While interviewed on the Phil Donahue program, "Donahue just literally shouted us off the air when we were on his show. He was just outraged by the obscenities, the explicit graphics and heavy metal in general. We nearly went out of business after that show because it was so negative for us."[41]

While the RIAA didn't seem to have any real fears from legislation they did have the unspoken threat of the piracy bill hanging over their heads. Bill HR2911, the Home Audio Recording Act, had been languishing in the House for some time. It was the latest of several such measures the RIAA had sought to get relief from piracy. Sponsored in the House by Representative Bruce Morrison (D-Connecticut) and drafted by the RIAA it would impose a tax of five percent to twenty-five percent on the price of all tape recorders and add one cent a minute to the cost of all blank cassette tapes. Thus, an hour-long cassette would cost sixty cents more. These monies would be pooled and returned to record companies and music publishers. It promised to bring untold millions to the companies.

At some point the bill would have to pass the Judiciary Committee, chaired by Senator Strom Thurmond, whose wife had been one of the signators to an early PMRC letter to Gortikov. In addition, the industry wanted continued help from the FBI and various other federal agencies in enforcing counterfeit and copyright laws. The RIAA did not want a lot of enemies in Washington and its stance of concession clearly influenced the rather slow response by the industry, perhaps hoping the storm would blow itself out. Gortikov repeatedly refused to discuss the home taping bill at all, and in doing so underlined its importance in the RIAA's thinking.

Others in the industry, such as Goldberg, Odegard, and Zappa, felt the industry was not taking a tough enough stand and were hopeful a stronger movement would emerge to thwart the PMRC. What galled artists like Zappa was the fact that the piracy bill would benefit the companies only. When someone taped an album at home the company lost sales and the performers and composers lost royalites. The home taping bill would recoup some of that loss for the companies but the performers and composers would gain nothing, provided people still taped at home. Thus the RIAA could be seen as selling out an artist's creative freedom, through censorship, for the benefit of the company. The artist would gain nothing financially, and lose creatively. However, the RIAA had offered only one concession and then adamantly refused to go further. The heads of four major labels, Capitol, CBS, RCA, and Warner Brothers, had been invited to testify at the hearings. None attended and only CBS bothered to even reply to the invitation. It might have been easier for the RIAA to yield more, but they didn't. At that point the RIAA could hardly be viewed as caving in, as Zappa felt.

While the industry showed signs of resistance, the other side picked up growing support. Around the time of the hearings the Reverend Jerry Falwell urged his Moral Majority followers to boycott porn rock and the sponsors of any outlets which broadcast such music. The vice-president of the retail record chain Camelot Music, James Bonk, told fellow retailers that shopping mall owners in San Diego had begun to insert clauses in leases giving them the right to demand that record stores "pull out merchandise that is morally objectionable."[42]

Evidence began to surface that the Washington wives did not enjoy total support outside the industry. *People* magazine did a report on lyrics and asked readers to send in comments. This generated 2,035 letters, the most of any article in the magazine's history and *People* reported that ninety percent of the writers were concerned not with supposed excesses of rock but by the threat of censorship.[43]

On September 30 Los Angeles Mayor Tom Bradley held a press conference to officially state his alliance with Musical Majority, and to firmly oppose the demands of the PMRC. The mayor had sent a written brief to the Senate hearing after being appraised of the situation by Frank Zappa. Bradley became the first elected official to publicly oppose such ratings.

The PMRC continued to pick up influential support. The controversy spilled over into the domain of syndicated columnist Ann Landers. A reader from Minnesota wrote to her and denounced rock as depraved and blamed the music for promoting dope use, suicide, sexual promiscuity, and teen violence. Another reader opined that the music caused permanent hearing loss and brain damage. Landers said the controversy caused her to finally listen to some of the songs. She believed herself, after over two decades of writing her column, to be virtually "shock proof" but found some lyrics "incredibly crude." According to Landers, she received some twenty thousand letters on the subject and the verdict was ninety-to-one in favor of rock and roll music. The majority praised rock as a healthy outlet for teens but this powerful show of sentiment did not sway the columnist. Landers wrote, "I still find many of the lyrics offensive. I support the Washington wives."[44]

The November 1985 issue of *Good Housekeeping* featured an article on "How Parents Can Stop Rock Songs." Essentially a recapitulation of the PMRC's stance, it claimed that lyrics to some songs were "too graphic to be printed here." The reader was urged to write and protest to groups such as the FCC, RIAA, and MTV. Addresses were thoughtfully supplied. The writer cited increased statistics on crimes committed by youth, teen suicide, and pregnancy. While admitting there was no psychological research proof to blame rock, nevertheless, by implication she did indeed link rock to these ills. Readers were urged to pressure local stations to keep offensive material off the air and hit the record industry where it hurt, at the profit line. Concerned parents were also urged to hold local meetings to discuss ways to combat the problem and to send donations to the PMRC to receive guidelines and informational tapes on the content of rock music.[45] The issue was on the newsstands by mid-October and by the first of November the record industry had already begun to receive protests from parents.[46]

President Ronald Reagan joined the assault during a speech on October 10 when he linked rock record companies with pornographers who hid behind the First Amendment, hinting that rock lyrics might fall outside the guarantee of free speech. During his speech at Crystal City, Virginia, Reagan said the music industry and the media provided children "with glorification of drugs, violence and perversity. . . . The First Amendment has been twisted into a pretext for license."[47] Some of the retailers' fears were beginning to come true as Sears and J.C. Penney announced they wouldn't handle any records with warning stickers. Wal-Mart, with hundred of outlets, stated they would scrutinize any stickered material much "more carefully."[48]

Senator Ernest Hollings kept the pressure on as his office announced, toward the end of October, that the senator was "seriously exploring" the possibility of a legislative solution to the issue of porn rock. To get around the First Amendment problem Hollings was researching a "truth-in-packaging" type of bill that would provide consumers with access to printed lyrics so the customer would know what they were buying. The senator's staff claimed a bill could be ready as early as December. They also claimed it was not a high priority with Hollings and that if the companies provided some "inter-industry response" the senator "would probably lose interest."[49] in his bill. What Senator Hollings was clearly doing was sending the record industry a not very subtle hint that they should quickly reach a solution with the PMRC and the PTA.

On November 1, 1985, at the National Press Club in Washington, D.C., a joint press conference was held by the RIAA, PMRC, and PTA at which time they announced an agreement had been reached in the porn rock controversy. When faced with a record which contained explicit material such as sex, violence and/or substance abuse the record company had two options. The first option involved placing a warning sticker on the album, or cassette, which was to read: "Explicit Lyrics – Parental Advisory." The second option involved printing the offensive lyrics on the back of the album or on lyric sheets inserted under the plastic wrap, which in either case, would be visible to the consumer. Cassettes were obviously too small to print the lyrics on so a company choosing the second option could place on the cassette a reminder sticker which would read "See LP for Lyrics." This was an obvious loophole since some sixty percent of music sales were cassettes, although the reminder sticker would likely quickly have the same force as a warning sticker, in the public mind. Gortikov said these new procedures would begin within sixty to ninety days.

The RIAA represented forty-four companies and twenty-two of them, accounting for eighty to eighty-five percent of the music sales in America, had agreed to the plan. They were: A&M, Arista, Atlantic, CBS Records, Capitol/EMI, Chrysalis, Columbia, Compeat, Crescendo, Elektra/Asylum, Epic, Manhattan, MCA, Mike Curb Productions, Motown, PolyGram, Portrait Records, RCA, Solar, Scotti Bros., Tabu, and Warner Bros. The previous mavericks, A&M and MCA, had rejoined the RIAA fold due to the option of printed lyrics. MCA had been particularly opposed to warning stickers. The one obvious place where the PMRC had lost was in defining "explicit lyrics." No standardized definition was to be adopted and each record company would decide on its own, using its own criteria, just what was, or was not explicit. The agreement, which applied to all types of music, was entirely voluntary of course, and not binding on anyone.

Tipper Gore said she was delighted with the agreement and wasn't worried about the lack of definition of "explicit." She claimed, "We have faith that they will make those judgments with the concern of the parents with young children in mind."[50] Ann Kahn, the PTA president, hailed the agreement as a major step forward to provide more information for parents and claimed it was "a win situation for everyone who is involved."[51] Gortikov claimed he was happy since he had satisfied the parents while at the same time being mindful of First Amendment guarantees. The RIAA had felt only a minute percentage of material would fall into the explicit category, although Gortikov acknowledged there could be a problem with artists whose contracts gave them complete control over their product and refused to participate. NAB head Eddie Fritts called the agreement a "responsible voluntary agreement" and a "good example of private citizen groups working constructively with industry."[52]

Not everyone was happy with the agreement. Danny Goldberg of the Musical Majority had mixed feelings. He remained adamantly against labeling but was not against the public reading lyrics. Thus he was encouraging other record companies to follow MCA's lead and use the second option. He said many members of the Musical Majority were against making any concessions and he didn't personally "believe in compromising with extremist groups. But it could have been worse."[53] Speaking for the ACLU, legislative counsel Barry Lynn termed the agreement "a defeat for free expression and the broadest possible artistic expression in this medium."[54]

The PMRC stated the group would continue to exert pressure on any record companies and artists which didn't abide by the agreement. That pressure would mostly take the form of informing parents about the offending material. They would monitor the agreement for a year and assess its effectiveness. The group was also said to be keeping a watchful eye on MTV. While PMRC felt that MTV had "toned down" somewhat, they weren't satisfied its efforts had been totally adequate. Still looming over the scene was Senator Hollings. Gortikov had denied the agreement had been in any way precipitated by any fears of Congressional intervention. The senator tried to keep the threat alive for after the agreement his press secretary, Mike Fernandez, announced the agreement was a welcome step in the right direction but wondered how it would be carried out. Hollings also planned to assess the program and wouldn't rule out the possibility of future legislation. "For now, no, we won't propose anything, but we'll be keeping a watchful eye."[55]

Perhaps the last word in this controversy goes to Frank Zappa who, on November 15, released an album on his Barking Pumpkin label called "Frank Zappa Meets The Mothers of Prevention." One track was a twelve minute cut titled "Porn Wars," an avant garde presentation which mixed music with the actual comments made by Zappa, seven senators, and Jeff Ling at the Senate hearings. On the cut Senator Paula Hawkins was heard chanting "burn" and "fire and chains and other objectionable tools of gratification in some twisted minds." Senator Hollings repeated the phrase "outrageous filth" while Senator Trible chanted "rape." Ling was heard barking, "I will drive my love into you." On one part a senator was heard asking why the hearings were held, then Zappa's voice breaks in and chants "sex . . . sex . . . sex." This was followed by Ling saying "Listen, you little slut." None of the senators featured on the record had any comment to make. The PMRC did comment and, obviously not sharing Zappa's sense of humor, declared, "We gave Frank Zappa more publicity than he could have bought. We revived a dying career."⁵⁶ Dee Snider also capitaliz-ed on the issue and on Twisted Sister's "Come Out and Play" album, released at the end of 1985, Snider expressed thanks to the PMRC on the album sleeve for providing the group with free publicity.

So who won and who lost the porn rock wars? Clearly rock and roll lost, but not as much as it appeared they might at the beginning. The PMRC saw very few of their initial demands met but they got their foot in the door. The hearings and all the publicity generated by the PMRC would never have been achieved had it not been for their connections. Had they been a group of un-connected Washington wives, it is likely they would have made few waves. There was more to it than that of course. The wives did need a "good" issue, one that would arouse publicity and support, and rock and roll was a very good issue. It had been everybody's favorite whipping boy since birth and had a very shady reputation. When the Washington wives threw up the image of mom desperately struggling to shield her helpless and innocent children from rock music, this savage and depraved beast, existing only to corrupt her children, it was easy to see why the media might pick up the issue, and whose side they might be on.

The music industry itself was slow to respond to the issue, allowing the wives to get a great deal of momentum going on their side. This slowness was partly due to the fear that antagonizing the wives might lead to a Congress not over-disposed to assist the RIAA with its other legislation, such as the piracy bill. That bill, as of 1987, still sat in Congress trying to work its way through. Manufacturers, mostly Japanese, of the tape recorders which would be taxed under the bill, had pledged to spend millions of dollars over the next decade to fight the bill. Passage of the bill, if ever, could be a long way off. Thus the RIAA concessions may, in the long run, yield them none of the hoped for benefits. When the industry finally did fight back, and it was mostly those out-side of the RIAA such as Zappa and Goldberg, public reaction indicated the wives did not have the solid backing of the general public. It was also obvious by then that any legislative action against the companies was unlikely. The hearings themselves helped to turn public opinion since the rockers scored a clear victory in terms of the debate. Denver, Zappa, and Snider came across as much more articulate, informed, and intelligent than those of the illogical, ir-rational PMRC. That was the time for the RIAA to toughen and refuse to con-cede anything at all. However, determined to create no enemies in Washington, the group still offered its concession. The PMRC perhaps by then had sensed a shift in momentum, and accepted.

The agreement was in that sense an RIAA sellout; they could have gotten off scot-free if they had pushed harder. Still, the RIAA is mostly a group of very large establishment companies and it would have been perhaps easiest of all for them to have initially yielded more to avoid the lengthy hassle. They did indeed put up some fight and held the line at a certain point. The real losers were the artists who have suffered a certain loss of creative freedom. Stickered products could find themselves unofficially blacklisted from radio airplay, retail stores and so on, causing an artist to consider this before creating a potentially "offensive" song. Worst of all a precedent had been established, a concession given. In the future it might be easier for the PMRC or some other groups to obtain still further concessions, to strip away still more freedoms.

By May of 1986 many of rock's bad boys had released new albums, including the Rolling Stones, Judas Priest, Prince, and Ozzy Osbourne but not one of these likely candidates got a warning sticker. The distinction for garnering the first such sticker apparently went to a PolyGram Records' artist who was rather obscure in North America. He was a French pop star named Serge Gainsbourg and, to make the situation even more ludicrous, he sang and recorded in French. Nevertheless, his album "Love on the Beat" merited a sticker, "Explicit French Lyrics: Parental Advisory."[57]

The PMRC did not rest on its laurels after the accord was reached. Through the early part of 1986 they were very active, although not in the high profile and media-intensive way of the past. The PMRC was busy sending speakers all over the country armed with an up-to-date porn rock slide show. The group was getting twenty to twenty-five requests each week for speakers and hoped to increase that number. The PTA had reached an agreement to cooperate with the PMRC and PTA president Ann Kahn had sent a letter to all fifty state chapters advising them of the availability of this free show. Another mailing went out to the twenty-four thousand local chapters. Speaking for the Washington wives, Susan Baker said her group was trying to activate parents and get them, on a grass roots level, to complain to local stations when they heard something offensive over the airwaves. In addition to educating parents about porn rock Baker said the group was building a ground-up movement "to pressure record companies, radio stations, artists and corporate sponsors to create, sell and support inoffensive products."[58]

On another front Tipper Gore of the PMRC was also vigilant. She had been monitoring new record releases and was upset that no warning stickers had been applied to any material by April 1986. She clearly felt many albums deserved such a fate and hoped the companies would soon "make good" on their word. Gore was particularly incensed with some heavy metal releases by independent labels, and while she admitted these small labels weren't part of the agreement, she complained that Gortikov had promised to "help us pressure the independents" to use stickers. The RIAA countered they had fulfilled the agreement by mailing a letter to the independent companies which outlined the accord. Industry sources were starting to worry that the PMRC might take the next step and publicly criticize a major label release. In April 1987 Mrs. Gore's *Raising PG Kids in an X-Rated Society* ("The book 10 million parents have been waiting for!") appeared with massive publicity, blaming rock for teen ills that ranged from pregnancy to murder, and alcoholism to suicide. Its cover was prominantly labeled *EXPLICIT MATERIAL – PARENTAL ADVISORY*.

While the PMRC was closely watching rock, the fans of the music weren't as equally aware of the danger. A columnist for *Billboard* surveyed over a thousand rock concert goers at the end of 1985 and early 1986 at five different sites and found the percentage who were aware of the PMRC ranged from twenty-seven percent to sixty-three percent. Of those aware of the PMRC eighty-five percent were opposed to the rating system.[59] It was clear that the kids were not taking the PMRC very seriously, something the industry had been guilty of, yet the group did pose a serious threat, witness what nearly happened after one of the PMRC mailings went to a Maryland woman named Judith Toth.

Toth was a Democratic member of the Maryland State Assembly and after receiving the PMRC mailing she was galvanized into action. In January, 1986 she introduced a bill into the Maryland House of Representatives which would have made it a crime, punishable by a fine up to $1,000 and/or jail term up to one year, for a retailer to sell any record containing obscene lyrics to a minor. The measure was actually an amendment to a long-standing Maryland bill outlawing the sale of obscene magazines and books to those under the age of eighteen. If the bill passed, Maryland would become the first state to ban the sale of x-rated records to minors. Such records would have to be kept in a special section of the store and a purchaser would be required to provide a birth date and identification.

Toth was inspired by the "stomach-turning" lyrics of many heavy metal groups and called the PMRC "instrumental" in providing information to Maryland lawmakers. She garnered support for her bill by passing around the PMRC file.[60] The Maryland House held a hearing on the proposal on January 14 and no opposition forces showed up. The industry was caught by surprise and almost all members of it didn't even hear about the hearing until after it was over. One exception was Tony

Steidler-Dennison, a Record Bar store manager who headed the Balti-more-based Recording Retailers Opposing Censorship (RROC). When he heard about the bill he called Toth and other legislators to inquire about the date for the hearing and subsequent vote, he was stonewalled and told that no hearing was scheduled although it took place that afternoon. When he inquired about the date for the vote he was again told that one was not scheduled although it also took place that day. Registered letters went unanswered.[61] Toth dismissed this complaint by noting, "We're not under any obligation to let our opponents know." Toth clearly had the PMRC's interest in mind when she mentioned the real impact of her bill was "persuasion: to put pressure on the manufacturers to keep up their agreement and to make sure that such material is clearly labeled."[62] Early in February the amendment passed in the House by a vote of 96–31 and then moved on to the Senate Judicial Proceedings Committee, preliminary to a full Senate vote.

At that point Toth was jubilant and predicted easy passage the rest of the way as well as a domino effect in which other states would press similar legislation. She gave credit again to the PMRC for having transcribed all the lyrics in the first place and held to the curious logic that only those of a certain age could understand rock lyrics. "Those of us who were over 18 couldn't understand the lyrics but once we got it in writing, we understood. I had no idea there was such pornographic material out there. . . . This is not the kind of stuff that kids should be listening to." She added ominously, "This is only the beginning."[63]

The industry was not caught flatfooted a second time and the RIAA moved to hire a lobbyist. Defects in the bill became obvious: it was badly written, it was unenforceable, and it involved tricky questions of interstate commerce. The chairman of the Judicial Committee called the proposal "the worst bill this session." A hearing was held on March 18 and this time both sides were represented. According to Toth, supporters of the measure were, "feminists, church people, psychiatrists, and kids damaged by records, including former druggies and child prostitutes."[64] The opposition was led once again by the intrepid Frank Zappa. The bill now had little chance of passing and Toth admitted her fight was now "uphill." She threatened to go after records on the grounds of x-rated visuals, already illegal in the state, and if her bill failed, she predicted picketing of record stores would develop as a grass roots movement. On April 1, 1986 the bill was defeated seven to four by the Senate committee and died.

Toth was livid and attributed defeat to "grandstanding" by opponents during an election year. She vowed to reintroduce the measure the following year, to rewrite all of Maryland's obscenity laws, and to look at existing laws and confer with state attorneys and police to take record companies to court. She hoped other states would try similar legislation just to keep the music industry "tied up." Judith Toth was by no means ready to quit for she said, "This is just the beginning of what I've been calling a war against recorded pornography."[65] For the moment rock had survived another skirmish.

However, all of this negative publicity had an effect and the image of rock as pornographic was firmly established. A telephone poll of almost fifteen hundred adults conducted in November 1985 by Media General/Associated Press surveyed attitudes on the music.[66] Predictably, the older the respondents the less the enthusiasm for the music. Overall, fifty-six percent liked rock, fifty-one percent believed rock had a bad effect on kids, and fifty-five percent thought the records should be rated like movies. Even in the eighteen to thirty-four age group, most of whom liked rock, thirty-nine percent thought rock had a bad effect. The music was blamed for encouraging violent behavior, laziness, drug use, sexual activity, disobedience, and disregard for authority. With regard to lyrics, eigthy-eight percent of those polled felt teenagers could understand them and forty-seven percent felt preteens understood the words.

Such was the image of rock yet there was no evidence to back that up. Toward the end of 1985 two California State University, Fullerton, professors were approached by a probation officer of Orange County and asked for research which linked punk rock and heavy metal to juvenile delinquency. They found none. Lorraine Prinsky and Jill Rosenbaum did, however, survey some three hundred southern California high school and junior high school students. The kids were asked to list their three favorite songs and give a brief description of what each was about. Of the 662 songs listed, only seven percent were considered by the students to be about drugs, violence, sex, or Satanism. The kids were unable to explain thirty-seven percent of their favorite songs, often giving literal interpretations, such as Led Zeppelin's "Stairway to Heaven" being about climbing stairs on the way to heaven. The conclusion reached by the researchers was that rock lyrics about violence, sex, drugs, and Satanism had very little effect on most teenagers. As Prinsky said, "Specific lyrics seem to be of little consequence to most kids, the musical beat or overall sound of a recording is of greater interest to teenagers."[67]

None of this is likely to deter the rock opposition, however. They are true zealots driven on by the "rightness" of their cause. By 1987 a standoff on the porn rock issue existed between the RIAA on one side and the likes of the PMRC and Toth on the other. How long it will last only time will tell. There is a serious threat and the industry had always been lethargic in its response, preferring to try and mount a defensive action after an attack, rather than take any offensive action. The next attacks may come from the PMRC or Toth, or someone or some group entirely new. The only certain thing is that at some point in the future rock and roll will again antagonize someone and yet another attempt will be made to destroy the beast.

Rock and roll music has been under attack for over thirty years. In 1956 Elvis Presley shocked and horrified the adult world. In 1966 Mick Jagger sent waves of revulsion and disgust rolling across the land. In 1976 Johnny Rotten and the Sex Pistols sent fear and loathing into the hearts of the establishment. Sometime soon someone will surface again who will have much the same effect — bank on it.

The attacks on rock have produced many hardships for people in the business. Alan Freed's career was ended completely. Chuck Berry and Jerry Lee Lewis had their careers weakened significantly. John Lennon was harassed by the U.S. government for years. Jagger and Richards were hasseled by the law. Jim Morrison was busted on stage and had trouble getting any more bookings for showing what men now show month in and month out in *Playgirl*. The Sex Pistols were blocked from playing almost everywhere. Heavy metal did not receive the kind of radio airplay its popularity entitled it to.

The government has hounded rock and roll numerous times over the years. In the late 1950s the music was accused of contributing to delinquency and of being of such poor quality that it took payola to get it on the air. In the early 1970s the administration damned rock for promoting drug use. In 1985 the music was banned for being pornographic, foisting its smutty little self on the public behind a First Amendment shield.

Rock and roll records have been broken and burned in public displays in the 1950s, 1960s, 1970s and 1980s. Religion has fulminated long and loud at the devil's music. Early rockers like Lewis and Little Richard underwent enormous turmoil over the moral dilemma of being a rocker. Groups like AC/DC and the Rolling Stones were denounced as the devil incarnate.

Rock and roll music allegedly doomed the young to deafness but the loudness of rock was a form of defiance and a demand to be heard that adults resented. There was Jesse Jackson, the man who would be president, implying, in the late 1970s that listening to rock and roll made teens pregnant. More ominous attempts have been made to imply that rock somehow was partly responsible for the behavior of murderers such as Charles Manson or the Night Stalker. It has also been blamed for any and all "riots" at concerts, even though they may have been provoked by police over-reaction. In all these years none of rock's critics have ever been able to come up with any proof that rock causes any of these ills.

The lyrics have been subject to a constant storm. From leerics, to drug songs, to sex rock, to porn rock. The name may change but the complaints remain the same. The upright and uptight were, and are, determined to tame and/or destroy the "beast." Those who complained about "dirty" lyrics in rock music probably complained about the same thing in books and other forums. But the issue for anti-rock forces goes much deeper. The main bone of contention, and antagonsim, is the conflict between youth and adults. After all, rock and roll is music that mom and pop don't like. The adult establishment can be relied upon to attack rock again and again in the future, but rock will survive. Youth will not let it die, or be tamed. Rock is too important for youth. It is the only thing in society over which they exercise a degree of control. They will fight for their music. And they should. The music is a healthy outlet for the challenge of growing up. ROCK ON!

Notes

1. Rock and Roll Rises and the Opposition Forms

1. Palmer, Tony. *All You Need Is Love.* New York: Grossman, 1976, p. 161.

2. Chapple, Steve. *Rock 'n' Roll Is Here to Pay.* Chicago: Nelson-Hall, 1977, p. 28.

3. Ibid., p. 31.

4. Gillett, Charlie. *The Sound Of The City.* New York: Outerbridge & Dienstfrey, 1970, p. 300.

5. Frith, Simon. *Sound Effects.* London: Constable, 1983, p. 32.

6. Schulman, John. Effect of the Copyright Act of 1909 on the quality of American music. *National Music Council Bulletin.* 16:11 May 1956.

7. Chapple, Steve. *Rock 'n' Roll Is Here to Pay,* p. 29.

8. Ibid., p. 235.

9. Ibid., p. 35, 43, 44.

10. Ibid., p. 46.

11. Ibid., p. 47.

12. Shaw, Arnold. *The Rockin' '50s.* New York: Hawthorn Books, 1974, p. 266–67.

2. Leerics

1. Blames A&R Men for Poor Music Tastes. *Billboard.* 66:19 September 11, 1954.

2. Holly, Hal. What about R&B "leer-ics?" *Down Beat.* 22:31 May 4, 1955.

3. MPPA in rap at dirty songs. *Variety.* 197:46 December 8, 1954.

4. Trade views off-color disk situation with mixed feelings. *Billboard.* 66:19 October 2, 1954.

5. Ibid.

6. Indie diskers back WDIA's bans. *Billboard.* 66:16 October 30, 1954.

7. WDIA's got a broom. *Billboard.* 66:16 October 30, 1954.

8. The fast buck vs. juve morale. *Variety.* 196:49 November 19, 1954.

9. A warning to the music business. *Variety.* 197:2 February 23, 1955.

10. Clean your doorstep. *Billboard.* 67:13 April 2, 1955.

11. Negro D.J. Raps spread of "filth" via R&B disks. *Variety.* 198:54 March 23, 1955.

12. WINS sez teenagers "hate" Haymes for his WCBS pan of R&B music. *Variety.* 198:60 March 9, 1955.

13. Feather, Leonard. Feather's Nest. *Down Beat.* 22:6 May 4, 1955.

14. Kennedy, Jimmy. Fears U.S. will make negative global impression via R&B tunes. *Variety.* 198:49 March 9, 1955.

15. Bundy, June. Censored R&R on new MBS disk service format. *Billboard.* 70:2 August 18, 1958.

16. Shaw, Arnold. *The Rockin' '50s.* New York: Hawthorn Books, 1974, p. 234.

17. Charts clean lyrics contest. *Billboard.* 70:6 July 14, 1958.

18. Shaw, Arnold. *The Rockin' '50s*, p. 235.

19. Bundy, June. Censorship eases on aired lyrics as acceptance grows. *Billboard.* 71:2 January 19, 1959.

20. Morrison, Don. Return of the leer-ics. *Variety.* 225:45 January 3, 1962.

3. "Riots" in the Streets

1. Bundy, June. Obscene R&B tunes blasted in New England. *Billboard.* 67:18 April 2, 1955.

2. Stage show at the State. *New York Times.* May 21, 1955, p. 11.

3. Haddock, Laura. Cambridge acts after teen riot. *Christian Science Monitor.* March 12, 1956. p. 2.

4. Haddock, Laura. Cambridge bans "hop" disk jockey. *Christian Science Monitor.* March 13, 1956, p. 2.

5. Ibid.

6. New rock, roll 'n' riot storm. *Variety*. 202:47, 54 March 28, 1956.

7. Teenagers riot in Massachusetts and cause rock and roll ban. *Down Beat*. 23:13 April 18, 1956.

8. New rock, roll 'n' riot storm, p. 54.

9. Ibid.

10. Rock 'n' roll B. O. dynamite. *Variety*. 202:1 April 11, 1956.

11. Ibid., p. 60.

12. Rocking and rolling. *Newsweek*. 47:42 June 18, 1956.

13. Rock-and-roll gate slowed to a waltz. *New York Times*. July 12, 1956. p. 25.

14. Swenson, John. *Bill Haley*. London: W.H. Allen, 1982, p. 76–77.

15. Kids dance in bathing suits, San Antonio pool bans rock 'n' roll disks. *Variety*. 203:41 July 11, 1956.

16. R&R battered and badgered. *Variety*. 203:46 July 18, 1956.

17. Rock 'n' roll banned. *New York Times*. September 20, 1956, p. 29.

18. *Rock around the Clock*. *New York Times*. April 12, 1956, p. 10.

19. Rock and roll disturbances. *Times* (London). September 4, 1956, p. 5.

20. No rock and roll film on Sunday. *Times*(London). September 6, 1956, p. 10.

21. Rock and roll disturbances. *Times* (London). September 11, 1956, p. 8.

22. Ronan, Thomas P. British rattled by rock 'n' roll. *New York Times*. September 12, 1956, p. 40.

23. Rock and roll film ban. *Times* (London). September 12, 1956, p. 4.

24. Stimulus behind rock 'n' roll disturbances. *Times* (London), September 15, 1956, p. 4.

25. *Rock around the Clock* raises rumpus in Britain; many towns ban pic. *Variety*. 204:84, September 19, 1956.

26. Rock 'n' roll disorders. *Times* (London). September 17, 1956. p. 8.

27. Ronan, Thomas P. Rock 'n' roll 'n' riots. *New York Times*. September 23, 1956, sec. 4, p. 4.

28. Queen's curiosity aroused, her kingdom much upset by rock 'n' roll film. *Variety*. 204:2, 61 September 26, 1956.

29. Stimulus behind rock 'n' roll disturbances. *Times* (London) September 15, 1956, p. 4.

30. Rock 'n' riot. *Time*. 71:50 May 19, 1958.

31. Ibid.

32. Goodsell, James Nelson. Rock 'n' roll wrangle looms. *Christian Science Monitor.* May 9, 1958, p. 13.

33. Goodsell, James Nelson. Rock 'n' roll opposition rises. *Christian Science Monitor.* May 8, 1958, p. 3.

34. Several N.E. cities face rock-'n'-roll ban issue. *Christian Science Monitor.* May 6, 1958, p. 31.

35. Jersey Guard bans rock 'n' roll show in Newark Armory. *New York Times.* May 8, 1958, p. 31.

36. Hopkins, Jerry. *Elvis.* New York: Simon and Schuster, 1971, p. 142.

37. "His Honor" twirls a mean dial. *New York Times.* June 16, 1958, p. 14.

38. Onward 'n' downward with R 'n' R. *Variety.* 210:58 May 28, 1958.

39. Rock 'n' roll opponents are due for big break. *New York Times.* January 13, 1958, p. 49.

40. St. Louis station smashes records to end the sway of rock 'n' roll. *Business Week.* January 25, 1958, p. 78.

41. These rock & riot shows. *Melody Maker.* 34:1, 16 May 9, 1959.

4. Combat the Menace

1. White council vs. rock and roll. *Newsweek.* 47:32 April 23, 1956.

2. Negro music protested. *New York Times.* April 10, 1956, p. 20.

3. Segregationist wants ban on "rock and roll." *New York Times.* March 30, 1956, p. 39.

4. Jungle music cry at Randall U.S. show. *Melody Maker.* 31:1 May 26, 1956.

5. Norman, Phillip. *The Stones.* London: Elm Tree, 1984, p. 26.

6. Kaplan, Mike. Civil liberties and rock and roll. *Variety.* 203:52 August 15, 1956.

7. R&B boom won't stick: Elgart. *Down Beat.* 22:1 March 23, 1955.

8. Bennett, Tony. Regarding rock 'n' roll. *Music Journal.* 19:32 September 1961.

9. Crosby, Bing. Requiem for rock. *Music Journal.* 20:38 January 1962.

10. Houser, John G. Col's Percy Faith sees music getting better, but big beat is here to stay. *Variety.* 220:57 October 5, 1960.

11. Walsh, Jim. "Pops" on pop music biz today. *Variety.* 207:45 June 5, 1957.

12. Songwriter Johnny Green likens R&R to tarragon. *Down Beat.* 23:44 September 19, 1956.

13. Musicians argue values of rock and roll. *Down Beat.* 23:12 May 30, 1956.

14. Crosby, Bob. Rock 'n' roll is our own fault. *Music Journal.* 16:14 September 1958.

15. Mel Torme sez U.S. disk jockeys off-key. *Variety.* 223:45 July 19, 1961.

16. "Payola popularized bad songs." *Variety.* 217:66 January 20, 1960.

17. Break that sound barrier. *Melody Maker.* 35:2–3 December 10, 1960.

18. Grevatt, Ren. The man who makes the stars. *Melody Maker.* 32:3 November 30, 1957.

19. Chapple, Steve. *Rock 'n' Roll is Here to Pay.* Chicago: Nelson-Hall, 1977. p. 47.

20. Rock 'n' roll assaulted. *Instrumentalist.* 13:92 September 1958.

21. Samuels, Gertrude. Why they rock 'n' roll. *New York Times Magazine.* January 12, 1958. p. 19.

22. Frith, Simon. *Sound Effects.* London: Constable, 1983, p. 93.

23. Rock 'n' roll's pulse taken. *New York Times.* October 27, 1956 p. 35.

24. Rock 'n' roll is keeping IQ down. *Music and Dance.* 52:16 November 1961.

25. Sir M. Sargent on "tom-tom thumping." *Times* (London). September 18, 1956, p. 5.

26. British bandleader blasts "pop rot."; MU blames U.S. imports. *Billboard.* 70:11 November 24, 1958.

27. Casals, Pablo. A disgrace to music. *Music Journal.* 19:18 January 1961.

28. Clerics "rock 'n' roll hubbub in Hub:" not immoral, but too commercial. *Variety.* 205:43 January 30, 1957.

29. Spellman in plea to save U.S. youth. *New York Times.* October 1, 1956, p. 22.

30. Telegram in brief: Malta. *Times* (London). April 26, 1957, p. 8.

31. Moon, Barbara. What you don't need to know about rock 'n' roll. *Maclean's.* 69:51, 52 July 7, 1956.

32. Pop songs being used by enemies of church. *Melody Maker.* 30:12 February 6, 1954.

33. Rock 'n' roll likened by cleric to jungle tomtoms. *Variety.* 204:33 September 5, 1956.

34. Chi Cardinal nixed R&R; disk sales stay steady. *Billboard.* 69:20 March 16, 1957.

35. Race, Steve. "Ban evil music." *Melody Maker.* 33:9 January 11, 1958.

36. Tobler, John. *25 Years of Rock.* Middlesex, England: Optimum, 1980, p. 36.

37. Soper, Donald. Artistic suicide. *Melody Maker.* 33:5 March 29, 1958.

38. Ex-R 'n' R star turned evangelist says despite polish, beat's still evil. *Variety.* 224:69 October 25, 1961.

39. Moon, Barbara. What you don't need to know, p. 15.

40. U.S. scenes recall "jungle bird house at the zoo." *Times* (London). September 15, 1956, p. 4.

41. Samuels, Gertrude. Why they rock and roll, p. 20.

42. Rock-and-roll called communicable disease. *New York Times.* March 28, 1956, p. 33.

43. Keeping up with Jones on rock 'n' roll; Prof puts beat on a couch. *Variety.* 206:55 May 1, 1957.

44. Dr. Howard Hanson blasts "rock and roll." *School Musician.* 34:39 November 1962.

45. Orman, John. *The Politics of Rock Music.* Chicago: Nelson-Hall, 1984, p. 4.

46. Dunn, Sam. The music of violence. *Music and Dance.* 51:13 March 1961.

47. Pintchman, Charles. The "rock 'n' roll" controversy. *Music Journal.* 19:60 April 1961.

48. Crazes: now and then. *New York Times.* February 26, 1957, p. 16.

49. Jahn, Mike. *Rock: From Elvis Presley to the Rolling Stones.* New York: Quadrangle/The New York Times Book Co., 1973, pp. 40–41.

50. Passing fad. *Musical America.* 77:4 March 1957.

51. Editorially speaking. *Music Journal.* 16:3 February 1958.

52. Race, Steve. *Melody Maker.* 31:5 May 5, 1956.

53. Race, Steve. Now we're at rock bottom. *Melody Maker.* 33:2–3 February 8, 1958.

54. Pop Rot! *Melody Maker.* 33:3 November 8, 1958.

55. Gibe at royal jive. *New York Times.* November 12, 1957, p. 39.

56. Wilson, John S. How no-talent singers get "talent." *New York Times Magazine.* June 21, 1959, p. 16.

57. Ibid., p. 52.

58. Brown, Tony. Rubbish on records. *Melody Maker.* 32:2 May 25, 1957.

59. Rahs 'n' raps on rock 'n' roll. *Variety.* 204:1 September 26, 1956.

60. Rock 'n' roll ebbs; D.J. de-accented on indie outlets. *Variety.* 211:57 June 25, 1958.

61. Seattle's KING-IBM pop poll shows only kids like "raucous" rockers. *Variety.* 216:86 October 21, 1959.

62. Bundy, June. DJ's dramatize R&R sneer campaign via colorful tactics. *Billboard.* 70:1 April 21, 1958.

63. Ibid., p. 4.

64. Ibid., p. 52.

65. Leblanc, Don. We don't have to put up with rock 'n' roll. *Maclean's.* 70:82 September 28, 1957.

66. Palmer, Tony. *All You Need Is Love.* New York: Grossman, 1976, pp. 221–23.

5. From the Waist Up

1. Beware Elvis Presley. *America.* 95:294 June 23, 1956.

2. Warn Elvis the Pelvis. *Variety.* 204:2 September 19, 1956.

3. Elvis Presley-digitation churns up teen tantrums, scribes raps, so-so B.O. *Variety.* 202:46 May 30, 1956.

4. Lees, Gene. Rock, violence, and Spiro T. Agnew. *High Fidelity.* 20:108 February 1970.

5. Nobody likes Presley in Canada except the kids. *Variety.* 208:52 September 18, 1957.

6. Goldman, Albert. *Elvis.* New York: McGraw-Hill, 1981, p. 181.

7. Ibid., p. 266.

8. Hopkins, Jerry. *Elvis.* New York: Simon and Schuster, 1971, p. 123.

9. Goldman, Albert. *Elvis,* p. 177.

10. Presley on pan but cash keeps rolling. *Billboard.* 68:18 June 16, 1956.

11. Ibid.

12. The music goes on & on & on. *Variety.* 203:51 June 13, 1956.

13. Hopkins, Jerry. *Elvis,* pp. 143–44.

14. Harris, Michael David. *Always On Sunday.* New York: Meredith Press, 1968, p. 116.

15. Gould, Jack. Elvis Presley. *New York Times.* September 16, 1956, sec. 2, p. 13.

16. Ibid.

17. "Mud" on the stars. *Newsweek.* 48:58 October 8, 1956.

18. Hopkins, Jerry. *Elvis,* pp. 171–72.

19. Principals toss a rock at Presley-mimic role. *New York Times.* February 25, 1957, p. 48.

20. Editorially speaking. *Music Journal.* 16:3 February 1958.

21. Marcus, Greil. *Mystery Train.* New York: E. P. Dutton, 1975, p. 147.

22. Find it risky to ban Presley disks on air. *Variety.* 204:1 September 5, 1956.

23. Hopkins, Jerry. *Elvis,* p. 198.

24. Presley's "poison" to Vancouver air. *Variety.* 209:57 December 4, 1957.

25. Toronto and Presley not in tune at yuletide. *Variety.* 209:57 December 11, 1957.

26. Hopkins, Jerry. *Elvis,* pp. 224–25.

27. Ibid., p. 211.

28. Goldman, Albert. *Elvis,* p. 318.

6. Stars Eclipsed

1. Swenson, John. *Bill Haley.* London: W. H. Allen, 1982, p. 52.

2. Ibid.

3. Ibid., p. 105.

4. Gillett, Charlie. *The Sound of the City.* New York: Outerbridge & Dienstfrey, 1970, p. 26.

5. B.B.C. bans rock 'n' roll "Rye." *New York Times.* September 18, 1956, p. 10.

6. Irving, Gordon. The Haley story. *Variety.* 205:16 February 27, 1957.

7. U.S. censors, press rap rock-and-roll. *Melody Maker.* 31:4 June 16, 1956.

8. Swenson, John. *Bill Haley,* p. 121.

9. Ibid., p. 123.

10. Palmer, Tony. *All You Need Is Love.* New York: Grossman, 1976, p. 217.

11. Negro singer jailed. *New York Times.* August 29, 1959, p. 38.

12. Lydon, Michael. Chuck Berry. *Ramparts.* 8:55 December 1969.

13. Ibid., p. 50.

14. Hagarty, Britt. *The Day the World Turned Blue.* Vancouver: Talonbooks, 1983, p. 53.

15. White, Charles. *Little Richard: The Quasar of Rock.* New York: Harmony Books, 1984, pp. 40, 49, 51.

16. Ibid., p. 60.

17. Ibid., p. 65–66.

18. Ibid., p. 67.

19. Ibid., p. 88–89.

20. Shaw, Arnold, *The Rockin' '50s.* New York: Hawthorn Books, 1974, p. 210.

21. White, Charles. *Little Richard*, p. 118.

22. Ibid., p. 197.

23. Lewis, Myra. *Great Balls Of Fire.* New York: William Morrow, 1982, p. 72.

24. Ibid.

25. Tosches, Nick. *Hellfire.* New York: Delacorte Press, 1982, p. 129.

26. Lewis, Myra. *Great Balls Of Fire.* p. 149.

27. Grevatt, Ren. Two views of Jerry Lee Lewis. *Melody Maker.* 33:7 May 24, 1958.

28. Tosches, Nick. *Hellfire*, pp. 156, 158.

29. Lewis, Myra. *Great Balls Of Fire*, pp. 169, 171.

30. Grade, Leslie. Why I dropped Jerry Lee Lewis. *Melody Maker.* 33:20 May 31, 1958.

31. Lewis, Myra. *Great Balls Of Fire*, pp. 173, 177.

32. Ibid., p. 183.

33. Shaw, Arnold. *The Rockin' '50s*, p. 189.

34. Tosches, Nick. *Hellfire*, p. 245.

7. Rock around the World

1. Refuse German theatres anti-riot insurance on *Rock around the Clock. Variety.* 204:13 October 24, 1956.

2. Belgian town bans U.S. Film. *New York Times.* December 17, 1956, p. 36.

3. Jakarta parties cite intimidation. *New York Times.* March 2, 1957, p. 3.

4. Cuba bans rock 'n' roll. *New York Times.* February 14, 1957, p. 55.

5. Caruthers, Osgood. Rock 'n' roll cuts swath in Egypt. *New York Times.* June 23, 1957, p. 24.

6. Egypt bans rock 'n' roll as sinuous imperialism. *New York Times.* June 17, 1957, p. 3.

7. Red lands seek better jazz. *New York Times.* November 1, 1958, p. 3.

8. French want to ban rock — by law. *Melody Maker.* 36:5 July 29, 1961.

9. R&R on the rocks in West Germany. *Variety.* 211:45 June 11, 1958.

10. Jahn, Mike. *Rock: From Elvis Presley to the Rolling Stones.* New York: Quadrangle/The New York Times Book Co., 1973, pp. 44–45.

11. Shaw, Arnold, *The Rockin' '50s.* New York: Hawthorn Books, 1974, p. 239.

12. Leipzig Presley fans jailed. *New York Times.* November 3, 1959, p. 19.

13. Reich stations ban "Presleyized" old folk song. *Variety.* 222:48 March 15, 1961.

14. Global report on rock 'n' roll. *New York Times Magazine.* April 20, 1958, p. 62.

15. Tooters' head vows clean sweep of Mex R 'n' R's "Municipal hoodlums." *Variety.* 224:61 October 4, 1961.

16. Green, Abel. Russian tastes and taboos. *Variety.* 206:2 March 27, 1957.

17. Lash Soviet pop singer as a fifth columnist for torchy Western music. *Variety.* 212:1 November 12, 1958.

18. Frankel, Max. Rock 'n' roll ring broken in Soviet. *New York Times.* January 13, 1960, p. 6.

8. ASCAP, Payola, and Alan Freed

1. Haverlin, Carl. ASCAP vs. BMI-II. *Saturday Review.* March 2, 1957.

2. Ibid., p. 10.

3. Ibid., p. 33.

4. Shaw, Arnold. *The Rockin' '50s.* New York: Hawthorn Books, 1974, p. 228.

5. R&R has "had it" here, O'seas not hot: ASCAP top. *Variety.* 204:54 October 17, 1956.

6. Congress investigation of rock 'n' roll. *Times* (London). September 19, 1956, p. 8.

7. Rock 'n' roll laid to B.M.I. control. *New York Times.* September 19, 1956, p. 75.

8. Ibid.

9. Shaw, Arnold. *The Rockin' '50s*, p. 158.

10. Ibid., p. 224.

11. Green, Abel. Cellar blasts BMI at ASCAP dinner where web execs are honor guests. *Variety*. 210:97 April 19, 1958.

12. ReMine, Shields. Payola. *American Mercury*. 9:34 March 1960.

13. Hammerstein, Oscar II. ASCAP vs. BMI. *Saturdy Review*. 40:15 February 23, 1957.

14. Haverlin, Carl. ASCAP vs. BMI-II, p. 10.

15. Ibid., p. 33.

16. Ibid.

17. Gould, Jack. TV: assessing effect of life under the table. *New York Times*. November 20, 1959, p. 63.

18. The slipped disc. *Reporter*. 21:4 December 10, 1959.

19. ReMine, Shields. Payola, p. 35.

20. Lewis, Anthony. House unit plans payola remedies. *New York Times*. May 4, 1960, p. 34.

21. *Responsibilities of Broadcasting Licensees and Station Personnel*. Hearings before a subcommittee of the Committee on Interstate and Foreign Commerce. House of Representatives. 86 Congress. 2nd Session on Payola and Other Deceptive Practices in the Broadcasting Field. Part 1. Washington, 1960, pp. 899–905.

22. Ibid., pp 489–90, 868, 870.

23. Ibid., pp 248, 622.

24. Ibid., p. 92.

25. Ibid., p. 250.

26. Ibid., p. 39.

27. Ibid., pp. 620, 868.

28. Ibid., pp 34, 249.

29. Facing the music. *Time*. 74:17 November 30, 1959.

30. ReMine, Shields. Payola, p. 39.

31. *The Rolling Stone Illustrated History of Rock & Roll*. New York: Rolling Stone Press, 1976, p. 92.

32. Whelton, Clark. He was king of rock 'n' roll. *New York Times*. September 24, 1972, sec. 2, p. 15.

33. Alan Freed, disk jockey, dead. *New York Times*. January 21, 1965, p. 31.

24. Jahn, Mike. *Rock: From Elvis Presley to the Rolling Stones*. New York: Quadrangle/The New York Times Book Co., 1973. p. 72.

35. Ibid., p. 48.

36. Freed is indicted over rock 'n' roll. *New York Times*. May 9, 1958, p. 49.

37. Disk jockey Freed. *New York Times.* November 13, 1959, p. 21.

38. Alan Freed, disk jockey, dead. p. 31.

39. Bundy, June. Freed replies to R&R press slurs. *Billboard.* 68:19 April 28, 1956.

40. Rock 'n' roll pied piper. *New York Times.* May 20, 1960, p. 62.

41. Whelton, Clark. He was king of rock 'n' roll, p. 15.

42. Shepard, Richard F. Alan Freed is out in "payola" study. *New York Times.* November 22, 1959, p. 1.

43. Adams, Val. Alan Freed loses 2nd broadcast job. *New York Times.* November 24, 1959, p. 31.

44. Goldman, Albert. *Elvis.* New York: McGraw-Hill. 1981, p. 315.

45. Freed, publisher refuse to sign immunity waiver. *Variety.* 217:55 December 2, 1959.

46. Roth, Jack. Alan Freed and 7 others arrested in payola here. *New York Times.* May 20, 1960, p. 62.

47. Shaw, Arnold, *The Rockin' '50s,* p. 267.

9. 1960–1962: Emasculated Rock

1. American Twist . . . or twisted Americans? *Senior Scholastic.* 79:13 January 10, 1962.

2. Holder, Geoffrey. The Twist? "It's not a dance." *New York Times Magazine.* December 3, 1961, p. 78.

3. British Safety Council raps "death cult" angle of "Laura" type pop disks.*Variety.* 220:57 September 21, 1960.

4. Betrock, Alan. *Girl Groups.* New York: Delilah Books, 1982, p. 35.

5. Ibid., p. 114.

6. Ibid., p. 115–16.

7. Marcus, Greil. *Mystery Train.* New York: E. P. Dutton, 1975, p. 181.

8. R&R Straws in the B.O. wind. *Variety.* 271:55 February 3, 1960.

9. Bundy, June. Air dogfight continues to rage. *Variety.* 73:1 August 14, 1961.

10. Gross, Mike. FM throws block at rock. *Variety.* 223:43, 47 August 16, 1961.

11. Chapple, Steve. *Rock 'n' Roll is Here to Pay.* Chicago: Nelson-Hall, 1977, p. 247.

12. Clark, Dick. *Rock, Roll And Remember.* New York: Thomas Y. Crowell, 1976, p. 67.

13. Ibid., p. 80.

14. Ibid., p. 82.

15. Ibid. (Count done by authors.)

11. Out of Sight

1. Rome solon hits TV's "Beatle style" singers. *Variety*. 242:193 May 4, 1966.

2. Air pollution. *Newsweek*. 66:76 August 16, 1965.

3. Grammar school bans Beatle haircuts. *Times* (London). November 18, 1963, p. 6.

4. M.B.E. returned to the Queen. *Times* (London). June 15, 1965, p. 12.

5. Author returns his military medal. *Times* (London). June 22, 1965, p. 10.

6. More protests over the Beatles. *Times* (London). June 22, 1965, p. 10.

7. For service. *Times* (London). June 16, 1965. p. 13.

8. Two to one against the Beatles. *Times* (London). June 17, 1965, p. 6.

9. Ibid.

10. Brown, Peter. *The Love You Make: An Insider's Story of the Beatles*. New York: McGraw, 1983, p. 183.

11. Sanchez, Tony. *Up and Down With the Rolling Stones*. New York: William Morrow, 1979, p. 22.

12. Norman, Philip. *The Stones*. London: Elm Tree, 1984, p. 96.

13. Ibid.

14. Judge, M.P.'s debate whether Rolling Stones are "Morons." *Variety*. 239:41 July 14, 1965.

15. Carr, Roy. *The Rolling Stones: An Illustrated Record*. New York: Harmony, 1976, p. 22.

16. Sanchez, Tony. *Up and Down*, p. 47.

17. Pop's bad boys. *Newsweek*. 66:92 November 29, 1965.

18. Norman, Philip. *The Stones*, p. 132.

19. Ibid., p. 242.

20. Sanchez, Tony. *Up and Down*, p. 297–98.

21. Goldman, Albert. On and on Mick's orgy rolls. *New York Times*. November 23, 1969, sec. 2, p. 19.

22. Ibid.

23. Ibid.

24. Morrison's penis is indecent. *Rolling Stone.* No. 13 April 19, 1969, p. 6.

25. Ibid.

26. Ibid.

27. Denisoff, R. Serge. *Solid Gold: The Popular Record Industry.* New Brunswick, N.J.: Transaction Books, 1982, p. 398.

28. Morrison's penis is indecent, p. 6.

29. Ibid.

30. Orman, John. *The Politics of Rock Music.* Chicago: Nelson-Hall, 1984, p. 148.

31. Hopkins, Jerry. *No One Here Gets Out Alive.* New York: Warner Books, 1980, p. 302.

32. British M.P. asks ban on Alice Cooper, blasts its sadism, necrophilia. *Variety.* 271:57 May 30, 1973.

33. Henderson, David. *'Scuse Me While I Kiss The Sky: The Life of Jimi Hendrix.* New York: Bantam, 1981, p. 114.

12. Ban the Beat

1. Chapple, Steve. *Rock 'n' Roll is Here to Pay.* Chicago: Nelson-Hall, 1977, p. 147.

2. Glasgow hall bars Liverpool sound. *Variety.* 232:45 October 16, 1963.

3. Ibid.

4. Irving, Gordon. Glasgow bans singers, beat groups with "disorderly" fans from civic halls. *Variety.* 240:63 October 27, 1965.

5. Norman, Philip. *Shout! The Beatles in their Generation.* New York: Simon & Schuster, 1981, p. 188.

6. Ibid.

7. Near riot at Clark 5 Carnegie Hall concert points up "menace" of R&R. *Variety.* 235:2 June 3, 1964.

8. Ibid.

9. Ibid., p. 86.

10. Balto. Ctr. Chief: acts themselves spark rock riots. *Variety.* 243:1 July 20, 1966.

11. Ibid.

12. Norman, Philip. *The Stones.* London: Elm Tree, 1984, p. 132.

13. Booth, Stanley. *Dance with the Devil: The Rolling Stones and Their Times.* New York: Random House, 1984, p. 180.

14. Jahn, Mike. *Rock: From Elvis Presley to the Rolling Stones.* New York: Quadrangle/New York Times Book Co., 1973, p. 152.

15. Herbst, Peter. *The Rolling Stone Interviews*. New York: St. Martin's, 1981, pp. 172–73.

16. Vancouver votes stiffer curbs on R&R shows in wake of Stones' riot. *Variety*. 244:59 August 24, 1966.

17. Booth, Stanley. *Dance with the Devil*, p. 315.

18. Sanchez, Tony. *Up and Down with the Rolling Stones*. New York: William Morrow, 1979, p. 61.

19. Norman, Philip. *The Stones*, p. 133.

20. Ibid.

21. Soul concert ends in a teen-age riot. *New York Times*. November 25, 1966, p. 44.

22. Knight, Curtis. *Jimi: An Intimate Biography of Jimi Hendrix*. New York: Praeger, 1974, p. 100.

23. Hopkins, Jerry. *No One Here Gets Out Alive*. New York: Warner Books, 1980, p. 210.

24. Ibid., p. 211.

25. Berry-Haley won't rock Albert Hall; Mgt. cancels gig. *Variety*. 255:52 July 23, 1969.

26. Ibid.

27. Chi's McCormick Place to blacklist rock combos that generate violence. *Variety*. 268:50 October 4, 1972.

28. Friedman, Myra. *Buried Alive: The Biography of Janis Joplin*. New York: William Morrow, 1973, p. 178.

29. Ibid., p. 317.

30. N.Y. state law fences in pop fests with long list of stiff regulations. *Variety*. 259:47 June 24, 1970.

31. British backlash vs. pop festivals. *Variety*. 259:2 July 29, 1970.

32. Edinburgh bans rock from city's auditoriums. *Variety*. 260:39 October 7, 1970.

33. Two rock fests kayoed in Tucson by local squawks. *Variety*. 261:41 December 2, 1970.

34. Norman, Philip. *The Stones*, p. 302.

35. Herbst, Peter. *The Rolling Stone Interviews*, p. 202.

36. Anson, Robert Sam. *Gone Crazy and Back Again: The Rise and Fall of the Rolling Stone Generation*. Garden City, New York: Doubleday, 1981, p. 158.

37. Herbst, Peter. *The Rolling Stone Interviews*, p. 201.

38. Sanchez, Tony. *Up and Down*, p. 189.

39. When a rock festival moved in on an Iowa town. *U.S. News & World Report*. 69:46 August 31, 1970.

40. Ibid., p. 47.

41. Ibid.

42. Feather, Leonard. Rock festivals: crunch and crisis. *Down Beat.* 37:20 October 29, 1970.

43. Ever feel they don't dig us? *Rolling Stone.* No. 58 April 2, 1970, p.8.

44. Ibid., p. 10.

45. Ibid.

46. Garlock, Frank. *The Big Beat a Rock Blast.* Greenville, S.C.: Bob Jones University, 1971, p. 34.

13. Against the Groove

1. Irate AFM flips over invasion of rocking records and culture. *Variety.* 234:49 March 25, 1964.

2. Henderson, David. *'Scuse Me While I Kiss The Sky: The Life of Jimi Hendrix.* New York: Bantam, 1981, p. 281.

3. Bennett, Marty. Audio's quality ires disk prods. *Variety.* 251:54 August 14, 1968.

4. Ibid.

5. Carr, Roy. *The Rolling Stones: An Illustrated Record.* New York: Harmony, 1976, p. 23.

6. Ibid., p. 27.

7. Norman, Philip. *The Stones.* London: Elm Tree, 1984, p. 133.

8. Sanchez, Tony. *Up and Down with the Rolling Stones.* New York: William Morrow, 1979, p. 48.

9. Rocker blasts "persecution" by disk biz and TV. *Variety.* 254:59 April 23, 1969.

10. Ibid.

11. TV webs don't give rock music an honest break; John Denver. *Variety.* 268:25 October 4, 1972.

12. Prof. looks at effects of pop music on school choirs. *The School Musician.* 44:25 June-July 1973.

13. Ibid.

14. Danziger, Harris. Popular music in the schools. *Music Journal.* 29:16 November 1971.

15. Ibid.

16. Ibid.

17. Chapple, Steve. *Rock 'n' Roll is Here to Pay. Chicago: Nelson-Hall,* 1977, p. 211.

18. Ibid.

19. Marsh, Dave. *Before I Get Old: The Story of the Who*. New York: St. Martin's, 1983, p. 237.

20. Ibid.

21. Rolling Stones: they don't really perform . . . they just stand there. *Melody Maker*. 41:3 June 18, 1966.

22. Koffman, Moe. Why do kids dig rock? *Maclean's*. 82:47 December 1969.

23. Ibid., p. 48.

24. Powell, Mel. The debasement of new music. *High Fidelity*. 20:MA–15 September 1970, section 1.

14. Rockers Go Home

1. Saigon regime bans songs for twisting. *New York Times*. April 2, 1963, p. 9.

2. Guild, Hazel. Crackdown on "liberal" Pix, play and music in Iron Curtain countries, only the twist okayed by Russos. *Variety*. 230:25 May 1, 1963.

3. Anderson, Omer E. Germany, in lather over beat band craze, lowering the boom. *Billboard*. 78:20 January 1, 1966.

4. Ibid., p. 37.

5. Avoid West's rock music, E. Germany warns its deejays. *Variety*. 272:38 October 2, 1973.

6. Reds rap Beatles. *New York Times*. August 12, 1965, p. 10.

7. All Cuban stations bar U.S. pop music. *New York Times*. April 22, 1973, p. 63.

8. Bans on "ereki" concerts cancel 16 Japan gigs of Beach Boys, Ast'nauts. *Variety*. 241:41 December 29, 1965.

9. Spain's foreign play curb hits rhubarb roadblocks. *Billboard*. 81:85 May 17, 1969.

10. "Foreignism": A dictatorship clamps down. *Rolling Stone*. No. 28, March 1, 1969, p. 4.

11. Greek official urges penalties for music aping hippie tunes. *New York Times*. February 4, 1970, p. 22.

12. Concerts to mourn lost rock cruises. *New York Times*. February 6, 1970, p. 28.

13. Peru expels rock band as U.S. "Imperialists." *Variety*. 265:60 December 15, 1971.

14. Ibid., p. 1.

15. The Communist Plot

1. Denisoff, R. Serge. *Solid Gold: The Popular Record Industry.* New Brunswick, N.J.: Transaction Books, 1982, p. 385.

2. Ibid.

3. Beatles unwitting agents of Red subversion, sez one Right-wing group. *Variety.* 244:2, 54 September 7, 1966.

4. Ex-Kenton sideman hears Red plot in rock sounds; propaganda with a beat. *Variety.* 259:1 May 20, 1970.

5. Ibid.

6. Bentley, Eric. For the right to wear our hair long. *New York Times.* August 20, 1970, sec. 2, p. 25.

7. Young, Scott. *Neil and Me.* Toronto: McClelland and Stewart, 1984, p. 107.

8. Brown, Peter. *The Love You Make: An Insider's Story of the Beatles.* New York: McGraw, 1983, p. 413.

9. Orman, John. *The Politics of Rock Music.* Chicago: Nelson-Hall, 1984, p. 112.

10. Anson, Robert Sam. *Gone Crazy and Back Again: The Rise and Fall of the Rolling Stone Generation.* New York: Doubleday, 1981, pp. 135–36.

11. Ibid., p. 189.

12. Orman, John. *The Politics of Rock Music,* p. 97.

13. Ibid., p. 98.

14. Ibid.

15. Anson, Robert Sam. *Gone Crazy and Back Again,* p. 189.

16. Orman, John. *The Politics of Rock Music,* p. 62.

17. Denisoff, R. Serge. *Solid Gold,* p. 383.

18. Ibid., p. 384.

19. Ibid., p. 405.

20. Ibid., p. 386.

16. A Deafening Noise

1. Acoustic trauma from rock and roll. *High Fidelity.* 17:38 November 1967.

2. Ibid.

3. Geerdes, Harold. Does rock create deafness? *Music Journal.* 31:26 December 1973.

4. Acoustic trauma from rock and roll, p. 38, 40.

5. Lebo, Charles. Acoustic trauma from rock and roll. *California Medicine.* 107:378 November 1967.

6. Not exactly music to your ears. *Consumer Reports,* 33:349 July 1968.

7. Ibid., p. 350.

8. Lamberg, Lynn. Rock music—turn it down while you can still hear it. *Today's Health.* 51:11 February 1973.

9. Ibid.

10. Ibid.

11. Sullivan, Dan. Ear-injury reports stir rock-music community. *New York Times.* August 21, 1968, p. 47.

12. Ibid.

13. Ibid.

14. Ibid.

15. Your ears are in good hands. *Rolling Stone.* No. 24 January 4, 1969, p. 4.

16. Ibid.

17. Nader sees deaf generation from excessive rock 'n' roll. *New York Times.* June 2, 1969, p. 53.

18. Lamberg, Lynn. Rock music—turn it down, p. 71.

19. Ward, Jeff. Cum on kill the noize! *Melody Maker.* 48:3 December 8, 1973.

20. Ibid.

21. Ibid.

22. Study shows rock music damages listeners' hearing. *Music Trades.* 118:48 March 1970.

23. Lamberg, Lynn. Rock music—turn it down, p. 71.

24. Careful you might harm your ears. *Melody Maker.* 45:26 February 7, 1970.

25. Ibid.

26. Lamberg, Lynn. Rock music—turn it down, p. 11.

27. Silver, Sidney L. Rock music & noise pollution. *Popular Electronics.* 3:31–32 March 1973.

28. Nicolosi, Lucille. *Terminology of Communication Disorders.* 2nd ed. Baltimore: Williams & Wilkins, 1983, p. 240.

29. Lamberg, Lynn. Rock music—turn it down, p. 11.

30. Ibid.

31. Silver, Sidney L. Rock music & noise pollution, p. 30.

32. Ibid.

33. Ibid.

34. Ibid., p. 33.

35. Ibid., pp. 32–33.

36. Ibid., p. 33.

37. Coronado, Merino. Hard rock's high dB's — and your hearing. *Radio Electronics.* 44:89 March 1973.

38. Speaks, Charles. Hearing loss in rock-and-roll musicians. *Journal of Occupational Medicine.* 12:218 June 1970.

39. Ibid.

40. Ibid.

41. Eddins, Dorothea. A second thought. *Health Digest.* November 1971, pp. 1–3.

42. Hagness, Don E. Does rock create deafness? *Music Journal.* 31:18–19 May 1973.

43. Geerdes, Harold. Does rock create deafness? *Music Journal.* 31:27 December 1973.

44. Snider, Arthur J. Is "rock" singing dangerous? *Science Digest.* 73:44 February 1973.

45. Ibid.

46. Ibid.

47. Loud rock linked to loss of lust. *Rolling Stone.* No. 54 February 14, 1974, p. 22.

48. Garlock, Frank. *The Big Beat a Rock Blast.* Greenville, S.C.: Bob Jones University, 1971, p. 24.

49. Ibid., pp. 33–34.

50. Ibid., p. 39.

17. Holy Rollers

1. Pope warns youth on wild outbursts over entertainment. *New York Times.* July 5, 1965, p. 2.

2. Killingsworth, Kay. "Beat" mass in church near Vatican draws teenagers & orthodox raps. *Variety.* 251:45 May 29, 1968.

3. Ibid.

4. Cleall, Charles. Pop in church — is it conducive to worship? *Musical Opinion.* 93:541 July 1970.

5. Ibid.

6. Ibid., p. 543.

7. Ibid.

8. Ibid., p. 545.

9. Brown, Peter. *The Love You Make: An Insider's Story of the Beatles.* New York: McGraw, 1983, p. 210.

10. "Beatles" U.S. personals may be dented by religioso rhubarb & DJ blackout. *Variety.* 243:70 August 10, 1966.

11. Ibid.

12. Ibid.

13. Ibid.

14. Norman, Philip. *Shout! The Beatles in Their Generation.* New York: Simon & Schuster, 1981, p. 266.

15. Beatles now legal in South Africa. *Melody Maker.* 46:12 June 19, 1971.

16. Brown, Peter. *The Love You Make*, pp. 212--13.

17. Ibid., p. 213.

18. Tex radio outlets don't accept Lennon's apology as sincere; ban still on. *Variety.* 244:51 August 24, 1966.

19. Ibid.

20. Ibid.

21. Beatles' disk ban spreading; will sales hurt? *Variety.* 225:55 June 4, 1969.

22. Beatle's single stirs storm — Anti-Christ? *Billboard.* 81:4 June 7, 1969.

23. Denisoff, R. Serge. *Solid Gold: The Popular Record Industry.* New Brunswick, N.J.: Transaction Books, 1982, p. 392.

24. Garlock, Frank. *The Big Beat a Rock Blast.* Greenville, S.C.: Bob Jones University Press, 1971, p. 19.

25. Denisoff, R. Serge. *Solid Gold*, p. 401.

26. Garlock, Frank. *The Big Beat*, p. 22.

27. Ibid.

28. Ibid., p. 26.

29. Ibid., p. 37.

30. Ibid., pp. 41, 45, 49.

18. See No Evil, Hear No Evil

1. Rob a blind man blurb dropped. *Times* (London). March 17, 1965, p. 5.

2. Ibid.

3. Taste for graffiti. *Time.* October 11, 1968.

4. Ibid.

5. Norman, Philip. *Shout! The Beatles in Their Generation.* New York: Simon & Schuster, 1981, p. 291.

6. Ibid., p. 347.

7. Mulligan, Brian. EMI spurns nude Lennon and Yoko Ono "2 Virgins" LP. *Variety.* 252:20 October 23, 1968.

8. Ibid.

9. Brown, Peter. *The Love You Make: An Insider's Story of the Beatles*. New York: McGraw, 1983, pp 320–21.

10. Wiener, Jon. *Come Together: John Lennon in his Time*. New York: Random House, 1984, p. 85.

11. Henderson, David. *'Scuse Me While I Kiss the Sky: The Life of Jimi Hendrix*. New York: Bantam, 1981, p. 229.

12. Spicy tunes leave bad taste with radio program chiefs. *Billboard*. 79:3 January 21, 1967.

13. Air pollution. *Newsweek*. 66:76 August 16, 1965.

14. Orman, John. *The Politics of Rock Music*. Chicago: Nelson-Hall, 1984, p. 148.

15. Chapple, Steve. *Rock 'n' Roll is Here to Pay*. Chicago: Nelson-Hall, 1977, p. 105.

16. Air pollution, p. 76.

17. Chapple, Steve. *Rock 'n' Roll Is Here to Pay*, p. 115.

18. Ibid., p. 116.

19. Weber, Bruce. Riots laid to raucous records. *Billboard*. 79:4 August 5, 1967.

20. Disk programmer sets own "morality" ratings. *Variety*. 258:1 May 13, 1970.

21. Henshaw, Laurie. Censored. *Melody Maker*. 47:24 March 11, 1972.

22. Mullinax, Edwin. The question of dirty lyrics. *Billboard*. 80:18 April 6, 1968.

23. Hall, Claude. Radio in slap smut drive. *Billboard*. 82:10 September 5, 1970.

24. Purge. *Newsweek*. 69:114 May 8, 1967.

25. Ibid.

26. Chain broadcaster McLendon warns U.S. mothers of evils in disk leerics. *Variety*. 246:45 May 17, 1967.

27. Manners & morals socking it to 'em. *Time*. 89:53 May 26, 1967.

28. Hall, Claude. Anti-smut McLendon to set up a "fringe" panel. *Billboard*. 79:28 May 20, 1967.

29. Manners & morals socking it to 'em, p. 53.

30. Hall, Claude. Anti-smut, p. 28.

31. Ibid.

32. Ibid.

33. Fox, Hank. McLendon vs. labels; compromise in the wind. *Billboard*. 79:10 May 27, 1967.

34. Ibid., p. 11.

25. Ibid.

36. Many Texas AMers follow McLendon in banning disks with dubious lyrics. *Variety.* 247:51 June 21, 1967.

37. Hall, Mildred. Good and bad youths. *Billboard.* 81:6 February 22, 1969.

19. Turn On, Tune In, Drop Out

1. The record industry and the drug epidemic. *Congressional Record—Senate.* November 21, p. 37853.

2. Norman, Philip. *Shout! The Beatles in Their Generation.* New York: Simon & Schuster, 1981, p. 294.

3. Ibid.

4. Denisoff, R. Serge. *Solid Gold: The Popular Record Industry.* New Brunswick, N.J.: Transaction Books, 1982, p. 396.

5. Ibid.

6. Sanchez, Tony. *Up and Down with the Rolling Stones.* New York: William Morrow, 1979, p. 58.

7. Carr, Roy. *The Rolling Stones: an Illustrated Record.* New York: Harmony, 1976, p. 48.

8. Weiner, Jon. *Come Together: John Lennon in his Time.* New York: Random House, 1984, pp. 80–81.

9. U.S. radio ban—but no British ban planned. *Melody Maker.* 41:4 May 14, 1966.

10. Hopkins, Jerry. *No One Here Gets Out Alive.* New York: Warner, 1980, pp. 139–40.

11. Wiener, Jon. *Come Together*, pp. 139–40.

12. Spiro Agnew vs. The White Rabbit. *Rolling Stone.* October 29, 1970, p. 24.

13. Weaver, Warren. Gore joins receiving line for Agnew. *New York Times.* September 23, 1970.

14. Ibid.

15. Michie, Larry. TV ad slant vs. Agnew rock rap. *Variety.* 260:60 September 23, 1970.

16. Nixon requests broadcasters to screen lyrics. *Billboard.* 82:78 October 24, 1970.

17. Lees, Gene. Rock, violence and Spiro T. Agnew. *High Fidelity.* 20:108, 110 February 1970, sec. 1.

18. Littleford, William D. The call to action against drugs. *Billboard.*

82:30 April 11, 1970.

19. Lees, Gene. Rock, violence and Spiro T. Agnew, p. 134.

20. Fong-Torres, Ben. FCC discovers dope, does darndest thing. *Rolling Stone.* No. 79, April, 1, 1971, p. 1.

21. Linkletter raps drug disks. *Billboard.* 82:33 July 11, 1970.

22. Glassenberg, Bob. Nation's PD's giving disk lyrics once-over in no-preaching drive. *Billboard.* 82:34 June 27, 1970.

23. Zhito, Lee. It's reflector not purveyor. *Billboard.* 82:70 November 7. 1970.

24. Ibid.

25. Tiegel, Eliot. MGM busts 18 rock groups. *Billboard.* 82:70 November 7, 1970.

26. Ibid., p. 10.

27. Mike Curb and Richard Nixon battle dopers. *Rolling Stone.* No 71 November 26, 1970, p. 6.

28. Col. Prexy Davis blasts MGM's Curb for fake witch hunt vs. drug abusers. *Variety.* 261:69 November 18, 1970.

29. MGM's drug drive a smokescreen. *Rolling Stone.* No. 72, December 2, 1970. p. 16.

30. Ibid.

31. Goldman, Albert. *Elvis.* New York: McGraw, 1981, p. 467.

32. Ibid., p. 468.

33. Fong-Torres, Ben. FCC discovers dope, p. 6.

34. FCC warns broadcasters on lyrics backing drug use. *New York Times.* March 7, 1971, p. 28.

35. Fong-Torres, Ben. FCC discovers dope, p. 6.

36. Drug songs open generation gap at WDAS-FM; owner fires his son. *Variety.* 262:1, 76 March 17, 1971.

37. Hall, Mildred. Drug lyric ruling draws static from radio-Johnson hits FCC. *Variety.* 83:27 March 20, 1971.

38. Ibid.

39. Fong-Torres, Ben. FCC discovers dope, p. 6.

40. Hall, Mildred. FCC clarification note shaky bridge over troubled waters. *Billboard.* 83:3 May 1, 1971.

41. Ibid.

42. Ibid.

43. FCC warning on drug lyrics brings sharp reaction in broadcast industry. *New York Times.* April 11, 1971, p. 50.

44. Ibid.

45. Denisoff, R. Serge. *Solid Gold*, pp. 412–13.

46. Pop songs don't and can't push drugs disk industry tells govt. commission. *Billboard*. 268:2 April 19, 1972.

47. The record industry and the drug epidemic, p. 37849.

48. Ibid., p. 37852.

49. Ibid., p. 37853.

50. Ibid., p. 37851.

51. Ibid., p. 37853.

20. New Tunes, Old Fears

1. Durbin, Karen. Can a feminist love the world's greatest rock and roll band? *Ms*. 3:23–26 October 1974.

2. McCormick, Lynde. Rolling Stones tour: a critical look at rock royalty. *Christian Science Monitor*. June 26, 1975, p. 19.

3. Evearitt, Daniel J. The Rolling Stones: the darker side of rock. *Christianity Today*. 22:18–19 February 24, 1978.

4. Cobb, David. Margaret in wonderland. *Maclean's*. 90:64 March 21, 1977.

5. Evans, Nancy. How to succeed by compromising. *Crawdaddy*. No. 87 August, 1978, p. 29.

6. Franklin, James Leo. The effects of rock music on the reading comprehension of eighth grade students. *Dissertation Abstracts*. June 1977. vol. 37 (12-A, Pt. 1) #7597.

7. Pop records debasing, headmasters are told. *Times* (London). September 23, 1981, p. 28.

8. Notable & Quotable. *Wall Street Journal*. May 2, 1983, p. 30.

9. Hall, Doug. Sex rhythm spurs disco pull. *Billboard*. 91:12 June 2, 1979.

10. Rock: the bus stops here. *Billboard*. 97:14 February 16, 1985.

11. Stinnett, Caskie. I know its only rock 'n' roll, but I hate it. *Atlantic Monthly*. 240:26 August 1977.

12. Landers, Ann. That junk we call rock. *Sun* (Vancouver, B.C.). October 25, 1985, p. B3.

13. Grein, Paul. Promo men lament fragmentation. *Billboard*. 93:90 August 15, 1981.

21. Punk Perverts, Disco Sucks, Metal Menaces

1. Tobler, John. *25 Years of Rock*. Middlesex, England: Optimum, 1980, p. 207.

2. Ibid.

3. Jones, Peter. U.K. Sex Pistols fire a controversy. *Billboard.* 88:56 December 18, 1976.

4. Ibid.

5. Butt, Ronald. The grubby face of mass punk promotion. *Times* (London). December 9, 1976, p. 14.

6. Ibid.

7. Foul-mouthed "punk rock" cult looms as new pop menace. *Variety.* 285:2 December 8, 1976.

8. Brown, Mick. Punks. *Rolling Stone.* No. 231 January 27, 1977, p. 11.

9. Jones, Peter. Sex Pistols, p. 56.

10. Punk rock & responsibility. *Variety.* 285:65 December 15, 1976.

11. Boston, Virginia. *Punk Rock.* London: Penguin 1978, p. 15.

12. Pistols' 45 hits target despite ban. *Billboard.* 89:65 June 25, 1977.

13. Reed, Roy. Punk rock, Britain's latest fad, leaves trail of violence in wake. *New York Times.* July 11, 1977, p. 2.

14. Brown, Mick. Punk: something Rotten in England. *Rolling Stone.* No. 245 August 11, 1977, p. 15.

15. Boston, Virginia. *Punk Rock,* p. 27.

16. Brown, Mick. Punks, p. 11.

17. Young, Charles M. Rock is sick and living in London. *Rolling Stone.* No. 250 October 20, 1977 pp. 68–75.

18. Jones, Peter. Sex Pistols ads ruled off British airwaves. *Billboard.* 89:76 November 19, 1977.

19. Boston, Virginia. *Punk Rock,* p. 16.

20. "Rock" vs. sensationalism. *New York Times.* January 9, 1978, p. 24.

21. Boston, Virginia. *Punk Rock,* p. 15.

22. Johnson, Alexandra. I think I'll sit this one out, thanks. *Christian Science Monitor.* December 4, 1979, p. 21.

23. Random notes. *Rolling Stone.* No. 298 August 23, 1979, p. 34.

24. Jones, Allan. U.S. disco wars: Carter to resign? *Melody Maker.* 54:10 August 4, 1979.

25. Ibid.

26. Disco taboo on Rhodesia radio. *Billboard.* 91:36 April 7, 1979.

27. Connelly, Christopher. Rock radio: a case of racism? *Rolling Stone.* No. 384 December 9, 1982, pp. 53–55.

28. Ptacek, Greg. Majors return to nuts and bolts of pre-MTV metal marketing days. *Billboard.* 97:HM15 April 27, 1985.

29. Frost, Deborah. Heavy metal rears its ugly head again. *Rolling Stone*. No. 431 September 27, 1984, pp. 83–84.

30. Ivany, John. Lowering the boom on heavy metal. *Billboard*. 97:10 July 6, 1985.

31. Vare, Ethlie Ann. Satanic image questions industry's metal morals. *Billboard*. 96:HM16 April 14, 1984.

32. Ptacek, Greg. Majors return to nuts and bolts, p. HM3.

33. Duncan, Robert. *The Noise*. New York: Ticknor & Fields, 1984, pp. 36–37.

22. The Evil Beat Will Make You Weak

1. Turn it down. *Melody Maker*. 50:39 March 15, 1975.

2. Documentation: rock music is hazard. *Journal of Occupational Health and Safety*. 45:10 September/October 1976.

3. "Indoor rock" may cause permanent hearing damage. *School Musician*. 50:46 November 1978.

4. Roth, Robert. High volume sound threat to patrons of some clubs. *Billboard*. 91:62 March 2, 1979.

5. Rock music gets ear plug. *Variety*. 293:70 November 15, 1978.

6. Ibid.

7. Lipscomb, David M. Hearing loss of rock musicians. *Audio*. 60:32 March 1976.

8. Ibid., p. 34.

9. Ibid., p. 36.

10. Ex-censor applies for disability, claiming rock concerts hurt his nerves. *Variety*. 306:87 April 14, 1982.

11. Disco music makes pigs deaf and mice gay. *Music Trades*. 129:30 March 1981.

12. Medico finds root of many evils in a pesty rock beat. *Variety*. 288:77 September 28, 1977.

13. Ibid.

14. Kozak, Roman. Can certain music harm one's health? *Billboard*. 92:53 February 23, 1980.

15. Ibid.

16. Ibid.

17. Soviet doctors blast rock's "harmful effect." *Variety*. 314:1, 32 March 28, 1984.

23. The Decadent Music Abroad

1. South Korea banning "decadent" foreign music, including many protest songs. *New York Times.* December 28, 1975, p. 10.

2. Iranians buying pop music tapes to beat the ban. *New York Times.* July 2, 1980, p. A9.

3. Spahr, Wolfgang. German clips crackdown? *Billboard.* 97:31 August 10, 1985.

4. Browne, Malcolm. Soviet bloc acts to curb "plague" of alien styles. *New York Times.* December 12, 1976, p. 6.

5. Browning, Jim. Czech musicians silenced. *Christian Science Monitor.* December 13, 1977, p. 5.

6. Rightwing beat of pop from West too strong for mag. in E. Germany. *Variety.* 296:114 October 31, 1979.

7. Skvorecky, Josef. Hipness at noon. *New Republic.* 191:30 December 17, 1984.

8. Fraser, John. Peking tries to still the growing beat of rock 'n' roll. *Christian Science Monitor.* November 17, 1978, p. 9.

9. Wren, Christopher S. Off-key or off-color, tunes of West worry China. *New York Times.* October 28, 1982, p. A2.

10. Weisskopf, Michael. Chain finds rock music ideologically off-key. *Washington Post.* March 20, 1983, p. A25.

11. Wren, Christopher S. Off-key or off-color, p. A2.

12. Rauth, Robert. Back in the U.S.S.R. – Rock and Roll in the Soviet Union. *Popular Music & Society.* 8:5 n. 3–4, 1982.

13. Ibid., p. 7.

14. Pitman, Jack. Cliff Richard SRO in USSR. *Variety.* 284:94 September 15, 1976.

15. 4 Swedish singers no longer a hit at Kremlin. *New York Times.* March 7, 1982, p. 7.

16. Jones, Peter. Soviets crack down on discos. *Billboard.* 94:41 September 25, 1982.

17. Mitchell, James. Rock is rolled out of Soviet discos. *Christian Science Monitor.* August 5, 1983, p. 3.

18. Ibid.

19. Lettlander, Erik. Latvian rockers play with fire. *Christian Science Monitor.* August 28, 1984, p. 7.

20. Martin, Lawrence. Soviets take to Western rock. *Globe and Mail.* March 21, 1986, p. N.

24. Sex Rock

1. Sex rock. *Time*. 106:39 December 29, 1975.

2. Williams, Jean. Sex-oriented lyrics, titles stir a storm. *Billboard*. 88:19 December 25, 1976.

3. Ibid.

4. Ibid.

5. NAB expresses concern. *Variety*. 285:78 December 1, 1976.

6. Blacks in PUSH against "Sex rock." *Variety*. 285:78 December 1, 1976.

7. Ibid.

8. Williams, Jean. Sex-oriented lyrics, p. 19.

9. Schreger, Charles. Jackson pushes rating bd. setup for X-type disks. *Variety*. 285:107 December 22, 1976.

10. "Media-Ethics" pow aims campaign at disk-pix pandering. *Variety*. 285:2 January 19, 1977.

11. Ibid., p. 92.

12. Penchansky, Alan. A "no-play" listing for sex songs. *Billboard*. 89:10 January 29, 1977.

13. Nobody's contesting Rev. Jackson's stand. *Billboard*. 89:3 February 26, 1977.

14. Ibid., p. 90.

15. The seamy side. *New York Times*. February 18, 1977, p. 26.

16. Williams, Jean. Industry ethics stamped as topic at PUSH parley. *Billboard*. 89:3, 90 July 9, 1977.

17. Ahmet Ertegun suggests Stones alter "Some Girls." *Billboard*. 90:3 October 21, 1978.

18. Williams, Jean. Stones, stations face pickets irate about Stones' record. *Billboard*. 90:64 November 25, 1978.

19. No action so Jackson's seeking nationwide Rolling Stones boycott. *Variety*. 293:70 November 15, 1978.

20. Peck, Abe. Stone lyric protest. *Rolling Stone*. No. 278 November 16, 1978, p. 39.

21. Rev. Jackson's publicity stunt. *Rolling Stone*. No. 278 November 16, 1978, p. 39.

22. A flood of "x-rated" music hits airwaves, concert halls, record shops. *U.S. News & World Report*. 83:50 October 31, 1977.

23. Ibid.

24. Teigel, Eliot. Song lyrics in panel spotlight. *Billboard*. 90:30 April 22, 1978.

25. Questionable lyrics: an enigma. *Billboard.* 91:18 September 22, 1979.

26. What turns censors on. *Melody Maker.* 51:32 February 21, 1976.

27. Ibid.

28. Walley, David. *No Commercial Potential.* New York: E. P. Dutton, 1980, p. 176.

29. Brenner, Suzanne. "Physical" is censored in South Africa. *Billboard.* 94:6 July 17, 1982.

30. Harrison, Ed. Stations banning Olivia's "Physical." *Billboard.* 93:10 November 7, 1981.

31. Weinraub, Bernard. Confrontation on lyrics stirs Voice of America. *New York Times.* March 1, 1983, p. A18.

32. ABC censor zaps Easton tune; can't do "Sugar" on "Bandstand." *Variety.* 318:72 April 3, 1985.

33. Jones, Peter. No. 1 single banned by BBC. *Billboard.* 96:56 March 17, 1984.

34. Joan Jett. *Melody Maker.* 58:3 August 27, 1983.

35. Schipper, Henry. L.A. mayor urges radio outlets to broadcast "Sun City" disk. *Variety.* 321:119 November 13, 1985.

36. Goodman, Fred. PolyGram changes Scorpions' cover. *Billboard.* 96:72 May 5, 1984.

37. Kozak, Roman. N.Y. politico would kill drugs via tax. *Billboard.* 92:15 October 18, 1980.

38. Kozak, Roman. Moral Majority in; what's the future. *Billboard.* 92:58 November 15, 1980.

39. Conservative mood of country could restrict songs, says Drew. *Variety.* 301:93 January 21, 1981.

40. Harrison, Mike. Does censorship loom? *Billboard.* 94:27 March 13, 1982.

25. Stage Fright

1. Kunstler, Jim. Led Zep concert beaned in Boston. *Rolling Stone.* No. 81, February 27, 1975, p. 11.

2. Newman, Gerald. *Elton John.* New York: New American Library, 1976, p. 150.

3. Ibid., p.151.

4. Kunstler, Jim., Led Zep concert beaned, p. 11.

5. Rockwell, John. Is rock the music of violence? *New York Times.* December 16, 1979, sec. 2, p. D1.

6. Young, Charles M. Heavy metal. *Musician.* 71:43 September 1984.

7. Marsh, Dave. *Before I Get Old: The Story of The Who.* New York: St. Martin's Press, 1983, p. 513.

8. Ibid.

9. Rockwell, John. Is rock the music of violence?, p. D1.

10. Ibid.

11. Stuart, Reginald. Some in Cincinnati seek ban on rock after deaths. *New York Times.* December 6, 1979, p. A26.

12. Cincinnati plan seek to control perils in crowds. *New York Times.* July 8, 1980, p. A12.

13. New Pop's rated 'x'. *Melody Maker.* 51:1 March 13, 1976.

14. Ibid.

15. LeMoyne, James, and Jennings, Ann. Oi — Music to riot by. *Newsweek.* 98:35 August 31, 1981.

16. Ibid.

17. Jones, Peter. Do music acts incite U.K. violence? *Billboard.* 93:2 July 25, 1981.

18. LeMoyne, James. Oi, p. 35.

19. Clerk, Carol. And the Oi goes on . . . *Melody Maker.* 56:5 July 18, 1981.

20. Ibid.

21. Britain: rock riot. *The Nation.* 233:71. July 25–August 1, 1981.

22. LeMoyne, James. Oi, p. 35.

23. Coren, Michael. Steps to stop the right rocking. *New Statesman.* 102:4 September 11, 1981.

24. Benjamin, Sid. Oshourne concert scuttled in Scranton, "Due to Bad Reputation," *Variety.* 310:117 February 16, 1983.

25. Orodenker, Maurie. Court refuses to allow Osbourne to do concert. *Billboard.* 95:30 February 26, 1983.

26. Appeals court lifts rock concert ban; judge defines music. *Variety.* 312:158 September 26, 1983.

27. Sacks, Leo. Semi-smut. *Village Voice.* 29:47 November 6, 1984.

28. Ibid.

29. Rock band blacklisted after "vulgar" show. *Vancouver Sun.* December 7, 1985, p. C11.

30. Arnold, Thomas K. Problems for punk promoter. *Billboard.* 97:38 January 12, 1985.

31. Watt bans rock groups from July 4 celebration. *New York Times.* April 6, 1983, p. A18.

32. The art of being James Watt. *New York Times.* April 8, 1983, p. A30.

33. Shabecoff, Philip. Fans protest Watt's ban on rock bands at concert. *New York Times.* April 7, 1983, p. B28.

34. Ibid.

35. McCombs, Phil. Watt sets off uproar with music ban. *Washington Post.* April 7, 1983, p. A17.

36. Ibid.

37. Alpern, David M. James Watt: bad vibrations. *Newsweek.* 101:26 April 18, 1983.

38. Clines, Francis X. Watt reverses ban on rock music at concert. *New York Times.* April 8, 1983, p. A14.

39. Rock that is "not for kids." *Vancouver Sun.* November 14, 1985, p. D3.

40. Sutherland, Sam. One city mulls concert control in lyric row. *Billboard.* 97:72 September 21, 1985.

41. Promoter, parents group agree on warnings for concert acts. *Variety.* 320:81 October 23, 1985.

42. Levin, Eric. Lay off of them blue suede shoes. *People.* 24:44 November 24, 1985.

43. Schipper, Henry. Texas promoter to fight law banning teens at concerts. *Variety.* 321:1+ December 11, 1985.

44. Ibid., p. 143.

26. Visual Violations

1. Shore, Michael. *The Rolling Stone Book of Rock Video.* New York: Rolling Stone Press, 1984, p. 105.

2. Ibid., p. 195.

3. Ibid., p. 138.

4. Ibid., p. 108.

5. Ibid.

6. Elektra agrees to femme demand on album covers. *Variety.* 286:66 February 23, 1977.

7. Harrison, Ed. Women and Warners forgive and forget. *Billboard.* 91:3 November 17, 1979.

8. Ibid.

9. Feminists end album boycott. *Rolling Stone.* No. 309 January 24, 1980, p. 16.

10. Ibid.

11. Gold, Richard. Labels try to restrain explicit sex. *Variety.* 310:179 April 20, 1983.

12. Ibid.
13. Stones' clip too "nasty" for television in Britain. *Billboard.* 95:30 November 26, 1983.
14. Canadian coalition wants to bleep out rock video violence. 313:1, 140 January 25, 1984.
15. Ibid., p. 140.
16. Ibid.
17. Godfrey, Stephen. Mulligan's parting shot. *Globe and Mail.* September 5, 1985, p. N2.
18. Music videos rapped for "senseless" violence. *Variety.* 317:142 December 12, 1984.
19. Ibid.
20. Sex, violence on rock channel. *Sun* (Vancouver, B.C.). September 6, 1985, p. B7.
21. Kozak, Roman. Caution: MTV may be hazardous to your mind. *Billboard.* 94:60 September 11, 1982.

27. Thou Shalt Not Rock

1. Buglioso, Vincent. *Helter Skelter.* New York: Bantam, 1974, p. 323.
2. Unger, Craig. John Lennon's killer: the nowhere man. *New York.* 14:32 June 22, 1981.
3. Adelson, David. AC/DC is front page news in Los Angeles. *Cash Box.* 49:7 September 14, 1985.
4. CBS Osbourne sued in youth's suicide. *Variety.* 321:2 October 30, 1985.
5. Vare, Ethlie Ann. For once, Osbourne shuns publicity. *Billboard.* 98:38 February 8, 1986.
6. Adelson, David. Osbourne is distressed. *Cash Box.* 49:9 February 1, 1986.
7. Grindal, Bruce T. Creationism, sexual purity, and the religious right. *Humanist.* 43:20 March/April 1983.
8. Ibid.
9. Ibid.
10. Bane, Michael. Fahrenheit 250: Florida minister, flock, fire rock. *Rolling Stone.* No. 206 February 12, 1976, p. 15.
11. Royko, Mike. Music to get pregnant by. *Stereo Review.* 36:74 May 1976.
12. Cook, David T. Unwed teen mothers and rock lyrics. *Christian Science Monitor.* April 10, 1975, p. 19.

13. Ibid.

14. Zito, Tom. Rock is unrighteous? *Rolling Stone.* No. 337 February 19, 1981, p. 9.

15. Ibid., p. 12.

16. Ibid., p. 16.

17. Ibid.

18. Ibid., p. 12.

19. Peters, Dan. *Why Knock Rock?* Minneapolis: Bethany House, 1984, p. 188.

20. Ibid., p. 263.

21. Ibid.

22. No sympathy for the devil. *The Progressive.* 47:19 April 1983.

23. Sheppard, John. The devil in rock music. *Alberta Report.* 10:38 December 20, 1982.

24. Ibid., p. 39.

25. Ibid.

26. Sippel, John. "Demonic" messages are focus of Calif. proposal. *Billboard.* 94:4 May 15, 1982.

27. Holland, Bill. "Demonic" message bill is introduced in Congress. *Billboard.* 94:72 July 10, 1982.

28. Aranza, Jacob. *Backward Masking Unmasked.* Shreveport: Huntington House, 1984, p. 2.

29. Ibid., p. 4.

30. A Christian "heavy metal" band makes its mark on the secular industry. *Christianity Today.* 29:46 February 15, 1985.

28. Moms Horrified, Rollers Curl PMRC's Hair

1. McDougal, Dennis. "Porn rock" the sound draws fury. *Los Angeles Times.* November 1, 1985, pp. 1, 32.

2. Dupler, Steven. National PTA asks labels: institute ratings system. *Billboard.* 96:70 October 27, 1984.

3. Terry, Ken. RIAA leaves LP rating issue to labels. *Variety.* 317:132 November 21, 1984.

4. McDougal, Dennis. "Porn rock," p. 33.

5. Wharton, Dennis. D.C. bluebloods want X rating for porn rock. *Variety.* 319:108 May 22, 1985.

6. Holland, Bill. Washington mothers blast "pornographic" rock lyrics. *Billboard.* 97:80 May 11, 1985.

7. Ibid.

8. Stround, Kandy. Stop pornographic rock. *Newsweek.* 105:14 May 6, 1985.

9. Ibid.

10. Gergen, David. X-rated records. *U.S. News & World Report.* 98:98 May 20, 1985.

11. Ibid.

12. Holland, Bill. NAB president speaks out on "porn rock." *Billboard.* 97:6 June 1, 1985.

13. Ibid.

14. Holland, Bill. NAB's Fritts urges labels: supply radio with lyrics. *Billboard.* 97:73 June 15, 1985.

15. Raspberry, William. Filth on the air. *Washington Post.* June 19, 1985, p. A21.

16. Paige, Earl. Dealers brace for lyric battle. *Billboard.* 97:3 June 29, 1985.

17. Ibid., p. 73.

18. Freeman, Kim. Lyric review board proposed. *Billboard.* 97:12 July 13, 1985.

19. MTV meets with parents' groups to explain its "high standards." *Variety.* 320:73 July 31, 1985.

20. Ibid.

21. Terry, Ken. Diskeries to label explicit records. *Variety.* 320:68 August 14, 1985.

22. PMRC calls for panel to devise ratings guidelines. *Variety.* 320:63 August 14, 1985.

23. Record companies at a crossroad. *Variety.* 320:68 August 14, 1985.

24. Terry, Ken. RIAA rejects PMRC's demand for a panel on explicit lyrics. *Variety.* 320:123 August 21, 1985.

25. Lyrics: enough ground surrendered. *Billboard.* 97:10 August 24, 1985.

26. RIAA, parents fail to harmonize. *Billboard.* 97:68 August 24, 1985.

27. Zappa, Frank. Extortion, pure and simple. An open letter to the music industry. *Cash Box.* 49:3 August 31, 1985.

28. Moleski, Linda. NARAS panel confronts the record rating issue. *Billboard.* 97:73 September 21, 1985.

29. Holland, Bill. PTA, PMRC unite on lyrics. *Billboard.* 97:1 September 21, 1985.

30. Wolmuth, Roger. Parents vs. rock. *People.* 23:49 September 16, 1985.

31. Ibid., p. 48.

32. Ibid., p. 51.

33. Zucchino, David. Big Brother meets Twisted Sister. *Rolling Stone*. No. 460 November 7, 1985, p. 64.

34. Ibid., p. 65.

35. Harrington, Richard. Clash of the hill rockers. *Washington Post*. September 20, 1985, p. B6.

36. Zucchino, David. Big Brother meets Twisted Sister, p. 16.

37. Ibid.

38. Harrington, Richard. Clash of the hill rockers, p. B6.

39. Abrams, Earl B. The ratings "show" move to Washington, D.C. *Cash Box*. 49:36 September 28, 1985.

40. Zucchino, David. Big Brother meets Twisted Sister, pp. 9, 65.

41. Adelson, David. Ratings opponents find strong resistance. *Cash Box*. 49:7 September 28, 1985.

42. McDougal, Dennis. "Porn rock," p. 32.

43. Levin, Eric. Lay off of them blue suede shoes. *People*. 24:43 November 4, 1985.

44. Ann Landers. *Sun* (Vancouver, B.C.). October 25, 1985, p. B3.

45. Hoyt, Mary Finch. How parents can stop obscene rock songs. *Good Housekeeping*. 201:120, 122 November 1985.

46. McDougal, Dennis. "Porn rock," p. 32.

47. Holland, Bill. RIAA, PMRC call off announcement. *Billboard*. 97:4 October 19, 1985.

48. Levin, Eric. Lay off of them blue suede shoes, p. 44.

49. Holland, Bill. Senator Hollings mulls "porn rock" lyrics bill. *Billboard*. 97:6, 75 November 2, 1985.

50. Pagano, Penny. Warnings or lyrics will be printed on record albums. *Los Angeles Times*. November 2, 1985, p. 12.

51. Harrington, Richard. Accord on lyric warning. *Washington Post*. November 2, 1985, p. H1.

52. Pagano, Penny. Warnings on lyrics, p. 12.

53. Wharton, Dennis. RIAA, PMRC reach accord on record lyrics; labels agree to use stickers or print words. *Variety*. 321:85 November 6, 1985.

54. Pagano, Penny. Warnings on lyrics, p. 12.

55. Pact announced on record lyrics. *New York Times*. November 2, 1985, p. 12.

56. Rense, Rip. Senators unflapped by Zappa. *Los Angeles Times*. November 1, 1985, pp. 1, 24.

57. Goldstein, Patrick. French star's new love songs take a beating. *Los Angeles Times.* May 11, 1986, Calendar section, p. 69.

58. Schipper, Henry. Parent's center to grass roots over "evils" of porno music. *Variety.* 322:107 February 12, 1986.

59. Shalett, Mike. On Target. *Billboard.* 98:26 March 15, 1986.

60. Maryland House passes ban on obscene disks. *Variety.* 322:1+ February 19, 1986.

61. Adelson, David. MD obscenity bill breezes through House of Delegates. *Cash Box.* 49:7 March 1, 1986.

62. Holland, Bill. Maryland Assembly mulls bill on record obscenity. *Billboard.* 98:77 February 15, 1986.

63. Adelson, David. Toth: only the beginning. *Cash Box.* 49:5 February 22, 1986.

64. Maryland solons offered views on bill to ban obscene disks. *Variety.* 322:91 March 26, 1986.

65. Adelson, David. MD obscenity bill defeated. *Cash Box.* 49:9 April 12, 1986.

66. Holland, Bill. Lyrics have bad effect. *Billboard.* 98:3 February 1, 1986.

67. Lewis, Randy. Teenagers aren't getting the message. *Vancouver Sun.* June 14, 1986, p. E1.

Index

Indonesia: opposition to rock in, 80
Infra-Riot, 264
Institute of Living. *See* Braceland, Francis J.
Iran: attacks on rock in, 80, 242–43
Iron Maiden, 270
Isle of Wight, 138–39
"It's All Right to Make Love on the First Night," 251
Ivaney, John, 232
"I've Got You Under My Skin," 211

Jackson, Jesse, 53, 92, 260, 291, 313; and campaign to ban "sex rock," 251–55
Jackson, Michael, 217, 245, 274, 299
Jackson, Richard, 170
Jacksons, 252, 278, 285
Jacobs, John, 265
Jagger, Mick, 3, 61, 108, 114, 120–23, 125, 127, 132, 182, 186, 190, 218, 240, 254–55, 277, 286, 313; accused of black magic, 121; arrested for drug possession, 200; blamed for violence at Altamont, 140–41; chauvinism of, 161; on David Frost's show to debate morals, 122; philosophical about audience reaction, 134; refuses to participate in television show ending, 147; refuses to support Black Panthers, 161; and reports of drug use by, 201; sexual aspects of persona of, 120–21; stage presence of, 120. *See also* Rolling Stones
Jam, 228
Tommy James and the Shondells, 188
James, Rick, 274
Japan: backlash against rock in, 155
Jarry, Gaetan, 118
Jarvis, Al, 106
"Jeanny," 243
Jefferson Airplane, 114, 127, 134, 139, 143, 149, 158, 182, 191, 199
Jefferson Starship, 260
Jenkins, Gordon, 9

Jesus Christ Superstar, 182
Jet, 251
Jett, Joan, 259
Jewell, Don, 143
"Jewish Princess," 257
"Joan Crawford Has Risen from the Grave," 277
John Birch Society, 133, 157–58
John, Elton, 127, 169, 193, 217, 246, 250, 252, 261–62, 284
Johnson, Brian, 282
Johnson, Johnny, 32
Johnson, Nicholas, 192, 202–3, 209–10
Jones, Archie N., 51
Jones, Brian, 120, 121, 132, 201. *See also* Rolling Stones
Jones, Tom, 186
Joplin, Janis, 125, 138, 189, 206, 239
Journey, 286
"Joy to the World," 210
Judas Priest, 286, 292, 293, 299, 309
"Juke Box Jury" (television show), 15
Jump 'n the Saddle Band, 279
Junior National Audience Board, 23. *See also* National Audience Board
Juvenile Delinquency and Crime Commission. *See* "Wash-Out-the-Air" Committee

KAFM (Dallas), 295
KAZY (Denver), 231
KDEN (Denver), 57
KEAN (Brownwood, Tex.), 180, 197
KEEE (Nacogdoches, Tex.), 180, 197
KEX (Portland, Ore.), 61
KFMY (Provo, Ut.), 257
KGFL (Los Angeles), 250
KILT (Houston), 195
KING (Seattle), 56
KIOI (San Francisco), 210
KITE (San Antonio), 22
KKUB (Brownfield, Tex.), 197
KMA (Shenandoah, Iowa), 21
KMET (Los Angeles), 260
KMIL (Cameron, Tex.), 179
KMPC (Los Angeles), 66

Other DA CAPO titles of interest